AUSTRALIAN FOREIGN POLICY
1938–1965

To

M.M.W.

who shared the journey and
bore the greater burden

THE EVOLUTION OF
AUSTRALIAN FOREIGN POLICY
1938–1965

BY

ALAN WATT

Director of the Australian Institute of International Affairs

CAMBRIDGE
AT THE UNIVERSITY PRESS
1967

Published by the Syndics of the Cambridge University Press
Bentley House, 200 Euston Road, London, N.W. 1
American Branch: 32 East 57th Street, New York, N.Y. 10022

Printed in Great Britain
at the University Printing House, Cambridge
(Brooke Crutchley, University Printer)

CONTENTS

PREFACE

The broad purpose of the following pages is to distinguish the varying assumptions underlying Australian foreign policy during the period 1938–65, and to consider the extent to which these assumptions are still valid when viewed against the background of drastic world changes (including changes within the Commonwealth of Nations) which have taken place. In general, the record has been closed as of 31 December 1965, but a few significant developments which occurred during the first nine months of 1966 have also been included.

In describing the evolution of Australian foreign policy, I have had continually in mind three basic questions: first, whether Australians are sufficiently conscious of the actual changes which have taken place in the world in which they live; secondly, whether Australian foreign policy has been adapted successfully to meet new situations and problems which these changes have produced; and, thirdly, whether the methods used to implement and explain Australian policies are adequate. It is hoped that the text will throw some useful light on the serious personal and national effort likely to be required of Australians if their present democratic freedoms, their standards of living and, indeed, their survival as a nation are to be ensured.

Choice of 1938 as the date for the commencement of this story should not, of course, be taken to imply that Australia had no foreign policy worth examining before that year. The degree of Australian participation in the First World War, and the activities of Mr William Morris Hughes, Prime Minister of Australia, at the Versailles Peace Conference provide early evidence to the contrary. Nevertheless Australian policy towards the Sudeten German problem in Czechoslovakia, culminating in the Munich crisis, is a convenient starting point for a study designed to explain how current policy has developed.

At the time of Munich Australia, unlike Canada and South Africa, had *no* diplomatic missions in any *foreign* country. Despite the re-establishment in 1935 of a small and separate Department of External Affairs, and recruitment for this department of a few officers with overseas experience and training, Australia had as yet no sufficiently organised Foreign Office supported by diplomatic establishments overseas to provide essential information and comments necessary for the formulation of a distinctively Australian foreign policy.[1] It was inevitable therefore that the confidential material upon which Australian policy on the Sudeten German question was based came from and reflected the views of the British Government of the day.

The material used for this book is taken from public sources. As a member of the Commonwealth Public Service for twenty-five years I am, of course, bound by the restrictions applicable to all Australian officials. This has involved deliberate omission of certain facts acquired in an official capacity. It is my considered opinion, however, that the facts omitted do not distort the main outlines of the story—otherwise I would not have written it. Most people, in my experience, underestimate the amount of valuable material on foreign policy available from public sources. A close study of the public record—including in particular parliamentary debates, published State documents, memoirs of eminent statesmen and members of the armed forces who have held key positions, critical books by historians, articles in learned journals and in newspapers—reveals a surprising range of information.

The topics which I have chosen for discussion are inevitably somewhat selective. No attempt has been made to draw a detailed and exhaustive picture of all aspects of Australian foreign policy since 1938, partly because this would inevitably have exceeded the reasonable bounds of a single book, partly because certain points have already been dealt with in detail in books and articles already published, partly because in some fields, such as trade, others are more competent—but mainly because such a definitive study is in my opinion best left to someone who will have access to the full secret record.

The subjects examined in the following pages should therefore be regarded as illustrative rather than exhaustive, their choice being determined by the background of my own particular range of experience and my judgement of their importance. Their treatment has raised problems both of style and of good taste. As to the former, deliberate avoidance of the first personal pronoun has at times led to indirectness of expression: I have

[1] For details as to the exact situation in 1938, see below, pp. 21–2.

tried to write from the outside and not from the inside. As to the latter, I came to the conclusion that it was impossible to describe adequately the development of Australian foreign policy between 1938 and 1965 without saying something about the personalities of the main actors on the political stage, and without criticising certain policies or methods of implementing them when this seemed justified. Nevertheless, I felt precluded from attempting to draw character sketches of individuals under whom I have served, based upon knowledge of intimate details acquired solely through official association. In describing the personalities and activities of cabinet ministers, therefore, I have limited myself to facts readily obtainable from any book of reference and to comments published by others. Where I have criticised policy, I have tried to do so on the basis of judgements which could be made by any non-official who had studied the public record. I am conscious, however, that adoption of this method of approach risks some unevenness in the images drawn of different individuals: the definitive image must therefore await publication of biographies, preferably based upon access to official records.

My thanks are due to the Australian National University, and in particular to Sir John Crawford (Director, Research School of Pacific Studies) and to Professor J. D. B. Miller (Head of the Department of International Relations in the same School), for the opportunity for research afforded me while a Visiting Fellow and for the encouragement given me to pursue this work. My thanks are also due to members of the Commonwealth Council of the Australian Institute of International Affairs for their understanding of the desirability of this work being completed after I had assumed the responsibilities of Director of the Institute. Daily contact with various colleagues both within the Department of International Relations and the Institute of International Affairs, and regular discussion with them of different issues, has been both stimulating and pleasant. I wish to express my gratitude to all of them, and especially to Dr T. B. Millar.

Finally, I desire to acknowledge with thanks the assistance of Mrs Robin Ward, who checked the references in chapters 6, 7 and 8 and prepared a trial index for the book in manuscript; Miss Norma Buckman, who checked references in chapter 5; and Mrs Jill McLeod, my secretary, who not only checked the references in the first four chapters but also showed patience and assiduity beyond the call of duty in typing and re-typing the manuscript. The constant support and cheerful attention to detail of Mrs McLeod has been a very real contribution to the completed work.

Canberra, September 1966   A.W.

ACKNOWLEDGEMENTS

Grateful acknowledgement is made to the following for permission to draw upon material previously contributed by me:

Encyclopaedia Britannica Ltd., *Book of the Year 1965* (Australia and New Zealand Supplement).

Australian Institute of International Affairs:
Roy Milne Memorial Lecture 1964.
Journals: *Australian Outlook; Australia's Neighbours; World Review.*

Australian Institute of Political Science: *Australia's Defence and Foreign Policy; The Australian Quarterly* (journal).

Australian National University: Department of International Relations Working Paper.

I

MUNICH

I. 'BLACK WEDNESDAY'

At 11 p.m. on 28 September 1938, 'Black Wednesday',[1] Mr Joseph Aloysius Lyons, Prime Minister of Australia and Leader of the United Australia Party, rose to his feet in the House of Representatives, Canberra, to make a much-delayed statement on the international situation. The public galleries were crowded, and there was a general atmosphere of tension heightened both by the unusual hour for such a statement and general knowledge that its delivery had been postponed on several occasions. Lyons read his speech in his customary, somewhat declamatory style. The effect upon his audience was not particularly impressive, because he failed to convey the sense of complete familiarity with and mastery of the text. His concluding words were as follows:

It will be seen...that what the Government of Great Britain has been doing, with the support of the Government of Australia, has been to make every effort to preserve the world's peace...If war is to come to the world it will not come by reason of anything that any British nation has done or failed to do. Our hands are clean. We have done our best to keep the peace. We have no selfish interest to serve. Even as the clouds gather about us we still hope that peace may be preserved.[2]

The Prime Minister resumed his seat in a general atmosphere of bewilderment rather than alarm. Many of those present sympathised with the comment made as Leader of the Opposition by Mr John Curtin, Leader of the Labour Party, in a short speech delivered immediately afterwards: 'I am astonished that this somewhat dramatic sitting of the House should have resulted in what I shall describe as a most extraordinary anti-climax.'[3] Lyons, they felt, had said either too much or too little:

---

[1] Alan Bullock, *Hitler, A Study in Tyranny* (Odhams, London, 4th imp., 1959), p. 427.
[2] *Commonwealth Parliamentary Debates* (subsequently abbreviated as *C.P.D.*), vol. 157, p. 312.　　　　　[3] *Ibid.* p. 326.

if there was no immediate risk of war, he had said too much; if the risk was real and immediate, he had not sufficiently explained the facts.

We now understand, of course, the precise reason for the statement and for the timing. The Australian Government had been advised from London that if the Government of Czechoslovakia failed beyond 2 p.m. (G.M.T.) of 28 September (midnight, Australian time) to agree to Hitler's latest demands for withdrawal of Czech forces from Sudeten areas by 1 October, Hitler proposed to take over such areas by force.[1] The Prime Minister had made his statement to Parliament, therefore, at the latest moment practicable without risking the charge of having failed to forewarn Parliament and the nation that war was imminent before it actually broke out.

The crisis was far better understood in Great Britain and in France than in Australia. Sir John Wheeler-Bennett has described the situation in London and in Paris on 'Black Wednesday', 28 September, in the following words:

Men and women woke with the eerie feeling that this was 'the last day' and that by tomorrow night their homes might be in flames. In Paris they were fighting for seats on the trains, and the roads out of the city were choked with traffic; in London they were digging trenches.[2]

According to Churchill's record:

It seemed that the moment of clash had arrived...Just before midnight on 27 September the warning telegram was sent out from the Admiralty ordering the mobilization of the Fleet for the following day.[3]

War, however, did not break out at midnight on 28 September. Hitler accepted the offer of the British Prime Minister, Mr Neville Chamberlain, to fly once more to Germany to try to reach agreement on a negotiated settlement of the Sudeten problem. The Munich Agreement was signed on 30 September.

---

[1] *Documents on British Foreign Policy, 1919–1939* (3rd series, vol. II), ed. E. L. Woodward and Rohan Butler (subsequently abbreviated as *Documents on B.F.P.*), p. 570; also Bullock, *op. cit.* p. 422; Dame Enid Lyons, *So We Take Comfort* (Heinemann, London, 1965), pp. 267–8.
[2] J. W. Wheeler-Bennett, *King George VI* (Macmillan, London, 1958), p. 353.
[3] Winston Churchill, *The Second World War* (Cassell, London, 1948), vol. I, p. 243.

On the same day, Lyons sent the following message to Chamberlain:

My colleagues and I desire to express our warmest congratulations at the outcome of the negotiations at Munich. Australians in common with all other peoples of the British Empire owe a deep debt of gratitude to you for your unceasing efforts to preserve peace.[1]

Chamberlain's first reaction to signature of the Munich Agreement is indicated by his comment on his return to London from Germany that 'This is the second time in our history that there has come back from Germany to Downing Street peace with honour. I believe it is peace for our time'.[2] This statement he was soon to regret, and his latest biographer and apologist, Mr Iain Macleod, tries to explain it away by saying that it was used 'in a mental and emotional condition close to breaking point'.[2] Such sentences 'grated harshly on the ear'[3] of Viscount Halifax, the ablest defender of the Munich Agreement, who was Foreign Secretary at the time of its signature. In the latter's opinion '...the only possible defence of Munich, which was the genuine defence, was that it was a horrible and wretched business, but the lesser of two evils'.[3]

This attitude, however, was not shared at the time of Munich by Chamberlain himself. The views of the British Prime Minister find perhaps their most ironical reflexion in the terms of a letter which he wrote to the Archbishop of Canterbury on 2 October 1938:

I am sure that some day the Czechs will see that what we did was to save them for a happier future. And I sincerely hope that we have opened the way to that general appeasement which alone can save the world from chaos.[4]

II. AUSTRALIAN POLICY

What was the policy of the Australian Government in regard to the Sudeten German problem? Mr R. G. Menzies,[5] then Attorney-General in the Lyons Government, replying to the debate on 5 October after the official text of the Munich Agreement had been tabled in the House, rejected Opposition

---

[1] Iain Macleod, *Neville Chamberlain* (Frederick Muller, London, 1961), p. 270.
[2] *Ibid.* p. 256.
[3] The Earl of Halifax, *Fulness of Days* (Collins, London, 1957), p. 198.
[4] Wheeler-Bennett, *op. cit.* p. 355.   [5] Now Sir Robert Menzies.

charges that the Government 'had no policy on foreign affairs, that it was silent as to any contribution it might have made to the discussion of any of these matters, and that...it had made certain commitments gravely affecting the future of the Australian people and had said nothing about them'.[1] After Chamberlain had decided to intervene personally with Hitler by flying to Germany for direct discussions, said Menzies:

We kept in touch with the British Prime Minister. We said: 'This is a great work you are doing. We know that you are aiming at peace. We know that you are going to keep the British Empire and Europe out of war if you humanly can. We are behind you in that resolve. We are completely behind what you are doing to avoid war.'[2]

Earlier, Australia had told the United Kingdom that it was highly desirable that 'the government at Prague should itself contribute to the settlement by making proposals'.[3] The Attorney-General added that Australia had made no commitment to Great Britain to send troops out of Australia if war had broken out: indeed, Great Britain had never raised the question.

Parliament was, of course, already aware that the Australian Government supported Chamberlain's policy of avoiding war and securing a negotiated settlement of the Sudeten German problem. Lyons had made a brief statement to the House to this effect as early as 27 April.[4] Moreover, a close reading of the Australian Prime Minister's speech in Parliament in the late evening of 'Black Wednesday' should have made Australians, inside and outside of Parliament, aware that Australia had not merely endorsed British policy towards Czechoslovakia, but also positively urged the British Government to bring pressure to bear upon the Czech Government to offer 'the most liberal concessions' to Hitler.[5]

In fairness to the Lyons Government it should be added that its policy was influenced in some degree by the view that it was 'quite wrong to imagine that the dispute about the position of the Sudeten Germans was a dispute in which all the merits were one way...the merits were distributed'.[6] In his speech of 5 October Menzies made effective use of this argument by quoting extracts from a letter of 21 September from Lord

---

[1] *C.P.D.* vol. 157, p. 429.   [2] *Ibid.* p. 431.   [3] *Ibid.* p. 430.
[4] *C.P.D.* vol. 155, p. 537.   [5] *C.P.D.* vol. 157, p. 307.   [6] *Ibid.* p. 432.

Runciman to Mr Chamberlain. In his letter Runciman, who had been sent by Chamberlain to Prague some months earlier as an unofficial mediator to try to speed up agreement between the Czech Government and the Sudeten German leaders regarding their claims for self-determination, said that, although in his opinion responsibility for the final break must rest on the two Sudeten German leaders Henlein and Frank, he had 'much sympathy...with the Sudeten case'.[1] He had been

...left with the impression that Czechoslovakia's rule in the Sudeten area for the last twenty years, though not actively oppressive and certainly not 'terroristic' has been marked by tactless lack of understanding, petty intolerance and discrimination to the point where the resentment of the German population was inevitably moving in the direction of revolt.[1]

So far as the Australian Labour Party was concerned, there was never any suggestion that either the British or the Australian Governments should have given greater support to Czechoslovakia or opposed Hitler more firmly. Curtin, Leader of the Opposition, said in Parliament on 5 October:

...the interests of Australia can best be served by giving paramount consideration to the safety of our own people and the safety of our own soil. The defence of this nation is best served by a policy of national self-reliance rather than one which embroils us in the perennial disputes in Europe...I say that the Labour Party in Australia is opposed in principle and in practice to Australians being recruited as soldiers in the battlefields of Europe...We believe that the best service which Australia can render to the British Empire is to attend to its own business, to make certain that we manage Australia effectively, so that we shall have the necessary population and be able to rely upon ourselves in the event of an emergency.[2]

This expression of Labour Party policy drew from the Minister for External Affairs, Mr W. M. Hughes, the following tart reply:

The honourable gentleman [Mr Curtin] says that we must close our ears to the piteous cries of the oppressed, because otherwise we may be endangered...we must not listen to their cry for help. The day may come when this small nation will cry aloud to the world for help, but what will the world say if we adopt and pursue the policy

[1] *Ibid.* p. 432.
[2] *Ibid.* pp. 393-5.

of selfish isolation outlined by the Leader of the Opposition?...
Czechoslovakia was dismembered because, however much in the
right it was, it was weak.[1]

III. THE REAL BASIS OF CHAMBERLAIN'S POLICY

When Hitler marched into Prague in March 1939 the eyes of
Neville Chamberlain were at long last opened as to the nature
of the Nazi threat to world peace. 'Prague', says Alan Bullock,
'has rightly been taken as the turning-point in British foreign
policy, the stage at which the British Government, however
belatedly, abandoned hope of appeasing Hitler, and set to
work...to organise resistance to any further aggressive move
by the German dictator.'[2]

After the rape of Prague, Chamberlain did his utmost to
rearm Great Britain and made it clear to Hitler that aggression
against Poland, for instance, would involve war with Great
Britain as well. The very word 'appeasement' which, as Sir
Keith Hancock has pointed out,[3] was originally 'put into circulation' by Field-Marshal Smuts as early as 1919 and which
for long 'both in its French and English versions, signified
reconciliation', became 'a word of abuse'.[3]

Controversy still rages, however, as to whether the Chamberlain policy at Munich was justified at the time.[4] As a judgement
on this basic issue is relevant to the question whether Australian
interests were sufficiently protected in 1938 by a policy of relying predominantly upon British official sources of information,
and also to the question of long-term risks involved in policies of
'appeasement' today, it is proposed to consider the arguments
for and against in some detail.

Those who justify or excuse Chamberlain's policy in 1938
usually do so on one or more of the following grounds:

(i) British (and French) military strength was such that
Great Britain could not have fought in September 1938. By
avoiding war for approximately twelve months, Chamberlain
bought time in which Great Britain could rearm.

(ii) British public opinion would not have supported a
declaration of war in 1938.

---

[1] C.P.D. vol. 157, pp. 398–9.   [2] Bullock, op. cit. p. 447.
[3] Sir Keith Hancock, Smuts (Cambridge University Press, 1962), vol. 1, p. 512.
[4] See Macleod, op. cit.; also Sir Charles Webster, 'Munich reconsidered', International Affairs, vol. xxxvii, no. 2 (April 1961).

(iii) The Commonwealth would not have supported Great Britain in 1938 if war had resulted from a British policy of standing up to Hitler.

Justification of the policy of appeasement in 1938 as a means of gaining 'time' in which to rearm is found in distinguished quarters and has become something of a legend. As recently as 1955 the Prime Minister of Australia, Mr Menzies, still felt able to pay a tribute to Chamberlain's memory along these lines:

...he gave us time, even at the price of humiliation. There had been, under the Air Administration of Philip Swinton, a concentration upon quality in the Spitfire and the Hurricane; great 'shadow' factories had been set up and equipped. The Battle of Britain had already been partly won. Let us remember that it was won not only by the superb dash, individuality, and courage of the pilots, but also by the superior speed, manœuvrability, and fire-power of their aircraft...A year was worth a good deal. We were much stronger in 1939 than in 1938.[1]

Iain Macleod elaborates this argument at length, drawing attention as well to the improvement in radar defences: 'the chain of radar stations which during the Munich crisis had been in operation only in the Thames estuary now [in September 1939] guarded Britain from the Orkneys to the Isle of Wight'.[2] After reviewing in detail all the improvements in British armaments and defences from Munich to the time when war broke out, Macleod sums up as follows:

...by September 1939, Britain was still very far from having completed her preparations for war, but in the preceding year these preparations had greatly increased in scale and in urgency. We had improved our absolute strength in every respect, and in air power we had improved our relative strength. The capital of the Empire and the centres of armament production had had their nakedness covered. Our civil defences had been put in order. Far more fighter squadrons had been remounted on the modern aircraft that were to win the Battle of Britain. At the Admiralty, programmes had been pressed ahead to counter the menace of the U-boat. A fundamental revision of Army policy had enabled a sizeable British Expeditionary Force to be planned. Output of war-stores had risen and at quickening rates, and so had our industrial potential for war.

[1] R. G. Menzies, *Speech is of Time* (Cassell, London, 1958), pp. 68–9. (Sir Richard Stawell Oration, delivered 8 October 1955.)　　[2] Macleod, *op. cit.* p. 260.

All these gains are matters of historical fact. On the other hand, many of the 'losses' by which critics have supposed the gains to be outweighed are highly conjectural.[1]

The important point, however, as Macleod admits by implication in the above quotation, is not whether British strength increased between 1938 and 1939, but whether during that period British strength increased *relative to German strength*. In certain important respects it undoubtedly did, the most significant being aircraft (Hurricanes and Spitfires) and radar defence. But if we consider the whole range of military force, including trained manpower and material, a 'powerful argument' can be made (the phrase is Mr Macleod's[2]) to support the conclusion that 'from the purely military point of view, it would have paid us to go to war in 1938'.[3]

The strongest witness for the prosecution is Churchill himself. He considers at length the strength of the Czech army and fortifications in 1938; the comparative strength in numbers and quality of the French and German armies in 1938 and 1939; the hesitations and fears of the German generals as subsequently revealed; defects in the Siegfried line in 1938; the impossibility, in his opinion, of a decisive Air Battle of Britain taking place before the Germans had occupied France and the Low Countries and so obtained necessary bases for fighter aircraft to escort bombers; the 'vast tank production' with which the Germans broke the French front and which, he says, 'did not come into existence till 1940'.[4] But his main argument is put simply in the following words and, so far as I am aware, has not been seriously disputed:

...munition production on a nation-wide plan is a four years' task. The first year yields nothing; the second very little; the third a lot, and the fourth a flood. Hitler's Germany in this period was already in the third or fourth year of intense preparation...In 1938–39 British military expenditure of all kinds reached £304 millions, and German was at least £1,500 millions. It is probable that in this last year before the outbreak, Germany manufactured at least double, and possible treble, the munitions of Britain and France put together, and also that her great plants for tank production reached full capacity.[5]

[1] Macleod, *op. cit.* pp. 265–6.   [2] *Ibid.* p. 262.
[3] *The Memoirs of General the Lord Ismay* (Heinemann, London, 1960), p. 92.
[4] Winston Churchill, *op. cit.* vol. i, p. 265.   [5] *Ibid.* p. 263.

Lest it be thought that Churchill, as a political critic of Chamberlain's policy of appeasement, is not a sufficiently impartial witness, let us turn to the opinion of Major-General H. L. Ismay,[1] then Secretary of the Committee of Imperial Defence and thus technically qualified and well placed to judge. In his memoirs, published in 1960, he makes the following comments:

There are those who say that we would have done far better to fight in 1938...There are others who say that the year's breathing space saved us. It seems to me that, *from the purely military point of view, it would have paid us to go to war in 1938* [emphasis added]. It is true that we were hopelessly unready, but German preparations were by no means complete, and in war it is relative strength which counts. It is also true that we had an extra year to rearm, but everyone knows that Germany made much better use of those twelve months than we did.[2]

Ismay, it is true, then refers to the effect of lack of unity on the home front and within the Commonwealth in 1938, and points out that such lack of unity can be a factor more disastrous than inferiority of armaments. But this introduces the second and third lines of argument which will be considered below.

If the judgements of Churchill and Ismay are sound,[3] the defence of Munich put forward by Lord Halifax[4] is substantially weakened. For Halifax, the critics of the Munich Agreement

...were criticising the wrong thing and the wrong date. They ought to have criticised the failure of successive Governments, and of all parties, to foresee the necessity of rearming in the light of what was going on in Germany; and the right date on which criticism ought to have fastened was 1936, which had seen the German reoccupation of the Rhineland in defiance of treaty provisions.[5]

He had 'little doubt that if we had then told Hitler bluntly to go back, his power for future...mischief would have been broken'.[5] In the circumstances of 1938, however (so Halifax argued), the 'Foreign Secretary was like a player invited to stake, when he knew that if the fortune of the game turned against him he had nothing with which to redeem his pledge... once the Austrian Anschluss had taken place, whether you liked

---

[1] Later Lord Ismay.   [2] Ismay, *op. cit.* p. 92.
[3] Sir Charles Webster (see p. 6, n. 4 above) supports the argument that British military strength, *relative to Germany's*, decreased between September 1938 and September 1939.   [4] Halifax, *op. cit.* pp. 196–9.   [5] *Ibid.* p. 197.

it or not, Czechoslovakia was no longer a defensible proposition'.[1]

There are two further important pieces of evidence which convincingly dispose of the claim that Chamberlain's policy at Munich was determined basically by his consciousness of British military unpreparedness for war. First, there is the specific statement to the contrary by Sir Samuel Hoare,[2] one of the 'big four' members of the British cabinet directly involved in pre-Munich discussions and a close confidant of the Prime Minister. 'Throughout the critical days of 1938', he wrote in his memoirs,

there was never absent from our minds the vital question of British military strength. My long years at the Air Ministry had particularly made me conscious of the gaps in our air defences and the need for time to repair them. *None the less, it would not be correct to say that our military weakness was the principal cause of the Munich Agreement* [emphasis added]. The over-riding consideration with Chamberlain and his colleagues was that the very complicated problem of Czechoslovakia *ought* [emphasis added] not to lead to a world war, and must at almost any price be settled by peaceful means.[3]

The key word in the last sentence quoted is the word 'ought', the precise meaning of which will be investigated further below.

The second vital piece of evidence is set out in volume II of the Third Series of *Documents on British Foreign Policy (1919–1939)*, which contains a mine of information regarding diplomatic reports and discussions during the period leading up to the signature of the Munich Agreement, including almost brutally frank talks between British and French political leaders in London.

The records of Anglo-French discussions in London on 18, 25 and 26 September 1938[4] deserve far more detailed examination than they can be given here. In general, however, it can be said that they disclose strong and persistent pressure by Chamberlain and his British associates upon Daladier and his French associates with a view to establishing the military weakness of France and to securing the assent of the French Government to a policy of continued appeasement of Hitler. Yet despite the notorious telegram (received in London on 24 September

---

[1] Halifax, *op. cit.* pp. 196–8.   [2] Later Viscount Templewood.
[3] Viscount Templewood, *Nine Troubled Years* (Collins, London, 1954), p. 289.
[4] *Documents on B.F.P.* pp. 373–99, 520–35, 536–41.

1938) from Sir Eric Phipps, British Ambassador to France,
advising the Foreign Secretary that 'His Majesty's Government
should realise extreme danger of even appearing to encourage
small, but noisy and corrupt, war group here. All that is best
in France is against war, *almost* at any price...',[1] the official
record of Anglo-French discussions shows that the French President of the Council, M. Daladier, made continual and almost
prophetic protests against both the policy and the probable
effects of yielding to Hitler. During the discussions on 18
September Daladier expressed himself as follows:

M. Daladier...feared...that Germany's real aim was the disinte-
gration of Czechoslovakia and the realisation of pan-German ideals
through a march to the East. Roumania would be the next country
to suffer and here a German minority in Transylvania would be used
as a lever. The result would be that in a very short time Germany
would be master of Europe, and, in particular, of the wheat and
petrol of South-Eastern Europe. *Within one year we might expect her
to turn back against France and Great Britain, who would then have to meet
her in much more difficult circumstances than those existing to-day.*[2] [Em-
phasis added.]

And again, during the same day,

M. Daladier...regarded the present problem as very much less a
Czechoslovak problem than a general problem involving the peace
of Europe. If we were to accept the German ultimatum by conceding all her demands, we should have created a very serious
precedent. Further German demands would follow in due course and
Germany would conclude that we should again give way.[3]

On 25 September Chamberlain gave the French representatives an account of his discussions with Hitler at Godesberg and
went so far as to express the opinion that 'It would be poor con-
solation if, in fulfilment of all her obligations, France attempted
to come to the assistance of her friend [Czechoslovakia] but
found herself unable to keep up her resistance and collapsed'.[4]
This and similar arguments led to something of an explosion
from the French President of the Council.

M. Daladier was glad to reply to these questions. He was always
hearing of difficulties. Did this mean that we did not wish to do
anything? We were, after all, giving Herr Hitler $3\frac{1}{2}$ million Sudeten

[1] *Ibid.* p. 510.   [2] *Ibid.* p. 384.
[3] *Ibid.* p. 386.   [4] *Ibid.* p. 532.

Germans. He said this was not enough and wanted everything else as well. Was the British Government ready to give in and to accept Herr Hitler's proposals . . . ?

We must face up to the facts and decide what we wanted. If Herr Hitler put forward certain demands must we agree to them? He would then be master of Europe and after Czechoslovakia would come Roumania and then Turkey. He might even turn to France and take Boulogne and Calais. He might even afterwards land in Ireland . . . Must we always give way to Herr Hitler's ultimata? If we were agreed to do so it was useless to have meetings and appear to discuss these questions. He was ready to agree to certain measures of conciliation which were in accordance with moral sentiments, but a moment came to call a halt and that moment had in his opinion come.[1]

It can of course always be argued that M. Daladier was bluffing—that he was putting on a bolder front than a politically sick French Government and a Maginot-Line-minded French General Staff justified. On the other hand, it should be noted that the British Foreign Office received at 2.15 p.m. on 26 September a message from the British Ambassador in Paris in very different terms from the earlier message quoted above:

. . . I have just seen President of the Chamber who confirmed the complete swing-over of public opinion since Hitler's demands had become known. He assures me that an overwhelming majority in the Chamber will now be for resistance. He says there is no kind of enthusiasm for war in the country, but a firm and melancholy determination to resist.[2]

At 4.10 p.m. on the same day Chamberlain caused to be sent the following message to Sir Horace Wilson, then in Berlin as his special emissary to Hitler:

Since you left, French have definitely stated their intention of supporting Czechoslovakia by offensive measures if latter is attacked. *This would bring us in* [emphasis added]; and it should be made plain to Chancellor that this is inevitable alternative to a peaceful solution.[3]

On the same afternoon Lord Halifax authorised the issue of a Press statement containing, *inter alia*, these words:

. . . if in spite of all efforts made by the British Prime Minister a German attack is made upon Czechoslovakia the immediate result

---

[1] *Documents on B.F.P.* pp. 532–3.   [2] *Ibid.* p. 547.   [3] *Ibid.* p. 550.

must be that France will be bound to come to her assistance, and Great Britain and Russia will certainly stand by France.[1]

The reference to Russia is presumably to be regarded, in the current state of British knowledge of probable Russian intentions, as a calculated bluff: but not so the reference to Great Britain. Wilson carried out his instructions and on 27 September informed Hitler, with great precision, and in spite of interruptions, of the circumstances in which Germany would find herself at war with Great Britain.[2] Greater credibility was lent to Wilson's message in Hitler's eyes by the long-delayed mobilisation of the British Fleet. There is little doubt that it was this warning, together with the intervention of Mussolini at the request of Great Britain,[3] which led to Hitler's acceptance of Chamberlain's offer to meet him again in Germany, where, at Munich, the Chancellor showed just sufficient flexibility to enable him to get the substance of what he wanted without war.

It is clear, therefore, from the official documents, that Chamberlain committed Great Britain to go to war with Germany in defined circumstances *despite* British unpreparedness for war in 1938. The basic reasons for Chamberlain's policy must thus be sought elsewhere.

A stronger case can be made for the claim that neither British nor Commonwealth public opinion would have supported a British declaration of war at the time of Munich. All those who have defended Chamberlain's actions in 1938 stress this argument strongly. ' ...one fact', says Lord Halifax, 'remains dominant and unchallengeable. When war did come a year later it found a country and Commonwealth wholly united within itself, convinced to the foundations of soul and conscience that every conceivable effort had been made to find the way of sparing Europe the ordeal of war, and that no alternative remained. And that was the big thing that Chamberlain did.'[4] So also Mr Menzies: 'the twelve months after Munich, with their grim and hateful record of treachery and aggression, did much to marshal the decent moral opinion of the world, to harden the spirit of resistance to tyranny and crime'.[5]

---

[1] *Ibid.* p. 550.   [2] *Ibid.* p. 566.
[3] Dame Enid Lyons (*op. cit.* p. 268) claims that Australian intervention, at her own suggestion, urging an approach to Mussolini, had an important influence upon Chamberlain's decision to send a message to Mussolini.
[4] Halifax, *op. cit.* p. 198.   [5] Menzies, *op. cit.* p. 69.

Now it is true enough that public opinion in both Great Britain and in the Commonwealth was strongly in favour of peace and showed overwhelming relief when signature of the Munich Agreement raised hopes that mankind had in fact been spared the ordeal of a world war. But public opinion, so to speak, was scarcely given the opportunity of developing any other point of view: Commonwealth Governments without exception gave the lead only in the direction of appeasement. Even then, public opinion in Great Britain became so restive that on 23 September Lord Halifax found it necessary to warn Chamberlain, then in Godesberg, that the Government might be in danger of falling behind the electorate on this issue! 'It may help you', the Foreign Secretary telegraphed, 'if we give you some indication of what seems predominant public opinion as expressed in press and elsewhere. While mistrustful of our plan but prepared perhaps to accept it with reluctance as alternative to war, great mass of public opinion seems to be hardening in sense of feeling that we have gone to limit of concession and that it is up to the Chancellor to make some contribution.'[1] The stiffening of French public opinion as Hitler's demands increased has already been mentioned. Had there been a strong governmental lead in the direction of resisting Hitler's extreme demands and supporting Czechoslovakia provided France, too, supported her, is it an unreasonable hypothesis to assume that the British people would have responded to the call?

Commonwealth support for such a policy was indeed more doubtful. According to Halifax, '...there was grave doubt whether the Commonwealth would be at one in supporting the United Kingdom in a policy of active intervention on behalf of Czechoslovakia in 1938...'.[2] Iain Macleod has summed up the lack of Commonwealth support for a policy of stouter resistance to Hitler at the time of Munich as follows:

Mackenzie King of Canada told Churchill during the war 'that he very much doubted whether his country would have rallied to us at once'. Though the Australian Government considered that constitutionally it was not possible for Australia to be neutral in a British war, the Opposition were flatly against involvement in 1938.

[1] *Documents on B.F.P.* p. 490; see also references to the state of British public opinion in *Old Men Forget*, by Duff Cooper (Hart-Davis, London, 1954), pp. 232, 235, 251.   [2] Halifax, *op. cit.* pp. 197–8.

So far as South Africa was concerned, Hertzog and Smuts were agreed on a policy of non-belligerency.[1]

It can reasonably be argued that Australia and New Zealand, however reluctantly, would have followed a British lead in September 1938 against a policy of appeasement, particularly if Britain had become involved in war. The Prime Minister of New Zealand, Mr Savage, had declared that 'wherever Britain is, we must be'.[2] So far as Australia is concerned, it is unlikely that the Lyons Government would have differed from the view of its Attorney-General that when Britain was at war Australia was inevitably and automatically at war also.[3] A contemporary statement of this attitude was made by Mr Keith Officer,[4] Australian Counsellor at the British Embassy, Washington, to Jay Pierrepont Moffat, Chief of the Division of European Affairs in the State Department, on 22 September 1938. In his diary Moffat records a conversation with Officer during which the latter 'was quite clear in his own mind that the Australian advice to Britain had been not to be manœuvred into going to war for Czechoslovakia...On the other hand, should war break out Australia would immediately follow.'[5]

In South Africa the Prime Minister, General Hertzog, and General Smuts had agreed upon a policy of non-belligerency in the event of a European War.[6] Canada's Prime Minister, Mr Mackenzie King, would have regarded a policy of firmness towards Hitler as catastrophic, and would have done his utmost to modify it. He did not believe in the efficacy of the principle of collective security, as embodied in the League of Nations Covenant.[7] Moreover, he was not only an ardent supporter of Chamberlain's policy of appeasement, but had misinterpreted Hitler even more deeply and to a later stage than the British Prime Minister himself.

According to his own account, during the Canadian Prime Minister's conversation with Hitler in Berlin on 29 June 1937 he formed a 'very favourable' impression of the Führer, and found him a man of 'deep sincerity' who was not 'the

[1] Macleod, *op. cit.* p. 269.
[2] Nicholas Mansergh, *Survey of British Commonwealth Affairs, Problems of External Policy 1931–39* (Oxford University Press, 1952), p. 199.
[3] See p. 20 below.   [4] Later Sir Keith Officer.
[5] *The Moffat Papers, 1919–43*, ed. Nancy Hooker (Harvard University Press, 1956), pp. 208–9.   [6] Wheeler-Bennett, *op. cit.* p. 411.
[7] James Eayrs, *In Defence of Canada* (University of Toronto Press, 1965), vol. II, p. 59.

least excited' but a person who 'spoke with great calmness, moderation, and logically and in a convincing manner'.[1] On 6 September 1938 the Canadian Prime Minister informed the Governor-General of Canada that he believed 'it will be found in the end that Hitler is for peace, unless unduly provoked'.[2] After Hitler occupied Prague by force in March 1939—an event which caused Chamberlain to reverse his policy—Mackenzie King refused to draw the logical inferences which the British Government drew. The present Prime Minister of Canada, Mr Lester B. Pearson, spent an evening with King after the rape of Prague and noted on 16 July 1939 that King was 'not in sympathy with recent policies and prefers Chamberlain the appeaser to Chamberlain the avenger'.[3]

Yet in spite of this strong attachment to a policy of appeasement, strengthened no doubt by the complex problem of maintaining Canadian unity, it would appear that if war had actually come and Britain had been involved Mackenzie King too would have sought from Parliament 'Canada's immediate participation'.[4]

While therefore it may not be possible to establish with certainty that a bold British policy of firmness in dealing with Hitler's demands would in September 1938 have succeeded in overcoming the hesitations and doubts of the Dominions, it is also impossible to disprove this thesis, except in the case of South Africa. It is conceivable that Chamberlain may have believed that he could not have secured Dominion support for a firmer policy, but the question still remains whether this was a decisive reason for adhering to his own policy at the time of the Munich Agreement.

All the arguments advanced by apologists of Chamberlain as justifying his policy had indeed some influence upon him, but the basic reason was in fact different from those considered above. In my opinion, Chamberlain decided that Hitler's claims on Czechoslovakia in respect of the Sudeten German problem must be acceded to because the British Prime Minister could not bring himself to believe that British *vital interests* were involved—at least, until the rape of Prague in March 1939 opened his eyes to the real scope of Hitler's ambitions. France was a different matter. If France became involved in war with

---

[1] Eayrs, *op. cit.* p. 231.   [2] *Ibid.* p. 64.   [3] *Ibid.* p. 74.   [4] *Ibid.* p. 71.

beginning of the reckoning. This is only the first sip, the first foretaste of a bitter cup which will be proffered to us year by year unless,
by a supreme recovery of moral health and martial vigour, we arise
again and take our stand for freedom as in the olden time. . .[1]

No similar words are to be found in the utterances of leaders
of any Australian political party in late September or early
October 1938, although in his speech of 5 October W. M.
Hughes, Minister for External Affairs, did warn that 'in a
little while the clouds will gather again'.[2] In his memoirs the
late Sir Earle Page, then Deputy Prime Minister, Minister for
Commerce, and Leader of the Country Party, states that the
Lyons Government, in supporting Chamberlain, 'was not
blinded by flimsy hopes. We regarded the agreement merely as
a respite which extended the period during which we could
proceed with our preparations for the inevitable conflict.'[3]
Unfortunately this claim is scarcely sustained by the terms of his
own speech when he tabled the text of the Munich Agreement
on behalf of the Prime Minister on 5 October:

The whole world welcomed with relief the outcome of the negotiations at Munich, which removed the imminent threat of a general
war, and owes a deep debt of gratitude to those who made the success of the negotiations possible. . .it is to be hoped that the Munich
Agreement, which resulted in the solution of the Sudeten question,
will inaugurate a new era in international relations when differences
which inevitably arise from time to time between nations will be
settled by peaceful negotiations on the basis of reason and justice.[4]

IV. UNDERLYING AUSTRALIAN ASSUMPTIONS AND METHODS

It remains now to examine briefly the assumptions as to the role
of Australia in the field of foreign policy at the time of Munich,
and the operative methods then used to formulate that policy.
These are most readily discernible in the speech which Menzies
made in reply to the debate on the Munich Agreement on
5 October 1938. Speaking as Attorney-General, Menzies can
be regarded as the theoretician of the Government in regard to
Commonwealth constitutional relationships.

Rebutting Curtin's charge that the Government had no

---

[1] *Ibid.* pp. 255–7.   [2] *C.P.D.* vol. 157, p. 400.
[3] Sir Earle Page, *Truant Surgeon* (Angus and Robertson, Sydney, 1963), p. 259.
[4] *C.P.D.* vol. 157, pp. 388, 391.

foreign policy of its own, Menzies asked whether a Dominion should formulate a foreign policy and announce it, whether or not it was in line with Great Britain's: 'to adopt such a line of conduct would be suicidal', he said, 'not only for us, but also for the British Empire as a whole...I have always believed... that the British Empire exercises its greatest influence in the world...when it speaks with one concerted voice...'[1] On the other hand, he added:

...we ought to have minds sufficiently informed and sufficiently strong, positive and constructive, to be able to say useful things at the right time to the Government of the United Kingdom...But that means that that policy in relation to any individual matter has to be expressed to the Government of the United Kingdom.[1]

On the question of Australian involvement if Great Britain should be at war, the Attorney-General's view was clear and emphatic:

My doctrine in relation to the position of Australia has been stated over and over again...that so long as the British Empire is constituted as it is today, it is not possible for Australia to be neutral in a British war...But the extent to which Australia may participate in a war, the means by which she may participate, and the question whether Australian soldiers shall fight on Australian territory or on foreign soil, are matters for determination by Australia or, may I say, of (sic) the enemy.[2]

When war actually broke out in 1939 Menzies, then Prime Minister, acted in strict accordance with his view that, Britain being at war, Australia was automatically at war also.

Lastly, what were the methods approved by the Government for putting into effect their view as to the role of Australia in the international field? It should be remembered that the first Australian diplomatic mission to a foreign country was opened as late as 1940, after the Second World War had broken out, when Mr R. G. Casey[3] resigned his cabinet portfolio and became Australian Minister in Washington. In other words, before and during the Munich crisis Australia had no diplomatic mission in Germany, France, Russia, Italy, Japan or the United States, although in the last-mentioned country Mr Keith Officer had been appointed Australian Counsellor on the staff of the British Ambassador, Washington. In these circum-

[1] *C.P.D.* vol. 157, p. 429.   [2] *Ibid.* p. 431.   [3] Later Lord Casey.

stances, the primary and predominant source of Australian official information regarding the nature and development of the crisis was the British Government. It is scarcely a matter for surprise therefore that Australian policy in relation to Germany and Czechoslovakia coincided with British policy.

By 1938, however, some steps had indeed been taken to build up in Australia the nucleus of a career Diplomatic Service. In 1935 the Department of External Affairs, which from 1921 until 1935 had formed part of the Prime Minister's Department, was re-created as a separate department under Lt.-Col. W. R. Hodgson, and efforts were made to staff it with a small group of university graduates, some with overseas experience. As early as 1924 Casey had been posted to London at the request of the Australian Prime Minister, Mr S. M. Bruce,[1] and given a room in the office of Sir Maurice Hankey,[2] Secretary of the Cabinet and of the Committee of Imperial Defence.[3] Bruce, like W. M. Hughes before him, had been dissatisfied with consultation between London and Canberra on certain important issues, and it was his wish that Casey should supplement the information supplied by the Australian High Commissioner in London by informing Bruce directly of developing problems before they reached the point of crisis and decision. When Casey left Great Britain to enter Australian politics, his London post was filled by successive career diplomatic officers.

It is now known[4] that by 1937 the Department of External Affairs had made at least a serious attempt to formulate an overall foreign policy consistent with Australian interests. A memorandum on 'The Foreign Situation, March 1937', drafted in the Department for the use of the Australian Delegation to the Imperial Conference of 1937, reviewed the world situation from an Australian point of view, and drew attention, *inter alia* (one year before the event), to the 'serious' nature of the German 'move against Czechoslovakia, when it comes...'[5] Even more impressive were the papers prepared for the same delegation by the Australian Department of Defence.[6]

---

[1] Later Viscount Bruce.   [2] Later Lord Hankey.
[3] For a summary of early history of the Department of External Affairs, see R. G. Casey, *Friends and Neighbours* (Cheshire, Melbourne, 1954), pp. 28–9. Sir Earle Page has paid a generous tribute to Casey's work in London—see *Truant Surgeon*, p. 359.
[4] See Paul Hasluck, *The Government and the People (1939–41)* (Australian War Memorial, Canberra, 1952), pp. 56–8   [5] *Ibid.* p. 57.   [6] *Ibid.* pp. 58–66.

and partly because the Prime Minister's flair for ironic humour tended to antagonise friends as well as foes.

Menzies gave his first message to the Australian people as Prime Minister in a broadcast delivered on 26 April 1939. In dealing with problems of foreign policy in this broadcast he coined the phrase which ever since has been quoted by his fellow-countrymen as the best short-hand description of the basic issue of international affairs as seen from Australia, namely the issue of the survival of Australia, as a country of Western European cultural traditions and stock, in a geographical area off the southern rim of Asia. 'What Great Britain calls the Far East', said the Prime Minister, 'is to us the near north.' This sentence needs to be read in its context:

In the Pacific we have primary responsibilities and primary risks. Close as our consultation with Great Britain is, and must be, in relation to European affairs, it is still true to say that we must, to a large extent, be guided by her knowledge and affected by her decisions. The problems of the Pacific are different. What Great Britain calls the Far East is to us the near north. Little given as I am to encouraging the exaggerated ideas of Dominion independence and separatism which exist in some minds, I have become convinced that in the Pacific Australia must regard herself as a principal providing herself with her own information and maintaining her own diplomatic contacts with foreign powers. I do not mean by this that we are to act in the Pacific as if we were a completely separate power; we must, of course, act as an integral part of the British Empire. We must have full consultation and co-operation with Great Britain, South Africa, New Zealand and Canada. But all those consultations must be on the basis that the primary risk in the Pacific is borne by New Zealand and ourselves. With this in mind I look forward to the day when we will have a concert of Pacific powers, pacific in both senses of the word. This means increased diplomatic contact between ourselves and the United States, China and Japan, to say nothing of the Netherlands East Indies and the other countries which fringe the Pacific.

It is true that we are not a numerous people, but we have vigour, intelligence and resource, and I see no reason why we should not play not only an adult, but an effective part in the affairs of the Pacific.[1]

It is clear from this statement that the Prime Minister was not making, on behalf of Australia, a declaration of independence of British foreign policy. It suggests rather that he still held to

[1] *Sydney Morning Herald,* 27 April 1939.

the view expressed by him in the House of Representatives on 5 October 1938, namely that 'the British Empire exercises its greatest influence in the world...when it speaks with one concerted voice'.[1] This interpretation is supported by the Note handed by the British Embassy to the State Department on 30 November 1939, in connexion with the appointment of Casey as first Australian Minister to Washington, which includes the sentence: 'This arrangement was not to denote any departure from the diplomatic unity of the Empire.'[2] It is also supported by the method, adopted by Casey after taking up his appointment in Washington, of acting in closest consultation and co-operation with two British ambassadors, Lord Lothian and Lord Halifax.[3]

Nevertheless, the public announcement that Australia must regard herself as a 'principal' in the Pacific; that she required separate diplomatic contacts in that area; and that these contacts should provide 'her own information' represents an important step towards the creation of a separate Australian foreign policy and the building up in foreign countries of a special Australian 'image'. Men of the calibre and experience of Casey in Washington and, later, of Sir John Latham[4] in Tokyo and Sir Frederic Eggleston[5] in Chungking could not fail through their independent reports to influence the formulation of Australian policy in directions unlikely always to be identical with British policy. In future it would be possible to compare international developments in these countries as reported by British sources in London with developments as reported from Australian diplomatic missions in foreign countries. The latter would be based upon information derived from direct contacts with foreign political leaders and officials, with foreign journalists, educationalists, businessmen and others, and with a wide range of members of the diplomatic corps, including

---

[1] See p. 20 above.

[2] C. Hartley Grattan, *The United States and the Southwest Pacific* (Harvard University Press, Mass. 1961), p. 163.

[3] Lord Casey, *Personal Experience 1939–46* (Constable, London, 1962). See, for instance, pp. 34–5.

[4] Then Chief Justice of the High Court of Australia, and a former Minister for External Affairs.

[5] Eggleston practised as a solicitor in Melbourne, held various portfolios in the Victorian Parliament, was Chairman of the Commonwealth Grants Commission, first Australian Minister to China, and Australian Ambassador to Washington.

British diplomats on the spot. Moreover, the establishment in Australia of reciprocal foreign diplomatic missions, for which 'the diplomatic unity of the Empire' was for the most part simply irrelevant, inevitably brought the Australian Minister for External Affairs and officers of his department in Canberra into personal contact with foreign representatives who expressed their Governments' points of view directly.

In his broadcast statement of 26 April Menzies still maintained the constitutional view that Australia could not be neutral when Great Britain was at war. Speaking of Great Britain, he said: 'her peace is ours; if she is at war, we are at war, even though that war finds us not in European battlefields, but defending our own shores... The British countries of the world must stand or fall together.'[1] Somewhat surprisingly, however, he concurred in an interpretation of this view by the Minister for External Affairs in the latter's first speech on the international situation in Parliament, on 9 May 1939, which restricted somewhat its general applicability. Sir Henry Gullett explained, with his leader's concurrence, that the Prime Minister's words were

...not to be interpreted to mean that in any and every set of circumstances the foreign policy of a government of the United Kingdom, if it led to war, should or would automatically commit Australia to participation in that war...But in the circumstances in which the Government of the United Kingdom and the Government of the Commonwealth find themselves today there is no sort of disagreement...If, therefore, in pursuance of this policy, the Government of Britain is at any moment plunged into war, this Government will...make common cause with the Mother Country in that war.[2]

The Leader of the Opposition, John Curtin, immediately endorsed the Minister's 'qualification' of Menzies' words; supported the opening of Australian legations in the United States, Japan and China; and recommended the appointment of an Australian representative to New Zealand. Speaking of the procurement of information which the creation of such posts would facilitate, Curtin said:

...I believe that there would be a greater degree of confidence on the part of the Australian people if they knew that the information

[1] Hasluck, *Government and People*, p. 119.   [2] *C.P.D.* vol. 159, pp. 198–9.

upon which important decisions were to be made by the Australian Government was information gathered and verified by men who have no responsibility for colouring it in order to justify policies pursued by governments other than our own.[1]

These statements lead one to the conclusion that the logic of events, rather than any theory of Dominion status, had begun to force both Government and Opposition in Australia to realise that Australian vital interests demanded something more in the field of foreign policy than intelligent suggestions to London, based primarily on British sources of information, as to how the United Kingdom Government should conduct on behalf of the British Commonwealth as a whole a policy which its constituent members felt able to endorse.

Menzies became Prime Minister after the seizure of Prague by Hitler on 15 March 1939, and after Chamberlain, convinced at last that Hitler aimed at the domination of Europe, if not of the world, had given on behalf of the British Government an unprecedented British guarantee to Poland. Britain was rearming as fast as she could in view of the threat by Hitler to what were now accepted as British vital interests, and Australia too was stepping up her rearmament programme, because she believed that if Britain became involved in war, she too would be involved. In addition, the Australian Government was uneasy lest an outbreak of war in Europe would cause Japan to extend her own military operations southwards. On 16 November 1939, after war with Germany had broken out, the Minister for External Affairs, Sir Henry Gullett, while claiming that there had been some easing of tension in the Far East 'at least for the time being', made the following significant statement to the House of Representatives: 'Until the war had actually commenced there was positive apprehension that the Allies might have, even at the outset, to contend against more than one enemy. So far, at least, the only enemy is Germany.'[2]

War between Germany and Australia commenced on 3 September 1939, the form of the official notification and proclamation in the *Commonwealth Gazette* clearly implying that the Australian Government accepted the view that when Great Britain was at war, Australia was automatically at war, or, in other words, that the Crown was indivisible.[3] In his broadcast

---

[1] *Ibid.* p. 199.   [2] *C.P.D.* vol. 162, p. 1165.
[3] Hasluck, *Government and People*, pp. 154-5.

to the nation on 3 September Menzies told the Australian people that Great Britain had declared war on Germany and that 'as a result, Australia was also at war'.[1] The consistency of this view of the constitutional position with the 'qualification', as the Leader of the Opposition had described it, placed by the Minister for External Affairs on 9 May upon the attitude expressed by Mr Menzies in his broadcast of 26 April may be open to doubt. However, as Hasluck has pointed out,

A statement that Australia was at war because Britain was at war does not express the whole truth. A constitutional theory alone could not have led to so prompt a declaration if Australians had not approved the cause for which they were to fight; and the endorsement of the declaration by all political parties was not necessarily an endorsement by every one of them of the view which the Government had taken of Australia's position as a member of the British Commonwealth.[2]

What was the policy of the Australian Government in regard to the issues leading to war? And what action was taken to put this policy into effect? As in the case of the Sudetenland, the Australian Government followed the British lead, and expressed its views to the British Government. When the House of Representatives assembled on 6 September the Prime Minister tabled a White Paper on the events leading to war, and during his speech described Australian policy and action in the following words:

I suggested that he [Chamberlain] and the British Government should make it clear to Herr Hitler that we regarded the merits of Danzig and the Corridor as quite open to argument and that we should use our influence with Poland to procure some form of arbitrament or adjustment, so long as Germany was prepared to play its part, but we felt that the time was opportune for a general European settlement which would recognise Germany's obligations to Italy and ours to France. That had been mentioned in the German despatch. And we welcomed references to possible future limitation of armaments, because we felt that the present state of affairs must lead to a serious economic breakdown, in which Germany would suffer as much as any country. I went further and suggested that it should be emphasised that there was amongst all the British peoples a genuine desire for good relations with Germany, but this desire was not inconsistent with the determination to fight Germany in what

---

[1] Hasluck, *Government and People*, p. 152.   [2] *Ibid.* p. 155.

seemed a just cause, yet it would be a tragedy if we should fight, each believing his cause to be just when unprejudiced discussion and desire to understand each other's point of view might have avoided it; and that, from that point of view, a clear statement by Herr Hitler of his aims and desires should if possible be obtained. I went on to say that I would not dismiss proposals made by Herr Hitler simply because they were vague or occasionally meaningless, but that it was essential our approach to the whole problem should be liberal and generous so long as generosity was at our own expense and not at the expense of others. I said that we must not connive at a Polish settlement which would leave Poland at such a disadvantage in the negotiations as would render it probable that its future history would resemble that of Czechoslovakia.[1]

Hasluck distinguishes three reasons why Australia accepted the onerous obligations of war, despite the fact that Australia had not been consulted by Great Britain prior to the mother country deciding to guarantee Poland and despite the fact that Australia was not a party to the guarantee. These reasons were, first, because of the view held by the Government regarding the constitutional position of Australia as a member of the British Commonwealth; secondly, because the Government believed that the defeat of Great Britain would eventually threaten the overthrow of Australia either by Germany or Japan; and, thirdly, because of the Government's view of international morality and the foundations of a stable community of nations. The third reason unified the country, which accepted the necessity of resisting by force a rule imposed by force. 'That was the one theme common to the speeches from all sides of politics.'[2] There remained, however, wide differences of opinion as to the nature and extent of the part Australia should play in the prosecution of the war.

II. CASEY AS AUSTRALIAN MINISTER TO WASHINGTON

In view of the Prime Minister's public endorsement of 26 April 1939 of the policy of establishing Australian diplomatic missions in the Pacific, and the concurrence of the Leader of the Opposition in this view during the debate on the international situation in the House of Representatives on 9 May, it is surprising that almost one year elapsed before the appointment of

---

[1] *C.P.D.* vol. 161, p. 32.   [2] Hasluck, *Government and People*, p. 156.

an Australian Minister to Washington was formally completed when Casey, having resigned his cabinet portfolio and seat in Parliament, presented his credentials at the White House on 5 March 1940. It is even more surprising that Latham, the first Australian Minister to Japan, did not arrive in Japan to take up his appointment until the end of 1940. No doubt the long time-gap before theory was put into practice was due in part to the desire of the Government to appoint well-known Australians of distinction to these first, vital, diplomatic posts, and to the consequent difficulty of disengaging them from the cabinet and the High Court respectively. This might be regarded as sufficient reason had not the fear of impending war, and the actual outbreak of war required urgent action. Hartley Grattan, referring to 'The cold reaction of the Australians and New Zealanders to the thinking eventually embodied in the Statute of Westminster (1931)',[1] which gave legal form to the convention that Great Britain would no longer pass legislation affecting the Dominions without their consent and which was not adopted by Australia until late in 1942, comments that this attitude 'illustrates their semi-philosophical acceptance of what their more adventurous fellow dominions [like Canada and South Africa] could only regard as an arrested nationalism'.[1] This description, however, substantially underestimates the developed nationalism of Australia, particularly after, and largely because of, Australian achievements in the First World War.

The personality of the Australian could scarcely be confused with that of an Englishman by anyone who knew both well; nor was there any lack of pride amongst Australians in their own country and people—indeed, they could more justly be charged with somewhat aggressive self-confidence. But Australians (unlike Canadians and South Africans), overwhelmingly British in origin, isolated in their island continent from significant contacts with non-British peoples, did not feel the urge to underline in the constitutional field the nationalism they were more than ready to assert on the field of sport. They were pragmatic by tradition, unaccustomed to and thus suspicious of theorising, preoccupied with taming a reluctant continent and with wringing from it the necessary basis for a high average standard of living for the average man, and hesitant to move

---

[1] Grattan, *United States and the Southwest Pacific*, p. 142.

speedily into new fields of independent thinking and acting. It is perhaps not surprising that in the circumstances it required the massive threat which war posed to the continuance of the Australian way of life to force Australia, somewhat slowly, into separate diplomatic activity.

Once established, however, Australian diplomatic missions showed no lack of initiative either in reporting or in comment. They worked in close co-operation with British missions in furthering the adoption by foreign countries of some policy upon which there had been mutual Commonwealth agreement. But there is little if any evidence of 'arrested nationalism' amongst Australian representatives overseas either as regards uncritical acceptance of British embassy views, or reluctance to convey Australian views to foreign governments. Indeed, it could be argued that, after Pearl Harbour, when the security of Australia became increasingly endangered and somewhat divergent British and Australian interests developed, Australia pressed its own particular views and needs beyond the point justified by the world situation as a whole.

Because of American power and resources, the work of the Australian Legation in the United States from the time of its establishment until the entry of America into the Second World War was of outstanding importance. Some account is desirable, therefore, of how effectively the Washington post operated during this period.

Australians at the time were largely unaware—and few are sufficiently aware today—of the distinguished work done by Casey on behalf of his country in registering effectively an Australian 'presence', not merely in Washington, but also in the United States as a whole. When America entered the war after Pearl Harbor, Australia was known, and favourably known, to a wide range of Americans. This was due primarily to the energetic and successful activities of the first Australian Minister to Washington, who built upon the significant contribution to the Allied war effort played especially by Australian armed forces on the ground in the Middle East, in the air in Europe through the Empire Air Training Scheme, and on the sea wherever Australian naval vessels operated.

Casey was a happy choice of the Australian Government as first Minister to the United States. He was fifty years old when he took up his appointment, unusually ripe, for an Australian, in military, diplomatic and political experience. Born in Australia and educated at Australian schools, he had graduated in Engineering, with honours in Mechanical Science, from Cambridge University before enlisting in the Australian army in the first year of World War I. By the end of the war he held the rank of Major, and had been awarded both the D.S.O. and the M.C. Tall, physically well set, and with a good bearing and presence, he returned to Australia and began to practise as a mining engineer. In 1924, however, his sense of public responsibility, tempered, no doubt, by his overseas experience both in peace and in war, led him to accept the offer of Mr Bruce, Prime Minister of Australia, of the post of Australian Political Liaison Officer in London, which he held for no less than seven years. To quote Casey's own words:

What Mr Bruce was mainly concerned with was the point in time at which consultation [between Britain and Australia] took place. He wanted to have information from London about any matter that concerned Australia in its earliest stages, so that Australian views could be expressed when policy was still being worked out, and not when it was so far advanced as to be very difficult to alter. Mr Bruce believed that the only satisfactory way to achieve this was to have an Australian officer in London, in daily touch with the Foreign Office and in the confidence of the relevant Ministers and senior officials, who could report direct to him and also provide a direct channel of communication between the Australian and United Kingdom Governments on matters of external affairs that affected Australian interests...I reached London in December and soon afterwards became established in the office of Sir Maurice (now Lord) Hankey, Secretary of the Cabinet and of the Committee of Imperial Defence...Thanks largely to the help of Sir Maurice Hankey, the inevitable difficulties inherent in this new experiment ...were overcome, and within six months the new link was working satisfactorily.[1]

Casey's period of official service in England made him familiar with the inside working of one of the best-run Foreign Offices in the world, gave him contacts with the British 'establishment' which would prove of lasting value in future diplomatic or political life, and deepened his experience of the development and handling of world problems, at least to the extent that they were likely to affect Australia.

[1] Casey, *Friends and Neighbours*, pp. 30–1.

Returning to Australia after his service in London, Casey entered Parliament, was appointed Assistant Treasurer (1933–35), Treasurer (1935–39), Minister in charge of Development and Scientific and Industrial Research (1937–39), and Minister for Supply and Development (1939–40) in the Menzies Government. Before taking up his Washington appointment he had visited the United States several times. By temperament something of an extravert, interested in people and with an admiration for the successful business entrepreneur, he found no difficulty at all in making quick and friendly contact with Americans. Further, his university and official experience in England and his understanding of the English temperament and outlook made it possible for him to explain Englishmen to Americans and Americans to Englishmen, and often to bring together on informal social occasions representatives of the two countries whose direct contacts had been formal rather than close.

Casey was an excellent host, with a flair for starting a conversation and inducing men of different outlook and views to carry it on. His social activities were facilitated by the fact that he was a man of some private means. Though more sensitive than the usual Australian politician, he was no shrinking violet: indeed, he had come to believe perhaps too firmly in the importance of the arts of public relations. Both he and Mrs Casey flew their own light aeroplane and readers of the American Press soon came to know that Australia was represented in Washington by a 'flying diplomat'. Regular speeches were made every three weeks or so in different parts of the United States, and Casey's deliberate policy of fostering Press contacts ensured publicity about Australia.

It can be said with confidence that thousands of Americans, including many in high political and official places, became increasingly conscious before Pearl Harbor that Australia was a country geographically placed in the South-West Pacific—not, as many Americans had tended to think, somewhere in the vague Far East, perhaps near the Sea of Japan—whose inhabitants were not identical with Englishmen, who did not pay taxes to Great Britain, whose representatives were not 'reserved' but apt to be singularly frank in speech: people, in fact, in some respects not unlike Americans. By developing this favourable 'climate' of opinion towards Australia, Casey performed an outstanding service for his country in advance of the time, after his departure from Washington, when United States power became the main barrier standing between Australia and Japan.

Hartley Grattan, an intelligent, impartial and exceedingly well-informed American friend of Australia, underestimates the importance for Australia of its diplomatic representation in the United States in the period which preceded Pearl Harbor when he states that the Australians 'suffered in Washington from their low visibility'. Australia was undoubtedly perceived by the Americans as a close associate of the United Kingdom, not as an autonomous Pacific power, an ancillary character emphasised by Australia's own insistence upon maintaining the 'diplomatic unity of the British Empire'.[1]

It is true—and not surprising, in view of their comparative strength—that the United States looked to Great Britain in regard to matters of military strategy, as the private agreement between the two countries on a 'Beat Hitler First' policy clearly shows. It is true also that American eyes looked north rather than south of the equator in the early days after Pearl Harbor, and that few Americans understood the significance of Dominion status, even for Australia. But some public evidence is now available of the extent to which certain influential Americans turned to Casey on occasion as an intermediary between Americans and British.

Thus, after the death of the British Ambassador to Washington, Lord Lothian, in the latter half of 1940, there was a real possibility that Lloyd George might have been appointed to the post. President Roosevelt's reaction to such reports and informal British soundings along these lines was 'consternation', but it was felt to be impracticable for this attitude to be conveyed direct to the British. In the circumstances, Casey was asked 'privately and confidentially to see a personal friend of the President and of Cordell Hull', and this interview prompted telegrams to Menzies in Canberra, Bruce in London, the Australian High Commissioner in Ottawa, and a visit to the South African Minister in Washington. 'The result of my communications', Casey has written, 'was that within twenty-four hours, Mr Churchill received messages from Mr Mackenzie King, Mr Menzies, Field-Marshal Smuts, and Mr Peter Fraser, varying in their content but in one way or another expressing con-

[1] Grattan, *U.S. and the Southwest Pacific*, p. 172.

cern at the Press speculation about the possible appointment of Lloyd George, and explaining why...'[1] In the event, Lloyd George's name was never put forward formally, and Lord Halifax was sent to Washington instead.

Secondly, when in January 1941 Roosevelt decided to send Harry Hopkins to London as his personal representative to maintain contact with Churchill and others pending the appointment of a successor to Mr Kennedy as American Ambassador to Great Britain, Casey was approached by Justice Felix Frankfurter, a close friend of the President, with a view to ensuring that the contact with Churchill was successful in establishing mutual confidence. In reply to Casey's message to the Australian High Commissioner in London, Bruce replied, 'I saw the Prime Minister last night and conveyed your point. He is most grateful and will certainly act on it.'[2]

Thirdly, in the early stages after the arrival in Washington of Lord Halifax, the new British Ambassador, Casey acted as a link between the Americans and Halifax, whom for some time they continued to identify in their minds as one of the architects of 'Munich'. In his diary extract for 1 April 1941 Casey records the following:

In March, Dean Acheson, Assistant Secretary of State, told me that something must be done to bring Cordell Hull and Halifax closer together. I asked what the trouble was. He said that Hull was 'the old man from Tennessee', and basically very shy. He regarded Halifax as a combination of the holder of an ancient British peerage, a Viceroy of India, and a British Foreign Secretary, all rolled into one, and he was scared to death of him. Could I do anything about it? I talked to Halifax, who said, 'I hope he's not as scared of me as I am of him.' I suggested to Halifax that one way of breaking the ice would be for him to ask Cordell Hull to dinner, together with a few other hand-picked men, including a couple of close friends of Hull's and a couple of others who could be relied upon to keep things moving agreeably. Halifax agreed at once, and was good enough to ask me to be one of them. I told Dean Acheson of the idea. He thought well of it, and suggested one or two appropriate men, as well as the things that Hull liked to eat and drink, all of which I passed on to Halifax. We discussed suitable subjects that one or other of us might throw into the ring. In due course the dinner party came off, only four of us, Halifax, Cordell Hull, Norman Davis, head of the American Red Cross and an old friend of Hull's, and myself.

[1] See Casey, *Personal Experience*, pp. 46–7.   [2] *Ibid.*; for details, see pp. 51–2.

Norman Davis and I met beforehand and discussed the evening and acted as the honest brokers who made the running until the other two warmed up.[1]

It is impossible to believe that well-known and influential Americans would have turned in circumstances such as these to the Australian Minister if Casey had not established himself in the United States as a person of standing and influence whose discretion and integrity could be trusted; nor can we believe that Australian interests suffered in the process.

Finally, while Casey had not succeeded, during his two-year period of service in Washington, in establishing the same ease of personal relationships with President Roosevelt that he had with Harry Hopkins, the President's most trusted adviser, with Justice Frankfurter, a power behind the throne, and with men like Secretary for War Stimson, Vice-President Henry Wallace, Secretary for the Navy Knox and Assistant-Secretary Dean Acheson of the State Department, it is clear that Roosevelt had a high opinion of Casey, and was conscious of the possible value of Australian services in a kind of intermediary position between the United States and Great Britain, at least in the Middle East area. When, after the change of Government in Australia in October 1941 which brought the Labour Party to power, and after Pearl Harbor had brought the United States into the war, Casey accepted Churchill's offer of a seat in the British War Cabinet, combined with an appointment as British Minister of State in the Middle East based on Cairo—a unique offer by a British Prime Minister to a citizen of one of the Dominions—Roosevelt positively encouraged Casey to accept the offer. This appointment led to an acrimonious exchange of messages between Churchill and the new Australian Prime Minister, Mr Curtin, which did no good to the Allied cause, and the President was disturbed by its public echoes.[2] In a personal message to Churchill, Roosevelt spoke with great frankness:

The publicity from the Casey business disturbs me greatly...It would be desirable all round if any way can be found to avoid all further public discussion of this which, it seems to me, plays right into the hands of our enemies. I realise that the Casey appointment is only an incident. The more important issue is the basic relationship of Australia to Great Britain. I sense in this country a growing

---

[1] Casey, *Personal Experience*, pp. 63–4.   [2] See pp. 58–9 below.

feeling of impatience at what publicly appears to be a rather strained relationship at this critical time between the United Kingdom and Australia...I say this to you because I myself feel greatly responsible for the turn of events. I still consider the decision to send Casey to the Middle East is a wise one and I told him quite frankly that I hoped he would take this job because of his knowledge of the American and Australian as well as the British angles in the Middle East area.[1]

But successful 'public relations', however important, must be tested by the degree of participation in official discussions of policy and actual negotiation. Here, too, there is no doubt as to the degree of Casey's successful penetration of both British and American official circles, despite the fact that he was a newcomer to the diplomatic corps in Washington and the representative of a country of small population and limited military power. Part I of his book *Personal Experience 1939–46*, covering the period of his service in Washington, and based on diary records, makes abundantly clear the range of his activities.

In the nine months we were together in Washington I got to know Lothian [British Ambassador] very well. I saw him practically every day...On most matters of mutual concern we made a practice of going together to see Cordell Hull to save the time of all three of us [p. 43].

On January 24th 1941 Lord Halifax, the new British Ambassador, reached Washington...I found him not so easy to get to know as Lothian, but in the course of the year we were together in Washington, we had no fewer than sixty-seven discussions [p. 53].

December 22nd 1941. Harry Hopkins telephoned and cheered me up a good deal by saying that he thought I would be pleased at what was in train so far as Australia was concerned...December 23rd... the American Lend-Lease people got in touch with me. As a result I sent the following telegram to Canberra: 'United States Lend-Lease authorities are anxious to know urgently how lend-lease aid to Australia can be stepped up in the most effective way. They ask for a report within 24 hours for the President's information... [p. 79].'

What then was the Australian Government's policy in relation to the Pacific between the outbreak of war with Germany and the Japanese attack upon Pearl Harbor? The basic aim was, not unnaturally, to draw the strength, influence and resources of the United States to the side of the British Common-

---

[1] Robert E. Sherwood, *Roosevelt and Hopkins* (Harper, New York, 1948), pp. 508–9.

wealth in its struggle with the Axis powers for survival. After the fall of France, Australia had good reason to fear that Japan might decide that the moment had come, while European strength was engaged in Europe and the Mediterranean, 'to enable each nation to enjoy its proper station in the world'[1] by pressing southwards herself. Australian diplomatic efforts, therefore, in collaboration with Great Britain, were directed towards inducing America to take effective steps, preferably to deter Japan from such a move, or, if this proved impracticable, to prevent a Japanese move southwards from being successful.

The means to this end took many forms, varying with circumstances. As indicated above, one broad approach was to build up in official and private circles in the United States a favourable 'climate' of opinion towards Australia, and an understanding of its problems and of its substantial contribution to the war effort in the Middle East and elsewhere. Secondly, attempts were made to induce the United States to give a firm warning to Japan that further encroachments southward would lead to war with America; and if such a warning were unobtainable, because Congressional opinion would not allow the President to make so bold and clear a statement, to seek some demonstration of American 'presence' in South-East Asia— such as using Singapore as a base for American warships, or even the visit of an American fleet to Australia—which might lead the Japanese to infer that an attack on certain areas would risk American intervention. Thirdly, Australia wished to exhaust any available diplomatic means of 'gaining time' by delaying any move further south by Japan, for example, by keeping negotiations going, by seeking some temporary *modus vivendi*, and even by way of appeasement of Japan by agreeing temporarily to some demand by her, for example, to close the Burma Road supply route to China. In accepting some measure of 'appeasement' in the last resort, however, the Australian Government had little or no illusion, as it had about Hitler during the Munich crisis, that militarist Japan's appetite for conquest of territory would thereby be assuaged: the objective was to gain time, both for rearmament and in the hope that the war situation outside the Pacific area might develop more favourably to the anti-Axis powers. It was important, too, that

[1] Quoted in *The Chrysanthemum and the Sword*, by Ruth Benedict (Charles E. Tuttle Co., Tokyo, 1954), p. 44.

American understanding should be secured in advance for any such unpalatable measures of 'appeasement'.

Of course, Australian diplomatic activity was not limited to Washington. Messages passed constantly between Canberra and London, whither Sir Earle Page was sent in October 1941 to act as accredited Australian representative to the British War Cabinet, because the Australian Government had become convinced, following upon Menzies' visit to England in that year, of the need to exercise the most direct influence in London if it was to have any effective say in regard to the higher direction of the war.

There was continuing pressure upon the British Government by the Australian Government to strengthen Singapore, not only by stationing a battle fleet there, but also by sending air reinforcements. Consultations took place between the two governments as to the danger of the Japanese seizing control of the Portuguese section of the island of Timor, immediately to the north of Australia, and as to possible military action which might be taken to deny the island to the Japanese, preferably with the prior assent of the Portuguese Government. Reports, not always well-founded, were received from the new Australian Legation in Tokyo[1] reflecting views current at that post which had to be balanced in Canberra by information received from other posts.

In short, before Pearl Harbor, it can be said that the Australian Government, conscious of danger—though it still had to learn from bitter experience just how weak Singapore was—actively engaged in an energetic campaign in the international field with the aim of protecting Australian interests, and that, on the whole, it was well served by a small Department of External Affairs and by its diplomatic representatives overseas.[2] This was particularly true of the Washington post, where Casey had made the necessary contacts and participated personally in discussions held by the United States Government with representatives, in particular, of the so-called ABCD powers (Australia, Britain, China, Dutch) regarding the negotiations with Japanese representatives in Washington which preceded the final break when Japan attacked Pearl Harbor.

[1] Hasluck, *Government and People*, footnote to p. 550.
[2] For a more detailed account of Australian policy between September 1939 and December 1941, see Hasluck, *Government and People*, pp. 524–58; Grattan, *U.S. and the Southwest Pacific*, pp. 166–9.

Messages from Washington to Canberra gave a ball-to-ball account of the course of these negotiations and, towards the end, led the new Labour Party Government which came to power in Canberra in mid-October 1941 to encourage Casey to seize any opportunity of intervening in the negotiations. When (following Chinese protests) the American Secretary of State, Mr Cordell Hull, abandoned further efforts to find an acceptable *modus vivendi*, Casey, with the prior knowledge and assent but not necessarily the approval of Hull and Halifax, took the drastic step of discussing the matter on 30 November direct and alone in Washington with the Japanese special envoy, Saburo Kurusu, who towards the end of the conversation was joined by the Japanese Ambassador to Washington, Admiral Nomura. Casey's offer to act as an intermediary between Kurusu and Hull in regard to any new proposals Kurusu might wish to make proved ineffective, because Kurusu had no authority to do more than press Japanese proposals for a *modus vivendi* already found unacceptable by the Americans.[1] The conversation, however, reflected a last, determined Australian initiative to delay or avert the crisis.

The great value of the information available to the Australian Legation in the last few days before Pearl Harbor, and conveyed to Canberra, where it supplemented information received from London, can be gauged from the following record selected by Casey from his own diary:

Late in November, Mr Stimson, Secretary of War, told me confidentially that precautionary war warning telegrams had been sent on November 27th to the Commanders of the American Pacific and Atlantic Fleets. On November 30th 1941, Cordell Hull told me that he believed that 'the Japanese are even now, practically speaking, on the march'. On the evening of December 3rd, the Americans asked the Japanese, 'Why are Japanese reinforcements coming south to Indo-China in such numbers?' The answer was unsatisfactory and vague—'Reports much exaggerated', 'Chinese massing on northen border of Indo-China', etc. On the morning of December 6th forty-six Japanese transports with a strong Japanese naval escort were seen from the air to be rounding Cape Cambodia and entering the Gulf of Siam.

I lunched alone with Colonel Frank Knox, Secretary of the Navy, in the Navy Office on December 5th. He told me that the Japanese Embassy had had orders the day before to burn their papers.[2]

[1] For details see Hasluck, *Government and People*, p. 551; Casey, *Personal Experience*, pp. 57–8.   [2] Casey, *Personal Experience*, p. 58.

Pearl Harbor was bombed on Sunday 7 December 1941, and on the following day Roosevelt addressed Congress, informing members that 'hostilities exist'.[1] Late on the Sunday afternoon the small staff of the Australian Legation, Washington, met at the minister's residence. At that stage the extent of the damage done to the American Fleet and installations at Pearl Harbor was not known, although it was suspected that it had been severe. For this small band of Australians, however, regret for the loss of American lives, sympathy for relatives, chagrin that, despite all the warning information available, the American Fleet had been caught napping, merged into one dominant emotion: the United States was an ally in a war which, whatever trials lay ahead, would in the end result in the defeat of the Axis Powers.

There was some brief discussion of the nature of the future work of the legation. Before Pearl Harbor, the central objective in everyone's mind had been to avoid Australia finding itself at war with Japan without America at her side. The decision of Japanese military leaders to bomb American territory had solved this problem. Ahead lay now problems of technical war-time collaboration, rather than of politics, designed to ensure the most efficient prosecution of the war. According to Hartley Grattan, 'Correctly seen, Pearl Harbor was an Australian disaster as it was an American disaster'.[2] It was not so regarded by Australians in Washington on 7 December 1941.

[1] Sherwood, *op. cit.* p. 437. The Curtin Labour Party Government decided that Australia should make a declaration of war against Japan separate from the British Declaration; see *Current Notes*, vol. XI, no. 10 (1941), pp. 278–9. For the attitude of the Menzies Government towards war with Germany, see p. 26 above.
[2] Grattan, *U.S. and the Southwest Pacific*, p. 177.

3

THE AUSTRALIAN LABOUR PARTY IN OFFICE

PART ONE

I. PRIOR TO PEARL HARBOR

On 28 August 1941 Menzies announced his intention to resign from the Prime Ministership and his readiness to serve under Mr A. W. Fadden,[1] Leader of the Country Party, who was acceptable to both the United Australia and Country Parties as Prime Minister. In his public statement Menzies said that while his cabinet colleagues had personal good will towards himself, many felt he was unpopular with large sections of the Press and the people; that this handicapped the effectiveness of the Government; and that there were differences of opinion within the Government parties themselves which might not exist under another leader.[2]

Fadden[3] formed a ministry on 29 August with Menzies holding the portfolio of Defence Co-ordination. The Government parties, however, had merely prepared the way for their own downfall. After a defeat of the Government, with the help of two Independent Members, during discussion on the Budget Mr John Curtin, Leader of the Australian Labour Party, was commissioned by the Governor-General on 3 October to form a Government. The new Prime Minister took for himself the additional portfolio of Defence Co-ordination and chose as his Attorney-General and Minister for External Affairs Dr H. V. Evatt, who in 1940 had resigned his position as Justice of the High Court of Australia in order to enter Federal politics.

So commenced a new era in Australian foreign policy which lasted until the defeat of the Labour Party at the Federal elec-

[1] Later Sir Arthur Fadden.
[2] See Hasluck, *Government and People*, pp. 503–5, for details of the party manœuvres which led to this resignation.
[3] Fadden, a chartered accountant from Queensland, held several cabinet offices for short periods in 1940, was Acting Prime Minister during Menzies' absence from Australia in the early part of 1941, and was Commonwealth Treasurer 1949–58.

tions held in December 1949. Thus it was the Labour Party which was in power at the time of the Pearl Harbor attack, when Singapore fell, when an actual invasion of Australia by Japanese forces seemed probable, when this fear was calmed by American naval victories in the battles of the Coral Sea and of Midway, when the San Francisco Conference met in 1945 to adopt the Charter of the United Nations, when Germany and later Japan surrendered, and when much of the post-war policy in relation to defeated enemies had to be considered and discussed.

The advent to power of the Labour Party was nothing new in Australia. It had been out of power, however, for almost ten years, due mainly to internal strains and stresses which arose during the Great Depression years and the rift in the party which occurred when Lyons and others left it and joined the newly created United Australia Party under the leadership of Lyons. It fell to John Curtin, elected Leader of the Labour Party in 1935, to heal the deep scars left by the split in the party and to restore it gradually as an effective political force.

During the First World War Curtin had been a pacifist, and in later years he had advocated for Australia a policy of minding its own business, endeavouring to secure economic and social justice for itself and others and defending itself from its own shores. It is one of the ironies of history that Curtin came to office as Prime Minister when Australia was already engaged in a world war and when Japanese aggression southwards was shortly to call for the greatest military, economic and moral effort from Australians to enable their country to survive.

Within little more than two months after the Labour Party came to power, the Japanese struck at Pearl Harbor on 7 December 1941. At this time the main body of Australian troops was engaged in the Mediterranean area. Some seven weeks later Singapore fell, shattering any lingering Australian illusions that an 'impregnable' base sheltered their homeland from any probable attack from the north. It stands to Curtin's lasting credit that, during the period from Pearl Harbor to the battle of Midway when Australian morale was being subjected to its severest test, he gave the necessary leadership to bring Australia through the ordeal, even if, in the process, he made some mistakes. There is little doubt that the strains and stresses of war upon this man of peace contributed to his early death in office in 1945.

The Minister for External Affairs in the Labour Government, Dr H. V. Evatt, was a distinctive and unique personality in Australian political life who substantially determined Australian foreign policy—subject to some Prime Ministerial restraints in certain fields—for a period of eight years. His many visits and strenuous activities abroad helped to create in the minds of overseas countries a more vivid and somewhat harsh Australian 'image'. No clear understanding can be gained of the effects of Australian policy in the international field during this period without some preliminary consideration of the qualities of Evatt not only as a politician but also as a man.

The new Minister for External Affairs was born in East Maitland, New South Wales, in 1894, and was thus forty-seven years old when he assumed his portfolio, at the height of his mental powers. His academic record had been outstanding. During his Arts course at Sydney University he collected prizes in subjects as diverse as Philosophy, English, History and Mathematics, graduating as a Bachelor of Arts with triple first-class honours. He then became a Master of Arts and proceeded to study Law, graduating as a Bachelor of Laws with first-class honours and the University Medal for the best student of his year. Later he qualified as a Doctor of Laws, a degree which is comparatively rare in Australia except when conferred *honoris causa*.

Evatt practised as a barrister in Sydney and became a King's Counsel in 1929. In 1925 he entered State politics in New South Wales as a Labour Party member of the Legislative Assembly. In 1930, at the unprecedented age of 36, he was appointed by the Federal Labour Government as a Justice of the High Court of Australia, where he sat for ten years, resigning from that Court in 1940, after the outbreak of the war, to enter federal politics in the same year. He had not served one full term in Parliament before he became Attorney-General and Minister for External Affairs.

As Minister for External Affairs, Evatt made numerous visits overseas, at first in connexion with the war, and later in connexion with post-war problems, particularly in their United Nations aspects. He was the *de facto* Leader of the Australian Delegation to the Charter Conference of the United Nations at San Francisco in 1945, although Mr Francis Forde, technically his senior in the Curtin ministry as Deputy Prime Minister,

was also a member of the Delegation. As a trained constitutional lawyer, Evatt had a significant influence upon the Charter[1]
beyond any reasonable expectation of the representative of a
Small or Middle Power: indeed, it can be argued with some
force that the San Francisco Conference represented the peak
of his international influence, despite the many United Nations
offices he held later.

Evatt was Chairman in 1945 of the Policy Committee of the
Far Eastern Advisory Commission set up in Washington to deal
with questions of post-war policy in relation to Japan; Leader of
the Australian Delegation to the Paris Peace Conference, 1946;
President of the South Pacific Regional Conference, Canberra,
1947, which established the South Pacific Commission; Chairman of the British Commonwealth Conference on the Japanese
Peace Treaty held in Canberra, 1947; and President of the
General Assembly of the United Nations in 1948. He led the
Australian Delegations to General Assembly Sessions in 1946,
1947 and 1948, and in that capacity held various United Nations
offices, including the Chairmanship of the United Nations Ad
Hoc Committee on Palestine in 1947.

In the domestic political field, Evatt became Deputy Prime
Minister in 1946, and in 1951, after the death of Joseph Benedict Chifley—who had succeeded John Curtin on the latter's
death in 1945—Leader of the Labour Party and Leader of the
Opposition in the House of Representatives. He resigned his
seat in Parliament in 1960 to take up an appointment as Chief
Justice of the Supreme Court of New South Wales, but serious
ill health led to his retirement from the Bench in 1962 and to his
death in 1965. Evatt's publications include *The King and His
Dominion Governors*, *Injustice within the Law*, *Rum Rebellion*, *Australian
Labour Leader* and *The United Nations*, covering a wide range of
legal, constitutional, political and international subjects.

It was, of course, unusual for a man of Evatt's training and
background to achieve the highest political office in the Australian Labour Party, which historically has leaned rather
towards the identifiable trade unionist who has made his way
slowly to the top through the trade-union movement or through
the parliamentary Labour Party or both. He was a 'white-

[1] See chapter 4, § 2, below, for an account of Evatt's influence at the San Francisco
Conference, 1945; also chapter 4, §§ 3 and 4, for an account of international
reactions to his policy and methods.

collar' man whose academic achievements in themselves would have made Labour Party supporters and politicians suspicious and reluctant to elect him Leader of the Party. Even Chifley, a man of experience and character who won the respect of Australians as a whole as Treasurer under Curtin's leadership and, on the latter's death, as Prime Minister, was apt to criticise severely persons of academic training whom he described privately on occasion as 'bloody B.A.'s'. It is not so surprising that the Labour Party found Evatt's talents most useful in the portfolio of External Affairs, as members of the party have usually been far more familiar with domestic than international problems. Two contributing factors to his election as Leader of the Labour Party were no doubt the prestige and publicity acquired, at home and abroad, while Minister for External Affairs, and the fact that he was in position as Deputy Leader of the Party when Chifley died in 1951.

Evatt's academic record speaks for itself as regards his intellectual ability. His training had developed his analytical capacity; his ambition directed his energies unflaggingly towards its realisation; no mere theorist, he gave great attention to factual detail. So long as his ambition was limited to a legal career, he was extremely successful in a remarkably short time, despite the fact that public speaking did not come naturally to him, partly, perhaps, because he was not a particularly imaginative or original man, and lacked a saving sense of humour and the ability to make human contacts easily. Even as a lawyer, he was much less of a 'jury man' than an advocate before a Court of Appeal. When he entered the federal political field, however, and especially when as Minister for External Affairs he represented his country overseas, reactions to his style and tactics were often adverse.

Evatt was no man to rest content with being a power behind the throne; he sought the limelight, the full glare of favourable publicity, and, being avid for power, when acquired he used it to the full. His natural abilities certainly made it possible for him while Minister to influence events and people, but in the process he made few if any friends. The status, therefore, which he succeeded in winning for Australia during his overseas visits was diminished by his aggressive and thrusting manner, which took small account of the susceptibilities of other countries, including the United Kingdom.

Before the Labour Party came to office in October 1941, its Leader, John Curtin, had on several occasions refused offers from the Government Benches to join in an all-party Government. He declared that he was ready to give every assistance in the prosecution of the war, but believed that the continual existence of an Opposition Party in Parliament was in the country's best interest, because Government policy would thus be subjected to regular and public scrutiny and criticism. This attitude did not, however, prevent him from proposing the formation of an Advisory War Council, to be constituted by the appointment to it of senior members of both Government and Opposition. Such a Council was in fact set up under National Security Regulations on 28 October 1940 to 'consider and advise the Government with respect to such matters relating to the defence of the Commonwealth or the prosecution of the war as are referred to the Council by the Prime Minister'. It was also empowered to 'consider and advise the Government with respect to such other matters so relating' as it thought fit.[1] Members of the Advisory War Council took an oath of secrecy.

The establishment of this body represented a considerable gesture by the Government to the Opposition, which thereby gained secret information from Government sources without political responsibility. In the opinion of Professor Partridge:

The arrangement was certainly an advantage for the opposition; no opposition has ever been more generously treated by its opponents. It kept the leading members of the Labour front bench intimately acquainted with problems and developments; it gave them a forum, often public, where they could systematically criticise aspects of the war administration, without themselves having to accept responsibility; and it gave an opportunity for some of the men who were later to become the dominant personalities in the Labour government which was formed in 1941—including Curtin himself, Beasley and Evatt—to establish themselves as national figures.[2]

Hasluck regards the establishment of the Council as justified by the particular political situation which existed at the time; he argues against it, however, if regarded in a more general or permanent sense as 'a useful aid to the machinery of government'.[3] Hasluck refers to complaints by Government members

[1] Hasluck, *Government and People*, p. 270.
[2] *Australia, a Social and Political History*, ed. Gordon Greenwood (Angus and Robertson, Sydney, 1959), p. 373.   [3] Hasluck, *Government and People*, pp. 273-4.

regarding the disclosure in the Press of the Council's business, and comments that:

> ...however it may have come about, press reports were published which were an incomplete and partial account of Council proceedings ...these reports were likely to have created an impression unfavourable to the Government and...in several cases, they were likely to create an impression favourable to non-Government members, and on one occasion, to the chances of the Labour Party's taking office.[1]

Nevertheless, on the assumption that the Labour Party would in any event have come to office, previous service by senior Labour Party representatives on the Advisory War Council must be regarded as having been in the national interest, as it familiarised these men with vital current issues in such a way as to diminish the handicap of taking over the reins of Government at a time of crisis after long years spent in the political wilderness.

In the brief period between the accession to office of the Labour Party on 3 October 1941 and the Japanese attack on Pearl Harbor, the new Government pursued policies broadly similar to those of its predecessors. There was no question at that time of requesting the return to Australia of the Australian Imperial Force from the Middle East: indeed, plans to reinforce these troops were approved by the War Cabinet as late as 26 November.[2] This is not surprising, as Japan had not yet finally thrown down the gauntlet. There were hopes that time could still be bought by extending the current negotiations between the United States and Japan, perhaps by devising an amended *modus vivendi* more acceptable to the United States than that proposed by the Japanese.[3] Pressure upon the British Government to reinforce Singapore had brought a renewed assurance from Churchill that if Australia were 'gravely threatened', Britain would cut her losses in the Middle East and send substantial aid.[4] In addition, Curtin pressed Churchill in an effort to obtain definite British reactions to each of five listed cases of prospective Japanese aggression. The Australian view as summarised by Hasluck[5] in each of these hypothetical situations was as follows:

(1) If Japan intensified attacks on China, especially in Yunnan and on the Burma Road, China should be given all

---

[1] Hasluck, *Government and People*, footnote to p. 274. [2] *Ibid.* p. 544.
[3] *Ibid.* pp. 550, 551.   [4] *Ibid.* p. 548.   [5] *Ibid.* p. 554.

support short of declaring war unless American intervention was certain.

(2) If Japan attacked Thailand, armed Commonwealth support should be conditional on American involvement; as regards the Kra Isthmus, however, we should occupy the region if the Japanese definitely threatened it by force of arms.

(3) If Japan attacked Russia, Britain should declare war against Japan, provided Russia undertook to consider herself at war with Japan if the latter moved south and Britain were involved thereby in war with Japan in the Pacific.

(4) An assurance of automatic armed support for the Netherlands East Indies should be given if Japan should attack the Indies, irrespective of the American attitude. The Netherlands should give a reciprocal undertaking.

(5) If Japan should attack Portuguese Timor, Britain should declare war, again irrespective of the United States attitude; a reciprocal understanding should be concluded with Portugal.

On 7 December 1941 Japan made its surprise attack on Pearl Harbor. The immediate effect upon Australian opinion was shock, rather than dismay.[1] 'Singapore was impregnable and the newest British battleships were coming as reinforcements to the Far East.'[1] The United States had entered the war. Curtin described the situation as 'the gravest hour of our history', and besought all to 'go about their allotted task with full vigour and courage'.[2] In a national broadcast he referred to the 'imperishable traditions' of Australians, and roundly asserted 'We shall hold this country and keep it as a citadel for the British-speaking race and as a place where civilisation will persist'.[2] These were proud and brave words. As disaster followed disaster, however, and the safety of Australia itself was directly and immediately imperilled for the first time in history, signs of stress and strain began to appear.

II. FROM PEARL HARBOR TO CASEY'S DEPARTURE FROM WASHINGTON

The entry of Japan into the Second World War and her quick succession of victories at Pearl Harbor, in Malaya, Singapore, the Netherlands East Indies and Burma resulted not only in serious conflicts of interest between Great Britain and Australia

[1] *Ibid.* p. 557.   [2] *Ibid.* pp. 557–8.

but also public revelation of acrimonious exchanges of telegrams between the British and Australian Governments. Under
the emotional strains of war, honest differences of judgement
and of opinion became tinged with doubts as to courage and
good faith. It is open to argument that the scars left by these
disputes never healed completely, that from this period onwards throughout the war years, and even as late in the post-
war period as Britain's application to join the Common Market,
British–Australian relations never recovered fully their old
degree of intimacy.

It is true that Chifley, who became Prime Minister and Leader
of the Labour Party on the death of Curtin in 1945, enjoyed a
reputation both in his own country and in London for integrity,
and that his sympathetic attitude towards British post-war
difficulties, especially in the economic field, did much to improve
relations between London and Canberra.[1] Further, the advent
to power in December 1949 of an Australian Prime Minister,
R. G. Menzies, who never hesitated to describe himself as a
'Commonwealth man', was followed in 1951 by the appointment as Minister for External Affairs of R.G. Casey, well and
favourably known to British political leaders and the British
'establishment' because of his long service in London as Australian Liaison Officer, his appointment by Churchill in 1942 as
British Minister of State in the Middle East, with a seat in the
War Cabinet, and his activities as Governor of Bengal from
1944 to 1946. Nevertheless, the differences and misunderstand-
ings between two 'Old Commonwealth' countries of similar
tradition and stock during the years 1941–42 were so substantial
that they require close and careful examination if present-day
relations between them are to be understood.

In the following account considerable emphasis is laid upon
the chronology of events. The first group of seven dates faithfully reflects the shock to Australian public opinion of enemy
victories in the war, merging into fears of an actual invasion of
Australia by Japanese forces and the eventual dissipation of these
fears following upon American naval victories in the Pacific:

21 June 1940   Signature by France of armistice with
                    Germany

---

[1] See L. F. Crisp, *Ben Chifley* (Longmans, London, 1960), chapter XVIII; also pp.
273–4 below.

7 December 1941	Japanese attack at Pearl Harbor
15 February 1942	Fall of Singapore
19 February 1942	Japanese bomb Darwin (Australian Northern Territory)
6 May 1942	American forces at Bataan (Philippines) surrender to Japan
8 May 1942	Battle of the Coral Sea, which brought 'immense relief and encouragement to Australia and New Zealand as well as to the United States' [1]
4 June 1942	Battle of Midway, 'rightly regarded as the turning-point of the war in the Pacific' [2]

The period from 7 December 1941 to 4 June 1942 covers the period of greatest tension between Canberra and London. For the first time in its history, an Australian Government was faced with the immediate problem of trying to ensure the survival of Australia. In these circumstances it believed that, whatever its obligations to Great Britain, to other parts of the Commonwealth and to allies in the war against the Axis Powers, its primary duty was to the people of Australia. Australian interests therefore were placed highest in the scale of priorities.

Secondly, three other dates are important in regard to the question of Australian knowledge of agreed British–American strategy designed to 'Beat Hitler First' in a war involving not only Germany but also Japan. From January to March 1941 (that is, before the United States entered the war) secret staff talks were held in Washington between British and American service representatives, resulting in agreement—though not at the formal governmental level—upon a plan to 'Beat Hitler First'. This implied, of course, the waging of a defensive or holding war in the Pacific until Hitler was beaten in Europe. After Pearl Harbor this tentative plan was in fact followed up by agreement between Churchill and Roosevelt. The extent to which the Australian Government was aware of and realised the full implications of these agreements is not entirely clear.

There is no doubt that Australia knew that the secret staff talks were taking place. The Australian war histories not only

---

[1] Winston Churchill, *Second World War* (Cassell, London, 1951), vol. IV, p. 220.
[2] *Ibid.* p. 224.

refer to them specifically, but name three high Australian service officers who 'were represented at meetings of the British delegates but not at the joint meetings'.[1] Moreover, it is clear that the Australian Government was informed officially in February 1941, both from London and from the Australian Legation, Washington, that Roosevelt had told the British Ambassador in Washington that the United States would have to fight a 'holding war' in the Pacific even if they become involved in a war with Japan as well as with Germany.[2] Nevertheless, Hasluck, who had access to all the secret documents, has commented that 'there is considerable doubt whether Australian ministers had sufficient information about the [secret staff] discussions to be fully aware at that time of all the implications'.[3] Moreover, another official war historian has disclosed that on 28 May 1942 'Dr Evatt had cabled [apparently from London] to Curtin the text of an agreement between Great Britain and America expressing this [Beat Hitler First] policy and then wrote: "The existence of this written agreement came as a great surprise to myself and, I have no doubt, to you. We were not consulted about the matter."'[4] If in fact Dr Evatt was not aware, during his first visit to Washington as Minister for External Affairs in March and April 1942, that Churchill and Roosevelt had formally agreed upon a 'Beat Hitler First' strategy, this in itself would be sufficient to account for some of the frustrations which he experienced in trying to secure American agreement to an increased allocation of supplies for the South-West Pacific area.

Even before the Labour Party came to power in October 1941 an Australian request, initiated by the Fadden Government but later confirmed by the Curtin Government, for the relief of Australian forces in Tobruk had caused some illfeeling between London and Canberra. On 14 September 1941 Fadden, acting primarily on reports received from the senior Australian army commander in the Middle East, General Blamey,[5] that there was 'increasing and convincing evidence of a decline in physical powers'[6] of the Australian troops in

---

[1] Lionel Wigmore, *The Japanese Thrust* (Australian War Memorial, Canberra, 1957), p. 53.
[2] *Ibid.* p. 53, n. 4.   [3] Hasluck, *Government and People*, p. 353.
[4] Dudley McCarthy, *South-West Pacific Area—First Year* (Australian War Memorial, Canberra, 1959), p. 188.   [5] Later Field-Marshal Sir Thomas Blamey.
[6] See Hasluck, *Government and People*, p. 620.

Tobruk after the prolonged siege to which they had been subjected, cabled London insisting that they should be relieved. A
reply was received on 15 September agreeing to the request,
despite the obvious reluctance of Churchill and the British
Commander-in-Chief, Middle East, General Auchinleck. On
30 September, however, Churchill asked Canberra to reconsider
the decision. The Fadden Government resigned on 3 October,
but Fadden, having consulted with Curtin, Leader of the Labour Party, maintained the previous Australian attitude. On
13 October Churchill again asked Curtin to review the matter,
basing his argument on somewhat different grounds. This
request was considered and rejected by the Australian War
Cabinet on 15 October. Subsequently, the relief of all the remaining Australian forces in Tobruk was effected, except for
one battalion.[1]

Of greater significance, however, than the relief of Australian
forces in Tobruk was the whole question of land, sea and air
reinforcements to maintain the 'impregnable' base at Singapore. When at the Washington Conference of 1921–22, under
American pressure (and against the wishes of Australia), it
was decided that the Anglo-Japanese Alliance would not be
renewed, the decision to build a modern base at Singapore was
crucial for Australia. Henceforth Australian military planning
was based upon the legitimate assumption that in time of emergency a British fleet would be sent to the Far East sufficient to
restrain Japanese military ambitions to an area well north of
Australia. British assurances to this effect, however, became less
certain as early as 28 June 1940, when Canberra received from
London a telegram drawing attention to the fact that 'the
whole strategic situation has been radically altered by the
French defeat'.[2] The telegram added that 'because we cannot
spare a fleet for the Far East at present' it was all the more
important to try to improve land and air defences in Malaya.[3]

The Australian Government was greatly comforted, however, when it received a telegram despatched by Churchill on
11 August 1940 giving a categorical assurance in the following
words:

If...contrary to prudence and self interest, Japan set about invading Australia or New Zealand on a large scale, I have the ex-

[1] *Ibid.* pp. 621–4.   [2] Wigmore, *op. cit.* p. 19.   [3] *Ibid.* p. 20.

plicit authority of the Cabinet to assure you that we should then cut our losses in the Mediterranean and sacrifice every interest, except only the defence and feeding of this Island, on which all depends, and would proceed in good time to your aid with a fleet able to give battle to any Japanese force which could be placed in Australian waters, and able to parry any invading force, or certainly cut its communications with Japan...[1]

After Pearl Harbor and before the fall of Singapore, the Australian Government received strong warnings from its political and military representatives in Malaya and Singapore regarding the need for urgent and significant reinforcements if the fall of Singapore was to be avoided. On 16 December Lt.-Gen. H. Gordon Bennett, in charge of Australian military forces in Malaya, recommended that at least one Australian division from the Middle East should be transferred to Malaya.[2] Two days later Lt.-Gen. Sir John Northcott, Deputy Chief of the Australian General Staff, then visiting Malaya, strongly recommended to the Chief of the Australian General Staff the despatch of all possible reinforcements to Malaya, including a machine-gun battalion.[3] On 25 December the Australian Government representative at Singapore, Mr V. G. Bowden (later taken prisoner and killed by the Japanese), cabled to Canberra his assessment of the current position: 'As things stand at present fall of Singapore is to my mind only a matter of weeks...without immediate air reinforcements Singapore must fall. Need for decision and action is a matter of hours not days.'[4]

On the same day (Christmas Day) the Australian Prime Minister sent messages to Washington for Churchill and Roosevelt, where both were conferring, expressing the opinion that reinforcements earmarked for Singapore seemed 'utterly inadequate',[4] particularly as regards fighter aircraft. He added that if the United States so wished Australia would 'gladly accept United States command in Pacific Ocean area'.[4] In a separate message to Casey, Curtin said, 'Please understand that stage of suggestion has passed'.[4] Churchill's reply was immediate and sympathetic. He said that Roosevelt had agreed to the diversion of a brigade of the 18th British Division to Singapore from its original Middle East destination, in an American transport. Curtin was reminded that Churchill himself had

[1] Wigmore *op. cit.* p. 24.   [2] *Ibid.* p. 154.   [3] *Ibid.* p. 164.   [4] *Ibid.* p. 182.

suggested that an Australian division be recalled from Palestine to replace other troops going to Malaya, or sent direct to Singapore. Roosevelt was also willing to send substantial American forces to Australia, where the Americans were anxious to establish important bases for the war against Japan.[1]

On 27 December Curtin published an article in the *Melbourne Herald* which angered Churchill, aroused misgivings in London and caused controversy in Australia itself. The article stated that the Australian Government refused to accept the view that 'the Pacific struggle must be treated as a subordinate segment of the general conflict'.[2] Curtin continued as follows:

The Australian Government, therefore, regards the Pacific struggle as primarily one in which the United States and Australia must have the fullest say in the direction of the democracies' fighting plan. Without any inhibitions of any kind, I make it quite clear that Australia looks to America, free of any pangs as to our traditional links or kinship with the United Kingdom. We know the problems that the United Kingdom faces...But we know, too, that Australia can go and Britain can still hold on. We are, therefore, determined that Australia shall not go, and shall exert all our energies towards the shaping of a plan, with the United States as its keystone, which will give to our country some confidence of being able to hold out until the tide of battle swings against the enemy.[2]

According to Churchill, this statement produced the 'worst impression' in American and Canadian circles. He cabled to Attlee from Washington, 'I hope there will be no pandering to this, while at the same time we do all in human power to come to their aid'.[3]

As early as 2 December the battleship *Prince of Wales* and the battle-cruiser *Repulse* had arrived in Singapore. Their presence greatly encouraged the defenders of Singapore and Malaya, despite the fact that they had not been accompanied by an aircraft carrier. This relief, unfortunately, was short-lived, as both ships were sunk by Japanese aircraft on 10 December while on a sortie, without sufficient air cover, in an attempt to interfere with the landing of Japanese troops in Malaya.

This was a particularly painful blow to Churchill himself. In a reply on 14 January to a critical message from Curtin he felt entitled to comment that in Great Britain 'We have sunk all party differences and have imposed universal compulsory

---

[1] *Ibid.* pp. 182–3.   [2] *Ibid.* quoted at p. 183.   [3] Churchill, *op. cit.* vol. IV, p. 8.

service, not only upon men, but women'.[1] The implication was clear enough: a country like Australia which had no all-party government and which had not imposed conscription was not well placed to blame Great Britain, particularly after the fall of France, for failing to send to the Far East in time sufficient reinforcements to prevent the fall of Singapore.

Two other developments early in 1942 led to acrimonious exchanges of telegrams between London and Canberra. The first related to Churchill's proposal that the 7th Australian Division, returning from the Middle East, should be diverted to Burma; the second was the appointment of Casey as British Minister of State in the Middle East, with a seat in the British War Cabinet.

Singapore fell on 15 February. On the same day Lt.-Gen. Sir Vernon Sturdee, Chief of the Australian General Staff, advised the Government that in his view Australia was the only satisfactory strategic post from which the offensive in the Pacific could be launched when American aid was fully developed. In these circumstances he recommended, *inter alia*, the recall of A.I.F. divisions from the Middle East.[2] Two days later, Curtin telegraphed Churchill along the lines recommended by Sturdee. On 18 February a cable was received in Canberra from Sir Earle Page, Australian representative to the United Kingdom War Cabinet, stating that the Pacific War Council, London (consisting of the United Kingdom, Australia, New Zealand and Holland), requested Australian agreement to the diversion to Rangoon of the 7th Australian Division. Page added that the Council agreed that the 6th and 9th Australian Divisions in the Middle East should be sent back to the Australian area 'as fast as possible'.[3] This request was rejected by the Australian War Cabinet despite the strongest pressure by Churchill, who successfully enlisted Roosevelt's aid in the proposed diversion. In a direct cable to Curtin on 20 February Roosevelt informed Curtin, *inter alia*, that he proposed to send to Australia, in addition to forces already *en route*, 'another force of over twenty-seven thousand men'.[4] Churchill, however, was not content merely to secure Roosevelt's support; in addition, he misjudged

---

[1] Churchill, *op. cit.* vol. IV, pp. 10–11.
[2] Wigmore, *op. cit.* p. 445. For text of Sturdee's paper, see Wigmore, *op. cit.* appendix 5.
[3] *Ibid.* quoted at p. 447.   [4] Churchill, *op. cit.* vol. IV, p. 140.

Australia's reactions by warning Curtin that Australia was dependent upon support from the United States and that if Australia refused to allow its troops to be diverted to Burma 'a very grave effect will be produced upon the President and the Washington circle'.[1]

These messages and this warning failed to move the Australian Government from the firm position it had taken up. On 22 February Curtin telegraphed to Churchill referring to Australian contributions to the war effort, pointing out that if one Australian division became engaged in Burma it could not be left unsupported and expressing doubt whether the division could be safely landed in Burma, much less 'brought out as promised'.[2] The Australian Government therefore held to its former decision. In its opinion 'The movement of our forces to this theatre...is not considered a reasonable hazard of war, having regard to what has gone before, and its adverse results would have the gravest consequences on the morale of the Australian people'.[2] To make matters worse, Churchill had to reply to Curtin on the same day stating that he had been compelled to divert the convoy conveying the 7th Division northward towards Burma pending advice of the Australian decision on his request, and it could not now reach Australia without refuelling! This action of Churchill's seriously disturbed the Australian Government because it seemed to imply that the British Prime Minister's decision indicated that he regarded the considered views of the Australian Government as irrelevant or unimportant.

When it had become quite clear that Australia could not be moved on this issue, Roosevelt endeavoured to pour oil on the troubled waters by sending a message to Curtin which contained the sentence 'Under any circumstances you can depend upon our fullest support'.[3] It was only after the passage of many years, however, that Churchill found it possible to view the Australian decision with equivalent tolerance. In volume IV of *The Second World War*, published in 1951, Churchill recorded the British side of the case with a considerable degree of generosity towards Australia. He pointed out that the Australians had sent four

---

[1] *Ibid.* p. 139.
[2] *Ibid.* p. 142. For a retrospective justification of Curtin's attitude, see comments by Maj.-Gen. S. Woodburn Kirby in *The War against Japan*, vol. II (Official British History of the Second World War), pp. 103–4.   [3] *Ibid.* p. 145.

divisions of troops 'across the world to aid the mother country in the war, in the making of which and in the want of preparations for which they had no share'.[1] These troops had played a distinguished part in the desert war; had suffered in Greece; while an Australian division had been destroyed or captured at Singapore, until then regarded as the key to the defence of Australia. He continued as follows:

> In the remorseless tide of defeat and ruin which dominated our fortunes at this time the Australian Government could feel very little confidence in the British conduct of the war or in our judgement at home. The time had come, they thought, to give all the strength they could gather to the life-and-death peril which menaced their cities and people.[2]

At the same time he justifiably pointed out that when the British people had been exposed to similar danger in a more probable form in 1940 they had not lost their 'sense of proportion' or hesitated to add to their risks for the sake of other vital needs. Thus, in August 1940 they had sent half of their 'scanty armour' to the Middle East for the defence of Egypt. Moreover, he did not believe at the time that Japan would actually invade Australia and in any event he had obtained in January 1942 Roosevelt's 'promise to accept responsibility and use the United States Fleet for the ocean defence of Australia, and to send upwards of ninety thousand American soldiers there...'[3]

Finally, during the second half of March 1942, relations between Canberra and London were still further exacerbated through the appointment of the Australian Minister to the United States as British Minister of State in the Middle East. As a result, what might have been a dramatic precedent for the utilisation by the mother country of the abilities of a distinguished servant of another Government of the Commonwealth of Nations was turned instead into a precedent for extreme caution in making any such appointment.

It would appear from the account given by Casey himself[4] that the reactions to Churchill's proposal of the Australian Minister for External Affairs on the one hand and of the Australian Prime Minister on the other hand were quite different. When the matter was discussed by Casey with Evatt, in San

---

[1] Churchill, *op. cit.* vol. IV, p. 137.   [2] *Ibid.* pp. 137–8.
[3] *Ibid.* p. 138.   [4] See Casey, *Personal Experience*, pp. 93–7.

Francisco on 18 March 1942 'Dr Evatt agreed that, all things considered, there could be only one answer, and that the filling of the post of Australian Minister in Washington would cause no real embarrassment'.[1] Evatt's opinion was based upon the argument that, since the transfer to Australia from the Philippines of General Douglas MacArthur, the military link between Australia and the United States would be more effective than the link through the Australian Legation. Curtin, on the other hand, informed Churchill that a change of Australian representation in Washington at that particular juncture would be most undesirable.

In the event, the final decision was left to Casey, who accepted Churchill's offer. No doubt he was influenced in this decision by the opinions of President Roosevelt, Lord Halifax, Harry Hopkins and Justice Frankfurter, all of whom he had consulted on the matter and all of whom advised him to accept. Additional reasons may well have been the desire of a man with a distinguished record in the First World War to take responsibility closer to actual military operations, together with the doubt whether, as an ex-cabinet member of the United Australia Party, he would be given sufficient scope by Evatt to justify his remaining in Washington. Casey's own final comment on the effect of his decision upon British–Australian relations is as follows:

The acid and embarrassing exchange of telegrams between Mr Churchill and Mr Curtin was made public, on Mr Curtin's initiative, both in London and in Australia. However flattering it might have been to my vanity, I believe the fact was that I had come between the hammer of Mr Curtin and the anvil of Mr Churchill, between whom there had been considerable personal feeling.[2]

It should not be thought that the differences and tension between Canberra and London outlined above were due merely to the fact that in Australia the Labour Party was in office, while in the United Kingdom the all-party Government was led by a dominant Conservative in the person of Churchill. The seeds of discontent with British handling of matters affecting Australia can be seen in much earlier periods when other political parties were in power in Australia.

As early as 1922, while W. M. Hughes was still Prime

[1] *Ibid.* pp. 95–6.   [2] *Ibid.* p. 97.

Minister, the Australian Government was not amused when at the time of the Chanak crisis it suddenly found itself expected to give Great Britain military support, if necessary, in regard to an issue arising out of British policy on which Australia had not been consulted. Again, Prime Minister S. M. Bruce had sent Casey to London in 1924 as Australian Liaison Officer in an effort to fill gaps in consultation by enabling Australia to be aware of problems in the formative stage before important decisions were taken.[1]

After the outbreak of the Second World War Menzies, while still Prime Minister, had come to the conclusion that direct Australian representation in the British War Cabinet was necessary if Australian interests were to be protected adequately.[2] This view was strengthened by Australian losses in Greece and Crete. Australia had not been consulted by Great Britain before aid to Greece was promised—only regarding the actual employment there of Australian forces—although, after Britain had given its undertaking to Greece, such employment was in practice unavoidable.[3] According to Hasluck, after the return of the Australian Prime Minister from Britain in 1941:

Menzies...while extolling Churchill's great qualities, felt obliged to tell his colleagues both in the War Cabinet and the Advisory War Council, of his 'unsatisfactory attitude of mind' towards questions in which Dominion interests were involved. Menzies considered that Churchill had no conception of the British Dominions as separate entities and, furthermore, the more distant the problem from the heart of the Empire the less he thought of it.[4]

Again, Australia was deeply concerned, when Menzies was still Prime Minister, at the transference of the United States Pacific Fleet to the Atlantic by agreement between America and Britain 'with only tardy reference to Australia' and no prior hint to the Prime Minister during his two months stay in London.[5] Further, it was Prime Minister Fadden who first forced the issue with Churchill regarding the relief of Australian troops from Tobruk.

The tone and the manner of handling disagreements between the Australian and British Governments after Pearl Harbor no doubt reflected substantially the fact that a Labour Party

---

[1] See p. 32 above.   [2] See Hasluck, *Government and People*, p. 347.
[3] *Ibid.* p. 335.   [4] *Ibid.* p. 347.   [5] *Ibid.* p. 345.

Government, long out of office, came to power in Canberra almost at the time of maximum crisis to Australia following upon Japan's entry into the war. Yet the acute differences between Canberra and London which developed after Pearl Harbor stemmed less from differences in the political outlook of parties than from real conflicts of interest between Britain and Australia which, in the end, led Australia to develop a distinctive Australian policy and to pursue it vigorously, even against occasional strong British opposition.[1]

III. DR EVATT AND THE SEARCH FOR SUPPLIES AND INFLUENCE ON ALLIED STRATEGY

The dominant voice in the formulation and execution of Australian foreign policy from 3 October 1941, when the Labour Party assumed office, until the Liberal–Country Party Coalition returned to power in December 1949 was that of H. V. Evatt, Attorney-General and Minister for External Affairs. This is not to suggest that the two Prime Ministers under whom he served, Curtin and Chifley, were mere ciphers in this field, or that other senior cabinet ministers were without influence. Broadly speaking, however, Evatt's intellectual capacity, legal training, overseas contacts and conference experience during and after the war put him in an almost unchallengeable position as an interpreter of overseas opinion and of international trends.

Evatt was a 'theoretician' of a kind rarely found in the Australian Labour Party, well able to analyse the points at issue, to clarify objectives and to suggest appropriate means for attaining them. In a speech in the House of Representatives as early as 25 February 1942 (that is, ten days after the fall of Singapore) the Minister for External Affairs referred to the 'fundamental need for creating effective machinery to ensure there shall be not only Allied unity of command but a guarantee of a common Allied strategical plan backed by the pooling of Allied resources and the sound allocation of those resources to Allied forces'.[2] Such co-ordination required (a) machinery for the higher direction of the war, permitting quick decisions to be

[1] See analysis of Australian policy during this period in Grattan, *U.S. and the Southwest Pacific*, pp. 178–81.
[2] *Foreign Policy of Australia*, selected speeches of Dr H. V. Evatt (Angus and Robertson, Sydney, 1945), pp. 29–30.

taken, due weight being given to all phases of the conflict, (*b*) unified command, and (*c*) machinery to handle reinforcements and supply in accordance with decisions of higher authority.[1] Australian efforts to secure a permanent organisation, said Evatt, had so far been 'mostly unsuccessful', although she had accepted Churchill's proposal for the establishment of a Pacific Council in London, despite her preference for Washington as the meeting-place. It was idle to pretend, however, that the Australian Government regarded the existing machinery as satisfactory, because 'at no point whatever does any representative of this country meet any representative of the United States in any council, committee, or strategic body directly concerned in the controlling of the Allied war against Japan, or for that matter Germany or Italy'.[2]

In London the representative of Australia accredited to the British War Cabinet was invited to attend meetings whenever the British Prime Minister thought that matters of direct and immediate concern to Australia were under consideration. But the Australian Government felt that in time of war practically all matters of foreign policy and high policy affected all British Dominions; yet it had been unable to secure British assent to actual membership of the British War Cabinet.[3] A Raw Materials Board and a Munitions Assignment Board were now functioning in the United States, with parallel bodies in London. Only the United Kingdom and the United States were actual members of these Boards. Evatt suggested that 'the function of planning for the effective and timely reinforcement of key positions in Allied plans will best be performed by an authority which can dispose of divergent, conflicting or competitive claims or arguments on the body where the advice of all Allies can be given in consultation'.[4]

These were the ideas in the mind of the Minister for External Affairs when he left Australia in March 1942 on his first overseas Mission to the United States and Great Britain. The way had been prepared for him in advance by a broadcast message delivered on 14 March by the Australian Prime Minister. In this broadcast Curtin described the purposes of the mission as the securing of larger military supplies for the South-West

[1] Evatt, *Foreign Policy of Australia*, p. 30.   [2] *Ibid.* pp. 32–3.
[3] *Ibid.* p. 3.   [4] *Ibid.* p. 35.

Pacific and the establishment of more efficient machinery for
the co-ordination of the war effort in this area, especially in
regard to the allocation of supplies, munitions and shipping.[1]

Speaking directly to the people of the United States, the
Prime Minister referred to his published newspaper article of
27 December 1941, in which he had 'said on behalf of the
Australian Government that we looked to America as the paramount factor on the democracies' side of the Pacific'.[2] He
denied that there was any 'belittling of the old country in this
outlook...We Australians, with New Zealand, represent Great
Britain here in the Pacific...on us the responsibility falls.'[2]
Curtin added that it had been the Australian wish for the
Pacific War Council to be located in Washington. 'It is a
matter of some regret to us that, even now...we have not
obtained first-hand contact with America.'[3] He warned
Americans that 'Australia is the last bastion between the West
Coast of America and the Japanese'.[4]

The Minister for External Affairs arrived in San Francisco
from Australia on 17 March 1942 after the fall of Singapore
and well before the battle of the Coral Sea. These were dark
days for Australia, whose political leaders could not accept
what seemed to them the optimistic assumption of their distant
British cousins that the Japanese did not intend to invade the
mainland of Australia. As a result it is not surprising that the
activities in Washington of Evatt and the advisers he had brought
with him seemed prompted by a sense of acute emotional urgency. It may well be that Evatt himself believed that the survival
of Australia depended upon the success or failure of his mission.

Against this background it is difficult to understand Evatt's
attitude towards Churchill's proposal to appoint Casey as
British Minister of State in the Middle East. The value of the
Head of a Diplomatic Mission to his visiting Foreign Minister
is, of course, substantial. Over a period of time a Head of
Mission builds up contacts in the country to which he is accredited and an understanding of that country's approach to
problems which it is most unlikely that a Foreign Minister can
match—at least during his first visit. Advice from the Head of
Mission as to whom to see and how to say what is to be said is
of the first importance.

There is no doubt that Casey had made his mark in Washing-

[1] *Ibid.* pp. 42–6.   [2] *Ibid.* pp. 43–4.   [3] *Ibid.* p. 44.   [4] *Ibid.* p. 46.

ton and that he had the most friendly relations, for instance, with Harry Hopkins, who was President Roosevelt's most trusted adviser. Yet Evatt made no attempt to dissuade Casey from accepting the post offered by Churchill; nor did he himself act in such a way as to confirm the view attributed to him by Casey that the direct channel to Washington of General Douglas MacArthur would in future be the most effective way of influencing American opinion to respond to Australia's war-time needs.

One can only speculate as to the reasons for this difference of approach of Curtin and Evatt to the importance of Casey's position in Washington. Suspicious by temperament, Evatt would have found it more difficult than Curtin to believe that an ex-cabinet minister from a different political party would faithfully carry out instructions from a Government of another political colour. This supposition is supported by information now available as to his attitude in 1942 towards the Rt. Hon. S. M. Bruce, then Australian High Commissioner, London. Before Evatt left Washington for London, according to Bruce's biographer,

Evatt began to prepare the way for his descent in Britain. He sent a cable to Cripps, prefaced by the words *Most Secret* and the instruction that it was to be deciphered by Alfred Stirling (External Affairs Officer in London), and given to Cripps alone. Stirling carried out his orders, and Cripps promptly told him to show the message to Bruce![1]

Secondly, at this stage Evatt's name was unknown in the international field: his overseas reputation as Australian Minister for External Affairs had still to be made. Even within his own country his abilities as Minister for External Affairs had yet to be proved. From statements made after his return to Australia on the subject of his overseas mission one is entitled to infer that he was determined to claim for himself the full credit for any success achieved. There is also some available evidence tending to confirm the supposition that during his stay in the United States he had decided to take every possible step to ensure that no person came, so to speak, between him and the American administration.

Copies of the diplomatic list for the relevant period held in

[1] Cecil Edwards, *Bruce of Melbourne* (Heinemann, London, 1965), p. 338.

the Library of Congress disclose that Evatt had taken the un-usual step of having his own name included as Head of the Australian Diplomatic Mission in Washington. In the list he was described as 'E.E. & M.P.—apptd' and also as Attorney-General and Minister of State for External Affairs. 'E.E. & M.P.', of course, stand for 'Envoy Extraordinary and Minister Plenipotentiary', while the word 'apptd' is an abbreviation of the word 'appointed', which under the American system implies that the person referred to has not yet presented any credentials. No reference was made to this aspect of his visit to the United States in Evatt's speech in the House of Representatives on 3 September 1942 reporting on his overseas mission.

The Australian case for a voice in the higher direction of the war effort and a larger share of military supplies was pressed by Evatt in every conceivable direction in Washington, mainly with President Roosevelt himself. On 5 April the Minister for External Affairs made a broadcast speech which included the following:

For three months Mr Curtin has asked for the establishment of a War Council at Washington to determine how best the war against Japan can be carried to the offensive. This Council has now been established...On it are represented the United States, the United Kingdom, Canada, China, Netherlands, together with Australia and New Zealand.[1] I have represented Australia on this body and I can assure you we are getting on with the job...[2]

In his speech in Parliament on 3 September 1942 Evatt was constrained to add, however, that 'While the Council is not executive in character, important matters on the political side, and to some extent also on the military side, are finalised at the Council'.[3] This somewhat ambiguous statement tends to exag-gerate the significance of the Council, which was advisory only and thus took no decisions on basic strategy or allocation of weapons. After the war its activities were described in the following terms:

In other respects, however, the Washington Pacific Council failed to fulfil the hopes of its sponsors. At no time did it play any important part in the making of decisions, whether strategic or political. As Mr Mackenzie King had shrewdly surmised, from the outset it proved in fact to be a purely consultative body. At its first meeting, recorded

---

[1] Later the Philippines became a member.
[2] Evatt, *Foreign Policy of Australia*, p. 53.   [3] *Ibid.* p. 70.

Harry Hopkins, 'not much happened. The President outlined the problems in the whole Pacific Area, but kept away from the tough tactics which are now in progress. It is perfectly clear, however, that this body wants to talk about military strategy and the distribution of munitions.' This was an understatement. What some members wanted was for the Council not merely to talk but to take decisions. That it never did. The most that could be said of it was said by Mr Nash, who noted that it did good work and served a useful purpose by enabling the smaller countries represented on it to be kept fully informed about developments in the Pacific War and by giving them an opportunity of stating their case in the presence of those in whose hands major decisions continued to rest. Such an opportunity was a psychological necessity for the Pacific dominions, abruptly confronted with the actual danger of invasion and sensitive, especially in the case of Australia, lest their peril be overlooked in the making of global strategy. 'The war', wrote Mr Churchill, in a disparaging allusion, 'continued to be run by the old machinery, but meetings of the Pacific War Councils enabled those countries which were not represented in this permanent machinery to be consulted about what was going on.' He never fully realised how important that was to those close to the point of danger but far from the place of decision. But equally Dr Evatt did not appear to understand that the role of secondary powers in a major war must remain a secondary one and that no elaboration of machinery could sensibly modify a relationship determined by relative power.[1]

Nevertheless, the Pacific War Council in Washington, with its weekly meetings, did provide for its members the opportunity for regular physical access to President Roosevelt and thus the means of learning much of what was in his mind and of influencing him in directions desired. Such access could have been obtained by an Australian representative in no other way. Evatt is entitled to much of the credit for the establishment of the Council, but it may be doubted if his efforts would have been successful had not Harry Hopkins become convinced that 'it was essential that there be an opportunity for the various countries in the Pacific to find a common meeting ground',[2] despite American army and navy lack of 'enthusiasm' for the proposal. On 1 April 1942 Hopkins noted that 'While in Hyde Park on this past week end, I told the President that I thought the matter must be decided affirmatively, and he readily agreed'.[2]

---

[1] Nicholas Mansergh, *Survey of British Commonwealth Affairs, Problems of Wartime Collaboration and Post-War Change, 1939–52* (Oxford University Press, 1958), pp. 138–9.   [2] Sherwood, *op. cit.* p. 515.

Separate Australian representation on the Munitions Assignment Board and on the Raw Materials Board was not achieved by Evatt. This, however, was due to no lack of effort by him: no other country achieved membership, which remained British and American only. On the other hand, his presence and activities in Washington and later in London kept before the minds of British and American leaders the precarious position and the urgent military needs of Australia. The precise extent of his influence in the field of military supplies is not yet clear from public records, although some evidence is now available. For instance, in one of the Australian war histories there is a reference to 'The three Spitfire squadrons at Darwin'which'had been sent from the United Kingdom for the defence of Australia as a result of negotiations between Mr Churchill and Dr Evatt in 1942'.[1] Curtin at least had no doubts as to the effectiveness of the overseas mission of his Minister for External Affairs when on 23 June 1942 he sent to his colleague a generous letter which included the comment that 'The result has been that Australia is assured of the certainty that all our needs are known to our allies and will be afforded greatly increased strength of armaments'.[2]

In recognising, however, the importance of Evatt's strenuous efforts, particularly in the United States, to ensure that due attention was paid to Australia's war-time needs, it is necessary to realise that the United States did not decide to give vital assistance to Australia either from motives of pure friendship or because of any strength of representation and argument by Australians: help was given primarily because the fortunes of war made an American base in Australia essential to the protection of American interests in the Pacific.

Before Pearl Harbor American military planning for the Pacific had been directed to the area north of the Equator. Casey's record of his first conversation with Roosevelt after taking up his appointment in Washington is illuminating in this respect. In a discussion with Roosevelt, following presentation of his credentials, Casey asked the President about the attitude of the United States towards Australia in then existing

[1] George Odgers, *Air War Against Japan 1943–45* (Australian War Memorial, Canberra, 1957), p. 44.
[2] See Evatt, *Foreign Policy of Australia*; a copy of the text of Curtin's letter is inserted opposite p. 66.

circumstances. Roosevelt told him confidentially that sometime
earlier he had sought his cabinet's views on what the United
States should do in three sets of circumstances, namely, if
Canada, a Latin American Republic, or Australia and New
Zealand were attacked. Cabinet had no doubt that an attack
upon Canada must involve the United States. As regards the
Latin American Republics however, 'the element of distance
began to enter in' and American intervention would thus be
more likely if Latin American Republics close to the United
States were the subjects of aggression. So far as Australia and
New Zealand were concerned, the President implied that the
element of distance was so great that there could be no certainty
of American intervention if these countries were attacked.[1]

After Pearl Harbor, however, it soon became clear to the
Americans that the Japanese intended to overrun the Philippines quickly and were capable of capturing these islands.
President Eisenhower has now revealed[2] that as early as 14
December 1941 General Marshall, who had summoned Eisenhower to Washington to join his staff, described the situation in
the Pacific and then asked 'What should be our general line of
action?' Eisenhower, a brigadier at the time, asked for 'a few
hours' to consider his answer. He reflected on his past experience
which had taught him 'the acute dependence of all elements of
military life upon the industrial capacity of the nation'. He
came to the conclusion that

Australia was the base nearest to the Philippines that we could hope
to establish and maintain, and the necessary line of air communications would therefore follow along the islands intervening between
that continent and the Philippines.

If we were to use Australia as a base it was mandatory that we
procure a line of communications leading to it. This meant that
we must instantly move to save Hawaii, Fiji, New Zealand and New
Caledonia, and we had to make certain of the safety of Australia
itself.[3]

Eisenhower conveyed these views to Marshall who merely
replied: 'I agree with you...Do your best to save them.'[3]

---

[1] Casey, *Personal Experience*, pp. 10–11.
[2] Dwight D. Eisenhower, *Crusade in Europe* (Heinemann, London, 1948), see
pp. 21–5.   [3] *Ibid.* p. 25.

4

THE AUSTRALIAN LABOUR PARTY IN OFFICE

PART TWO. DR EVATT AND THE POST-WAR SETTLEMENT

I. PRIOR TO FORMULATION OF THE DUMBARTON OAKS DRAFT OF THE UNITED NATIONS CHARTER

By the second quarter of 1943 a qualitative change in favour of the Western Allies had taken place in the war situation. The war was still far from won, but the Axis Powers had suffered significant reverses in Europe, the Middle East and the Far East and were being placed increasingly on the defensive. The German surrender at Stalingrad dashed hope of an early German victory over the Soviet Union. In the Middle East, the Allied victory at Alamein and landings in Morocco and Algeria foreshadowed the defeat of Italy. Although 'Japan herself', writes F. C. Jones, 'had not as yet suffered any decisive defeat... The more far-sighted among her leaders could see the eventual end for Japan, as well, when once Germany and Italy should have been overwhelmed by the hostile coalition against them'.[1]

It is of interest to look at this period of the war through the eyes of Japanese diplomatic observers whose views have been made public since the war. According to Toshikazu Kase, when the news of the surrender on 31 January 1943 of the German army at Stalingrad reached Tokyo, a conference was held in the Japanese Foreign Office to study the European situation. The majority, he claims, thought that the power of Germany and Italy would gradually decline while the combined strength of the Allied Powers would rise; that there was little chance of victory for Germany; and that 'consequently Japan must re-orient her policy before Germany collapsed'.[2] Although this

---

[1] Jones, Borton and Pearn, *Survey of International Affairs 1939-46. The Far East 1942-6* (Oxford University Press, 1955), p. 111.
[2] Toshikazu Kase, *Journey to the 'Missouri'* (Yale University Press, New Haven, 1950), p. 67.

judgement was not shared by Japanese army leaders, Prince
Konoye, according to Kase, 'began to express pessimistic views
as early as February, 1943'.[1] The Prince found that Marquis
Kido, Lord Keeper of the Privy Seal, agreed with him that it
was necessary to end the war, and the latter reported their
conversation to the Emperor.

In April 1943 Ambassador Shigemitsu was called home from
China to become Foreign Minister. Kase comments as follows:

The choice fell on him largely because of his alleged acceptability to
the democratic powers...He is a man of confirmed liberal views....
On assuming his duties as foreign minister Shigemitsu began immediately to work for the return of peace...Shigemitsu exerted a
strong and subtle influence on the course of events, both internally
and externally...Shigemitsu often sought audience with the Emperor to inform him of current international developments. I have
reason to believe that these lectures had far-reaching effects in
moulding the Emperor's thoughts...Shigemitsu had more success
in paving the way to an early peace than could have been secured by
anyone else. By common consent he was perhaps the most far-sighted
foreign minister Japan has ever had.[2]

Shigemitsu has given us his own account of the significance of
the Battles of the Coral Sea and of Midway. In order to cross
from Timor to Darwin, he has written, 'it was necessary to have
a firm grip on Papua'.[3]

The plan was for a task squadron to escort troopships from Rabaul
round the eastern corner of New Guinea into the Coral Sea in
order to attack Port Moresby from the sea. At this point it ran into
an enemy aircraft-carrier squadron...The battle of the Coral Sea
was in itself a hard-won victory [for the Japanese] but strategically
it not only marked the turning-point of the war but it also led to a
severe reverse sustained in the battle of Guadalcanal.[4]

Of the subsequent Japanese defeat at Midway on 5 June 1942
Shigemitsu writes:

By the battle, parity with the U.S. Navy was lost and in succeeding
defeats mastery of the sea and air was soon transferred to the
Americans. 'Midway' was in fact the turning-point...This
defeat shattered Japanese plans. The details were never divulged
either to the nation or to the cabinet. They were even kept secret

[1] Toshikazu Kase, op. cit. p. 68.   [2] Ibid. pp. 68–70.
[3] Mamoru Shigemitsu, Japan and her Destiny (Hutchinson, London, 1958), p. 275.
[4] Ibid. pp. 275–6.

from all but a few in the Navy itself. The Japanese Army and Navy do not admit defeat. The public announcement left it to be inferred that American losses were greater than ours. This refusal to acknowledge a reverse is a firmly rooted weakness—a relic from feudal times.[1]

The thoughts and conclusions of Japanese diplomats were not, of course, known to Australian political leaders at the time, but they confirm, from the enemy camp, the justifiable grounds for the swing from pessimism to guarded optimism following upon developments in Europe, the Middle East and the Pacific during the period from the fall of Singapore on 15 February 1942 to the fall of Stalingrad on 31 January 1943. Bitter fighting in the war with Japan still lay ahead, but the fear of actual invasion of Australia by a ruthless enemy was lifted and the psychological effects of the shock of the fall of the Singapore bastion gradually passed away.

Subsequent statements by Curtin as Prime Minister or by his Minister for External Affairs were not always temperate—especially when it was believed that Australia, as a small Power, was being inadequately consulted by the Big Three—but they tended to lose the faintly hysterical quality which was on occasion apparent under the stresses and strains created by fear of an actual Japanese invasion. Australia continued to press for military resources in an effort to ensure that a 'holding' war in the Pacific would not turn out to be a losing war, and that a 'Beat Hitler First' policy should not be so interpreted as to preclude the allocation to the Pacific area of resources necessary not merely to hold the Japanese but also to make it possible to press them back towards their home islands.[2] On the whole, however, it was now possible for Evatt to concentrate his energies on attempts to influence the shape of the post-war world, especially the nature of the new world organisation which, it was hoped, would avoid the mistakes of the League of Nations or of its Member States, and really 'save succeeding generations from the scourge of war'.[3] This was a field of activity for which the Australian Minister for External Affairs had exceptional qualifications. An expert constitutional lawyer, his domestic and international political experience during the years 1942–45

---

[1] *Ibid.* p. 277.
[2] See Professor MacMahon Ball's introduction to Evatt's *Foreign Policy of Australia*,
    pp. v and vi.   [3] See Preamble to the United Nations Charter.

broadened his range of contacts and, in the process, deepened understanding of the issues involved.

As early as 27 November 1941, before Pearl Harbor, in his first speech in Parliament as Minister for External Affairs, Evatt had drawn attention to the terms of the Atlantic Charter which had been signed by Churchill and Roosevelt some three months earlier, and commented as follows:

Thus the objectives of the United States and of Britain are similar. In both countries there is a sure and certain hope, first, that, in the long run, it will not be possible for Germany to impose permanent serfdom upon great nations and great peoples such as France, Holland, Belgium, Norway, Poland, Greece, Yugoslavia and Czechoslovakia; second, and more positively, that international peace can be maintained only through international justice, and that the four great freedoms, freedom of speech, freedom of religion, freedom from fear, freedom from want, are meaningless unless they are enjoyed not in one or two countries, but as President Roosevelt insists— 'everywhere in the world'.[1]

The argument that peace could be maintained only through justice was to be a recurring theme throughout later speeches.

In his introduction to the second volume of Evatt's published speeches Sir Frederic Eggleston describes the principles underlying the Minister's policy towards post-war organisations:

A world order does not depend merely on the elimination of force as an instrument of national policy. Peace is not a negative concept...The keynote of the philosophy is found...in the stress laid on the promotion of human welfare and the elimination of want. The improvement of living standards among backward and primitive peoples and the elimination of unemployment in industrial countries would provide the most dynamic stimulus to the world economy.[2]

In Hartley Grattan's opinion, the policies pursued by Evatt were not merely personal, but were rooted in traditional Labour Party attitudes:

What the Australians and New Zealanders sought was national security and equality for small countries in a big-power world strongly disposed to power politics, accompanied by an assurance

---

[1] Evatt, *Foreign Policy of Australia*, p. 12.
[2] *Australia in World Affairs*, selected speeches of Dr H. V. Evatt (Angus and Robertson, Sydney, 1946); see the foreword, pp. viii–ix.

that socio-economic reforms, which they fully intended to pursue as nationalists, would have international support.[1]

It was the first Cairo Conference, held from 22 to 26 November 1943, and attended by Churchill, Roosevelt and Chiang Kai-shek, which acted as the catalyst of Australian and New Zealand thinking on post-war organisation. Neither Dominion was consulted about the Cairo decisions, and each of them learned only from the communiqué issued after the Conference that Japan was to be stripped of all the islands in the Pacific seized since the beginning of the First World War; that she was to restore Manchuria, Formosa and the Pescadores to China; and that Korea was to become free and independent in due course. This failure to consult fostered fear that post-war settlements would be determined by the Great Powers exclusively, despite the contributions to the general war effort made by smaller Powers, and despite the special interests of the two Dominions in the Pacific area. The strength of the reaction of the two Dominions is best seen in the terms of the Australian–New Zealand Agreement, signed at Canberra on 21 January 1944.

Pending publication of Hasluck's second volume on *The Government and the People* in the official series of books entitled 'Australia in the War of 1939–45', the best background source of information regarding the Australian–New Zealand Agreement 1944, based upon access to New Zealand secret documents, is that given by Professor F. L. W. Wood.[2] Hasluck has already given a tantalising foretaste of the account we may expect in his second volume in an address he gave on 27 July 1954 entitled 'Australia and the formation of the United Nations'.[3]

Both sources agree that the initiative for the conference between representatives of the two Dominions came from Evatt and that not only the New Zealand Delegation, but also official members of the Australian Delegation were taken by surprise at Evatt's sudden suggestion, made after the conference had opened, that items of agreement should be embodied in a treaty. The New Zealanders had envisaged merely an exchange of

---

[1] Grattan, *U.S. and the Southwest Pacific*, p. 189.

[2] Professor F. L. W. Wood, *Official History of New Zealand in the Second World War 1939–45. The People at War* (War History Branch, Department of Internal Affairs, Wellington, 1958).

[3] *Royal Australian Historical Society, Journal and Proceedings*, vol. XL, part III, pp. 133–78.

opinions, noted down in an agreed record of proceedings: they doubted 'the wisdom and the constitutional propriety of nego- tiating a formal treaty'.[1] Even after the New Zealand Prime Minister, Mr Peter Fraser, had agreed to sign a treaty, the New Zealand Cabinet 'felt some uneasiness' lest a bilateral pact should lead to criticism in the United States and weaken the spirit of unity among the United Nations.[2] According to Wood,

The documents as finally adopted...were much less open to such criticisms than at one time seemed likely. Some of the suggestions which would have been most likely to cause offence were dropped from the agreement on New Zealand's insistence, and some plain speech was deliberately cut out from the report of the proceedings which was sent to the Government of the United Kingdom. For example, New Zealand refused to support a suggestion from Aus- tralia that the administration of the Solomon Islands should be transferred to her, together with the British share, or possibly the whole, of the Franco-British condominium of the New Hebrides.[3]

Nevertheless, it is impossible to accept without reserve Evatt's statement to Parliament on 10 February 1944 that 'The Agreement has had a warm and encouraging welcome on all sides, especially in the United Kingdom and also among the other United Nations'.[4] Had the two Dominions, who had good reason to discuss and publicise their post-war aims in an endeavour to ensure that these were not overlooked or simply ignored by the chief Allied Powers, been content to issue a statement of principles, in permissible words, in a joint communiqué, some adverse international reactions might well have been avoided and no retainable ground would have been lost.

The text of the Australian–New Zealand Agreement[5] was tabled in the House of Representatives by Evatt on 10 February 1944. Its main provisions were as follows:

(a) The signatories agreed to consult together in such fields as defence, external policy affecting the Pacific, commerce between the two countries, and the fostering of full employment and social security (Art. 35). In order to facilitate consultation and collaboration, they established an Australian–New Zealand

---

[1] Wood, op. cit. p. 313.   [2] Ibid. pp. 315–16.   [3] Ibid. p. 316.
[4] Evatt, Foreign Policy of Australia, p. 171.
[5] For full text, see Current Notes (subsequently abbreviated to C.N.), vol. xv, no. 1 (January 1944), pp. 2–9.

Affairs Secretariat in their respective Departments of External Affairs (Arts. 38, 39).

(*b*) Both Governments claimed the right to representation at the highest level on all armistice planning and executive bodies (Art. 7). It was of 'cardinal importance' that they should be associated, not only in the membership, but also in the planning and establishment of the general international organisation referred to in the Moscow Declaration of October 1943 (Art. 14). The ultimate disposal of enemy territories in the Pacific should be effected only with the agreement of Australia and New Zealand, as part of a general Pacific settlement (Art. 26). There should be no change in the sovereignty or system of control of any of the islands of the Pacific without their assent (Art. 27).

(*c*) Each signatory promised the other full support 'in maintaining the accepted principle that every government has the right to control immigration and emigration in regard to all territories within its jurisdiction' (Art. 32).

(*d*) An International Air Transport Authority should be set up to Control international air trunk routes, under certain conditions; in default of this, both Governments undertook to support a system of air trunk routes controlled and operated by Governments of the British Commonwealth under Government ownership (Arts. 17–23).

(*e*) The doctrine of 'trusteeship' was declared applicable in principle 'to all colonial territories in the Pacific and elsewhere', the main purpose of the trust being the welfare of the native peoples (Art. 28). The signatories agreed to promote the establishment of a South Seas Regional Commission (subsequently established in 1947 as the 'South Pacific Commission'), with advisory powers (Art. 30). The functions of this Commission were defined in considerable detail, the overall purpose being 'to secure a common policy on social, economic and political development directed towards the advancement and well-being of the native peoples...' (Art. 31).

The provisions of the Agreement summarised so far were unlikely to cause any substantial flutter overseas, despite the fact that other countries, especially the Great Powers, might not support them—with the exception that Great Britain was unlikely to be pleased with the prospect of the two Dominions forcing the pace on the subject of trusteeship. Two Articles, however, caused irritation if not resentment in the United States, namely,

Art. 13. The two Governments agree that, within the framework of a general system of world security, a regional zone of defence comprising the South West and South Pacific areas *shall* [emphasis added] be established and that this zone should be based on Australia and New Zealand, stretching through the arc of islands north and north east of Australia, to Western Samoa and Cook Islands.

Art. 16. The two Governments accept as a recognised principle of international practice that the construction and use, in time of war, by any power, of naval, military or air installations, in any territory under the sovereignty or control of another power, does not, in itself, afford any basis for territorial claims or rights of sovereignty or control after the conclusion of hostilities.

Use in Article 13 of the word 'shall' in regard to the security of an area beyond the power of Australia and New Zealand themselves to maintain could only cause irritation. Moreover, the assertion in a formal, public, bilateral agreement between two claimant countries without Great Power status that the defence of the area under consideration 'should' be based on Australia and New Zealand scarcely seems the most diplomatic or effective method of achieving this particular objective.

But it was Article 16 which caused the strongest reaction in the United States. True, there were 'suggestions about bases current in the United States at the time',[1] but these could not be taken as indicating American Government policy. When the text of the Agreement was received in Washington, the first reaction was that Article 16 was either superfluous as a formal statement of the obvious, or, more probably, an insult to the United States, whose military power had saved the two Dominions from possible invasion, whose resources of manpower and material were being expended still in the defeat of Japan, and whose Government had not claimed rights which the Article denied.

When, however, the formal comments of the Secretary of State, Mr Cordell Hull, were despatched from Washington in due course, they were limited to puncturing the pretensions of the signatory Governments by reminding them that anything in the Agreement referring to territories other than those possessed by them 'was, of course, entirely without prejudice to

[1] Grattan, *op. cit.* pp. 193–4.

the rights of other countries'.[1] In addition, Mr Hull stressed that it was desirable 'to agree upon arrangements for a general international security system before attempting to deal with problems of regional security'.[1]

Some American military leaders and Members of Congress were not as restrained as Mr Hull. Senior American naval officers, for instance, interpreted the Australian–New Zealand Agreement as an attempt to exclude the United States from the South Pacific, and they became less willing to use forces from the two Dominions in operations against the Marshall and Caroline Islands which might found an Australian and New Zealand claim for a voice in their disposal.[2]

The British reaction to the agreement was more favourable. It may be asked, however, whether an important element in British approval was not the implied anti-American tone of the agreement which contrasted so strongly with the statement of Mr Curtin of 27 December 1941 that 'Australia looks to America, free of any pangs as to our traditional links or kinship with the United Kingdom'.[3] British opinion could be forgiven a degree of *Schadenfreude* if it interpreted the Agreement as evidence that the honeymoon period of relationships between the two Pacific Dominions and the United States was ending.

In short, the Australian–New Zealand Agreement was important 'not so much because of what the agreement contained but because of what it foreshadowed'.[4] It was evidence indeed that Australia in particular, through its Minister for External Affairs, intended to take vigorous initiatives in pressing publicly views on the post-war settlement without much regard to the susceptibilities of its greatest and closest Allies. Both Governments—as the Cairo Conference showed—had good reason to regard a firm initiative as necessary if their views were to gain the attention of the Great Powers. They overplayed their hand, however, both in choosing to sign a treaty and in the form of expression of several Articles, at some cost—at least in the case of Australia—to friendly relationships with the United States. It will be seen from subsequent developments that Evatt continued this trend during the remainder of his tenure of the portfolio of External Affairs.

---

[1] Wood, *op. cit.* p. 318.   [2] *Ibid.* footnote to p. 317.   [3] See p. 55 above.
[4] Mansergh, *Survey of British Commonwealth Affairs*, p. 181.

II. THE UNITED NATIONS CHARTER

Few if any aspects of Australian foreign policy have attracted as much interest, attention and comment inside and outside Australia as the activities of Evatt at the Charter Conference of the United Nations held at San Francisco from 25 April to 26 June 1945.[1] There were various reasons for this. First, the Charter Conference was a constitutional convention held in the full glare of world-wide publicity. The Second World War was not yet over. The consciousness of human suffering was so great, and hopes for the successful organisation of peace in the future so strong that the creation of the Charter was headline news. Secondly, there is no doubt that the initiative of Evatt was a central feature of this news.

Harper and Sissons describe Evatt as 'a man of great intellect and dominant personality' who

...subsequently emerged as one of the outstanding figures of the Conference, the champion of the smaller powers. A liberal socialist and a former member of the Australian High Court, he brought to the Conference a passionate conviction of the need for morality in international affairs, a sense of mission, and a belief in the need for world government by gradual stages. These were combined with a devotion to legal processes and a humourless determination to establish democratic principles as the basis for the conduct of international relations.[2]

Those Australians who find it difficult to accept without reservation this description of Evatt's convictions and motivation will nevertheless accept fully the tribute paid to him by Hasluck, a subsequent political opponent and critic of Evatt's methods who was closely associated with him during the Conference and in the best position to judge:

The political credit or criticism for achieving policy... belongs almost solely to Dr Evatt. For ceaseless determined activity I have never

[1] See, *inter alia*, *Report by the Australian Delegates* in Commonwealth Parliamentary Papers (subsequently abbreviated to *C.P.P.*), General Session 1945–46, vol. III, pp. 701–803; Dr Evatt's speech of 30 August 1945 (introducing the Bill to ratify the Charter) and subsequent debate (*C.P.D.* vol. 184, commencing on p. 5,016); Hasluck, 'Australia and the formation of the United Nations'; Harper and Sissons, *Australia and the United Nations* (Manhattan Publishing Co., N.Y., 1959); *Australia in World Affairs 1950–55*, ed. Greenwood and Harper (Cheshire, Melbourne, 1957), chapter by Professor Geoffrey Sawer, pp. 92–124; Grattan, *op. cit.* chapter 15; Wood, *op. cit.* chapter 26; Mansergh, *op. cit.* pp. 307–22.

[2] Harper and Sissons, *op. cit.* p. 48.

seen anything like his performance. Coming to the conference an almost unknown man internationally, he made himself one of the better-known figures in that multitude of people all striving to impress themselves on others. He made Australia the acknowledged activator and often the spokesman of the small powers.[1]

Foreign Ministers, of course, do not work in a vacuum; their effectiveness at a conference depends substantially upon the abilities and activities of their staffs and upon the adequacy of the preparatory work done before a conference opens. In these respects Evatt was well served. Of the five officials to whom he paid a tribute during his speech in Parliament on ratification of the Charter, one subsequently became Minister for External Affairs, two became Permanent Heads of that department, one became Solicitor-General, and one Secretary-General of the South Pacific Commission.

The completeness of the preliminary preparations for the conference was quite abnormal, due partly to hard work and partly to the accident of circumstance. Lest it should be thought that such adequacy of preparation for a conference is customary, it is necessary to point out that there are few more difficult aspects of the formulation of Australian foreign policy—with certain notable exceptions—than to secure ministerial attention to, understanding of and decisions upon complex submissions before a conference actually begins. A properly organised and experienced Foreign Office will always have prepared a substantial brief, including relevant documents, information about the views of other countries, and suggestions or recommendations on Australian policy to be pursued. But it has been rare for an Australian Minister for External Affairs attending a conference in person to have read the brief in full in advance, and unusual for the detailed application of general policy to be determined before the first Delegation Meeting at the place where the conference is held. Such a meeting is most frequently attended by an exhausted Minister and exhausted staff, most of whom have just arrived from various quarters of the globe, who have still, in many cases, to get their conference 'bearings'. Why then was the Australian delegation 'so carefully briefed'[2] on this occasion?

In his lecture on 'Australia and the Formation of the United

[1] Hasluck, 'Australia and the formation of the United Nations', p. 173.
[2] Harper and Sissons, op. cit. p. 48.

Nations',[1] Hasluck has given a detailed summary of preliminary organisation, studies and discussions bearing upon the development of Australian policy in this field. These included the establishment of a Reconstruction Division, created in 1940, in the Department of Labour and National Service; the setting-up of a short-lived Reconstruction Committee on External Relations which met once only—on 4 December 1941; Hasluck's own appointment as Head of a small Post-War Section of the Department of External Affairs; and the creation of an Inter-Departmental Committee on External Relations, dealing mostly with economic matters, whose first meeting was held on 3 June 1942. At this stage, he says, 'ministerial interest was not in the great international questions of power and military security and the composing of the interests of national states, but with what was termed 'economic security' and 'social justice'.[2]

During 1942 W. D. Forsyth was appointed to the Post-War Section, and gave special attention to colonial questions. In the same year, Hasluck was sent as an observer to the Mont Tremblant Conference of the Institute of Pacific Relations, where he gained valuable contacts with British, American, Canadian and Dutch officers engaged in similar work to his own, including Lord Hailey, Sir John Pratt, Sir George Sansom and Sir Frederick Whyte (U.K.), Sir Ramaswami Mudaliar (India), Sir Zafrulla Khan (Pakistan), and Leo Pasvolsky (U.S.). In the following year a 'great deal of work' was done in the Post-War Section preparing memoranda on world organisation, summarising views of other countries and stressing main Australian interests, 'but little use was made of these memoranda'.[3] Ministerial interest was still centred on questions of economic policy, especially problems likely to arise out of the application of Article VII of the Mutual Aid Agreement between the United States and the United Kingdom.

At the Hot Springs Food Conference and the I.L.O. Conference in Philadelphia, both held in 1943, the Australian 'full employment' theory later elaborated at San Francisco in 1945 was pressed strongly. Preparations were also made for the Bretton Woods International Monetary Conference to be held in 1944. Issues arising at all these conferences required decisions

---

[1] See Hasluck, 'Australia and the formation of the United Nations', pp. 134–66.   [2] *Ibid.* p. 139.   [3] *Ibid.* pp. 148–9.

at the ministerial level. But, despite general references in one or two speeches of Evatt's in 1943 to post-war security and the special long-term interests of Australia in the Pacific, it was not until the exchanges of views leading to the Moscow Declaration of October 1943, according to Hasluck, that political issues were examined seriously in Australia.

As already mentioned, the Cairo Conference took place in November 1943, and the absence of prior consultation by London with Canberra and Wellington was substantially responsible for the decision to hold the Australian–New Zealand Conference in Canberra in January 1944.[1] In August 1944 the Dumbarton Oaks Conference met in the United States to draft a Big-Power version of the United Nations Charter, the text being published in October of that year. This was considered by representatives of Australia and New Zealand who met in Wellington in November 1944, and the two delegations drew up twelve resolutions which were approved by the Australian cabinet during the same month. Hasluck states that these resolutions 'constitute the first formal decision by the Australian Government relating to the formation of the United Nations'.[2] They formed the basis of the amendments to the Dumbarton Oaks text submitted to the San Francisco Conference by the Australian delegation.

In February 1945 the Post-Hostilities Division of the Department of External Affairs, which in March 1944 replaced the Post-War Section, drew up detailed suggestions for amendments to the Dumbarton Oaks draft. During the following month, the sponsoring Great Powers issued invitations to attend a conference at San Francisco on 25 April to complete the Charter of the United Nations. Arrangements put in hand by the Department of External Affairs for the Australian delegation had to be changed owing to the personal intervention of the Prime Minister who, to Evatt's chagrin, decided to include in the delegation Francis Forde, the Deputy Prime Minister, who took with him a number of advisers not members of the Department of External Affairs. This led at San Francisco to an absurd and childish division of the Australian delegation into two camps, each living on a different floor of the same hotel. There was a 'perpetual contest for effective leadership between the two

[1] See p. 73 above.
[2] See Hasluck, 'Australia and the formation of the United Nations', p. 157.

6   WAF

Ministers, the contest being won by Dr Evatt'.[1] As to the officials, the strength of the 'Evatt team' lay primarily in the fact
that 'they were in possession of most of the documents'.[1] 'We
were discouraged', writes Hasluck, 'from sharing either our
knowledge or papers.'[1]

But before the United Nations Conference began, preliminary meetings were held in London attended by representatives of
the United Kingdom, Canada, Australia, South Africa, New
Zealand and India. It was here that Evatt began for the first
time to concentrate upon and master the problems inherent in
the proposed Charter.

Even as late as the day of his arrival in London he [Evatt] still had
little detailed knowledge of the contents of the Dumbarton Oaks
draft. He learned rapidly as he went along, and revealed a very
great ability to grab at the points which were significant, and to
demand the information which was vital to the arguments he began
to develop...he made his first strong impression...pursuing the
line of his thinking in a way that I think revealed even to the
British people, who had been steeped in this matter for months, some
of the flaws in the Dumbarton Oaks work. I remember that morning
as the beginning of the reputation which Dr Evatt established for
himself later at the San Francisco Conference as a forceful personality—a leader for those who agreed with him; a most difficult
man for those who did not.[2]

After further talks in Washington with the Department of
State, Evatt and the members of his Delegation left by special
conference train on a three-day journey across the continent to
San Francisco. This was a period of most intensive work, because the Minister had nothing else to do but think of these
problems at all times of the day or night. By the time the train
reached San Francisco, therefore, the Australian amendments
to the Dumbarton Oaks text had been carefully worked over
and the Minister and his staff could be said to be literally
experts on Great Power, Commonwealth and Australian policies towards the establishment of the World Organisation. To
vary the Churchill phrase, never in the history of Australian
Diplomatic endeavour at both Ministerial and official level have
so many concentrated so early on so much.

The opening statement on behalf of the Australian Delega-

---

[1] Hasluck, 'Australia and the formation of the United Nations', p. 160.
[2] *Ibid.* p. 164.

tion was made by Forde as the senior of the two cabinet members as early as 27 April. The text had been drafted by the delegation and determined by Evatt. Its substance can be summed up in one sentence:

> In our view the success of the Conference will be measured by one test. Will it bring into existence an organisation which will give to the peoples of the world a reasonable assurance of security from war and reasonable prospect of international action to secure social justice and economic advancement?[1]

On 3 May Evatt gave a press conference which symbolised his assumption of the *de facto* leadership of the delegation. On this occasion he explained the purposes of the Australian amendments as follows:

(1) To prevent the possibility of a single Great Power vetoing amendments to the constitution, providing such amendment is twice approved by a two-thirds majority of the General Assembly including three permanent members of the Security Council.

(2) To exclude the 'veto' of the permanent members from all arrangements relating to the peaceful settlement of disputes and to confine such 'veto' to decisions involving the application of economic and military sanctions.

(3) To require a pledge from all members to respect the territorial integrity and political independence of other members.

(4) To declare that justice and the rule of law shall be the principles guiding the action of the Security Council and for this purpose to require the maximum employment of the Permanent Court in determining the legal aspects of international disputes.

(5) To see that the Security Council is in fact composed of 'security' Powers, i.e. Powers which by their past military contribution to the cause of world security have proved able and willing to assume substantial security responsibilities, or which are willing, and by virtue of their geographical position in relation to regions of primary strategic importance are able, to make a substantial contribution to the maintenance of international peace and security.

(6) To require members to pledge themselves to take action both national and international for the purpose of securing for all peoples, including their own, improved labour standards,

---

[1] *C.P.P.* General Session 1945–46, vol. III, pp. 775–9.

economic advancement, employment for all and social security and, as part of that pledge to take appropriate action through the Assembly, the Economic and Social Council and the International Labour Organisation and, in particular, to make regular reports to the Assembly as to what they have actually done to carry out the pledge.

(7) To elevate the Economic Council into a principal organ of the World Organisation and to give the Economic Council under the General Assembly specific new functions, including power to initiate action for the making of international conventions on all matters not being dealt with by other specialised agencies.

(8) To give the General Assembly a wider jurisdiction over, and a fuller share in, the general work of the Organisation and in particular to vest the Assembly with power to prevent situations and disputes from becoming 'frozen' in the Security Council, as occurred in the League of Nations in the notorious cases of external aggression against China, Ethiopia, and Czechoslovakia.

(9) To lay down the principle that the purpose of administration of all dependent territories is the welfare and development of the native peoples of such territories, and to place an obligation on nations controlling particular dependent territories, to be specified by appropriate action, to report regularly to advisory bodies consisting of expert administrators.[1]

This was indeed an ambitious programme for the representative of a Small or Middle Power to announce in the face of Great Power agreement on a text which would require substantial amendment if the programme was to be put into effect. Nothing daunted, Evatt applied to his difficult task not only unflagging energy but considerable zest as well. 'Not for him the half-light in which Mr Mackenzie King delighted to move', writes Nicholas Mansergh, 'but the full glare of public attention and popular acclaim.'[2]

The *New York Times* published in San Francisco during the Conference a special daily edition which described and commented upon Conference developments and was read avidly by at least the representatives of Small Powers. The Australian Minister for External Affairs understood well the arts of pub-

---

[1] *C.P.P.* General Session 1945–46, vol. III, pp. 775–9.
[2] Mansergh, *op. cit.* p. 135.

licity in attacking entrenched positions of Great Powers. As a member not only of the Conference Steering Committee (which included the leaders of all delegations) but also of the important Executive Committee of Fourteen, and as the most active and probably the best informed head of any delegation present at San Francisco, he established himself as the leader of the campaign against important features of the Dumbarton Oaks draft. Whether or not one agrees with the policy he pursued or with his methods, his technical achievement in influencing the Conference was a *tour de force*.

This, indeed, was the peak of Evatt's international influence as Minister for External Affairs. In later meetings of the General Assembly of the United Nations inconsistencies began to appear in Australian policy, especially in regard to the interpretation of 'domestic jurisdiction'[1] (Art. 2, (7)); while Evatt found it difficult if not impossible to form an objective judgement on the growing evidence of Stalin's 'cold-war' policy. In particular, his pressure for a 'tough' Japanese peace settlement,[2] his handling of the Manus Island issue[3] and his intervention as President of the United Nations General Assembly in the Berlin issue[4] tended to antagonise the United States, relations with which it became the most urgent task of his successors to improve.

There are two extreme views of the influence of the Australian Minister for External Affairs at the San Francisco Conference. The first is that given by Evatt himself in his speech in the House of Representatives on 30 August 1945 when he moved the second reading of a Bill to approve the Charter of the United Nations. 'Of the 38 amendments of substance which Australia proposed no less than 26 were either adopted without material change or adopted in principle.'[5] This exaggerates the degree of success of the Australian delegation, minimises the part played during the Conference by other Middle or Small Powers, including Canada and New Zealand, in pressing views which often coincided with those of Australia, and blurs the degree of compromise at times accepted by Australia in order to secure Great Power assent—for instance in regard to the full-employment 'pledge'.

The second extreme view is that, when all the tumult and

[1] See Harper and Sissons, *op. cit.* chapter 6.   [2] See p. 101 below.
[3] See p. 100 below.   [4] See p. 99 below.   [5] *C.N.* vol. XVI, no. 6 (1945), p. 187.

shouting of smaller countries at San Francisco had died away, the Charter as it emerged was a Great Power Charter reflecting the inevitable facts of power. Thus even Mansergh, while admitting a 'creative contribution of the dominions...in respect of economic and social policy and the setting up of the Trusteeship Council',[1] comments as follows on the attitude of the United Kingdom to Middle Power pressure (including pressure from the Dominions) to limit the authority in the Security Council of the Permanent Members:

Her attitude was understanding but in important matters uncompromising, and the dominions, lacking the support of a great power, emerged from the Conference with concessions to their respective viewpoints which were of secondary importance so far as the political provisions of the Charter were concerned.[2]

This is an underestimate of concessions gained by Smaller Powers even in the political field, and an underestimate of the importance of the efforts made by the Smaller Powers even when these were unsuccessful.

The chief contest at San Francisco centred round the right of veto of the Permanent Members of the Security Council. It is important to remember that *all* such members—not merely the Soviet Union—supported the view that international peace and security must be based upon unanimous agreement between the Great Powers. They made it clear that they would not sign a Charter which did not recognise their right of veto, and by their influence managed to prevent a majority vote in favour of the Australian proposal that, 'while the veto should apply to proposals for enforcement action under Chapter VII (sanctions), it should *not* apply to proposals for the Pacific Settlement of Disputes (Chapter VI)'.

Nevertheless, while maintaining the Yalta formula unchanged (Art. 27), the Great Powers made one important concession as a result of Small Power pressure; in an interpretative statement issued by the sponsoring Powers it was made clear that the veto could not be used to prevent an item being placed on the agenda of the Security Council, or to prevent an item being discussed. The assent of the Soviet Union to this position was obtained only after the matter was taken up with Stalin personally in Moscow by Harry Hopkins, at the request of President Tru-

---

[1] Mansergh, *op. cit.* p. 319.   [2] *Ibid.* p. 315.

man.[1] This concession avoided the possibility that the Smaller Powers, for their part, might refuse to sign the Charter if even the right of discussion of a problem could be denied by exercise of a Great Power veto. The right of discussion in the Security Council, together with the power to remove a matter from the agenda of the Council by a simple majority vote and thus enable the General Assembly to consider it, has in practice proved to be of great significance in view of the abuse by the Soviet Union of its right of veto during subsequent years.

The statement by the sponsoring Powers interpreting the Yalta formula protested against any assumption 'that the permanent members, any more than the non-permanent members, would use their "veto" power wilfully to obstruct the operation of the Council'.[2] Evatt made the most of this statement after the defeat of the Australian amendment, by urging the Great Powers to accept in practice the position they refused to accept in principle:

I can only hope...that during the next few years the Great Powers will demonstrate to the world by their actions in the Council that they will not in practice exercise to the full the veto rights which they possess under the Charter. Certain public indications along these lines have already been made, and we all accept these indications thankfully and in good faith. If it can be agreed that all peaceful means of settling disputes must be adopted and exhausted and that in practice the veto will not be used to block such procedures, I am convinced that we will make a great step forward. This would remove many of the doubts which middle and smaller countries have felt regarding acceptance of the present text...The Great Powers can perform a great service to the world if they demonstrate in practice that the powers given to them under the Charter will be used with restraint and in the interests of the United Nations as a whole.[3]

This hope, alas! proved vain. To date the Soviet Union has used the veto on more than one hundred occasions. In particular, lack of unanimity amongst the Permanent Members of the Security Council has prevented both the effective working of the Military Staff Committee (Art. 47) and the conclusion of special agreements under which member states were intended to make

---

[1] See Sherwood, *Roosevelt and Hopkins, op. cit.* pp. 910–11. In assenting to the request Stalin told Hopkins 'it was a mistake to believe that just because a nation was small it was necessarily innocent'.

[2] *C.P.P.* General Session 1945–46, vol. III, p. 788.   [3] *Ibid.* p. 718.

available to the Security Council armed forces and facilities necessary for the purpose of maintaining international peace and security (Art. 43).[1]

Having failed to obtain further concessions regarding the right of veto of Permanent Members of the Security Council, the Australian delegation endeavoured to secure approval of a resolution which would at least have prevented a Great Power veto upon amendments to the Charter. It proposed that only a two-thirds majority vote of the General Assembly, including the votes of *three* Great Powers, should be necessary for the amending process. This proposal failed, due to Great Power opposition and pressure. It thus became more difficult to amend the Charter than to create it, since at the San Francisco Conference only a two-thirds majority was necessary for approval of the text. The inevitable result of such rigidity in the constitution of the Organisation was to encourage revision by way of interpretation, whether or not the new interpretation was legally justified.

The most notable success of Evatt during the San Francisco Conference was his influence on the 'domestic jurisdiction' provisions of the Charter. As finally accepted and incorporated in the Charter (Article 2 (7)), this reads as follows:

Nothing contained in the present Charter shall authorise the United Nations to intervene in matters which are essentially within the domestic jurisdiction of any state or shall require the Members to submit such matters to settlement under the present Charter; but this principle shall not prejudice the application of enforcement measures under Chapter VII.

This paragraph appears in Chapter I of the Charter, which deals with the purposes and principles applicable to the Charter as a whole; whereas in the Dumbarton Oaks draft the provision regarding domestic jurisdiction, in somewhat different form, was included only as a part of Section VIII dealing with the Pacific Settlement of Disputes (Section A, 7).

In the Australian view an amendment to this provision in the Dumbarton Oaks draft advanced at San Francisco by the sponsoring Powers was still defective because it appeared to empower the United Nations to impose a settlement of any dispute, provided there was an actual threat to the peace, even

---

[1] See p. 324 below for detailed comments on developments within the United Nations after 1945.

though the dispute arose out of a matter within the domestic jurisdiction of one of the parties. As Evatt subsequently reported to Parliament: 'This seemed to us to be virtually an invitation to an aggressor to threaten force, in the hope of extorting concessions from the State concerned as the price of support by the Security Council.'[1] Such a situation was viewed by the Australian delegation with serious concern. For instance, suppose some country demanded of Australia that she should permit the entry for permanent residence of one million immigrants, and, on the demand being rejected, threatened the use of force. If Australia then appealed to the Security Council for support and protection it was conceivable that the Council, acting under powers accorded it by the paragraph sponsored by the Great Powers, might make such support conditional upon Australia accepting a compromise—for example, by agreeing to permit to enter Australia as migrants, say, one-half or one-quarter of the number demanded. It was the purpose of the Australian amendment therefore to ensure that, in a dispute arising out of a matter of domestic jurisdiction, the authority of the Security Council to intervene should be limited to preventing aggression or defending the victim of aggression. While Evatt did not in his speeches at San Francisco refer specifically to the subject of immigration, the report of the Australian delegation which he presented to Parliament contains the direct comment that, under the Dumbarton Oaks draft, such matters as migration policy would have become subject to the jurisdiction of the Security Council immediately an aggressor threatened to use force.[2]

Much has been written since the San Francisco Conference as to the correct interpretation of Article 2 (7) of the Charter, including its relation to other parts of the Charter, the meaning of the word 'intervention', and the inconsistent interpretations which member countries, including Australia, subsequently placed upon it. Harper and Sissons sum up these developments as follows:

The crux of the matter is that few governments have attempted to adopt a purely legal interpretation of Article 2 (7), even if this were possible in view of the conflicts of judicial opinion. The attitude of governments on the meaning of the Article has been governed

[1] *C.N.* vol. xvi, no. 6 (1945), p. 187.
[2] *C.P.P.* General Session 1945–46, vol. iii, p. 729.

primarily by political considerations, based on the particular government's interest in giving a wide or a narrow meaning to the Article according to whether or not it wished to focus international attention on particular issues. Consistency of policy on, or interpretation of, Article 2 (7) has been somewhat exceptional.[1]

Nevertheless it is difficult for anyone who was present at San Francisco to doubt that the meaning of the Australian proposal was generally understood at that time. This is implied, for instance, in the critical statement of the Norwegian delegation that the Australian attitude was 'tantamount to saying that we are in favour of the Council maintaining or restoring the peace, but we will have it do so only on our own conditions'.[2] It is all the more remarkable that the decisive vote in committee during the San Francisco Conference approved the Australian proposal by the astonishing majority of 31 to 3, with 5 abstentions. This unusual success in securing substantial amendment to a text already agreed upon by the sponsoring powers was a *tour de force*, and in some degree at least to be interpreted as a tribute, quite apart from the merits of the argument, to Evatt's advocacy of the points of view of many Middle and Small Powers during the Conference as a whole.

In the report of the Australian delegation presented to Parliament, and in his second reading speech on the Bill to ratify the Charter, the Minister for External Affairs laid considerable stress on the importance to Australia of the domestic jurisdiction paragraph. Yet in his Oliver Wendell Holmes Lectures on the United Nations, delivered at Harvard University in October 1947 and subsequently edited and published under the title *The United Nations*,[3] this aspect of the San Francisco Conference is dealt with in only the most cursory fashion. By the time that the lectures were delivered, however, the policy of the Australian Government on the Indonesian, Spanish, and religious trials issues had involved the rejection by Australian delegations of several claims by other countries that issues before the United Nations were matters of domestic jurisdiction. In these circumstances it would not have been easy for Evatt to expound at Harvard the nature of his successful advo-

---

[1] Harper and Sissons, *op. cit.* pp. 176-7.
[2] Russell and Muther, *A History of the United Nations Charter* (Brookings Institution, Washington, 1958), quoted at p. 910.
[3] Oxford University Press, Melbourne, 1948.

cacy at San Francisco in 1945 without raising doubts as to the
consistency of arguments advanced then with arguments used
on several occasions in the intervening years.

Other important aspects of the Charter which, in the final
form of the text, show substantial influence by Evatt were
Chapter XI (Declaration Regarding Non-Self-Governing
Territories); Chapters XII and XIII (trusteeship); Chapter IX
(International Economic and Social Co-operation); Chapter X
(The Economic and Social Council); Chapter VIII (Regional
Arrangements); and the Powers of the General Assembly.

Australia and New Zealand had made clear their attitude
towards colonial territories as early as January 1944 in the
Australian–New Zealand Agreement. Their basic position
remained unchanged throughout the London consultations in
April 1945, despite strong British reservations, and throughout
the San Francisco Conference, where the New Zealand Prime
Minister, Mr Peter Fraser, acted as chairman of the committee
dealing with trusteeship matters. The Dumbarton Oaks draft
had contained no chapter on trusteeship, largely, it would
appear, due to the unwillingness of the United States to commit
itself on an issue regarding which there was still disagreement
within the American Government.[1] While at San Francisco the
two Dominions had to accept compromises, they and their supporters were successful in pressing the sponsoring Powers to
accept a text involving colonial Powers in a wider degree of
accountability to the United Nations in respect of colonial
areas than some at least of such powers would have desired.
For instance, the Australian view that metropolitan Powers
should undertake to transmit to the Secretary-General certain
information relating to economic, social and educational conditions in their non-self-governing territories is embodied in
Article 73 (e) of the Charter.

The Smaller Powers were also successful at San Francisco
in elevating the status of the Economic and Social Council,
which became one of the principal organs of the United Nations,
and in widening the range of its functions. A somewhat bitter
struggle took place on the 'full-employment' issue, which
Australia wished to see incorporated in the Charter in the form
of a specific international guarantee. In the end, Evatt had to

[1] Vandenbosch and Hogan, *The United Nations* (McGraw-Hill, New York, 1952),
p. 81.

rest content with the provision in Article 55, that the United Nations shall *promote* higher standards of living, full employment, and conditions of economic and social progress and development.

The provisions of Article 51 (which declares that nothing in the Charter shall impair the inherent right of individual or collective self-defence in the event of armed attack), and of Articles 52 and 53 (which permit 'regional arrangements' consistent with the purposes and principles of the United Nations relating to the maintenance of international peace and security), reflect some gestures by the sponsoring Powers additional to those contained in the Dumbarton Oaks draft designed to mollify the fears of Latin American countries and others (including Australia) that a Great Power veto in the Security Council might leave them helpless in the case of aggression. Senator Vandenberg, the United States representative on the Committee dealing with regional arrangements, publicly acknowledged Evatt's contribution towards the final text of these Articles.

Finally, Evatt was the central figure in the battle to enlarge the powers of the General Assembly. The Dumbarton Oaks proposals had tended to underline the subordinate responsibility of the Assembly in matters of international peace and security, by stressing the Assembly's right to discuss 'general principles'; by stating that where 'action' was desired in regard to such principles or other 'questions' discussed by the Assembly the matter should be referred to the Security Council; and by limiting the Assembly's power to make recommendations regarding international peace and security to matters not under consideration by the Security Council. These provisions were extended somewhat by the sponsoring Powers before the San Francisco Conference to include an Assembly power to recommend 'measures for the peaceful adjustment of any situation...likely to impair the general welfare or friendly relations among nations...'

An Australian amendment sought specific power for the Assembly to make recommendations on 'any matter affecting international relations', except in regard to a question which was before the Security Council. This was supported by a committee majority which modified slightly the Australian phrase to 'any matter within the sphere of international relations'. The Soviet delegation opposed such an amendment on the ground that it would permit discussion in the Assembly of matters of domestic jurisdiction—an interpretation contested by the Australian Minister for External Affairs, who argued that the domestic jurisdiction clause 'overrides all other powers granted to the General Assembly'. A compromise was eventually reached by a subcommittee consisting of Stettinius, Gromyko and Evatt, which accepted the phrase 'any matters within the scope of the...Charter'.

According to Harper and Sissons[1] the real purpose of the Australian amendment was to make clear the power of the Assembly to discuss questions relating to dependent peoples and full employment. No authority is quoted for this statement, and perhaps it is sufficient for the authors to rely on their further comment that Evatt, concerned at the exclusion of Australia from British–American direction of Allied war strategy, wished 'to establish the right of the Assembly to criticise the capricious use by any great power of its right of veto to prevent United Nations action on particular issues'.[2]

III. THE INTERNATIONAL EFFECTS OF EVATT'S POLICY AND PRACTICE AS MINISTER FOR EXTERNAL AFFAIRS

The examples given above establish clearly the exceptional influence of Evatt, the representative of a Small or at most a Middle Power, upon the text of the United Nations Charter as revised during the San Francisco Conference. It is now necessary to consider, first, the extent to which Australian interests were served by his personal success, and, secondly, the effect upon Australian–United States and Australian–British relationships of his policy and methods both during and after the Conference.

There are three main sources of criticism of Evatt's activities at the San Francisco Conference, namely: Hasluck, now a member of the Liberal Party and Minister for External Affairs; Menzies, Leader of the Liberal Party and Prime Minister of Australia during the period from December 1949 to January 1966; and McEwen, Leader of the Country Party (which since 1949 has formed a coalition Government with the

---

[1] See Harper and Sissons, *op. cit.* pp. 56–60, for a discussion of the powers of the Assembly.   [2] *Ibid.* pp. 59–60.

Liberal Party) and Minister for Trade and Industry. These three, of course, were all political opponents of Evatt, and this fact must be taken into account in considering their comments.

For reasons indicated above, Hasluck, an officer of the Department of External Affairs whose departmental functions and conference responsibilities involved close working relationships with his Minister, was best placed to form a judgement. He resigned from the Department of External Affairs in 1947, did not enter Parliament until 1949, and expressed some criticism in a book entitled *Workshop of Security*, published in 1948. Although his more detailed public comments were made in 1954,[1] after he had become Minister for Territories in the Menzies Government, these are consistent with those expressed in 1948.

In the last chapter of *Workshop of Security* Hasluck's main criticism is directed against methods rather than policy:

...Australian foreign policy in the past three or four years has suffered from a passion for doing something on every occasion without enough thoughtful concern over doing what is best and doing it at the right time. There has also been a sort of larrikin strain in Australian foreign policy—a disposition to throw stones at the street lights just because they are bright. It is not a habit that helps the general illumination. We have also stamped the foot and thumped the table a little too often...Then we have sometimes butted unnecessarily into other people's arguments without waiting to consider whether the argument was getting on all right without us. We are not as considerate of other people's honour as we are of our own and are rather careless of other people's corns.[2]

He argues that Australia, which is not a Great Power, must rely for its influence not on size or strength, but on 'quality'. Her influence will depend upon the respect in which she is held, and this in turn will depend upon 'modesty as well as courage ...wisdom and good faith'.[3] Australian policy should aim at improving relationships between the Great Powers and supporting international co-operation within the provisions of the Charter. This can best be achieved by contributing 'clear, objective, honest thinking...firm, logical and unprovocative delivery of...views and...unswerving goodwill in the steady pursuit of the ideal of international co-operation'.[3]

---

[1] Hasluck, 'Australia and the formation of the United Nations', especially pp. 173–8.
[2] Paul Hasluck, *Workshop of Security* (Cheshire, Melbourne, 1948), p. 178.
[3] *Ibid.* p. 180.

In his lecture on 'Australia and the Formation of the United Nations', delivered six years later, Hasluck again criticises heavily the methods adopted by Evatt at San Francisco. In his opinion the reputation of Evatt and of Australia built up at the Conference 'was a reputation for activity and determination and aggressiveness in meeting criticism or opposition rather than for wisdom...A tremendous amount of the achievement was just hammering on the door.'[1] He describes Evatt as 'first and last a successful politician':[2]

...he was working for a success at San Francisco rather than addressing himself to the continuing tasks of good international relations. He was eager to play a leading role in making the Charter and of being the champion of small powers. His ambition was clearer than his policy.[3]

Policy, according to Hasluck, should be based upon a country's needs and interests, which need not always be 'narrow, selfish and without idealism'.[3] These interests have to be reconciled in some way with the interests of other countries, whose support should be sought not for the sake of a mere conference success, but in order to make more secure the interests of one's country. This objective may not be attained by setting Small Powers against Great Powers, or by trying to divide the Great Powers amongst themselves. The security provisions of the Charter were based upon the view that it was essential for decisions to be based upon the principle of the unanimity of the Great Powers. Hasluck concludes his lecture as follows:

What the San Francisco Conference did was to dig away at this foundation, and one of the most ardent, even if not fully conscious diggers, was Australia. We may have helped to make a slightly better document, but I don't think we helped to make a better world situation.[4]

During the debate in the House of Representatives on ratification of the Charter, Menzies, Leader of the Opposition, praised Evatt's technical skill and pertinacity in pursuing at San Francisco what he thought to be the right line of decision; on the other hand, he criticised strongly the Minister's attitude during the Conference and subsequently towards Great

---

[1] Hasluck, 'Australia and the formation of the United Nations', p. 174.
[2] *Ibid.* p. 176.   [3] *Ibid.* p. 177.   [4] *Ibid.* p. 178.

Britain: '...the practice of carrying into the public Press matters of dispute or conflict with Great Britain, which ought to be the subject of private discussion', he said, 'seems to me to be deplorable'.[1]

For the rest, Menzies sounded a note of warning which was repeated many times after he became Prime Minister in 1949. He supported wholeheartedly ratification of the Charter 'as a great gesture towards peace', because 'Every honest attempt to produce collective security by bringing the nations of the world into harmonious association with each other deserves the good wishes of mankind.' Nevertheless, it was also necessary to realise that 'it would be a tragedy for the world if we believed that the ratification of the world Charter would of its own force either create or protect the peace'.[1] Peace would depend essentially upon co-operation between the Great Powers, and if the spirit of co-operation were lacking, 'no writing will prevent war'.[2] In his opinion,

...we have here in this Charter a provision for a species of alliance between the United States, the United Kingdom, Russia, China and France, to which there is attached for many useful purposes of discussion and co-operation a great number of smaller powers. The function of these smaller powers will be to influence, so far as they can, the Great Powers, and when the Great Powers have unanimously decided upon a certain course, to play their part in its enforcement. But the vital issue of peace or war, so far as it concerns the world as a whole, will be determined by the Great Powers—by a core of alliances within the general structure of the Charter.[2]

In his speech during the same debate, McEwen, who had been a member of the Australian delegation to the San Francisco Conference in the capacity of 'consultant', supported Menzies' criticism of Evatt's public differences of opinion with the British delegation. He praised the dignity, correctness and conscientious devotion to his duties displayed by Forde, but complained that Evatt 'completely disregarded the existence of the dozen consultants and advisers appointed by the late Prime Minister (Mr Curtin)'.[3] Evatt, said McEwen, 'displayed a technical knowledge of the Dumbarton Oaks draft, and the implications of the innumerable amendments, which was probably second to none at the conference. He worked un-

---

[1] *C.P.D.* vol. 184, pp. 5,111–12.   [2] *Ibid.* pp. 5,114–15.   [3] *Ibid.* p. 5,159.

tiringly, and no man in that whole assembly could have devoted himself more completely to the work in hand.'[1] But the Australian delegation at San Francisco was 'a one-man band';[1] indeed, in McEwen's opinion, the views put forward by Evatt were his 'personal views', rather than the foreign policy of Australia.[2] It was the duty of a Foreign Minister to safeguard the interests of his own country, and these, in the case of Australia, were not 'capable of being protected by ourselves alone'.[2] Our safety and destiny lay in our membership of the British Commonwealth, and our strength was the total strength of the British Commonwealth. In these circumstances, every time Evatt publicly reproached the British Government or revealed publicly a disagreement on an important issue with the United Kingdom, he was steadily whittling down the authority internationally attached to the voice of the United Kingdom. Evatt, after all, was 'Minister for External Affairs', not 'Foreign Minister', and his very title should have indicated that his duties were concerned largely with Australian relations with the United Kingdom and with other Dominions. However attractive from the point of view of cultivating Australian nationalism, or gaining personal publicity, the development of a separate foreign policy by Australia, or by any other British Dominion, would reduce the British Commonwealth to its component parts, and they all would be outside the ranks of the Great Powers.[3] McEwen concluded his criticism in the following words:

The right honourable gentleman is unquestionably a man of great ability, extraordinary industry, and of notable force of character; but with these qualities go an obvious burning personal ambition to be a great figure, and an insatiable desire for publicity. If ever the British Empire were unlucky enough to have at the same time a group of Dominion Foreign Ministers as well equipped as Dr Evatt and practising the same tactics, the British Commonwealth would disintegrate like the atom.[3]

The great need was for understanding and tolerance and good faith, and without these ingredients the Charter could not be relied upon to work.

These criticisms of Evatt's methods and, to some extent, of his policy by political opponents are, of course, open to the charge of conscious or unconscious political bias. Until a wider

[1] *Ibid.* p. 5,159.   [2] *Ibid.* p. 5,160.   [3] *Ibid.* pp. 5,160–1.

range of official documents and personal memoirs become accessible it is not possible to form a completely balanced judgement as to the general effect upon Australian relations with her two most important friends and allies, Great Britain and the United States.

So far as Great Britain is concerned, any adverse effects do not appear to have been deep or lasting. While British political leaders and officials were certainly not amused by certain aspects of the policy and methods of the Australian Minister for External Affairs, their long national experience of handling difficult children—such as the American Colonies, Ireland and South Africa—made it easier for them to roll with the punch, maintain silence in public, pursue their own policies tenaciously and wait until individual Australian children matured, died, or were replaced in office.

The effects upon the United States were more important, and here at least some evidence of adverse American reactions is available which, whether justified or not, is not open to the charge of being politically tainted. This covers a period stretching from 1943 to 1948, and therefore refers not merely to Australian policy at the San Francisco Conference but also to Australian pressure for greater allocation of war material to the Pacific area, the Australian–New Zealand Agreement, the 'Manus Island' controversy, Australian policy towards a peace treaty with Japan, and Evatt's intervention in the Berlin problem while President of the United Nations General Assembly.

In Fleet-Admiral William D. Leahy's memoirs[1] there are only two brief references to Evatt, both of them unfavourable. Each refers to Australian requests for more aeroplanes, and each reflects a degree of distaste if not distrust. Reference has already been made to the unfavourable reactions of senior American naval officers and some Congressmen to certain paragraphs of the Australian–New Zealand Agreement, 1944.[2]

Entries in the Forrestal diaries (New York, 1951) are particularly critical. J. V. Forrestal had been appointed Secretary of the Navy in 1944, and in 1947 became Secretary of Defence, a post which he held until his resignation in 1949. On 22 November 1948 he made the following note in his diary:

Lunch with the President today. Cabinet plus Mr Harriman.

Marshall reported on the activities at U.N. from which it would

---

[1] William D. Leahy, *I Was There* (Gollancz, London, 1950), pp. 182, 205–6.
[2] See p. 77 above.

appear that our situation *vis-à-vis* Berlin, and the Russian situation in general, is rapidly deteriorating. Evatt, who is President of the General Assembly, is an active source of both irritation and uncertainty. The results of his activities and, to a lesser extent, Bramuglia's (Juan A. Bramuglia, Foreign Minister of the Argentine), who is Chairman of the Security Council, has been greatly to undermine the American position among the neutral nations. He has succeeded in giving the impression that, after all, the Russian demands are not so extreme and unmeetable.[1]

117538

It is important to note that the views expressed are, by implication, those of Secretary of State Marshall rather than of Forrestal, however much the actual words used may be those of the latter. Professor Geoffrey Sawer finds criticism of Evatt's intervention in the dispute about Berlin and the Berlin blockade 'unreasonable' and argues that such an intervention by the President of the General Assembly was 'in accordance with the spirit of its founders'.[2] The point to which primary attention is drawn here, however, is the nature of the American reaction, not whether the reaction was justified.

A second diary entry, for 20 December 1948, relates to Indonesia:

Cabinet—Indonesia—Australia
...Lovett [Robert A. Lovett, Undersecretary of State] discussed Indonesia and the action of the Dutch in seizing the capital and taking into custody the governmental leaders. He expressed annoyance at the gratuitous interference of Dr Evatt, the Foreign Minister of Australia, who had, although not a member of the Security Council (they are a member of the Good Offices Commission), addressed a communication to the Security Council expressing the view that if the U.S. had taken firm and preventive action with respect to the intent of the Dutch government to interfere in the affairs of the Republic, the present situation might have been avoided. He (Lovett) reported that in an interview with Ambassador (Norman J. O.) Makin of the Australian Embassy, he had expressed himself in the strongest terms as to our government's dissatisfaction with this unilateral action on the part of Evatt.[3]

But the fullest and best account of United States reactions to policies pursued by the Australian Minister for External Affairs between 1944 and 1949 is that given by Hartley Grattan, an

---

[1] *The Forrestal Diaries*, ed. Walter Millis (Cassell, London, 1952), p. 496.
[2] *Australia in World Affairs 1950–55*, p. 113.   [3] *Forrestal Diaries*, p. 504.

American friend both of Australia and of Evatt.[1] According to Grattan, Evatt saw in the United Nations a means of escape from Big-Power politics. This idea was not bad in itself; unfortunately, Evatt tried to act out his policy at a time when the world was 'rapidly degenerating into hostile power blocs, polarised around the United States and the U.S.S.R.'[2] The development of the Cold War—to which the Australian Minister for External Affairs found it very difficult to adapt himself—made it necessary to supplement the United Nations by other arrangements. Grattan comments as follows:

> ...there necessarily developed a certain measure of ambiguity in relations with the United States...The wartime accord early began to lose some of its warmth. It was further cooled by virtue of the fact that the United States was a central figure of the Cold War power struggle, a struggle of which Evatt disapproved and which he appeared to 'blame on' the Americans, explaining Russian actions as defensive.[3]

Differences also arose between Australia and the United States with regard to Manus Island, a part of Australian New Guinea where the Americans had built a powerful base during the Second World War. Shortly after the war, according to Grattan, the Americans considered making Manus Island the 'southern anchor' of a defence perimeter in the Western Pacific, and also showed interest in New Zealand's Trust territory of Samoa and in the British territory of Christmas Island. Soundings as to the Australian attitude towards the use of Manus elicited the response that Australia would require a *quid pro quo* in the form of American agreement for joint use of other American bases in the Pacific. Grattan also alleges, without supporting evidence, that Australia prevented the United States from acquiring Christmas Island, which Great Britain would have been prepared to transfer. In the event, the Americans abandoned Manus altogether and made Manila their 'southern terminus'. Grattan gives no firm answer to the question whether this decision was due to onerous conditions made by Australia in relation to the Manus Base, or to American 'rethinking' of American strategy, but there is little doubt that Australian–American relations suffered some further deterioration as a result of the Manus controversy.

---

[1] Grattan, *op. cit.* pp. 199–205.   [2] *Ibid.* pp. 199–200.   [3] *Ibid.* p. 200.

Further, Grattan refers to delay by the Australian Government in accepting American proposals to use the balance due to the United States under war-time Lend–Lease arrangements to finance exchange of university students and teachers, and also to Australia's refusal of a double-taxation agreement between the two countries. Here, however, it is easier to see the shadow of the hand of the Department of the Treasury at that particular stage than the hand either of Evatt or of the Labour Party. *Per contra*, there is no doubt that the Minister for External Affairs was himself strongly committed to a 'hard' policy towards Japan, designed to limit and control Japanese armament and to break up the old economic monopolies (Zaibatsu). Such a policy the United States was unwilling to enforce, largely because of the development of Stalin's cold-war policy and Communist victories in mainland China, which induced a gradual change in the American attitude towards Japan. 'The Labourites were reluctant to admit that the locale of menacing power in East Asia had shifted from island Japan to the continent...'[1]

Evatt would readily have accepted any challenge to his policy towards Japan, which he strongly defended during debates in the House of Representatives when Bills to ratify the Japanese Peace Treaty and the military alliance between the United States, Australia and New Zealand (ANZUS) were being considered in 1952. At that stage the Labour Party was in Opposition, and formally voted against ratification of the Japanese Peace Treaty. While accepting the ANZUS Treaty, the Opposition minimised its significance, and Evatt argued that 'the price that has had to be paid for it', namely, approval of a 'soft' peace with Japan, was too high.[2]

On the other hand, Evatt violently rejected during the ANZUS debate criticism of his handling of the Manus Island controversy, claiming that 'A silly and wicked campaign' had been carried on against the Chifley Government in regard to this issue, including an alleged leakage to a newspaper of secret information from official files. The substance of his defence is contained in the following extract from his speech:

My colleagues and I did not become Ministers of the Australian Government in war-time in order to give Australian territory to any

---

[1] *Ibid.* p. 205.   [2] See *C.P.D.* vol. 216, p. 598.

country. We wanted a regional agreement of this [ANZUS] kind...
The Chifley Government was anxious to conclude an agreement
which provided that Pacific bases should be made available for use
by the British Commonwealth and the United States of America...
The Menzies Government has obtained the agreement we are now
considering at the price of agreeing to the rearmament of Japan and
I consider that that was too great a price to pay for it...We...
offered the United States of America, in connexion with a mutual
defensive pact of this character, the use of any bases in Australia on
condition that Australia should have the right to use American
bases for the common defence of the two countries.[1]

To which Casey, Minister for External Affairs at the time of the
ANZUS debate, replied that the only charge he made against
Evatt in his handling of the Manus Island problem was that
'he over-played his hand'. Evatt, said the Minister,

...aimed too high, and misjudged the temper and mood of the
United States of America at that time. It is not to his discredit that
he failed to get a regional arrangement in the Pacific. The Americans
cooled off...Australia lost what I think was a tremendous opportunity to retain the militant interest of the world's greatest power in
a position of immense value to us...[2]

IV. UNDERLYING ASSUMPTIONS AS TO AUSTRALIAN POLICY AND METHODS, 1941–49

It remains to summarise now the assumptions as to policy and
methods adopted by Evatt during his period of office as Australian Minister for External Affairs. In doing so it is necessary
to remind ourselves again that he took over cabinet responsibilities at a time when Australia was at war with Germany,
while within a few months the Japanese onslaught southwards in
the Pacific placed the survival of Australia in jeopardy for the
first time in her history.

The first assumption was that Australia must pursue an
independent foreign policy directed to the maintenance of her
own vital interests, and that this frequently required the public
expression of her views despite the fact that they might differ
from those of her friends and allies, including Great Britain. As
the representative of at most a Middle Power, Evatt was frustrated and angered by Great Power dominance and exclusive-

[1] *C.P.D.* vol. 216, pp. 594–6.   [2] *Ibid.* p. 747.

ness in the running of the Second World War, and by the desire of such Powers to determine the substance of the post-war settlements. Thus the Australian–New Zealand Agreement of 1944 was an explosive protest—at least on the part of Australia—against the principle so complacently stated by McNeill, namely, 'Inasmuch as the Anglo-American monopoly of strategic decision reflected the realities of military and economic power, the [war-time] system worked well enough...Powerful nations have never yet been willing to submit their actions to majority vote of small Powers.'[1]

The second assumption was that Australia and New Zealand, especially the former, were destined to carry out in the Pacific area after 1945 certain regional responsibilities for the Commonwealth of Nations as a whole or for those members of the Commonwealth with interests in the Pacific. Reference has already been made to Australian interest in taking over British responsibilities in the Solomon Islands and the New Hebrides at the time when the Australian–New Zealand Agreement was negotiated.[2] Subsequent developments were summed up by Evatt in a B.B.C. broadcast delivered on 10 May 1946:

It should be recognised that new methods have necessarily been devised to meet new situations. One recent example of the flexibility of British Commonwealth consultations and procedures is the appointment of an Australian to represent not only Australia, but the United Kingdom, India and New Zealand as well, on the Allied Council for Japan in Tokyo. Again, an Australian general has been appointed as officer commanding all British Commonwealth occupation forces in Japan. In some respects, therefore, we are reaching a stage in British Commonwealth relations at which there is a division of functions on a *regional* basis for certain purposes. It has become possible for a Dominion to act not only for itself but also for the United Kingdom and other Dominions as well.[3]

It was perhaps not unnatural that this assumption was at its strongest during a period when Great Britain was trying desperately to recover from the effects of a world war and was substantially preoccupied with European affairs and her difficult economic situation, and when she was still suffering the psychological shock caused by considerable loss in power and

[1] William Hardy McNeill, *Survey of International Affairs 1939–46, America, Britain and Russia, Their Co-operation and Conflict, 1941–46*, at p. 156.
[2] See p. 74 above.   [3] Evatt, *Australia in World Affairs*, p. 189.

prestige in the Pacific area, following upon Japanese victories in South-East Asia. The new Liberal–Country Party Government which came to power in Australia in 1949 did not proceed on the basis of such an assumption, although during Spender's brief tenure of office as Minister for External Affairs there was some evidence of special Australian interest in such adjacent islands as the New Hebrides, New Caledonia and Timor.[1] Moreover, developments in the defence field from 1949 onwards, expanding informal arrangements between the United Kingdom, New Zealand and Australia in respect of the Malayan area (ANZAM), signature of the Security Treaty between Australia, New Zealand and the United States (ANZUS) and of the South-East Asia Collective Defence Treaty (SEATO), and Australian and New Zealand decisions to station ground troops in Malaya in time of peace, provided a new framework for Commonwealth and Allied activities in South-East Asia. These developments will be considered in detail in the following chapter.

Evatt's third, and perhaps most important, assumption was that a Middle or Small Power had a better chance of influencing international developments through the United Nations than by any other means, despite the privileged position in the Security Council of the Permanent Members of the Council as laid down in the Charter. At the San Francisco Conference of 1945 Evatt directed all his efforts, with conspicuous though limited success, towards the creation of a United Nations Organisation which would minimise the controlling influence of the Great Powers, maximise the influence of the Middle and Small Powers, bind all member states to adhere to principles of 'justice' as reflected in the economic and social views of the Australian Labour Party, and provide a public, international forum for the leaders of the smaller Powers in which to stir up world public opinion through mass-media reporting. Subsequently, in the Security Council, in the General Assembly, and as the holder of high United Nations offices, including the Presidency of the Assembly, Evatt pursued an energetic policy in accordance with which important world problems would be brought to the United Nations for consideration, investigation, conciliation and determination. Though not uncritical of some of the work of the United Nations, as his Oliver Wendell Holmes

[1] See, for example, Spender's speech of 9 March 1950, *C.P.D.* vol. 206 at p. 633.

Lectures delivered at Harvard University in 1947 show, he continued to the end of his period of office as Minister for External Affairs to turn to the United Nations as the first and best hope of securing international peace and justice.

As a public speaker on the world stage, Evatt's style was always assertive if not actually aggressive—the traditional lawyer fighting for his client and demanding recognition of the latter's rights. He did not understand the value of occasional diplomatic silence, or the need to balance present successes against possible long-term losses. Thus in trying to restrict the Great Power right of veto, he gave little thought to the possibility that some day Australia might be glad to seek the exercise of a British veto in defence of a vital Australian interest; while in pressing for an increase in the powers of the General Assembly beyond those contained in the Dumbarton Oaks draft, his imagination did not lead him to foresee that the votes of Small Power *blocs* in the General Assembly might in due course be directed, not merely against Great Power policies, but also against the policies of smaller Powers like Australia—for instance, in regard to trust and non-self-governing territories.

Finally, the Australian Minister for External affairs showed himself at times too rigid in policy and methods when formulated or developed, refusing to admit facts calling for reappraisal of past assumptions. Thus, he found great difficulty in accepting the harsh facts of Stalinist post-war policy, while his personal 'commitment' to the United Nations made him over-optimistic as to what could be achieved by reference of political problems to the world organisation.

As a political personality Evatt made his mark on the world stage and, at the time of the San Francisco Conference, increased Australia's standing amongst Middle and Small Powers. But his style and methods did not attract friends—least of all amongst the Great Powers. In particular, the balance of available evidence suggests that Australia lost ground between 1945 and 1949 in her relationships with the United States, the dominant power in the Pacific.

5

THE LIBERAL–COUNTRY PARTY IN OFFICE—LEADERS, GENERAL OUTLOOK, AND ATTITUDE TOWARDS DEFENCE

I. THE PRIME MINISTER—ROBERT GORDON MENZIES

Federal elections were held in Australia in December 1949, and the Labour Party, which had held office for eight years, was defeated. The Liberal–Country Party Coalition came to power, under the Prime Ministership of Robert Gordon Menzies, as an avowedly anti-Communist Government which had promised to outlaw the Communist Party in Australia.

Domestically, Communist-dominated trade unions had held the Australian community to ransom through a strike at coal mines which dislocated industry, put some 600,000 fellow-Australians out of work, and compelled a Labour Government to send troops to work open-cut mines!

Internationally, in the Europe–Atlantic area, Stalin had unsuccessfully blockaded Berlin (1948–49); Czechoslovakia had come under Communist control (1948); Russia had forbidden her eastern European partners to accept Marshall Plan aid (1948); misuse of the Soviet veto and development of the cold war had prevented the establishment under the Security Council of the international security system envisaged by Articles 43–47 of the Charter, and had indirectly fostered the creation of the North Atlantic Treaty Organisation (1949). In Asia, Communist insurrections had broken out in Indonesia and Malaya (1948), while in 1949 Mao Tse-tung had gained control over mainland China. It is not surprising that against this background the Australian electorate favoured a government to the right of centre. What is more surprising is that the same Government has remained in office, at the time of writing, for some sixteen years—a period unprecedented in Australian political history.

A Prime Minister who held office for sixteen consecutive

years must have exceptional qualities. Before analysing differences between the foreign policy of the Labour Party and of the Coalition—and drawing attention to some important similarities—it is desirable to say something of the man who dominated the cabinet for such a long period.

As his name implies, Robert Gordon Menzies is of Scottish descent. He was born in the State of Victoria on 20 December 1894. After a brilliant academic record at the University of Melbourne, where he studied Law, he soon began to make his mark at the Victorian Bar where, had he chosen to concentrate on a legal career, he would undoubtedly have reached the highest ranks. In 1928, however, at the age of 33, he entered Victorian State politics, and by 1932 he had become Attorney-General, Minister for Railways and Deputy Premier in the Victorian Legislative Assembly. In 1934 he transferred his political activities to the Federal sphere, becoming in the same year Attorney-General for the Commonwealth. Since that date he has held Federal office as Treasurer, Minister for Trade and Customs, Minister for Co-ordination of Defence, Minister for Information and for Munitions, and Prime Minister. In other words, for approximately 35 years his primary energies have been directed to parliamentary affairs, while still maintaining some degree of private practice at the Bar during those periods when this was practicable and permissible.

Menzies has never been a dry-as-dust lawyer who could argue successfully in a Court of Appeal but bore a non-legal audience to tears. Born with the gift of speech, and well-versed in orthodox English literature, his firm, clear, modulated voice and his capacity for irony and repartee place him among the chosen few outstanding speakers of the English-speaking world. After a speech to the National Press Club in Washingdon, D.C.—not the least critical audience in the world—in 1941, following a visit to England, American echoes reached the Australian Embassy in the following form: 'Can't he stay around for a while and speak to wider audiences? He is No. 2!' By which last phrase was meant that Menzies as a speaker was second only to Churchill, not excluding Roosevelt. Whatever the Prime Minister has had to say during his political career—whether as Parliamentarian, speaker from a public platform, after-dinner speaker or plain raconteur—has never lost in effectiveness from the form in which the ideas have been conveyed.

The best and at the same time the most generous delineation of Menzies' style and character is that given by Hasluck in 1951 in the capacity of a war historian.[1] Hasluck, now Minister for External Affairs, wrote that 'the new Prime Minister had the disadvantage of his own brilliance' in facing the difficulties of office:

A man of fine presence, ease of manner, poise and style, he incurred the suspicion of being vain, of lacking sincerity, and of being aloof. A man of keen intellect he inevitably had often made lesser men seem foolish. A man who had consciously devoted himself to public service from early manhood both in State and Federal politics, he incurred the accusation of being ambitious for office...Part of the disadvantage of Menzies, as indeed of Bruce before him, was that he flew in the face of the whole of Australian myth and legend which places its hearts of gold only in rough cases, makes its wisest men laconic and ungrammatical, and insists that a man who is careless and vulgar in his own speech and manners is sure to be careful of his neighbour's interests...Above all, Menzies suffered that disability of the great advocate and of the logical mind in a world of political conduct governed and obstructed by political motives. Having reached an impeccable conclusion by faultless logic and demonstrated the argument clearly to the public he had a sense of achievement and an expectation that from that conclusion the inescapably correct consequences would flow. Of course they seldom did.[1]

Other critics—and not merely his political opponents—have been less kind. One well-known Australian journalist and author has described Menzies as 'the great survivor'—a 'great actor', 'lazy in his reading', 'essentially arrogant, although courageous', with a preference for surrounding himself with a 'firebreak of mediocrity'.[2] An Australian historian is outraged by what is interpreted as 'overweening pride and arrogance', and claims that the Prime Minister has 'three all-consuming passions', namely, the 'spur to fame' (with 'contempt and disdain' for associates); 'almost superstitious respect...for British institutions', and a desire to 'ridicule all who offered a way forward, who wanted "progress"'. The only virtue admitted by the latter writer is 'dignity and courage...in the hours of adversity'.[3]

---

[1] See Hasluck, *Government and People*, p. 115.
[2] See Donald Horne, *The Lucky Country* (Penguin Books, Adelaide, 1964), pp. 152–8.
[3] Professor Manning Clark, *A Short History of Australia* (Mentor Books, New York, 1963), pp. 218–19, 222.

To understand the Prime Minister's attitude towards problems of foreign policy it is necessary to start with his reverence for British parliamentary democracy and for the British legal tradition, with its distrust of written constitutions, and pragmatic Common Law approach.

These traditions—parliamentary and legal—did more than influence Menzies: they became part of his blood and bones, and substantially fashioned his mental outlook. Hence, largely, his attachment to the conception of the British Commonwealth, and to the British constitutional monarchy. 'I am a Commonwealth man'—'We are all the Queen's men', he was apt to say, at least until the time when the handling of the South African question at the Commonwealth Prime Ministers' Conference in 1961, and the British decision to apply for entry to the European Common Market in 1962, deeply disturbed and troubled his faith in the future of the Commonwealth as he had understood or conceived it.

Hence, in some degree, his distrust of the effectiveness of the United Nations, with its written constitution and its artificial stress upon the 'sovereign equality of all its members', which enables the weakest member to cast a vote in the General Assembly equal to that of the United States or the Soviet Union, irrespective of capacity to carry a reasonable share of the economic or military burden of responsibility for carrying out policies recommended.

For the Prime Minister, realism required a decent respect for the principles and purposes of the United Nations, but also clear recognition of its impotence, in certain cases, to resolve vital problems of security. In his view, a country like Australia should be ambitious, not for publicity or for Small-Power popularity, but to acquire 'great and powerful friends', able and willing to support policies designed to further Australian interests. Criticism of views of such friends not shared by Australia should be voiced privately, not publicly. Ironically enough, this general principle was never in practice adhered to by cabinet ministers concerned with problems of international trade.

Whereas it was Evatt's instinct to refer international disputes immediately to the United Nations for examination, investigation and decision or recommendation, Menzies claimed and often asserted that mere reference to the United Nations was not a policy in itself: Australia had to decide what the ultimate effect

—good or bad—of such reference might be, and what policy she proposed to follow when the issue came before the United Nations. In the forefront of his foreign policy, therefore, he placed good relationships between Australia and Great Britain, and between Australia and the United States. He was not antagonistic to the United Nations, but sceptical of its effectiveness, especially in the field of international peace and security.

As regards Asia, the Prime Minister was cautious. He accepted in principle the view that Australia, a country of European cultural tradition, must, if only because of its permanent geographical situation off the southern rim of Asia, study, understand and co-operate as closely as practicable with its Asian neighbours of the 'near north'. The events of the Second World War had been sufficient in themselves to demonstrate this. But the philosophy and religion of Asia were almost closed books to a man of his temperament, just as tropical climates oppressed his massive physical frame. His imagination at fullest stretch could not comprehend what induced an Indian fakir to lie down on a bed of nails, or a Japanese samurai to commit suicide out of loyalty to his lord. Actions such as these were to him simply irrational, evidencing a lack of any sense of proportion, or humour. His own faith was in the pragmatic life of action and of reasonable compromise, seeking equity in this present life, not immortality in the next or oblivion in Nirvana.

To Menzies, equality for all nations in the world as we know it was illusion; world government was so far over the horizon as to be invisible; power was a fact of life, whether we liked it or not. No country in the world had devised a better or fairer government for its citizens than had Great Britain, which had developed the democratic parliamentary tradition to the highest point yet reached. Australia should do all it could to strengthen Great Britain and thus the Commonwealth as a whole, and bend its best efforts towards ensuring that Commonwealth policies marched at least in the same direction as the policies of the United States, which in the last resort alone had the power, since 1942, to protect if it so wished vital Australian interests in the Pacific area against pressure on a major scale. Not for Australia the policy of 'non-alignment', which would only isolate her from her powerful friends. The Korean War, developments in Malaya and in the old 'Indo-China' had shown the necessity for such friends—to say nothing of an unstable Indonesia and the possibility of a resurgent Japan. Friendship with Asian countries? Yes, as witness trade with Japan and economic aid through the Colombo Plan; but in matters of defence and security at least co-operation with Great Britain and alliance with the United States was essential, whether or not such a policy was distasteful to Asian countries.

In short, until 1962 at least, one could say that for Menzies the central driving force of his foreign policy was his faith in the British Commonwealth (as he long continued to call it), tempered by his realistic judgement that, in view of the diminution of British strength brought about by two world wars, the power of the United States must be taken into account as the most important factor in the Pacific. On the first point, his deepest emotions were involved. 'When the Commonwealth ceases to be an inner feeling', he said in 1950, 'as well as an external association, virtue will have gone out of it.'[1]

...our true brotherhood must be a matter of feeling and not merely a matter of thought...an unquenchable sense of common destiny and common duty and common instinct. To many people the British Commonwealth is a curious machine that has worked... relied upon by mankind twice during this century, to their great deliverance...Unless the Commonwealth is to British people all over the world a spirit, a proud memory, a confident prayer, courage for the future, it is nothing.

> It may be that the gulfs will wash us down:
> It may be we shall touch the Happy Isles,
> And see the great Achilles, whom we knew.
> Tho' much is taken, much abides; and tho'
> We are not now that strength which in old days
> Moved earth and heaven; that which we are, we are;
> One equal temper of heroic hearts,
> Made weak by time and fate, but strong in will
> To strive, to seek, to find, and not to yield.[2]

On this occasion the Prime Minister publicly unveiled, in almost lyrical form, his deep sentiment for the Commonwealth. One may judge the better against this background the underlying sadness of a speech made by him in Parliament on 16 October 1962 on the subject of Britain's application to join the

---

[1] Menzies, *Speech is of Time*, p. 17.   [2] *Ibid.* pp. 18–20.

Common Market, in the course of which he confessed that 'The old hopes of concerting common policies have gone'.[1]

One of Menzies' last acts as Prime Minister, prior to his voluntary retirement from public office early in 1966 at the age of 71, was to announce the Government's decision not to be represented at the Lagos Commonwealth Conference on Rhodesia by the Prime Minister or a member of the cabinet, but only by an observer. This decision was criticised in some quarters in Britain as showing lack of interest in the Commonwealth of Nations, and was characterised by the Prime Minister of Malaysia as 'callous' and 'rotten'.[2] Menzies, remembering his own support for British policy during the Suez crisis of 1956, and Australian military aid to Malaya during the 'Emergency' and to Malaysia in face of Indonesian confrontation, must have found such comments deeply ironical.[3]

II. MR SPENDER[4] AS MINISTER FOR EXTERNAL AFFAIRS

The first full review of the foreign policy of the new Coalition Government was made in the House of Representatives on 9 March 1950 by the new Minister for External Affairs and External Territories, Mr P. C. Spender.[5] As a statement by a minister of only three months standing, who had not yet been 'processed' through visits to London, Washington and the United Nations in New York, it is surprisingly comprehensive and, in most instances, sure in touch as an expression of the policy which the Government was to pursue for many years to come.

Spender was born in 1897, and graduated from Sydney University with first-class honours in Law and the University Medal. A successful barrister, he took silk at the early age of 38. At the age of 40 he entered federal politics as an independent candidate, subsequently joined the United Australia Party, and held ministerial office for brief periods as Minister without Portfolio (1939), Treasurer and Vice-President of the Executive Council (1940), and Minister for the Army (1940–41). In 1940 he became a member of the Advisory War Council, and re-

---

[1] *C.N.* vol. xxxiii, no. 10 (October 1962), p. 35.
[2] *The Canberra Times*, 10 January 1966, p. 5.
[3] For a detailed account of Menzies' changing views on the Commonwealth of Nations, see chapter 7 below.
[4] Later Sir Percy Spender.   [5] See *C.P.D.* vol. 206, pp. 621–40.

mained a member, after the Labour Party took office in October 1941, until the end of the War. He was Minister for External Affairs from December 1949 to March 1951, when he became Australian Ambassador at Washington until 1958. While in Washington he was Leader of Australian delegations to a number of sessions of the United Nations General Assembly. In 1958 he was elected a member of the International Court of Justice at The Hague, and became President of the Court in 1964. As Minister for External Affairs Spender played a distinguished part in the successful negotiations for a Security Treaty between Australia, New Zealand and the United States (ANZUS)[1] and in securing agreement upon a Commonwealth plan for economic aid to underdeveloped countries (Colombo Plan).[2]

Spender was no starry-eyed idealist, but a realist who liked to regard himself as a 'man of the world'. In his speech of 9 March 1950 he made it clear that the Menzies Government did not intend to place the United Nations as high in the list of Australian foreign-policy priorities as had Evatt. First emphasis was given to the 'maintenance of our security and our way of life'. Pursuit of these objectives involved closest co-operation with the British Commonwealth, especially Great Britain, and with the United States. The United States was the greatest Pacific Power: it was therefore essential that Australia should maintain the closest and best possible relations with her and initiate and carry out Australian Pacific policies as far as possible in co-operation with her. In stressing the outstanding importance of Australian–American relations, the Minister indicated that he had in mind something more than a war-time or merely military alliance:

Indeed, as far as possible, it is our objective to build up with the United States somewhat the same relationship as exists within the British Commonwealth...we desire a full exchange of information and experience on all important matters and consultation on questions of mutual interest. Where we conceive our interests to diverge from those of the United States on any fundamental issue, we shall, of course, firmly maintain our own point of view. But where our general objectives coincide, we shall seek to have done with petty disagreements and follow broad avenues of co-operation.[3]

[1] § III below. [2] See p. 116 below, and chapter 6, pp. 197–9 below.
[3] See *C.P.D.* vol. 206, pp. 635–6.

It was only 'fourthly' that the Minister referred to the United
Nations, obligations to which Australia must be in a position to
discharge. Even here, however, certain reservations were stated.
Spender referred to the danger of exaggerating, not the importance of the aims or purposes or principles of the United
Nations, but the extent to which in present circumstances it
could exert real influence for the maintenance of peace in the
world. Australia would continue to apply the principles of the
Charter in its own foreign policy, and give continuing support
to the operations of the United Nations 'so long as the United
Nations itself operates in accordance with those principles'.[1]

Where the United Nations was manifestly unable to protect
Australian interests, it was the duty of the Government to follow
simultaneously a policy of making supplementary arrangements
among those known to be friends. As so far in the United
Nations the 'major disputants' had not been brought together,
and as there was no immediate prospect of agreement between
them in the future, the basis of Australian foreign policy and
defence policy must be adjusted accordingly. Australia lived in
a dangerous world, and must look immediately to means additional to the United Nations, 'not necessarily to other principles', to defend its interests.[2]

Spender urged therefore 'that all Governments...directly
interested in the preservation of peace through South and South-
East Asia and in the advancement of human welfare under the
democratic system should consider immediately whether some
form of regional pact for common defence is a practical possibility'.[3] Australia, the United Kingdom and other Commonwealth countries might form the nucleus. But the Minister
had in mind 'particularly the United States of America, whose
participation would give such a pact a substance that it would
otherwise lack. Indeed, it would be rather meaningless without
the United States.'[3] The pact should not be merely 'defensive',
but should have positive aspects as well. It should aim at promoting democratic political institutions, higher living standards,
increased cultural and commercial ties. The Government would
spare no effort in pursuing this objective.

So far, main emphasis in the Minister's speech had been
placed upon military means of ensuring Australian security.
It is important to note, however, that Spender was fully

[1] *C.P.D.* vol. 206, p. 636.   [2] *Ibid.* pp. 637–8.   [3] *Ibid.* p. 632

conscious as well of the need for a non-military approach to the problem of stabilising non-communist governments in South and South-East Asia. 'The problem in Asia', he said, 'lies in the poverty that exists within the region itself, no less than in the pressure from external forces.'[1] He referred to low consumption standards, pressure of population and insufficiency of capital investment, and stated that the Government was concerned 'that there is lacking as yet any concerted attempt to check and reverse through international measures the deterioration in the political and economic situation...the economic advantages of the rest of the world from the development of the output of food and raw materials in the region are...self-evident'.[1] Results were needed quickly. A start had been made, so far as Commonwealth countries were concerned, at the Colombo Conference[2] at which Australia had pressed strongly for the creation of an organisation the objectives of whose members would be the grant of economic assistance to under-developed countries in South and South-East Asia. The Australian Government had approved the Colombo Plan proposals and would act as host to other governments as soon as the latter indicated their assent also, in order to get the scheme under way.

After passing references to Australian interest in the problems of Europe, and the broad principles to be considered in any Japanese peace settlement, Spender concluded his speech by disclaiming any belief that there was some simple or magic cure for the world's ills; declared that two world wars had shown that 'authority which depends on force alone rests upon hollow foundations if it is not sustained by honesty of purpose, and a recognition of the value of individual human beings';[3] and proclaimed his faith that man, 'a civilised, rational being', was bound to seek 'means to escape his own destruction'.[3]

In the light of subsequent developments, Spender's analysis and foresight, as evidenced by his first formal exposition in Parliament of international problems from the point of view of the new coalition Government, were remarkable.

Largely through his own efforts, the ANZUS Treaty was negotiated, signed and ratified by 1952. Subsequently, in 1954, the South-East Asia Collective Defence Treaty came into existence, embracing as member states the United States, Great

[1] *Ibid.* p. 629.   [2] Held in Colombo, Ceylon, from 9–14 January 1950.
[3] *C.P.D.* vol. 206, p. 640.

Britain, France, Australia, New Zealand, Thailand, Pakistan and the Philippines. Article 3 of this Treaty bound the parties to 'strengthen their free institutions and to co-operate with one another in the further development of economic measures, including technical assistance, designed both to promote economic progress and social well-being and to further the individual and collective efforts of governments towards these ends'. Although economic action taken under this Article was limited in scope—to the dissatisfaction of the three recipient signatory governments, namely, Thailand, Pakistan and the Philippines—this was due mainly to the fact that the Colombo Plan was in operation and that donor governments preferred the latter vehicle for economic aid.

The Consultative Committee established as a result of discussions at the Colombo Conference of January 1950 met in Sydney in May of that year and agreed upon a broad programme of capital aid and technical assistance to underdeveloped countries, Spender himself being substantially responsible for the emphasis placed upon technical assistance, which later proved to be the most successful feature of the Colombo Plan. Since 1950 membership has been expanded to include Australia, Canada, Ceylon, India, New Zealand, Pakistan, the United Kingdom, Malaysia, the United States, Afghanistan, Burma, Cambodia, Indonesia, Laos, Nepal, the Philippines, Thailand, Vietnam, Japan, Korea, Bhutan and the Maldive Islands.[1] By 30 June 1965 Australia alone had contributed a total of £58,641,744 under the Colombo Plan, of which £41,295,157 had been spent on economic development projects and £17,346,587 on technical assistance schemes.[2]

On 8 June 1950 during a statement in reply to the debate in the House of Representatives on the Minister's speech of 9 March, Spender responded to a request by Evatt for further clarification of his earlier statement that the Government would support the operation of the United Nations so long as that organisation acted in accordance with the principles of the Charter. The Minister drew attention to the terms of the 'domestic jurisdiction' clause (Article 2 (7)), and commented upon the 'increasing tendency of the Assembly to overstep its competence in relation to non-self-governing territories';

[1] See *C.N.* vol. xxxvi, no. 1 (January 1965), pp. 8–15.
[2] *Year Book of the Commonwealth of Australia*, 1965, p. 1,226

criticised the 'exaggerated interpretation of its powers' by the United Nations in relation to clauses of the Charter dealing with human rights and fundamental freedoms; and deplored 'the tendency to use the United Nations as a sounding board for propaganda'.[1] His general summing-up is remarkably pertinent when viewed from the vantage-point of 1966:

The basic objective of any world organisation must be the maintenance of peace. The purposes of the United Nations are well expressed in Article 1 of the Charter: in the short term the removal of threats to the peace, and in the long term adjustment of economic and social tensions which lead to war. But there is danger of the United Nations losing sight of these overall objectives through embarking on activities which are not strictly in accord with these objectives; through ill-considered intervention in situations without carefully considering its own limitations and adapting its approach to those limitations; and through dissipating and duplicating its energies over fields of little or no return.[1]

In short, although Minister for External Affairs for a period of some fifteen months only, Spender undoubtedly left his mark upon the development of Australian foreign policy. On his appointment to Washington in March 1951 he was succeeded by Mr R. G. Casey, who held the portfolio of External Affairs for a period of approximately ten years.

III. THE ANZUS TREATY

1. Proposals for some form of Pacific pact during the period 1936–1950

The ANZUS Treaty—so called because the three partners to the military alliance which it constituted were Australia, New Zealand and the United States—was initialled in Washington on 12 July 1951, tabled in the Australian House of Representatives on the following day and signed in San Francisco on 8 September. The actual debate on the Bill to ratify the treaty was not opened until 21 February 1952. After approval of the Bill by the Australian Parliament, the treaty came into force on 29 April 1952, when instruments of ratification were deposited in Canberra.

Few Australians, if any, who listened to or read Spender's first ministerial review of foreign policy in Parliament on 9 March 1950 would have believed in the practicability of such a development within a period of some two years. Indeed, prior

[1] *C.N.* vol. xxi, no. 6 (June 1950), p. 411.

to the outbreak of the Korean War on 25 June 1950 available evidence pointed in the contrary direction. In particular, there had been public leakages of the views expressed on 10 January 1950 to a private meeting of the Senate Foreign Relations Committee by the American Secretary of State, Mr Dean Acheson. After the meeting the Committee Chairman, Senator Connally, quoted Acheson as saying that the United States line of defence in the Pacific lay east and not west of Formosa, and comprised Japan, Okinawa and the Philippines. 'With bases on those territories', the Secretary of State was reported to have said, 'the United States of America would have an impregnable defence.'[1] Two days later Acheson himself publicly confirmed this view of the American defence perimeter in a speech to the National Press Club.[2]

Spender, of course, was not the first Australian to show interest in some form of security alliance in the Pacific area; nor has advocacy of a Pacific pact been limited to any one Australian political party.[3]

Following ministerial references during the year 1936 in both Houses of Parliament, against the background of possible reform of the League of Nations Covenant, the Australian Prime Minister, Joseph Lyons, raised the matter in broad terms in his opening speech to the Imperial Conference held in London in 1937.[4] He also took the unusual course, for an Australian Prime Minister, of discussing the proposal in London with the Ambassadors of the United States, the Netherlands, France, the Soviet Union, China and Japan.[5] The Pacific Powers gave it a 'cool reception'.[6] Later in the year the Attorney-General, Robert Menzies, informed the House of Representatives that conversations had been suspended 'for the time being' because of the Sino-Japanese dispute.[7]

---

[1] *Chronology of International Events and Documents*, vol. VI (1949–50), p. 60.
[2] See Frederick S. Dunn, *Peace-Making and the Settlement with Japan* (Princeton University Press, 1963), at pp. 80–1, 194.
[3] For an exhaustive account of Australian proposals for a Pacific Pact during the period 1936–49, see now J. G. Starke, *The Anzus Treaty Alliance* (Melbourne University Press, 1965), pp. 4–27.
[4] For evidence of the important part played by Sir George Pearce, then Minister for External Affairs, in the Pacific Pact proposal, see Peter Heydon, *Quiet Decision* (Melbourne University Press, 1965), pp. 128–31.
[5] Hasluck, *Government and People*, pp. 69–70.
[6] Harper and Sissons, *Australia and the United Nations*, p. 30.
[7] Hasluck, *Government and People*, p. 70.

On 14 October 1943, after the battles of the Coral Sea and Midway had relieved Australian fears of actual Japanese invasion, Evatt reviewed in Parliament Australia's war aims. He made specific reference to the Solomon Islands, New Hebrides, New Caledonia, Timor, Papua and New Guinea, and said:

...I visualise New Guinea, both Australian and Dutch, as an integral part of the Pacific zone with which Australia will be vitally interested in collaboration with Britain and New Zealand on the one hand, and the Dutch, French and Portuguese on the other.

The Commonwealth Government is convinced that, in order to prevent future aggression, measures should be concerted for the permanent defence of this area as one of the zones of security within the international system that must be created.[1]

Some three months later, while Labour Party governments still held office in both Dominions, Article 13 of the Australian–New Zealand Agreement, signed at Canberra on 21 January 1944, asserted that 'a regional zone of defence comprising the South-West and South Pacific areas shall [*sic*] be established'.[2]

On 13 March 1946 Evatt reported at length in Parliament on recent missions to London and Washington. Under a main heading 'The Pacific', and a sub-heading 'Bases', the Minister elaborated his views in some detail. He spoke of the great complexity of the task of making a lasting peace settlement for the whole Pacific area, and the need to avoid precipitate action and a piecemeal approach. Though the Australian Government was fully conscious of the importance of making security arrangements in the Pacific, it would not be party to any hasty arrangements for the re-allocation of territory or the disposition of military bases in the Pacific; nor would it enter into any commitments which would lessen the control of the Australian people over their own territories. Evatt declared:

...Any consideration of plans for the joint *use* of any bases in Australia's dependent territories should be preceded by an overall defence arrangement for the region of the Western Pacific, including the islands formerly mandated to Japan; as an incident to any such arrangement, Australia should be entitled to reciprocal use of foreign bases in the region...

The detailed means of implementing a security policy for the Pacific have yet to be decided, but...Australian security is very

[1] *C.P.D.* vol. 176, p. 574.   [2] For full text of Article 13 see p. 76 above.

largely dependent on our closest co-operation with the British Commonwealth and the United States of America...[1]

Again, when Evatt enumerated to Parliament on 8 April 1948 the principles of Labour Party foreign policy followed during his term of office, he listed as one of them 'To strengthen Pacific security by appropriate regional arrangements in co-operation with the United States of America and other Pacific nations'.[2]

It is clear therefore that at one time or another during the period 1936–50 *all* Australian political parties have advocated negotiation of some form of Pacific security pact as an essential element in Australian foreign policy. Before 1951, however, the nature of the pact had not been closely defined, nor the prospective members precisely determined. The Menzies Government pressed the issue more keenly than the Curtin and Chifley Governments for a number of reasons. First, it had less confidence than the preceding governments in the capacity of a world organisation to maintain international peace and security, primarily because of the ruthless use of the veto in the United Nations Security Council by the Soviet Union. Secondly, it had less ambition than Evatt to try to 'bargain' with the United States for reciprocal rights to use American bases as an 'incident' of an overall defence arrangement for the region of the Western Pacific. Thirdly, the Menzies Government came to office at a time when it had become increasingly clear that Stalin's 'cold-war' policy had ended the war-time honeymoon between the Western Allies and the Soviet Union.

2. *Why ANZUS became negotiable*

Australian wishes would not in themselves have been sufficient to attract American support for a Pacific pact which included Australia, had it not been for the appearance of an unusual constellation of circumstances which the Menzies Government read aright, and had not the Government taken firm and prompt action to seize the initiative. Richard Rosecrance describes the situation as follows:

...Up to the middle of 1950 the United States had tended to assume that the Communists believed Europe to be the decisive sphere and

[1] *C.P.D.* vol. 186, pp. 200–1. For references to the Manus Island controversy, see pp. 100–2 above.   [2] *C.N.* vol. XIX, no. 5 (May 1948), p. 268.

the most inviting area for Communist expansion. Accordingly, the United States had supported the creation of NATO to deter Communist advance...The Korean War, however, abruptly changed American assessments of the priority of Communist goals. The Far East, after Korea, seemed an independent objective, not merely a way-station on the road to Bonn, Paris, or London. The logical result of such a realisation was a more favourable view of defence arrangements that might prevent further Communist victories. A Pacific pact, of whatever composition, would fill that requirement. The Congress was not unamenable to this line of reasoning, and on 11 July the House Foreign Affairs Committee 'endorsed unanimously proposals for a mutual defence pact throughout the Pacific area patterned after the North Atlantic Treaty...'[1]

Moreover, the Korean War underlined, from the American point of view, the dangers to Japan from Communist pressure and the need to ensure that Japan did not become a 'military vacuum'.[2] In short, a Pacific pact in the particular form of the ANZUS Treaty became for the first time negotiable against the background of, first, American pressure for an early and generous peace treaty with Japan, and, secondly, military aid readily and swiftly given by Australia during the Korean War.

(a) The peace treaty with Japan

The Australian attitude towards a peace treaty with Japan was well known to the United States and to the world at large. After the harsh experience of the war in the Pacific, *all* Australian political parties distrusted Japan. During Evatt's regime as Minister for External Affairs Australian representatives on the Far Eastern Commission in Washington and on the Allied Council for Japan pressed for the adoption of policies which would ensure that Japan should be made incapable of revived military aggression. To this end they argued in favour of a peace treaty which would keep Japan disarmed and subject to post-treaty controls. Speaking as Leader of the Opposition in Parliament on 19 March 1947 Menzies said: 'There is, I think, common ground between us that—I use the Minister's words—"Japan must never again be permitted to develop the means of

---

[1] R. N. Rosecrance, *Australian Diplomacy and Japan 1945–1951* (Melbourne University Press, 1962), p. 183.

[2] Phrase used by Spender in a speech in the House of Representatives on 28 November 1950 (*C.P.D.* vol. 211, p. 3,171).

waging war".'[1] But when the Menzies Government came to power it soon discovered—especially against the background of the Korean War—that Australian views could not decide the kind of peace which Japan would in fact be accorded.

On 6 April 1950 President Truman appointed John Foster Dulles Foreign Policy Adviser to the Secretary of State, and Dulles 'indicated a preference for work on the peace settlement with Japan'.[2] In September of the same year the President directed the State Department to 'begin a new effort to reach agreement on a Japanese treaty' and the 'seven principles' produced by a drafting committee under John Allison as Chairman made it clear by way of omission that, in the American view, there should be no restrictions on Japanese rearmament: indeed, the emphasis was shifted instead to security of Japan from attack.[3]

Subsequently, in January 1951, the question of a peace settlement with Japan was one of the matters considered in London at a Commonwealth Prime Ministers' Conference. As Spender told the House of Representatives on 14 March 1951:

> The London talks revealed...that the change in the world situation had...had a marked effect on the approach of the United Kingdom Government and other British Commonwealth governments to the Japanese settlement. It was clear that the understandings on the basis of which a general measure of agreement had been achieved in 1947, when the Japanese peace settlement was discussed at the British Commonwealth Conference in Canberra, were no longer completely or even largely accepted...it was now argued that Japan should be allowed the means to defend itself against aggression.[4]

In these circumstances, notwithstanding Opposition claims to the contrary when ratification of the actual Peace Treaty was under discussion in Parliament, no action by Australia could have resulted in general acceptance of a more restrictive treaty. Menzies described the position succinctly in an article published in *Foreign Affairs*:

> It [the Australian Government] very soon discovered that its own advocacy of a prohibition of Japanese rearmament...had no hope of success. The United States and the United Kingdom, the two principal free nations, made it clear that they were not prepared to prohibit a substantial measure of Japanese rearmament. And if these

[1] *C.P.D.* vol. 190, p. 852.   [2] Rosecrance, *op. cit.* pp. 172–3.
[3] *Ibid.* pp. 188–90.   [4] *C.P.D.* vol. 212, p. 483.

Great Powers were not willing to prohibit, and to enforce that prohibition by supervision and occupation if necessary, how could Australia by herself make a prohibition effective...? No Australian party or leader has been prepared to say that Japan should be kept unarmed *and* that Australia should be the policeman for the purpose.[1]

The Peace Treaty favoured by the United States would have come into existence whether or nor Australia opposed it. It remained for the Australian Government to seek security by other means. By accepting a treaty which in some important respects it did not approve, Australia was able the more effectively to press the United States to agree to become a party to a security treaty designed, *inter alia*, to guarantee the territorial integrity of metropolitan Australia, and its island territories, against armed attack.

(b) *Australian participation in the Korean War*

The second factor which made negotiation of the ANZUS Pact practicable has received too little notice in Australia, although it has not escaped the attention of Professor Rosecrance:

When the Korean attack occurred an Australian air contingent was ordered into the fighting in support of the United Nations forces and on 26 July it was announced that Australia would commit...units from all three services to the Korean struggle. The military cooperation of the two nations heralded the re-establishment of the comradeship in arms which had existed in 1945. America was hard pressed in Korea and the offer of Australian ground forces at such a critical time must have been warmly welcomed in all sections of the American Government. It would probably be correct to say that Australian–American relations attained a degree of cordiality in the summer of 1950 which they had not known since the days of the Pacific War.

When Prime Minister Menzies visited Washington in July, the warmth of his reception exceeded the normal requirements of diplomatic etiquette. In August the Australian Prime Minister received an overwhelming ovation from the United States Congress, and succeeded in obtaining a loan of $250 million.[2]

To sum up: a Pacific Pact in the form of the ANZUS Treaty became for the first time a practicable proposition against a

---

[1] *Foreign Affairs*, vol. xxx, no. 2 (January 1952), pp. 189, 194; R. G. Menzies, 'The Pacific settlement seen from Australia'.

[2] Rosecrance, *op. cit.* pp. 183–4.

specific international background. First, the commencement of the Korean War strengthened the developing American conception of a role for Japan in the post-war world as a possible ally in the containment of Communism. Such a conception called for a peace treaty with Japan which was 'moderate' and which did not positively forbid some degree of eventual Japanese rearmament. In these circumstances it was highly desirable, though perhaps not strictly necessary, for the United States to obtain Australian assent to a peace settlement with Japan which Australians believed likely to increase their own security problems. Secondly, American goodwill towards Australia flowing substantially from the speed of that country's military contribution in aid of American forces fighting in the Korean War made a guarantee of Australian security politically acceptable in the United States. The opportunity presented itself, not for the kind of wider treaty which both Evatt and Spender had originally envisaged, but for a military alliance with narrower membership which, in the words of Casey, 'gives Australia access to the thinking and planning of the American Administration at the highest political and military level and gives us in turn the means of putting our own views forward at the same level in complete frankness and friendliness'.[1] Had this opportunity not been seized by the Australian Government when it occurred there is no certainty that it would have recurred in any foreseeable future.

3. *The meaning and significance of the ANZUS Treaty*

(a) *Are obligations under ANZUS 'weaker' than those under NATO?*

It is a curious fact that the ANZUS Treaty—the most successful initiative taken by the Australian Government in the field of foreign affairs in the post-war period—has until comparatively recent times been consistently criticised and 'written-down' by Australians both inside and outside Parliament. The reasons for this will be examined in due course. The most persistent line of attack has been to damn ANZUS with faint praise by comparing it unfavourably with what is alleged to be the 'tighter' obligation undertaken by the parties to NATO. The late Professor Leicester C. Webb for long stood alone in contesting this inter-

---

[1] *C.N.* vol. XXIV, no. 11 (November 1953), p. 657.

pretation of ANZUS, which close study of the relevant texts does not support, although his view has now been broadly endorsed by J. G. Starke, a well-known Australian writer in the field of international law, and by Dr Albinski of Pennsylvania State University.[1]

The key articles of the respective treaties are as follows:

ANZUS: Art. IV (1). Each Party recognises that an armed attack in the Pacific Area on any of the Parties would be dangerous to its own peace and safety and declares that it would act to meet the common danger in accordance with its constitutional processes.

Art. V. For the purpose of Article IV, an armed attack on any of the Parties is deemed to include an armed attack on the metropolitan territory of any of the Parties, or on the island territories under its jurisdiction in the Pacific or on its armed forces, public vessels or aircraft in the Pacific.

NATO: Art. V (1). The Parties agree that an armed attack against one or more of them in Europe or North America shall be considered an attack against them all and consequently they agree that, if such an armed attack occurs, each of them, in exercise of the right of individual or collective self-defence recognised by Art. 51 of the Charter of the United Nations, will assist the party or parties so attacked by taking forthwith, individually and in concert with the other parties, *such action as it deems necessary* [emphasis added] including the use of armed force, to restore and maintain the security of the North Atlantic area.

During the debate in Parliament on the Bill to ratify ANZUS, Mr Arthur Calwell, Deputy Leader of the Labour Party, drew attention to the difference in wording between ANZUS and NATO and commented:

There is an obligation on the United States of America and on all the other participants in the European treaty to go to each other's aid. The only guarantee that is given in the Pacific treaty is that the nations will consult in common...There is no real obligation in the [Pacific] treaty on anybody and on some grounds it would be better to have no treaty at all.[2]

---

[1] Leicester C. Webb, 'Australia and Seato', in *SEATO: Six Studies*, ed. G. Modelski (Cheshire, Melbourne, 1962), pp. 56–7; Starke, *op. cit.* pp. 118–19; Henry S. Albinski, *Australia's Policies and Attitude Towards China* (Princeton University Press, 1965), p. 79.　　　　[2] *C.P.D.* vol. 216, p. 741.

Outside Parliament, Professor MacMahon Ball commented: 'The reference to "the use of armed force" does not appear in the Pacific Pact. It is a notable omission and suggests that the United States was not prepared to commit herself as far in the Pacific as in Europe.'[1]

Mr David Sissons carried this line of argument further when he wrote:

...the [ANZUS] Pact...has been referred to as a 'watered-down version of the North Atlantic Treaty Organisation'. The extent of the dilution can hardly fail to give comfort to those whom its purpose was to discourage...The wording of the two treaties is in many clauses identical. Accordingly any differences are significant. The corresponding obligation in the Pacific Pact is much weaker...Is this not an open proclamation to the world that America regards the Pacific as of secondary importance and that she is reluctant to commit herself to extreme measures there?[2]

Professor Norman Harper, who gives a balanced account of the ANZUS Treaty as a whole, nevertheless agrees that the ANZUS formula 'was a much more diluted obligation than the provision in the North Atlantic Pact'.[3] Professor Dunbar has commented that ANZUS was 'framed in somewhat less compromising terms' than NATO.[4]

Now it is true that the ANZUS Treaty does not contain the psychologically comforting and politically reassuring phrase of NATO that 'an attack against one...shall be considered an attack upon all'. But the important point, surely, is not what an attack is considered to be, but what each party is bound to do when an attack on one party comes. If one examines the text of the NATO formula, it is clear that, in the event of an attack upon one of the parties, each party is bound under the terms of the treaty itself to take only 'such action as *it* [emphasis added] deems necessary'. Further, the interpretation placed by Professor Julius Stone on the NATO phrase 'including the use of armed force' is contrary to that of Professor MacMahon Ball. In Professor Stone's opinion, the use of armed force under the NATO formula is permissive, not mandatory. He reads the

[1] 'The Peace Treaty with Japan', *Australian Outlook*, vol. v, no. 3 (September 1951), p. 139.
[2] 'The Pacific Pact', *Australian Outlook*, vol. vi, no. 1 (March 1952), p. 23.
[3] *Australia in World Affairs, 1950–55*, p. 159.
[4] *International Law in Australia*, ed. O'Connell (The Law Book Co. Ltd., Sydney, 1966), p. 402.

phrase as meaning 'including (though not necessarily) the use of armed forces [*sic*]'.[1]

The Australian Minister for External Affairs, Mr R. G. Casey, was justified in his statement to Parliament on 13 July 1951 that '*As in the case of the North Atlantic Treaty* [emphasis added]...the precise action to be taken by each party is not specified'.[2] The reason why the NATO formula was abandoned by the United States for all subsequent treaties was not to indicate less American interest in other regions than in Europe, but to avoid unnecessary confusion and debate in the United States Senate. In an article on 'Security in the Pacific' John Foster Dulles explained the position as follows:

This language of the North Atlantic Treaty gave rise to an extended constitutional debate in the United States Senate, a debate in which I participated. Many Senators felt that if the United States by treaty determined that an attack upon Western Europe would be the same as an attack upon the United States, the President would then be under an affirmative duty to use our armed forces for an area defense of Western Europe just as for the defense of the United States itself. Some Senators felt that this unduly enlarged the responsibility and authority of the President as against that of the Congress.

It seemed unnecessary and unwise to revive this domestic constitutional issue in connexion with the Pacific security treaties. Australia, New Zealand and the Philippines, *with good reason* [emphasis added], were quite satisfied with the security which would result from a treaty declaration, in Monroe Doctrine language...[3]

NATO countries were perfectly well aware that the NATO formula, in itself, involved no automatic commitment to war by parties to the Treaty when there was an attack upon one party. Sir Anthony Eden,[4] in his book *Full Circle*, takes this for granted:

When I saw M. Schuman at the Quai d'Orsay, I repeated the view which I had put to Dr Stikker. It was well known, I said, that the reason why the North Atlantic Treaty had been drafted so as to *exclude* [emphasis added] 'automatic' commitments was that the United States were constitutionally unable to commit themselves automatically to go to war.[5]

[1] J. Stone, *Legal Controls of International Conflict* (Maitland Publications, Sydney, 1954), p. 260.   [2] *C.P.D.* vol. 213, p. 1,709.
[3] *Foreign Affairs*, vol. xxx, no. 2 (January 1952), pp. 174–97.
[4] Later the Earl of Avon.
[5] Anthony Eden, *Full Circle* (Cassell, London, 1960), p. 43.

This was also the view expressed by Casey, when he told Parliament that, in the event of an armed attack upon one of the parties to ANZUS: 'There is no obligation on Australia to make any immediate formal declaration of war; the United States, for its part, could not constitutionally accept such a binding obligation. But the broad intention is that an attack on one shall be regarded as an attack on all.'[1]

Dulles himself gave further weight to this interpretation of ANZUS in January 1952. He told the Senate Foreign Relations Committee that 'There is really no doubt in any quarter that an armed attack upon Australia, New Zealand, or the Philippines would in fact involve the United States.'[2]

(b) Is ANZUS meaningless, unimportant or disadvantageous to Australia?

The debate on the Bill to ratify the ANZUS Treaty which opened in the Australian Parliament on 21 February 1952 makes painful reading today. It was bedevilled throughout by the Manus Island controversy—an issue irrelevant to the subject under discussion. Although Evatt, as Leader of the Opposition, 'welcomed' the ANZUS Treaty, while regretting 'the price that has had to be paid for it'[3] (that is, the Japanese Peace Treaty), practically the whole of his speech was devoted to a vigorous defence of the policy of the Chifley Government in rejecting tentative American advances in the immediate postwar period for retention of the vast military base they had constructed at Manus Island, unless the British Commonwealth, including Australia, was granted in return the right to use American bases in the Pacific. As Mr Haylen (A.L.P.)[4] said, 'the [ANZUS] issue has been muddied at the source'.[5] Members of the Opposition charged that confidential information from official files had been disclosed to the Press in an endeavour to prejudice the reputations of Evatt and the Labour Party.

Whatever the reason, there was a deplorable lowering of the standard of debate on an issue vital to Australia, and a persistent writing-down of the significance of the treaty by the

[1] C.P.D. vol. 216, p. 218.
[2] Quoted in Rosecrance, op. cit. p. 205.
[3] C.P.D. vol. 216, p. 598.
[4] Australian Labour Party.
[5] Ibid. p. 603.

Opposition, despite formal acceptance of the pact in principle. Thus Haylen declared:

We know that it [ANZUS] is the pay-off to the Japanese Peace Treaty, and though we are still grievously worried about the repercussions of that atrocious document, we accept this pact. But when we ask ourselves what is in it, we must be honest and admit that it does not give us anything that we have not already got, although it does make existing understandings more valid by putting them in writing ...This Pact has teeth, but they are irregular and are not a complete set...In my opinion, the agreement will impose more obligations on the Australian people than it will impose on the Americans...[1]

Mr Kim Beazley (A.L.P.) conceded that 'Every person who seriously studies this pact will welcome it. The Opposition believes it to be good.' He then delivered the following broadside against the Treaty:

This pact adds nothing to the world situation; it simply expresses in writing what has always been a fact, that is, the community of interest that exists between Australia and the United States...No country is in a position to attack Australia in the first instance without moving elsewhere on a scale that would inevitably cause a world war. Therefore the chances that the United States of America will be called upon to honour this Pact in the event of an attack being made upon Australia are at most only one-tenth of the chances that Australia will be called upon to honour this pact in the event of the United States becoming involved in a world war. I do not make that statement in criticism of the pact[2]...Australia will not be attacked from Asia, or from anywhere in the Pacific, unless a war first occurs in Europe. That is as true today as it was in 1939.[3]

To Mr Ward the proposed Treaty was a 'meaningless document':[4]

Actually it is an innocuous pact. It will not be very important, as far as this country is concerned, whether it is ratified or rejected...The Pacific pact does not commit the United States of America to send forces to defend Australian territory in the event of an attack being made upon us. In fact, the Americans came to the aid of Australia during World War II without the obligation of any pact...I believe that no pact is necessary now.[5]

[1] *Ibid.* p. 604.
[2] This sentence awakens echoes of Shakespeare's version of Mark Antony's speech on the death of Julius Caesar.
[3] *C.P.D.* vol. 216, pp. 609–10. [4] *Ibid.* p. 616. [5] *Ibid.* pp. 614–15.

If one looks beyond the Parliamentary debates to the political commentators the story is much the same. To Professor Mac-Mahon Ball: 'this Pact is a commendable, if not convincing, effort to comfort the fearful and credulous'.[1] To Mr David Sissons:

...it seems certain, almost beyond reasonable doubt, that circumstances under which Australia may invoke American assistance under the pact will not arise. Australia is unlikely to be attacked by Asian Communist forces except incidentally in an overall Great Power struggle. In this she already would be allied with America...This unreal right to assistance in unlikely circumstances is an empty recompense for the real obligation which it is not impossible that we may be called upon to discharge.[2]

To Dr John Burton, sometime Secretary of the Department of External Affairs (though not at the time when ANZUS was negotiated), the ANZUS Treaty

...extends the areas of possible conflict, antagonises all Asian neighbours who have been excluded from it, and draws Australia into any and every conflict in which America might become involved in the Pacific...Australia has left itself no more freedom of action than if it were a state of the American Union...By the ANZUS Pact Australia has joined the United States in the fight against 'communism', though, like Britain, it has no vital interests being threatened by Communism. In so doing it has antagonised its neighbours, and made its future relations with Asia more difficult, and therefore has prejudiced its security more than before.[3]

These strong criticisms of a central feature of Australian foreign policy cannot be ignored; yet there seems to have been no attempt at the political or official levels to consider them collectively and to answer them in detail. This failure of successive Menzies Governments to expound ANZUS and to refute criticisms led to a lack of public understanding of the treaty which became even more serious when Australia signed the South-East Asia Collective Defence Treaty (SEATO) in 1954. The meaning of neither treaty was adequately expounded by Australian political leaders. Public opinion for many years was substantially unaware of the important differences between the two treaties, and some Australians were even inclined to believe that the earlier treaty had merged in the latter.

[1] 'The Peace Treaty with Japan', *Australian Outlook*, 1951, p. 138.
[2] 'The Pacific Pact', *Australian Outlook*, 1952, pp. 21–2.
[3] John Burton, *The Alternative* (Morgans, Sydney, 1954), pp. 74–6.

(c) Was acceptance of the Japanese Peace Treaty too high a price to pay?

Both Government and Opposition disliked certain important features of the Japanese Peace Treaty—especially the absence of restrictions on armaments. For Evatt, acceptance of the Peace Treaty was 'too great a price to pay' for ANZUS. The Government, on the other hand, believed that such a price would have to be paid in any event, irrespective of ANZUS, as Australia could not prevent such a Peace Treaty coming into effect. In these circumstances, the Government regarded ANZUS, not as consideration for a price paid, but as a collateral benefit—a welcome measure of guarantee against, *inter alia*, the possible resurgence of a militarist Japan.

Further, the Government was conscious of a certain weight of argument against a 'hard and bitter' peace with Japan. 'What we have to do', said Casey, '...is to steer a path between the alternative perils of an aggressive and fully armed Japan which can again threaten us single-handed...and a defenceless and economically prostrate Japan that will present an easy prey to Communism and which might become an important part of the general Communist threat to world peace.'[1]

(d) Was ANZUS unnecessary?

Ward's statement that 'the Americans came to the aid of Australia during World War II without the obligation of any pact...I believe that no pact is necessary now' omits, of course, all reference to the fact that war was forced upon a reluctant American Congress and people by the Japanese attack upon Pearl Harbor. Isolationist opinion in the United States was strong, and there must still be doubt whether, had the Japanese attacked only British territory in December 1941, President Roosevelt could have mustered a majority in Congress for a declaration of war against Japan.

In his book *Personal Experience 1939–46*, Casey has thrown some light upon the warnings he received in high quarters on taking up his appointment as first Australian Minister to the United States early in 1940. Adolf Berle, Assistant Secretary of State, expressed the belief that 'in the United States more than

[1] *C.P.D.* vol. 216, p. 1,710.

in any other country, public opinion made itself felt on Government policy, and...it was practically impossible for the President or his Administration to put over a policy of which a majority of the people disapproved'. Stanley Hornbeck, Far Eastern Adviser to the Secretary of State, when asked what the United States would do in the event of any extreme Japanese action, replied that it was impossible to tell. 'It is dependent', he said, 'on the state of public opinion more than on any settled policy of the Administration.'[1]

Reference has already been made[2] to President Roosevelt's explanation, when Casey presented his credentials as Australian Minister at Washington, that 'the element of distance' denoted a declining interest on the part of the United States in regard to countries as far away as Australia and New Zealand. Casey comments that 'The President said it in a kindly and less direct way than this, but this was clearly what he meant. However, fortunately, this attitude was to alter dramatically.'[3]

It is true that on 5 December 1941, immediately before Pearl Harbor, the Australian Government was informed by the British Government that President Roosevelt had given to the British Ambassador in Washington an assurance of American 'armed support' in a number of eventualities involving further aggression by Japan (including an attack upon British territory), but the probable reactions of Congress to a request by the President for a declaration of war in such circumstances is still a matter for speculation.[4] In the result, therefore, the most important element in the dramatic alteration of the American attitude was, first, the Japanese attack on Pearl Harbor, which forced convinced isolationists in Congress to support a declaration of war against Japan, and, secondly, a series of Allied military disasters in the Pacific north and south of the equator. Hartley Grattan comments that:

It was disaster in war in the north that forced the use of Australia as a primary base. After the collapses in Malaya, Java, and Burma, the allied forces were split, some driven westward into India, others south-westward into Australia. When that great dispersal of survivors took place, Australia became *by force of circumstances* the

---

[1] Casey, *Personal Experience*, pp. 13, 14.
[2] See pp. 67–8 above.   [3] Casey, *Personal Experience*, pp. 10–11.
[4] See Raymond A. Esthus, *From Enmity to Alliance* (Melbourne University Press, 1965), pp. 132–4.

anchor of the American line of defence in the Pacific. The Americans, therefore, did not (to employ the words an Australian military historian used in undermining an Australian myth) arrive in Australia 'solely to help Australia and in response to Australian appeals'.[1]

Further, it cannot seriously be disputed that the existence of a solemn obligation to 'act to meet the common danger', approved by the United States Congress, would be a factor of great importance in influencing American decisions; otherwise all treaties are 'meaningless', including NATO. Moreover, those who have argued that ANZUS was unnecessary have failed to take sufficiently into account the fact that the mere existence of such a public treaty obligation tends in itself to deter possible aggression.

(e) *Is ANZUS more advantageous to the United States than to Australia?*

There is, of course, no comparison between the military power of the United States and that of Australia. *Prima facie*, therefore, the balance of advantage in a military alliance binding both countries to 'act to meet the common danger' in the event of armed attack would appear to favour Australia. However, it can be argued that, whereas circumstances are unlikely to arise calling for fulfilment of the American obligation to Australia, Australia could easily be involved in war through the operation of American policy in the North Pacific, in which Australia would allegedly have little or no influence.

Many critics of ANZUS have been consistently reluctant, at least until the last three or four years, to consider the possibility of an armed attack upon Australia or its territories by an Asian country other than Communist China or Japan. They have chosen to interpret the Treaty as directed against attack by one or other of these two countries only. But the basic fact, from the Australian point of view, is that ANZUS comes into effect when an armed attack is made on any party by *any* country, Communist or non-Communist, ex-enemy or otherwise. There is, in ANZUS, no reservation, as in the Manila Pact of 1954, which limits American obligations to instances of 'aggression by means of armed attack' by Communist countries. This is of particular importance when considering the possibility of an attack upon

---

[1] Grattan, *U.S. and the Southwest Pacific*, p. 183.

the Australian Trust Territory of New Guinea or upon the Territory of Papua. While the applicability of the Treaty in such circumstances was never uncertain, its interpretation by America and Australia was emphasised in public statements made during 1963 by the U.S. Under-secretary of State for Political Affairs, Mr Averell Harriman,[1] and by Menzies,[2] both of whom specifically affirmed that the ANZUS Treaty covers an armed attack on New Guinea.

Since the establishment of Malaysia on 16 September 1963, and President Sukarno's decision to continue to 'confront' Malaysia, the scope of the ANZUS Treaty in covering Indonesian 'armed attack' upon Australian forces outside Australia and its territories has become a question of crucial importance. Following the decision announced by the Australian Prime Minister on 25 September 1963 to help Malaysia and the United Kingdom defend the territorial integrity and political independence of Malaysia, Australian military forces in Malaya and in Malaysian Borneo, and Australian naval forces in Malaysian waters, have become directly involved in operations against Indonesian infiltrators. Public doubts have been expressed both inside Parliament and outside as to whether Indonesian attacks upon such forces would justify Australia in invoking the ANZUS Treaty.

During a Parliamentary debate, Arthur Calwell, who had become Leader of the Labour Party Opposition, challenged a statement made at a press conference on 17 April 1964 by the Minister for External Affairs, Sir Garfield Barwick, that 'The [ANZUS] Treaty expressly covers attacks on Australian military personnel or aircraft or ships in the Pacific area. Borneo was, for this purpose, in the Pacific area... America is not in doubt about this.'[3] Calwell, however, revealed during his speech that Averell Harriman had told him (Calwell) 'that America does believe that its commitment [under ANZUS] does include the protection of Australian troops already in Malaya'.[4] If the Malayan peninsula, in the American view, is 'in the Pacific', it is scarcely conceivable that Sabah and Sarawak are not. W. J. G. Starke has advanced an additional argument in support of the

---

[1] *The Sydney Morning Herald*, 4 June 1963, p. 5.
[2] *Ibid.* 13 November 1963, p. 7.
[3] Quoted in *Australia's Defence*, by T. B. Millar (Melbourne University Press, 1965), p. 75.   [4] *C.P.D.*, H. of R., vol. XLII (21 April 1964), p. 1,274.

claim that North Borneo is within the 'Pacific area': he points out that during the Second World War the 'South-West Pacific Area', as defined for joint operations by American, Australian and New Zealand forces, included Borneo.[1] In this connexion, however, it is necessary to keep in mind the reply made in Parliament by the Australian Minister for External Affairs on 26 February 1959 to a question, upon notice, asked by Mr Whitlam (A.L.P.). Casey had been asked 'Which of the islands off the coast of China are included in the term "Pacific Area" in the Security Treaty between Australia, New Zealand and the United States?' He replied as follows:

The broad phrase 'Pacific area', as used in several places in the Anzus Treaty, is not precisely defined. In view of the intimate relationship between the three Governments this is something that is well left for decision from time to time in the light of changing circumstances.[2]

On the other hand, it is true that under the ANZUS Treaty Australia accepted wide commitments 'in the Pacific area', some of which, conceivably, she might have preferred to avoid. This, no doubt, was part of the price she had to pay for securing the promise of American support under the Treaty. In stressing this point, however, the critics have not taken into sufficient account certain important considerations. As previously pointed out, the terms of the Treaty are such as to give Australia at least some degree of security against complete involvement in circumstances she might disapprove. If in fact America should become involved in war in the Pacific through injudicious action in the determination of which Australia has played no part, the form and scope of action to be taken by Australia is still a matter to be determined by the Australian Government. In Casey's words, 'There is no obligation on Australia to make any immediate formal declaration of war'.[3] Secondly, while it would be idle to pretend or assume that all partners to an alliance have equal influence on one another— irrespective of their comparative military and economic resources—it is unwise to assume that Australia can have *no* influence upon the policy of the United States, particularly when the two countries can speak frankly to one another in the

---

[1] For a detailed examination of the scope of the phrase 'in the Pacific area', see Starke, *The Anzus Treaty Alliance*, pp. 126–9.
[2] *C.P.D.*, H. of R., vol. xxii, p. 405.   [3] *C.P.D.* vol. 216, p. 218.

capacity of military allies. Thirdly, it may reasonably be asked whether, in the event of the United States becoming engaged in a major war in the North Pacific, an Australian Government might not decide that vital interests required Australia to join the United States whether or not she was legally obliged, under such a treaty as ANZUS, to 'act to meet the common danger'.

(f) Has ANZUS estranged Australia from Asian countries like India?[1]

The most serious objection to ANZUS is the claim that Australia, by signing the treaty, prejudiced her relationships with non-aligned countries, especially India, whose goodwill is in the long term thought to be essential to her survival. This poses the question whether Australia, as a country of European descent and cultural tradition geographically placed off the southern rim of Asia, should give absolute priority to her friendly relationships with Asian countries, many of which pursue or have pursued policies of non-alignment?

There are those who, like Burton,[2] would claim that close relationships between Australia and non-aligned countries would actually increase rather than diminish Australian security, even if the price of such friendly relations were the cancellation of a military alliance with the United States. Such a claim has not been strengthened by India's recent experience of Chinese military pressure, despite acceptance by both countries of the Five Principles (Panchsheel), which include mutual respect for each other's territorial integrity, non-aggression, and peaceful co-existence. More commonly, it is argued that Australia should not have entered into the ANZUS or SEATO Treaties unless and until countries like India were ready to join in a regional pact.

No one will deny the importance to Australia of harmonious relationships with Asia, and leaders of *all* Australian political parties have supported such a policy in principle and tried, in their different ways, to pursue it in practice. Strong support for the Colombo Plan, which has been responsible for thousands of students from Asian countries coming to Australia for technical

---

[1] For a discussion of post-war relationships between India and Australia, see chapter 6 below, pp. 220–36.   [2] See p. 130 above.

training, together with the opening-up of a wide range of diplomatic posts in South and South-East Asia, are evidence of more than lip-service to the principle of good relationships. Faced with the alternative, however, of depending solely on Asian goodwill or joining a military alliance, the only Australian Government which has been in power since an alliance became a practical possibility has chosen the latter rather than the former, while at the same time maintaining its efforts, through the Colombo Plan and in other ways, to create friendly links with Asian countries. The background to this choice has been well described by Hartley Grattan as follows:

... while the Australians sought good relations with the Asian states, they did not feel that this meant that they must conform their own policies to Asian policies... [Australia's] policies should, by preference, be sympathetic to the Asian states in every respect in which this was possible, but if Australian interests dictated support of policies the Asians were little likely to regard with any enthusiasm as policies they themselves could adopt, the plunge had to be made...[1]

India, in fact, showed far less concern about the creation of ANZUS than about the subsequent establishment of the South-East Asia Collective Defence Treaty (SEATO). There were no Asian members of ANZUS—Pakistan was not a party, nor Burma, Thailand, Laos, Cambodia, Vietnam (North or South), the Philippines or Indonesia. The south-west Pacific areas of Australia and New Zealand, both metropolitan and non-self-governing, were not part of 'Further India', where Indian cultural influence had been substantial. If the treaty area of ANZUS was technically the 'Pacific' as a whole, so that Australia and New Zealand could conceivably become involved if, for instance, war developed following upon American support to the Republic of China in the Formosa area, such a war could scarcely be regarded as avoidable if only ANZUS had not existed.

It may be doubted whether Mr Nehru, while firmly rejecting for India a policy of 'alignment', was really critical of Australia and New Zealand for aligning themselves with the United States as partners in a security treaty. According to Dr S. N. Varma, India's 'attitude to individual military alliances has

---

[1] Grattan, *U.S. and the Southwest Pacific*, p. 222.

been pragmatic'.[1] Thus she was comparatively indifferent to the
Rio Pact and the Brussels Treaty, though strongly opposed
to the proposed Middle East Defence Organisation and to
SEATO. As regards ANZUS, India had criticised the proposed
ANZUS Pact on the ground that such a step was likely to
aggravate the already unsettled conditions in Indonesia and
Indo-China. However, her opposition to its formation and later
to its existence was not very vigorous.[2] In any event, in spite of
ANZUS and in spite even of SEATO, India—hard-pressed by
China in 1962 on her northern borders—showed appreciation
of sympathy and assistance, not merely from Great Britain and
the United States, but also from Australia. Since that date links
between India and Australia have been strengthened by visits
at various levels, while the successive posting to New Delhi as
High Commissioners of two Australian diplomats of the highest
rank, namely, Sir James Plimsoll and Sir Arthur Tange, has
been appreciated by the Indian Government, providing as it
does clear evidence of the importance which Australia attaches
to Indo-Australian relations. In short, with benefit of hind
sight it is now possible to judge that the ANZUS Treaty has *not*
been a fatal bar to the maintenance and development of cordial
relations between the two countries.

(g) Is ANZUS anti-British?

There is a final line of criticism of ANZUS which requires
consideration, namely the so-called 'exclusion' of Great Britain
from membership. This 'exclusion' was resented not merely by
some sections of opinion in Great Britain, but also, in a degree, in
Australia and New Zealand. There is no doubt that many
British people or people of British descent were distressed by the
fact that two of the 'Old Dominions' were prepared to enter
into a military alliance with a foreign country despite the fact
that the mother country, the most important member of the
Commonwealth of Nations and its strongest military power, was
not included as a member. Various questions arise. Did Great
Britain, before the treaty was signed, seek to be included? If so,
was she deliberately excluded, and by whom, for what reasons?
Did Great Britain facilitate the creation of ANZUS, or did she

[1] *Aspects of India's Foreign Relations*, India Paper no. 1, prepared for the 13th Conference of the Institute of Pacific Relations (Lahore, 1958), p. 6.
[2] *Ibid.* p. 7.

endeavour to prevent its coming into existence? Complete and authoritative answers to these questions must wait until official records are made available to historians.[1]

So far as the present *public* record stands, all that can be said is as follows. There is no doubt that the United Kingdom was fully consulted by Australia and New Zealand before signature of the treaty, and that she did not try to dissuade the two Dominions from becoming parties. Sir Esler Dening, a senior British diplomat, was present in Canberra during the Dulles visit, and was kept generally informed regarding the discussions.[2] The Minister for External Affairs told Parliament on 21 June 1951 that 'The United Kingdom government was given the fullest possible information regarding the discussions in Canberra. During the many weeks which elapsed between Mr Dulles's departure from Canberra and the making of President Truman's statement various messages were exchanged between London and Canberra.'[3] On the other hand, the British Foreign Secretary, Mr Herbert Morrison, speaking in the House of Commons on the ANZUS Treaty, said that 'it would not have been unwelcome to us if we had been included in the proposed pact'.[4] Later, when Churchill had returned to power, he told Parliament:

I did not like the ANZUS pact at all. We did not have an entirely clean sheet on the matter when we took over power. I did not like it at all, and I am greatly in hopes that perhaps larger, wider arrangements may be made which will be more satisfactory than those which are at present in force. But, as I say, it is not a matter where one can give directions. One has to endeavour to use influence and allow time to work.[5]

In the event, however, time did not work in the sense of enabling the United Kingdom to join ANZUS; instead, SEATO was created in 1954 and the United Kingdom joined in this wider grouping of powers.

The best account so far available of the 'exclusion' of Great Britain from ANZUS is that given in an article by Dean E.

---

[1] For an account of the attitude of the British Government, without indication of the sources upon which it is based, see Dunn, *Peace Making and the Settlement with Japan*, p. 197.
[2] See Casey, *Friends and Neighbours*, p. 72; Starke, *op. cit.* p. 39.
[3] *C.P.D.* vol. 213, p. 281.
[4] *U.K. Parliamentary Debates*, H. of C., vol. 486 (1951), cols. 2007–8.
[5] *U.K. Parliamentary Debates*, H. of C., vol. 516 (1953), col. 973.

McHenry and Richard N. Rosecrance which gives a wide cover-age from available public sources of the various reasons which allegedly influenced the ANZUS partners in limiting member-ship to the three Treaty Powers.[1] The writers point out that all the partners accepted responsibility for the decision, although they claim that Menzies, on one occasion, passing through America after the Coronation in London, 'broke the diplo-matic front with the United States' by giving to the *New York Times* the following explanation:

Australia sympathised with Britain's desire to be included in the pact, but if the United States was not willing to extend a member-ship to Britain there was nothing that Australia or New Zealand could do about it short of denouncing the Treaty and this Australia would not do, nor did Britain wish her to do so.[2]

Of course, had Britain been admitted, the immediate question would have arisen whether some or all of her colonial territories in South-East Asia and the Pacific were covered by the Treaty.

Commenting on the 'exclusion' of Great Britain from membership of ANZUS, Hartley Grattan has said that:

...the oddest aspect of the whole affair was that it was Australian Conservatives, led by an Imperialist Prime Minister, whose actions inspired the fuss and who were not shaken thereby in their deter-mination to take independent action in the national Australian interest.[3]

In truth, however, Australia and New Zealand became allies of the United States in ANZUS not because they had come to love America more and Great Britain less, but because the facts of power in the Pacific had changed during and subsequently to the Second World War. The old assumptions underlying policy had simply proved unjustified. Singapore had not been an impregnable bastion. British undertakings to reinforce, defend and hold Singapore in time of emergency had proved impossible to carry out in the unforeseen circumstances of a war at one and the same time in Europe, the Mediterranean and the Pacific, during which France had fallen at an early stage. German submarines were taking their deadly toll of shipping and Britain was fighting for survival. American military power became

---

[1] 'The exclusion of the United Kingdom from the ANZUS Pact', *International Organisation*, vol. XII (1958), pp. 320–9.
[2] *Ibid.* p. 323.   [3] Grattan, *op. cit.* p. 219.

predominant in the Pacific. Australia and New Zealand therefore had to face what Professor F. L. W. Wood has called 'the Anzac dilemma'.[1] The justification for coining this phrase, he wrote: 'lies in the tension felt by Australia and New Zealand in the planning of their overseas policies; a tension produced by the pull between old habits of thought and emotion and the necessities imposed by geography and the present state of world affairs'.[1]

The only way to plan intelligently for the future, he argued, was to face the facts, however, disagreeable. It was a disagreeable fact that during the past half-century there had been a diminution in British power and prestige.

The Pacific...is no longer under the wing of the Royal Navy...It is a striking fact that during the past war New Zealand and Australia quietly acknowledged that they were within the American field and the responsibility of the United States fleet...This involved the tacit repudiation of the most basic axiom of our thinking, or more accurately perhaps of our feeling, in matters of defence and physical security.[2]

To those in Great Britain who criticised the ANZUS Treaty on the ground that it might 'commit the United Kingdom to go to war on account of actions taken by independent British Communities in the South Pacific', Professor Wood pointed out that Australia and New Zealand had 'twice in recent years and without question followed Britain into European wars in which the Commonwealth commitment arose directly from British actions'. In his opinion the ANZUS Treaty, though 'not a perfect document', had been somewhat unfairly criticised:

It is most certainly not anti-British, but is essentially an attempt by small Powers living in a danger area to reach, ahead of the crisis, a workable understanding with the Great Power predominant in that area. It is true that it might lead to the two Dominions being involved in war by American policy; but it is hard to envisage a major crisis involving the United States which would not bring them in—as happened in 1941 and 1950.[3]

Australia and New Zealand had already entered into informal arrangements with the United Kingdom for the defence of the Malayan area (ANZAM)[4] before ANZUS was negotiated. Both Dominions contribute to the Commonwealth Strategic

---

[1] *International Affairs*, vol. xxix (April 1953), p. 184.
[2] *Ibid.* p. 188.   [3] *Ibid.* p. 191.   [4] See pp. 163–6 below.

Reserve in Malaya, and their forces co-operated in the fight against Communist terrorists during the 'Emergency' and in resistance to Indonesian armed incursions into Malaysia when President Sukarno decided to 'confront' Malaysia. It is clear therefore that, in the post-war years, there has been no lack of readiness to co-operate with the mother country in the defence of an area of great importance to Australia and New Zealand; nor has there been any lack of appreciation in these two Commonwealth countries of the extent of Great Britain's self-imposed burden in making available substantial military forces for the defence of Malaya, Singapore, Sabah and Sarawak. Yet 'brush-fire' wars are one thing, aggression on the grand scale another. In preventing or countering the latter in the Pacific, Australia and New Zealand have regarded the maintenance of American power as essential. Hence ANZUS and, later, SEATO.

4. *Summing up*

It is a mistaken view to regard the ANZUS Treaty merely as the result of a well-timed and clever diplomatic move by Australia in securing a 'pay-off' or 'reward' for its assent to the Japanese Peace Treaty. It represents rather the fruit of efforts over the years, during the war and after the war, by political leaders and servicemen, to create and maintain a relationship of confidence and common purpose between the United States, Australia and New Zealand. Its benefits to the individual parties may not be equal, but they are certainly of vital importance for the smaller Powers, and of considerable importance for the United States. On the latter point it is appropriate to listen to an American voice:

On the American side, the usefulness of the treaty was that it associated the United States with what World War II had proved to be, on the one hand, the principal sources of strength in the South-West Pacific, and, on the other, had also proved to be bases of infinite value in dealing with aggression originating in the Western Pacific. As inheritors of total responsibility in the Western Pacific, the Americans could hardly do less than to gain all the support, and take out all the insurance, in the general area they could gain or take out. ANZUS was both insurance and support for the United States... the benefits were in the end mutual...[1]

[1] Grattan, *op. cit.* p. 220.

IV. THE SOUTH-EAST ASIA COLLECTIVE DEFENCE TREATY

The South-East Asia Collective Defence Treaty, usually referred to as SEATO, was signed at Manila on 8 September 1954 by the representatives of Australia, France, New Zealand, Pakistan, the Philippines, Thailand, the United Kingdom and the United States. On 27 October 1954 a Bill to authorise ratification of the Treaty was introduced into the House of Representatives by Mr R. G. Casey, Australian Minister for External Affairs. This Bill was approved by Parliament, and the Treaty came into force on 19 February 1955.

Ratification of the Treaty was not opposed by the Labour Party which, however, has become increasingly critical of SEATO over the years. Its Leader, Mr Arthur Calwell, expressed the opinion in 1963 that it should be 're-planned on a cultural, educational, medical and technical assistance basis and not on a military basis', and that it 'should include all the peoples of South-East Asia'.[1]

Much has now been written in Australia and elsewhere about SEATO.[2] Here it is proposed merely to try to clarify the circumstances in which SEATO came into existence; to set out the main provisions of the Treaty with a view to distinguishing it from NATO and ANZUS; to cover certain points raised during the debate in Parliament; and to consider some current criticisms of the value of the Treaty.

A. HISTORICAL BACKGROUND

1. *Need to supplement ANZUS*

As Casey pointed out during the parliamentary debate on the Bill to ratify ANZUS, the Australian Government never regarded ANZUS as a 'complete and final answer to the problem of security in the Pacific', but rather as a 'great advance along the road' to Pacific security.[3] ANZUS itself contained a pre-

---

[1] Arthur Calwell, *Labor's Role in Modern Society* (Lansdowne Press, Melbourne, 1963), p. 181.

[2] See, for example, *SEATO: Six Studies*, ed. Modelski; *Australia in World Affairs 1950–55*, pp. 179–93; Russell H. Fitfield, *Southeast Asia in United States Policy* (Praeger, New York, 1963), chapter 5.

[3] *C.N.* vol. 22, no. 7 (July 1951), p. 403.

amble in which was stated the desire of the parties 'further to co-ordinate their efforts for collective defence for the preservation of peace and security pending the development of a more comprehensive system of regional security in the Pacific area...'. The system of collective defence envisaged by Articles 43–47 of the Charter of the United Nations had failed to materialise, due mainly to the development of the 'cold war' and the ruthless use of its right of veto in the Security Council by the Soviet Union. In an attempt to meet this situation in the Atlantic and Pacific areas, NATO and ANZUS had been formed. 'However', said the Minister for External Affairs, during the SEATO debate, 'a gap remained in South-East Asia, and it was to meet this gap that the South-East Asia Collective Defence Treaty was drawn up at Manila'.[1]

Casey had been continually conscious of this gap from the time when, shortly after taking over the portfolio of External Affairs in 1951, he had made a 'good-will' visit to the countries of South-East Asia, supplemented by brief visits to Hongkong, Japan and Korea. The Minister's report to the House of Representatives on 27 September 1951 clearly reflected a deeper interest in the countries surrounding Malaya and Singapore and a greater realisation of their significance for Australia. Casey had become convinced that it was urgently necessary to strengthen and expand Australian diplomatic representation in South-East Asia. This central theme in his speech was expressed as follows:

The third main conclusion which I reached is that of the great importance of Indo-China and Burma to the security of Malaya—and indeed of South-East Asia as a whole. I believe that the realisation of this particular point was probably the most important single result of my trip. If Indo-China and Burma were lost to the Communists—indeed, if either of them were lost—Thailand would be immediately outflanked, and it would be difficult, if not impossible, for Thailand successfully to resist heavy Communist pressure unless very substantial help were afforded her from without...Australia has always shown a special interest in...Malaya—with good reason, as the last war showed. It seems to me only logical that Australia must pay greater attention to developments in areas to the north of Malaya on which the security of Malaya may well substantially depend...I propose in the near future to recommend to the

---

[1] *C.P.D.*, H. of R., vol. v (October 1954), p. 2,382.

Government for its consideration a review of Australian representation in South-East Asia. It is essential that we should have our own posts reporting quickly and directly to Australia so that we can follow developments and be in a position to take diplomatic and any other action which appears appropriate and practicable.[1]

Following upon this 'review', Australian diplomatic representation in South-East Asia was in fact substantially strengthened and expanded. This included the stationing at Singapore from 1954 to 1956 of a senior External Affairs Officer with the personal rank of Ambassador. His functions were not limited to the representation of Australia in Singapore, Malaya and the Borneo Territories; they involved also a degree of co-ordinating responsibility for Australian diplomatic posts in South-East Asia as a whole. Meanwhile, Casey himself made frequent visits to the area, and built up very close contacts with Malcolm MacDonald, British Commissioner-General for South-East Asia, with other British civil and military authorities in Singapore and Malaya, with French and local authorities in Indo-China, and with the governments of independent States. As a result, the information available to the Australian Government from first-hand sources increased greatly, strengthened its belief in the seriousness of the situation in Indo-China in particular, and made it all the more anxious to press on at the earliest practicable moment with the creation of a Mutual Defence Pact which would be wider in scope than ANZUS.

2. *The Geneva Conference of 1954*

(a) *Australian attitude*

Before attending the Geneva Conference 1954 on Indo-China and Korea—Australia was formally represented only at discussions in respect of Korea, but the Australian delegation was also in closest touch with numerous other delegations directly involved in discussions on Indo-China—the Australian Minister for External Affairs again made a personal visit to Saigon. No doubt his judgement of the current situation in Vietnam substantially affected the attitude of the Australian Government during the period of Anglo-American tension in April 1954 when Dulles was sounding-out British readiness to

---

[1] *C.N.* vol. XXII (1951), p. 514.

join with the Americans in a policy of Allied intervention from the air at Dien Bien Phu.

While in Saigon Casey had reached the conclusion, as he subsequently reported to Parliament on 10 August 1954, that 'such intervention would be wrong...it would not have the backing of the United Nations. It would put us in wrong with world opinion, particularly in Asia. It would probably embroil us with Communist China. It would wreck the Geneva Conference...'[1] He had felt that Australia should look for political settlement of the problem in Indo-China—a negotiated settlement—recognising the realities of the situation.[1]

The Australian Government, however, was in a serious dilemma. How could it avoid precipitate American action in Indo-China which it believed to be mistaken, without stifling the new American interest in the security of part of the mainland of South-East Asia? In the event, Australian opposition to an air-strike at Dien Bien Phu became submerged in the deepening crisis in British–American relations arising from Britain's blunt rejection of the American approach.

(b) British attitude

Before dealing with British policy at the time of the Geneva Conference, it is essential to consider British reactions to contemporary information regarding the devastating power of early hydrogen-bomb tests by the United States. Indeed, it is scarcely an exaggeration to suggest that subsequent British foreign policy can be understood only with difficulty unless one keeps constantly in mind British preoccupation with avoidance of action which, in the opinion of the British Government, might escalate into an atomic war during which Great Britain might be the first and worst victim.

British reactions are perhaps best revealed in the words of the British Prime Minister, Mr Churchill—a man whom no one will charge with want of courage—in a speech delivered in the House of Commons on 1 March 1955, almost a year later:

There is an immense gulf between the atomic and hydrogen bomb. The atomic bomb, with all its terrors, did not carry us outside the scope of human control or manageable events in thought and action,

[1] *C.P.D.*, H. of R., vol. IV (August 1954), p. 97.

in peace or war. But when Mr Sterling Cole, the Chairman of the United States Congressional Committee, gave out a year ago— 17 February 1954—the first comprehensive review of the hydrogen bomb, the entire foundation of human affairs was revolutionised, and mankind placed in a situation both measureless and laden with doom...apart from...blast and heat effects over increasingly wide areas there are now to be considered the consequences of 'fall-out', as it is called, of windborne radioactive particles...The broad effect of the latest developments is to spread almost indefinitely and at least to a vast extent the area of mortal danger.[1]

The effect of Sterling Cole's report of 17 February 1954 was heightened by the results of American thermonuclear tests in the Marshall Islands which began on 1 March of that year. On 11 March an official American statement was issued disclosing that 28 Americans and 236 Marshall Islanders had been exposed unexpectedly to some radiation during the test. Five days later it was disclosed that the crew of the *Fukuryu Maru* had been exposed to radioactive fall-out although, it was claimed, the ship had been engaged in fishing some 20 miles outside the designated danger area. On 20 March, prior to the second explosion, this danger area was increased by the United States from 50,000 square miles to 315,000 square miles.

British opinion was seriously alarmed by these developments, and a debate was held in the House of Commons on 5 April 1954 on an Opposition motion, the introductory clauses of which were as follows: 'That this House, recognising that the hydrogen bomb with its immense range and power as disclosed by recent experiments, constitutes a grave threat to civilisation, and that any recourse to war may lead to its use...'[2]

Speaking on this motion, Churchill said: 'the hydrogen bomb carries us into dimensions which have never confronted practical human thought...To us in this overcrowded island, and to the densely populated regions of Europe, the new terror brings a certain element of equality in annihilation...'.[3]

In these circumstances, no more unsuitable time could have been conceived for an American Secretary of State to approach a British Foreign Secretary to secure agreement upon a course

---

[1] *C.N.* vol. xxvi, no. 3 (1955), pp. 225–7.
[2] *U.K. Parliamentary Debates*, vol. 526, col. 36.   [3] *Ibid.* cols. 48–9.

of action which the latter believed could result in atomic war. Anthony Eden wrote subsequently:

I am fairly hardened to crises, but I went to bed that night [23 April 1954] a troubled man. I did not believe that anything less than intervention on a Korean scale, if that, would have any effect on Indo-China. If there were such intervention, I could not tell where its consequences would stop. We might well find ourselves involved in the wrong war against the wrong man in the wrong place.[1]

The Foreign Secretary returned hastily to London to consult the British Prime Minister and his cabinet colleagues. According to Eden, Churchill summed up the position by saying that the United Kingdom Government was being asked to assist in misleading Congress into approving a military operation, which would in itself be ineffective, and which might well bring the world to the verge of a major war. The British Cabinet agreed that the United Kingdom must decline to give any undertaking of military assistance to the French in Indo-China.[2] On 27 April Churchill formally announced in the House of Commons that 'Her Majesty's Government are not prepared to give any undertakings about United Kingdom military action in Indo-China in advance of the results of Geneva'.[3]

This British refusal led to serious tension in British–American relations which was not eased until Churchill visited Washington during the last week of June 1954. As between Eden and Dulles, however, it may be doubted whether the mutual lack of confidence which increased during this period was ever subsequently overcome before the Suez crisis of 1956 created such fundamental distrust between the two men that it became extremely difficult for either to work with the other. In the event, illness removed both statesmen from the political scene.

In view of the deep impression made upon both British political leaders and British public opinion by the results of the hydrogen bomb tests in early 1954, it is scarcely surprising that British policy since that date, from Berlin to Laos, has been marked by extreme caution and has been designed primarily to avoid or prevent action which might lead to atomic war. Lord Home, speaking as British Foreign Secretary, expressed this attitude succinctly when he said on 28 December 1961 in a

[1] Eden, *op. cit.* p. 102.
[2] *Ibid.* p. 105.   [3] Quoted in *SEATO: Six Studies*, p. 59.

speech at Berwick-on-Tweed: 'Peace, for ours is a most vulnerable island, is the first of British interests.'[1] This statement is not to be interpreted as advocacy of a policy of peace at any price, as subsequent British military support for Malaysia, for instance, has shown; but it indicates determination to pursue a policy of great caution and readiness to pay a high price in order to avoid possible escalation of local war into atomic war.

British insistence that no action should be taken in the direction of establishing a South-East Asia Collective Defence Organisation, until the possibilities of securing an agreed settlement on Indo-China at the Geneva Conference, upset Dulles. He could point to the terms of a joint communiqué issued after his talks with Eden in London between 11 and 13 April containing the statement that 'we are ready to take part, with the other countries principally concerned, in an examination of the possibility of establishing a collective defence, within the framework of the Charter of the United Nations, to assure the peace, security and freedom of South-East Asia and the Western Pacific'.[2] Yet when Dulles called a meeting in Washington for 20 April to set up a working group to study this subject, Eden forbade the British Ambassador to attend and the meeting had to be converted into a general briefing on the coming negotiations at Geneva.

Eden based his objection largely on the fact that Dulles had chosen to omit India and Burma from the list of countries invited, arguing that this omission would be 'insulting to… both'.[3] In support of his attitude, Eden subsequently published the text of a British minute of the conference stating that both parties had agreed that in any statement to the House of Commons the Foreign Secretary would explain that the whole question of membership was a matter for further consideration and would be discussed with the Governments of India and Pakistan.[3] While, however, the attitude of India and Pakistan—particularly the former—was regarded by the British Government as important, there is little doubt that Eden's main objection to the meeting called by Dulles was the fear that it might prejudice a settlement at Geneva. To the Americans defence discussions of this kind might be a useful lever upon the Communist powers in securing a more favourable Geneva

---

[1] *The Times* (London), 29 December 1961, p. 5.
[2] Eden, *op. cit.* pp. 97–8.   [3] *Ibid.* p. 98.

settlement; to the British such a weapon could not be employed, because it might make more difficult the task of securing the assent of Russia and China and the approval of India.

That the British attitude towards a Pacific Pact at the time of the Geneva Conference was cautious in the extreme is clear from the eight points prepared by Eden for the British cabinet and approved by cabinet. They included the following (emphasis added):

(4) We can give an assurance now that *if* a settlement is reached at Geneva, we shall join in guaranteeing that settlement and in setting up a collective defence in South-East Asia...

(6) If no such settlement is reached, *we shall be prepared at that time to consider* with our allies the action to be taken jointly in the situation then existing.

(7) But we cannot give any assurance now about possible action on the part of the United Kingdom in the event of failure to reach agreement at Geneva...

(8) We shall be ready to join with the United States Government now in *studying* measures to ensure the defence of Thailand and the rest of South-East Asia, including Malaya, in the event of all or part of Indo-China being lost.[1]

It was not until the last week of June that the United States obtained Churchill's approval to British participation in the first discussions which eventually led to the creation of SEATO. A joint communiqué issued in Washington by Eisenhower and Churchill stated that the two governments had agreed to 'hasten the planning of Asian defence against Communism and to set up an Anglo-American working party to consider the problem of security in the area'.[2]

The attitude of the British Government towards the creation of some defence organisation covering South-East Asia has been elaborated at length because it throws light upon the history of SEATO since its establishment. Subject to certain important reservations mentioned below, formal action by SEATO has required the assent of all its members. The final communiqué issued in Bangkok on 25 February 1955 after the first meeting of the SEATO Council stated specifically that 'Decisions of the Council will be taken by unanimous agreement'.[3] In these circumstances any 'radical divergence between the strategic

[1] Eden, *op. cit.* pp. 105–6.
[2] Quoted in *SEATO: Six Studies*, p. 64.   [3] *C.N.* vol. XXVI (1955), p. 125.

priorities as seen from Washington and London', as suggested by Professor Julius Stone,[1] would inevitably tend to restrict the scope of vigorous SEATO action.

3. After the Geneva Conference

In view of the doubts and hesitations about commencing negotiations for a South-East Asian Defence Treaty before the completion of the Geneva Conference, the speed with which SEATO was eventually established may at first sight seem surprising. A number of important factors contributed to this.

So far as Great Britain was concerned, some attempt had to be made to heal the serious rift with the United States, if only to ensure that the latter country refrained from active opposition to the settlement reached at Geneva. The most likely way to achieve this was for Great Britain to assent at least to preparatory discussions regarding a possible South-East Asia Security Pact. For Australia, the return to office on 29 May 1954 of the Menzies Government enabled Casey to take new initiatives. Backed by cabinet decisions on 4 June, Casey sought to promote a regional defensive arrangement in support of an Indo-China settlement, but, 'of course, with a more extensive purpose'.[2] The Government's own desire for such a pact was stimulated by Press attacks in Australia accusing it of shilly-shallying despite evidence that the American interest in a South-East Asian security pact was 'cooling fast'.[3]

But the main incentive to speedy action was the general lack of confidence that the agreement reached at Geneva would in fact prove to be a lasting settlement. Indeed, many delegates leaving Geneva after the Conference feared that the 17th parallel, now dividing North from South Vietnam, might be found to be a very temporary boundary; that, within a period of one or two years, pressure from the North might be successful in undermining the Government of the Republic of Vietnam; and that, with the whole of Vietnam lost, the position of the non-Communist governments of Laos and Cambodia might prove to be untenable.

It seemed essential therefore, especially to Australia, to create a security organisation which would include those

---

[1] *Australian Journal of Politics and History*, vol. 1 (1955–56), p. 7.
[2] Quoted in *SEATO: Six Studies*, p. 62.   [3] *Ibid.* p. 63.

Asian members willing to join, rather than to delay its establishment in the hope that other Asian countries, particularly India, might at some much later stage agree to participate. One could always hope that non-members would in time come to see that it might be in their own interest to join the organisation; if they did not, and if they were critical of the organisation established without them, this could not be helped. The current situation in South-East Asia was regarded as so serious that the Australian Prime Minister took the unprecedented step of announcing Australia's willingness, in time of peace, to accept military commitments in advance for the defence of South-East Asia:

...before long we may be forced to regard the Communist frontier as lying on the southern shores of Indo-China...this...gloomy view...can be falsified if...we are able not only to give economic and spiritual encouragement to the non-Communist elements in Indo-China, but also to rally the weighty opinion and influence of the great new democracies of South and South-East Asia...[1]

The Geneva Conference ended on 21 July 1954. Seven weeks later the South-East Asia Collective Defence Treaty was signed in Manila.

4. *Summing up*

American initiatives toward the establishment of a defence organisation for South-East Asia before and during the greater part of the Geneva Conference were frustrated primarily by the rigid opposition of Great Britain, which feared that even consultations might endanger a negotiated settlement at Geneva and antagonise non-aligned countries like India. Before deciding whether or not to become a party to such an organisation, the British Government wanted to be sure that a settlement (between Communist and non-Communist Governments) had been reached. American approaches regarding military intervention in Indo-China by the United States, the United Kingdom and others were also rejected by the United Kingdom, partly because the British Government believed that such intervention would not be successful, but mainly because it feared that such a war was likely to escalate and increase the risk of the British Isles suffering atomic attacks.

[1] *C.P.D.*, H. of R., vol. IV (5 August 1954), p. 65.

Australia stood somewhere between Great Britain and the United States, sharing the former's view that military intervention in Indo-China would be ineffective and would arouse strong resentment in Asia, but anxious to begin at the earliest possible moment the task of creating a defence organisation in South-East Asia which might in some degree 'shore-up' the Geneva settlement or act as a barrier to further Communist encroachments in the area or both. The Australian Government feared that, if steps towards such a defence pact were not taken speedily, the American Government might lose its new interest in the mainland of South-East Asia.

The speed with which SEATO was created after the Geneva Conference reflected primarily the strong fear, current at the time at least in American and Australian circles, that the 17th parallel would prove to be merely an imaginary and temporary line, and that the whole of Vietnam and perhaps also Laos and Cambodia would come under effective Communist control within a period of one or two years. While Great Britain in particular—but also Australia—had hoped that countries like India could be brought in as parties to a defence organisation in the area, the situation in South-East Asia was held to be far too urgent and dangerous to delay action further in the hope of securing wider membership. In the event, India's reaction showed that further delay and encouragement would not in fact have induced her to join. While Nehru was comparatively restrained in his criticism of the Manila Treaty, his friend and associate Krishna Menon attacked SEATO violently.[1]

B. NATURE AND SCOPE OF SEATO OBLIGATIONS

In its essential paragraph SEATO incorporates substantially the ANZUS formula and not that of NATO.[2] Article IV (1) of SEATO is in the following terms:

Each party recognises that aggression by means of armed attack in the Treaty Area against any of the Parties or against any State or Territory which the Parties by unanimous agreement may hereafter designate, would endanger its own peace and safety, and agrees that it will in that event act to meet the common danger in accordance with its constitutional processes...

[1] See pp. 226–7 below.
[2] For a comparison of the NATO and ANZUS formulae see pp. 124–8 above.

Article IV (3) made it clear that no action could be taken on the territory of a 'designated' State without the consent of the Government of that State. Further, the 'Treaty Area' as defined by Article VIII excluded from the operation of the Treaty 'the Pacific area north of 21 degrees 30 minutes north latitude'; that is, it excluded, *inter alia*, Formosa and Hong Kong.

As Dr Evatt, Leader of the Opposition, pointed out during the parliamentary debate on ratification of the Treaty, the word 'aggression' does not occur in the corresponding Articles of ANZUS or NATO: 'It has to be not merely armed attack, but aggression by means of armed attack. . . It does not follow that the nation which strikes the first blow is necessarily the aggressor.'[1]

A vital distinction between ANZUS and SEATO is the limitation under SEATO of the American obligation to cases of 'Communist aggression'. This special reservation was agreed to with reluctance by the other parties to the Treaty.

For the rest, SEATO has a special Article (III) binding the parties to 'co-operate with one another in the further development of economic measures, including technical assistance'; contains a special clause (in Article II) designed to 'prevent and counter subversive activities directed from without against their [the Parties'] territorial integrity and political stability'; formally 'designates', in a protocol, 'the States of Cambodia and Laos and the free territory under the jurisdiction of the State of Vietnam'; and has attached to it a 'Pacific Charter', introduced by the Government of the Philippines, binding the parties primarily to 'uphold the principle of equal rights and self-determination of peoples'.

The United States' reservation affirms the readiness of that country to consult with the other parties, in accordance with the provisions of Article IV (2), if any party considers that its territory or political independence, or that of a designated State, 'is threatened in any way other than by armed attack or is affected or threatened by any fact or situation which might endanger the peace of the area. . .'

C. DEBATE IN PARLIAMENT

On 27 October 1954 Casey introduced into the House of Representatives a Bill to approve ratification of SEATO. In

[1] *C.P.D.*, H. of R., vol. v (1954), p. 2,575.

his speech he frankly admitted that 'the [Geneva] settlement greatly strengthened the position of the Communists in South-East Asia and exposed the whole area to increased danger from Communist domination'. He also admitted that there were a 'number of countries that we would have liked to see there' who were not represented at Manila, but claimed that the countries who had signed the Treaty constituted a 'strong and effective nucleus'. While the Australian Government appreciated the 'desire for peace' of 'neutral' countries, it considered that 'peace can be assured only if it is made clear to a potential aggressor that an act of violence on his part will be met with effective resistance'.[1]

Australian participation in SEATO, the Minister asserted, was essential:

> ...the time has gone by when Australia could rest securely within its own borders. Instead of living in a tranquil corner of the globe, we are now on the verge of the most unsettled region of the world... It is no longer possible for any country to rely entirely for its security on its own strength and resources. There can be no safety in isolationism: it has to be sought through a sound system of collective defence...After the war it was hoped that the United Nations could provide a basis for collective security, but the organisation is paralysed because the right of veto is held by the major source of danger to the world's peace—the Soviet Union. To meet this situation...other mutual defence organisations have been formed... However, a gap remained in South-East Asia, and it was to meet this gap that the South-East Asia Collective Defence Treaty was drawn up at Manila.[2]

Anticipating comment in Australia—as in the case of the ANZUS Treaty—that the obligation of the parties under the terms of Article IV (1) was weaker than the corresponding obligation under NATO, Casey flatly contested the validity of this argument:

> This formula has been the subject of much discussion, and at Manila we were careful to make certain that the wording adopted was just as effective as that used in the North Atlantic Treaty...Mr Dulles made it clear to us that, as far as the American constitutional position was concerned, the formula adopted at Manila, deriving from the Monroe Doctrine...gives all the freedom of action and power to act that is contained in NATO...[3]

[1] *Ibid.* pp. 2,383, 2,384.   [2] *Ibid.* p. 2,382.   [3] *Ibid.* p. 2,386.

The Minister for External Affairs was on more difficult ground when he claimed that 'the primary purpose of the treaty is to combat Communism'. Casey explained that the American delegation originally wanted Article IV (1) itself to be limited in scope to instances of 'Communist aggression' only—in which case, of course, the American obligation under Article IV (1) would have been identical with the obligation of each of the other parties. The Minister took great pains to stress, however, the view of the Australian Government that:

> ...resistance to Communism is the immediate objective of the treaty, and it is for this principal purpose that the Australian Government is prepared to commit itself to this treaty. In fact, we cannot at present see any other circumstances in which we would be obliged to intervene...I wish to state categorically that the Australian Government would never regard itself as being committed, contractually or morally, to military action against any other member of the Commonwealth...The Pakistan Foreign Minister was informed of our position on this point before the treaty was signed.[1]

During the debate which followed, Evatt made a strong and effective attack upon the Government's acceptance, at Manila, of obligations wider than those of the United States. The inclusion in the preamble of the Bill of a reference to Communism, he said, made the preamble resemble a 'manifesto against Communism', but this reference was irrelevant and of no binding effect. It was absurd, he said, to make that emphasis in an agreement, so far as Australia was concerned:

> ...Australia's obligation under this agreement is to act—including military action—against Fascist or nationalist aggression as well as against Communist aggression. Therefore, why does the preamble to the Bill refer only to one class of aggression?...If there were Japanese aggression in the treaty area...and parties to the agreement were affected, the United States, under this agreement would not be obliged to take action with regard to that aggression...If there were an attack on Dutch New Guinea, by, say, Indonesia, and the Netherlands Government requested intervention under this treaty—and the area was designated unanimously under Article IV—would such aggression be termed 'Communist aggression'?... That is a defect in the treaty, and it is our duty to recognise it...I cannot imagine why the difficulties were not confronted more boldly at Manila...It is quite wrong in principle...that Australia's obli-

---

[1] *C.P.D.*, H. of R., vol. v (1954), p. 2,387.

gation under this treaty should be unlimited, and that the United States should have only a limited obligation. Who is to judge whether the particular aggression alleged to have occurred is Communist aggression...[1]

In criticising this aspect of SEATO, the Leader of the Opposition discovered considerable virtue in the ANZUS Treaty which, when ANZUS was under discussion in Parliament, he had greeted without enthusiasm:

From the point of view of Australian security...I maintain emphatically that our obligations under the ANZUS pact are clearer. That agreement is enormously more important to our security than is this treaty. Under ANZUS there is an obligation on all three parties to the pact, including the United States, to intervene against aggression, wherever it may take place, if it be directed against any of the parties, and whether it be Communist aggression, fascist aggression, nationalist aggression, or any other kind of aggression... The ANZUS pact was drafted in strict accordance with the principles of the Charter, but the same position does not arise under the present agreement.[2]

It was part of Evatt's argument that a treaty directed solely against 'Communist' aggression would be contrary to the United Nations Charter. Regional arrangements, he maintained, must be consistent with the purposes and principles of the Charter, and such arrangements under the Charter must be concerned only with 'the maintenance of international peace and security' in relation to the region.[3]

Speaking in reply, Casey frankly admitted that the preamble to the Bill had 'no legal significance'. He answered Evatt's criticism by making three brief assertions; first, that the United States Congress would not have ratified the treaty if the American obligation under it had been wider than 'Communist' aggression (since only in such circumstances would Congress have concluded that there was a danger to American security); secondly, that some Asian parties to the treaty might not have ratified it if the treaty itself had been restricted to cases of Communist aggression; and, thirdly, that a treaty limited to

---

[1] *Ibid.* pp. 2,575–9.   [2] *Ibid.* p. 2,579.

[3] See also Fifield, *Southeast Asia in United States Policy*, p. 116. In Professor Fifield's opinion 'The treaty comes under Article 51 of the United Nations Charter, "the inherent right of individual or collective self-defense" clause, and not Article 52 concerning regional arrangements where a Soviet veto could apply to enforcement measures'.

communist aggression 'would have attracted the animosity of some of the Asian countries that are not signatories'.[1] Further explanation of the reasons for the remaining parties to SEATO signing a treaty containing obligations which, *prima facie*, are wider in scope than the obligation assumed by the United States must await publication of official records.

The two amendments moved by the Leader of the Opposition in Parliament, namely, that Australia should not ratify the Treaty unless the United Kingdom, New Zealand and the United States also ratified, and that no armed forces should be contributed by Australia under the Treaty without the prior approval of Parliament, were defeated on a party vote.

D. CRITICISM OUTSIDE PARLIAMENT

Since SEATO was established it has been subjected to considerable criticism. Non-aligned countries, such as India, have opposed its basic conception, and their attitude has stimulated use, by some Australians, of the argument that Australian membership of military alliances makes it impossible to establish good relations with Asian countries which are not members, especially India. So far as ANZUS is concerned, this criticism has already been considered;[2] the effect upon relations with Australia of Indian antagonism to SEATO is dealt with in chapter 6.[3]

Secondly, some member countries, notably Pakistan, the Philippines and Thailand, consider that their more powerful or richer partners have failed to contribute sufficient economic aid as envisaged by Article III of the Treaty. They object to being 'taken for granted'[4] and feel entitled to some economic compensation, as Asian countries which have, so to speak, embarrassed themselves in their relations with other Asian countries through agreeing to join in a predominantly Western military organisation. But it was never the intention of the 'donor' countries that economic aid under SEATO should take the place of aid to under-developed countries outside the framework of SEATO. Mr Casey has put the Australian point of view as follows:

Australia does not wish to duplicate or replace through SEATO the valuable work being done in this field through other agencies. In

---

[1] *C.P.D.*, H. of R., vol. v (1954), pp. 2,695, 2,696.
[2] See pp. 136–8 above.   [3] See pp. 226–7 below.
[4] Quoted in *SEATO: Six Studies*, p. 105.

the Colombo Plan and in United Nations activities, Australia and other countries have made appreciable contributions towards raising living standards in Asian countries. But we think that there is a clear role for SEATO also in relation to its members. A country's defence and security cannot be placed in a separate compartment of its own. It is a vital interest of the community and must have a sound economic basis. We use SEATO machinery to review economic problems affecting the ability of member countries to pursue the Treaty objectives, especially in the field of defence, and we examine possibilities of mutual aid and co-operation to meet them.[1]

In fact, Australia has made gifts, under Article III of the Treaty, amounting to several million pounds, designed 'to provide assistance in the form of equipment and services (especially training) needed for the defence programmes' of Asian member-countries, though such aid 'does not cover weapons or munitions'.[2]

Thirdly, and most important, is the criticism that SEATO has been over-cautious, at times even to the point of timidity. This has been attributed to 'the modesty of its resources, the supremacy of governmental interests within it, and...its sensitivity to criticism from member and non-member countries alike'.[3] It has also been suggested that the Far East has now become for Great Britain and France an area of only secondary, if not of tertiary interest.[4] None of the Great Power members of SEATO is indigenous to the treaty area, and when they disagree, SEATO is allegedly powerless.[5]

Considerations such as these have led Mr B. A. Santamaria, an Australian publicist well-known for his outspoken political comments and connexion with Catholic Action and other organisations, to declare:

Since each Power has a right of veto over the decisions of the collective entity, SEATO consecrates disagreement—and therefore impotence. Britain and France, both in the twilight of Empire, regard the Orient as a region in which they no longer have any real interest. The available wealth has long since been absorbed, the bases are gone, and what is spent there today in terms of military or economic power is good money chasing bad. Further, the Americans, who have two frontiers, one of which faces China, must be restrained from committing to the Orient troops or treasure which

[1] R. G. Casey, *Friends and Neighbours* (Michigan State University Press, East Lansing, 1958), pp. 117–18.   [2] *Ibid.* p. 118.
[3] *SEATO: Six Studies*, pp. 27–8.   [4] *Ibid.* p. 4.   [5] *Ibid.* p. 5.

might better be devoted to the Western Hemisphere. Hence, every dispute in the SEATO area must be dampened down before a latter-day Dulles commits the crowning imprudence of dragging the United States into the 'wrong war in the wrong place'. Any war in the Pacific—whatever has to be sacrificed to avoid it—is the 'wrong war in the wrong place' for Powers whose interests are overwhelmingly European.[1]

This criticism, though illustrative of an attitude of mind in a section of Australian opinion, is clearly exaggerated. For instance, it underestimates the importance of British interests in Hong Kong and Malaysia, the continuance of British bases and military forces there, and British readiness to use such forces in certain circumstances, despite the financial and military burden involved: for example, in support of Malaysia against Indonesian confrontation. An important development since Santamaria wrote has been the public recognition by the British Labour Government that 'It is in the Far East and Southern Asia that the greatest danger to peace may be in the next decade, and some of our partners in the Commonwealth may be directly threatened. We believe that it is right that Britain should continue to maintain a military presence in this area.'[2]

Moreover, it is necessary to remember that United Kingdom policy has shown great caution in Europe as well as in the Far East; for example in the handling of various crises over Berlin, despite British steadfastness in maintaining the obligation to help defend Berlin if Communist pressure brought the issue to an actual boiling point.

Nevertheless, there is an important element of truth in Santamaria's view that South-East Asia must, for European countries, be an area of at least secondary importance. It could be argued that the eventual readiness of Great Britain and France to join in creating SEATO reflected less a desire to make it a positive, effective body than a decision, while maintaining prestige as world powers, to prevent SEATO from taking any action which might lead to a war likely, in their opinion, to escalate in due course into an atomic war in Europe.

[1] *The Bulletin* (Sydney), 16 February 1963, p. 30.
[2] Statement on British Defence Estimates by Mr Denis Healey, British Defence Minister, 25 February 1966, issued by the British High Commission, Canberra (G42/a/SUB).

Much of the criticism of SEATO misses the main point, namely that the Treaty binds the United States to 'act to meet the common danger' in the event of 'Communist aggression' by means of armed attack in the Treaty area against any of the parties or against any state or territory which the parties by unanimous agreement have designated under Article IV. As has already been pointed out in regard to Korea,[1] America has been hesitant to undertake such an obligation on the mainland of Asia. In fact, since the creation of SEATO, no such armed attack has occurred on the territory of any of the eight signatory parties, and this is no doubt due substantially to the mere existence of SEATO.

On the other hand, critics understandably point to developments in recent years in Laos and Vietnam, where SEATO has not prevented deterioration advantageous to Communist powers or forces. They point to differences of opinion amongst SEATO members as to what action has been desirable or practicable in these States, and blame SEATO for inaction or timidity which, in the case of Laos, led to the withdrawal of that country in 1962 from the shelter of the SEATO 'umbrella' after a second Geneva Conference. They fail to take into sufficient account the inherent difficulties which lie in the way of helping these States, inexperienced in methods of democratic government, to help themselves: the nature of the terrain; the complexity of devising means of counteracting modern, revolutionary insurgency, based upon terror, and supported and directed from Communist countries with a common border; the inevitable differences of outlook amongst members of any military alliance, not excluding NATO; and the fact that when the United States agreed to become a party to SEATO it did not regard as practicable the establishment in South-East Asia of a tight military organisation of the NATO kind.

Moreover, an interpretation has now been placed upon the 'unanimity rule' in SEATO[2]—and apparently not contested by the members—which is of great importance. At a time when Thailand was very disturbed at developments in Laos and extremely concerned that SEATO seemed unready or unable to

---

[1] See p. 118 above.
[2] The final communiqué issued, on 25 February 1955 after the first meeting of the SEATO Council at Bangkok, stated that 'Decisions of the Council will be taken by unanimous agreement.' See *C.N.* vol. xxvi (1955), p. 125.

take more positive action, the Dean Rusk–Thanat Khoman joint statement of 6 March 1962, issued in Washington, introduced an important gloss upon the text of the Treaty. In this statement the American Secretary of State affirmed that the obligation of the United States to assist Thailand in case of Communist armed attack against that country 'does not depend upon the prior agreement of all other parties to the Treaty, since this Treaty obligation is individual as well as collective'.[1] Equally important for Australia, this interpretation was specifically endorsed by the Minister for External Affairs, in answer to a parliamentary question on 8 March. After quoting the Rusk–Thanat statement in full, Sir Garfield Barwick added:

Although the SEATO Treaty envisages collective resistance to aggression, each party agrees under Article IV (i) that, in the event of armed attack in the Treaty area against any of the Parties or against a State designated in the Protocol, it will act to meet the common danger in accordance with its constitutional processes. It is therefore plain, as the Secretary to State said, that 'the treaty obligation is individual as well as collective'. The Treaty provides the basis for collective action by the signatories and much detailed planning has been done in an effort to make such action effective. However, it is a matter for each of the partners individually to determine in advance or at the time, the precise manner in which it carries out the obligations which it has accepted. Of course, in making its decisions, the Australian Government will take into account the consultation and planning within the SEATO organisation and the action which other members are prepared to take, collectively or individually, but at the appropriate time will decide itself how it will perform its obligations under the Treaty.[2]

The United States, Great Britain and Australia sent air squadrons to Thailand in 1962, at the invitation of the Thai Government. The United States also sent ground forces while New Zealand sent a small force of parachute troops. This significant precedent for action by certain members of SEATO would appear to have widened the scope of possible action under the Treaty and to have restricted the scope for obstruction by any one member of the organisation. Even if no such action formally objected to by one member can properly be described as action under SEATO, the practical effect may be the same.

---

[1] *SEATO: Six Studies*, p. 293.   [2] *C.N.* vol. xxxiii (March 1962), p. 36.

Another way to test whether or not SEATO is a 'paper tiger', weak and useless, is to consider the probable situation in South-East Asia if it were abolished. Few will deny the strategic importance of Thailand, both directly for Malaya and indirectly for Australia. During the Second World War Thailand, faced with overwhelming Japanese strength and the uncertainty of effective support from Western countries, came to an accommodation with Japan. If SEATO did not exist, its interpretation strengthened by the Rusk–Thanat statement of 1962, might not Thailand, under extreme pressure from Peking, feel that an accommodation with Peking was unavoidable? And if this happened, what would be the effect upon Malaysia?

To question the justification for many of the criticisms of SEATO, however, is not to suggest that it is a perfect instrument for combating 'Communist aggression' or 'subversive activities directed from without'. The main purpose of this review has been to clarify the historical background to SEATO in order to explain why it came into existence when it did and in the form it actually assumed.

SEATO, of course, is only one means of pursuing international objectives in South-East Asia: others include the United Nations Organisation, ANZUS, the Colombo Plan, the Economic Commission for Asia and the Far East (ECAFE), and ordinary diplomatic activity. If one accepts the view that Australia, as a country geographically situated off the southern rim of Asia, should enter *no* military alliances but should concentrate solely upon cultivating the goodwill of Asian countries, then SEATO inevitably stands condemned. This is an arguable point of view, though not one which is acceptable to the great majority of Australians.

V. THE AUSTRALIAN CONTRIBUTION TO THE DEFENCE OF THE MALAYAN AREA

A. HISTORICAL BACKGROUND

1. *ANZAM*

In the period since the end of the Second World War, the United Kingdom, Australia and New Zealand have given close attention to the security of the Malayan area. In view of Japan's war-time victories, culminating in the fall of Singapore, this is scarcely cause for wonder; what is surprising, however, is the singular lack of clarity in public statement by political leaders as to the precise nature of the rights acquired and obligations undertaken by the three Commonwealth countries in regard to the defence of this area. So far as Australia is concerned, such statements have often been obscure or inconsistent.

The word ANZAM stands for the Australian, New Zealand and Malayan area. At one stage it was a more-or-less classified word, never mentioned in public by officials; later, Prime Ministerial use of the word made adherence to this rule or convention absurd. When the British Prime Minister, Mr Harold Macmillan, visited Australia in 1958, he said publicly on 5 February, 'British defence plans in this area are based on two things: our membership of SEATO and of ANZAM.'[1] This bare mention of ANZAM can scarcely be regarded as any more illuminating than the passing reference of the Australian Prime Minister on 20 April 1955 to 'the ANZAM Defence Committee, representing Great Britain, Australia and New Zealand'.[2] No precise indication was given of the purposes of ANZAM or of the functions of the ANZAM Defence Committee.

Until comparatively recently, the clearest account of ANZAM was that contained in a report prepared by a study group of the Royal Institute of International Affairs and published in 1956. As this group met under the chairmanship of Marshal of the R.A.F. Sir John Slessor, and included amongst its members senior British service officers, it can reasonably be regarded as authoritative as far as it goes. The report includes the following paragraph:

In 1949[3] the Governments of Australia, New Zealand and the United Kingdom had agreed to co-ordinate defence planning in an area known as the ANZAM region, which includes the Australian and New Zealand homelands and the British territories in Malaya and Borneo, together with the adjacent sea areas. ANZAM planning was at first limited to the defence of sea and air communications in the region, while co-ordination was conducted at Service level and did not involve firm commitments by the Governments concerned. Subsequently, however, planning responsibility under ANZAM was extended to cover the defence of Malaya and in the spring of

---

[1] *C.N.* vol. xxix (1958), p. 113.   [2] *C.P.D.*, H. of R., vol. vi (April 1955), p. 51.
[3] Actually, the year was 1948—see *C.P.D.* vol. 208, p. 3465.

1955 Australia and New Zealand agreed to station military units in Malaya. The acceptance of commitments of this character was an important development in Australian and New Zealand policy. It will be noted, however, that ANZAM covers only the southern part of the Manila Treaty area.[1]

Subsequently, further light was thrown on ANZAM by General Sir Richard Hull, Chief of the British Imperial General Staff, during a visit to Australia in 1963. In a press conference in Canberra on 27 February, and a television interview over channel 7 (Canberra) on 5 March, General Hull made the following points. ANZAM was not a treaty or written agreement, but a term used to denote a consultative arrangement by which Australia, Great Britain and New Zealand co-ordinate defence interests in this part of the world. It dealt with matters in the Malayan area. ANZAM met in Canberra on an 'as required' basis. Australia was represented on it by the Australian chiefs of staff, and the United Kingdom was represented normally by the Head of the British Defence Liaison Staff in Australia. New Zealand was represented by the New Zealand Military Representative in Canberra, but as New Zealand was close, its representative was sometimes a New Zealand chief of staff. The United Kingdom tried to be represented once a year by one of the chiefs of staff. The deployment of the Commonwealth Strategic Reserve in Malaya[2] was determined under the ANZAM consultative arrangements.

The most comprehensive account of ANZAM now available is that given by Dr T. B. Millar.[3] He confirms that there is no formal ANZAM treaty, and that ANZAM is an agreement to consult and to co-ordinate military planning and activities originally entered into by the Labour governments of Britain, Australia and New Zealand and continued by their successors in office. Technically, the ANZAM Defence Committee consists, according to Dr Millar, of the Australian Defence Committee and the Chiefs of Staff Committees of Britain and New Zealand. As these can never all get together, meetings take place in three places—London, Singapore, and Canberra. 'The group that meets in Canberra is the one referred to as the "ANZAM Defence Committee". It is chaired by the Secretary of the Australian Department of Defence, and includes the

---

[1] *Collective Defence in South-East Asia* (Oxford University Press, 1958), p. 20.
[2] See p. 170 below.   [3] See Millar, *Australia's Defence*, pp. 69–76.

Australian Chiefs of Staff Committee, plus representatives of the British and New Zealand Chiefs of Staff.'[1]

While the Commonwealth Strategic Reserve is, in a general sense, 'under the command of the ANZAM Defence Committee'—to use Sir Richard Hull's phrase—its operational employment is a responsibility of the British Commander-in-Chief, Far East, operating within the terms of a general directive issued by the ANZAM Defence Committee after approval by the three Governments concerned. New developments not covered by the existing directive would require its modification. The British Commander-in-Chief, Far East, of course, has other responsibilities as well. He is responsible to the United Kingdom Government for all British forces not assigned to the Commonwealth Strategic Reserve.[2]

2. *Post-war Change in Australian strategic plans*

We have seen that ANZAM was at first 'limited to the defence of sea and air communications'. Its subsequent extension to 'planning responsibility...for the defence of Malaya' was related, presumably, to the serious deterioration of the situation in French Indo-China, especially in Vietnam. Dien Bien Phu fell to the Vietminh on 7 May 1954 and one day later the Powers assembled at Geneva began their discussion of the problems of Indo-China. On 17 June Pierre Mendès-France became Prime Minister of France. He announced publicly his intention of reaching a settlement at Geneva by 20 July, and of resigning in the event of failure.

A cease-fire agreement was in fact signed on 21 July. Vietnam was partitioned provisionally at the 17th parallel and an international commission established to supervise the carrying-out of its terms. Provision was made in a Final Declaration for the holding of elections to unify Vietnam in July 1956, although it should be noted that neither the United States nor the Republic of Vietnam accepted the Declaration.[3] Reference has already been made to the speed with which, after the Geneva Conference concluded, the South-East Asia Col-

---

[1] Millar, *Australia's Defence*, p. 71.   [2] *Ibid.* pp. 72–3.

[3] For the text of the Declaration by the representative of the United States, see *Select Documents on International Affairs*, no. 1 of 1964 (Department of External Affairs), p. 17; for the text of the Declaration by President Ngo Dinh Diem, see *ibid.* p. 22.

lective Defence Treaty Organisation was negotiated, and the reasons for this.[1]

SEATO was signed on 8 September 1954 and came into force on 19 February 1955. In an important speech to the House of Representatives on 20 April 1955, reporting on the recent Prime Minister's Conference held in London and his subsequent visit to Washington, the Australian Prime Minister, Mr Menzies, informed Parliament that before SEATO was signed, Australia, Great Britain and New Zealand, 'through their military staffs', had sat down to the task of working out how the defence of Malaya and therefore of the islands and of Australia and New Zealand themselves could be effected. At the London talks it had been recognised that, if war came, Great Britain, Australia and New Zealand would need to find much greater forces than a strategic reserve. In the event of a 'hot' war, Australia itself must be ready to contribute forces 'probably... of the order of two divisions'.[2] In the meantime, she would contribute to the strategic reserve 'to be stationed in Malaya' two destroyers or frigates, an aircraft carrier on an annual visit, additional ships in an emergency, an infantry battalion with supporting arms and reinforcements in Australia, a fighter air wing of two squadrons, a bomber wing of one squadron and an airfield construction squadron.[3]

The decision of the Australian Government to station Australian troops in Malaya in time of peace, announced by the Prime Minister on 1 April 1955, was strongly opposed by the Labour Party when the issue came before Parliament on 20 April. Professor Norman Harper has commented on the decision as follows:

Strategically, it involved a revolutionary switch in Australian policy. In the last two world wars, Australian troops had fought as part of a British defence force in the Middle East. Malaya had now become the pivot of Australian defence, and the Middle East had been tacitly abandoned, with British consent, as an Australian responsibility. It meant the peacetime commitment of Australian ground troops outside Australia's territorial limits. While a bomber and transport wing of the Royal Australian Air Force had previously been temporarily stationed in Malaya, this was in fact a significant departure in Australian defence planning.[4]

---

[1] See pp. 151–2 above.   [2] See *C.N.* vol. xxvi (1955), p. 289.
[3] *Ibid.* p. 288.   [4] *Australia in World Affairs, 1950–55*, p. 189.

Professor Harper states that 'Top-level staff discussions in Melbourne and Singapore had produced a decision to concentrate defences...at the Kra Isthmus at the southernmost extremity of Thailand. Before deciding to station Australian troops in Malaya, Mr Menzies discussed the broad strategic problem in Washington.'[1]

The Australian Prime Minister went to unusual lengths to justify before the bar of Australian public opinion this important development in Australian policy. In his statement of 1 April, announcing that Parliament would be asked to endorse the Government's decision to station Australian ground forces in Malaya, Menzies stressed the stern necessity for this decision in the following words:

There was a time when we permitted ourselves to think that we were remote from the dangers of the world, and that any great war would be thousands of miles away from us. But that day has gone...I call upon all Australians to realise the basic truth...that if there is to be war for our existence, it should be carried on by us as far from our own soil as possible. It would be a sorry day for the security of Australia if we were driven to defend ourselves on our own soil, for that would connote the most disastrous defeats abroad and the most incredible difficulties for our friends and allies desiring to help us.

Two things are unbelievable. One is that any responsible Australian should think that we could be effectively defended either by our own efforts within our own borders or by resolutions of the United Nations rendered impotent by the Communist veto. The simple English of this matter is that with our vast territory and our small population we cannot survive a surging Communist challenge from abroad except by the co-operation of powerful friends, including in particular the United Kingdom and the United States...we cannot accept the collaboration of our friends and allies in a comprehensive defence against aggressive Communism unless we as a nation are prepared to take our share of the responsibilities.[2]

During the debate in Parliament the Prime Minister, in his speech of 20 April 1955, spelled out in detail the overall objectives of Australian foreign policy and the principles adopted by the Government in pursuit of those objectives. Menzies listed five objectives, namely (a) the securing of peace with justice; (b) cultivation of 'powerful and willing friends' to aid

---

[1] *Australia in World Affairs, 1950–55*, p. 189.
[2] *C.N.* vol. xxvi (1955), pp. 278–9.

Australia if war should come; (c) readiness to defend not only Australian rights, but also the rights of others; (d) the raising of living standards both for Australians and for the people of other nations; (e) readiness to live and let live—that is non-interference with the internal affairs of other people so long as they pursue the same principle.

In pursuit of these objectives six main principles were to be applied: (1) support for the United Nations Charter; (2) support for a close co-operation with the British Commonwealth; (3) closest co-operation between the British Commonwealth and the United States; (4) development of 'good neighbour' policies towards Asian countries in this section of the world; (5) encouragement of the world's peaceful trade, including Australian trade; (6) justification of the co-operation of other nations by ourselves accepting obligations and doing what is necessary at home to make those obligations performable.

In supporting adherence to the United Nations Charter, the Prime Minister stressed that it was no substitute for power:

Those who refer blithely to the United Nations and think that such a reference disposes either of our defence problem or of the defence problem of the free world, are living in a state of pathetic and dangerous illusion...in the present set-up of the world...no great power is likely to be found voting to condemn its own actions, or to impose military sanctions upon itself.[1]

He criticised those who speak of 'the Charter' and of 'power politics' as opposed, and then draw the conclusion that the acquisition of national military power is against the spirit of the Charter. The fact was that the Charter contemplated power and the use of force, and therefore depended upon the existence of national power.

Menzies argued that the closest understanding and the highest possible community of action between the British Commonwealth and the United States were 'vital to the security of all of us'.[2] There was not a country in the world, he asserted, more completely British than Australia, nor one more devoted to the throne and person of Her Majesty the Queen. We were a proud member of a Crown Commonwealth, and would ever continue to be so. Yet Australians would be blind if they could not see that the United States had become, in the most literal sense,

---

[1] *Ibid.* pp. 282–3. [2] *Ibid.* p. 284.

vital to the existence of the free world. 'When we turn from the world scene to consider our own position in this corner of the world', he added, 'it would be hard to find any Australian of this generation who did not recognise that the friendship and co-operation of the United States are vital to our own safety.'[1]

The Prime Minister, before announcing the decision to station Australian ground forces in Malaya, made every effort to ensure that he had the support and encouragement of the United States Government. Returning to Australia from the London Prime Ministers' Conference by way of Washington, he had discussed the problem with President Eisenhower and John Foster Dulles, and had been authorised by them to make public an agreed statement of American policy. While less than a specific commitment, this statement was a definite encouragement to Australia to proceed with its plans, and Menzies used the statement during his speech in the House of Representatives on 20 April in an attempt to meet the possible criticism that the Australian Government did not have American support for its policy:

> ...in the general task of preventing further Communist aggression, the United States considered the defence of South-East Asia, of which Malaya is an integral part, to be of very great importance...I raised the question whether in the event of Great Britain, Australia and New Zealand undertaking to station substantial forces in Malaya, we could be assured that the United States would be prepared to give us effective co-operation. I was informed that though the tactical employment of forces was a matter which would have to be worked out in detail on the Services level, the United States considered that such effective co-operation was implicit in the Manila Pact...[2]

3. *Commonwealth Strategic Reserve*

The precise range of purposes for which the Australian component of the Commonwealth Strategic Reserve was sent to Malaya has not been set out clearly in official statements. At some stages the relevance of the Reserve for SEATO purposes has been stressed; at other stages, the SEATO aspect has been played down or denied.

There is no doubt that Australian soldiers sent to Malaya were intended to be used in the campaign against the 'terro-

---

[1] *C.N.* vol. XXVI (1955), p. 285.   [2] *Ibid.* pp. 289–90.

rists' in the Malayan jungle: they have in fact been so used. Again, it is clear that they are *not* to be used 'in relation to any civil disturbances or in the internal affairs of the Federation or Singapore'.[1]

In his statement of 1 April 1955 Menzies said that Australia proposed to 'participate in the establishment in Malaya, as a very important part of the Manila Treaty area, as a contribution to the defence of the treaty area of a strategic reserve in which the United Kingdom and New Zealand will participate'.[2] Again, in his speech in Parliament on 20 April 1955 the Prime Minister referred to 'the particular example which represents the most advanced stage of planning against the background of the Manila Treaty',[3] and added that United Kingdom, New Zealand and Australian troops in Malaya would 'represent not only a true defence in depth for Australia itself', but 'also a source of strength to our Asian friends'.[3] Moreover, in the same speech the Prime Minister obviously attached importance to the message he had received from the Acting Chairman of the Manila Treaty Council Representatives Meeting at Bangkok:

...at its informal meeting, April 7, the Council Representatives of the SEATO have taken note of the statement made by Your Excellency on 1st instant, and welcomes the decision of the Australian Government to seek parliamentary approval for participation by Australian forces in a strategic reserve to be established in Malaya as an important part of the Treaty area.[3]

Clearly, the SEATO Representatives themselves regarded the Commonwealth Strategic Reserve in Malaya as a possible source of strength for SEATO purposes.

Subsequently, however, the tendency of Government leaders to relate the Strategic Reserve in some degree to SEATO was damped down, though not consistently—partly, perhaps, because of the strong opposition shown in Parliament by the Labour Party to the decision to send ground forces to Malaya in time of peace, and partly because of the sensitiveness of Malayan political leaders on the subject of SEATO. The first elections were held in Malaya on 27 July 1955 and a Chief Minister was appointed—Tunku Abdul Rahman—who became Prime Minister when the Federation of Malaya became an

---

[1] See statement of the Prime Minister of 16 June 1955 in *C.N.* vol. xxvi (1955), p. 419.   [2] *Ibid.* p. 279.   [3] *Ibid.* p. 287.

independent State on 31 August 1957. As from the latter date Malaya was no part of British territory to which the Manila Treaty applied, and the Federation Government showed no desire to apply for separate membership of SEATO. Like Singapore, Malaya tended to view SEATO with hesitation if not suspicion, fearing that any direct relationship with it might 'attract' trouble.

Thus, when the Melbourne newspaper *The Age* reported on 5 July 1955 a statement by Major-General T. B. L. Churchill, i/C Administration at G.H.Q., Far East Land Forces, Singapore (then on a visit to Australia), that 'As I see it, the Australian contribution is to be a strategic reserve, which could be used anywhere in South-East Asia', the Minister for Defence, Sir Philip McBride, issued an immediate denial. After General Churchill's statement the Leader of the Opposition, Dr Evatt, had claimed that 'General Churchill's statement was in direct conflict with the assurance given to Parliament by the Menzies Government that the troops would be in front-line duties against the Malayan terrorists'.[1] As reported in *The Age*, the Minister for Defence 'emphatically denied' General Churchill's statement, adding that the Prime Minister had made it clear to Parliament that the forces would be located in Penang as part of the strategic reserve for the defence of Malaya. They would also be used for anti-terrorist operations in this area. The suggestion by the federal Opposition Leader that there were wider commitments for Australian troops was entirely without foundation.[1]

On 19 December 1955 Menzies confirmed that Australian troops in Malaya 'could...be available for use against the Communist terrorists'. He concluded with the platitudinous or ambiguous comment that 'The Australian Forces, like other British Commonwealth Forces, are in Malaya to add to the strength of Malaya.'[2] Yet on 19 September 1957, speaking in Parliament mainly on the subject of the proposed defence agreement between Great Britain and Malaya, the Prime Minister again reintroduced the SEATO theme:

SEATO represents the overall predominant conception, and I should therefore emphasise that not only the forces which we can deploy ahead of war, as we now do in and around the Malayan

---

[1] *The Age*, 6 July 1955, p. 3.   [2] *C.N.* vol. xxvi (1955), p. 859.

Peninsula, but also the forces which could be quickly used in the event of war, and which would thereafter be powerfully reinforced from our partly trained reserves of strength, will be constantly related to SEATO defence.

Indeed, in time of war it is quite certain that SEATO will establish overall commands and that our forces, by suitable arrangements, will be under them.[1]

After referring to the proposed defence agreement between Great Britain and Malaya, and to the intention of Australia and New Zealand to 'associate ourselves with its terms', Menzies drew attention to Article 3 of the Agreement, under which Malaya granted to Great Britain the right to maintain in the Federation a Commonwealth Strategic Reserve for the purpose of assisting Malaya in the external defence of its territory and 'for the fulfilment of Commonwealth and international obligations'. He added that it was the belief of the Australian Government that Australian forces, by their very presence in the region in a state of readiness, 'add strength and confidence to the countries of the region and are available to meet demands of an emergency'.[2]

Finally, in his important pronouncement of 25 September 1963, indicating Australian support for Malaysia in the face of Indonesian confrontation, the Prime Minister told Parliament that 'The establishment of the Commonwealth Strategic Reserve, of SEATO—to the functions of which the Reserve was relevant—the negotiations [*sic*] of the ANZUS pact', were 'all of the same pattern'.[3] There had been some suggestion that Australian forces in Malaya went there primarily for purposes of internal security. That was not so. Menzies continued as follows: 'As I have indicated, they went there and are there as a part of a strategic reserve with the United Kingdom and New Zealand and as a contribution to the defence of the South-East Asian area.'[4] No statement would appear on its face to be clearer. Yet an examination of the terms of the United Kingdom–Malayan Defence Agreement, and consideration of action under it, again throws doubt upon the extent of the purposes for which the Strategic Reserve can be used—at least without the consent of the Government of the Federation of Malaya.

---

[1] *C.N.* vol. xxviii (1957), p. 724.   [2] *Ibid.* pp. 729–30.
[3] *Select Documents on International Affairs*, no. 1 of 1963, *Malaysia*, issued by the Department of External Affairs, p. 202.   [4] *Ibid.* p. 203.

4. *Interpretation of the United Kingdom–Malayan Defence Agreement*[1]

Under Article 1 of the British–Malayan Agreement on External Defence and Mutual Assistance, 1957, the United Kingdom undertakes to afford assistance to Malaya 'for external defence of its territory'. Malaya agrees, under Article III, to 'afford' [*sic*] the United Kingdom the right to maintain in the Federation 'such naval, land and air forces including a Commonwealth Strategic Reserve as are agreed between the two Governments to be necessary for the purposes of Article 1 and for the fulfilment of Commonwealth and international obligations'.

Article VI provides for mutual consultation on measures to be taken jointly or separately in the event of a threat of armed attack against the territories or forces of Malaya or the territories or protectorates of the United Kingdom in the Far East (or British forces therein) or other threat to the preservation of peace in the Far East. If there is an actual armed attack upon any of the territories or forces listed in Article VI, the two Governments undertake to co-operate and to take such action as each considers necessary. If, however, there should be a threat to the peace or an actual outbreak of hostilities 'elsewhere than in the area covered by Articles VI and VII', then under Article VIII the United Kingdom must obtain Malaya's 'prior agreement. . .before committing United Kingdom forces to active operations involving the use of bases in the Federation of Malaya; but this shall not affect the right of. . .the United Kingdom to withdraw forces from. . .Malaya'.

From the strictly legal point of view, it would appear that Article VIII of this Agreement required the consent of the Government of Malaya (before British forces could be committed to active operations involving the use of bases in Malaya) only in circumstances which could scarcely arise, namely in the event of an outbreak of hostilities *other than in the Far East*. British forces could operate from Malayan bases, not only in the event of armed attack against any of the territories or forces of Malaya (Article VI), but also, without Malayan assent, (*a*) in the event of an attack upon 'any of the territories [for example, Hongkong] or protectorates [for example, Brunei] of the United Kingdom in the Far East' or upon British forces in such ter-

[1] For text, see *ibid.* pp. 204–5.

ritories or protectorates or in Malaya (Article VII), and (*b*) in the event of a 'threat to the preservation of peace in the Far East' (Article VI). Under this interpretation of the Treaty the United Kingdom would appear to have the legal right to operate, for instance, aircraft from Butterworth base in Malaya for SEATO or other purposes if peace in the Far East were threatened or disturbed.

This, however, was not the interpretation placed upon the Agreement by the Prime Minister of Malaya when it was decided to send Commonwealth air squadrons to Thailand during the crisis in Laos of 1962. At that time Tunku Abdul Rahman is reported to have said in Kuala Lumpur on 20 May 1962 that, under the mutual defence agreement with Great Britain, Commonwealth forces in Malaya could not be used, except for the defence of Malaya and British territories in South-East Asia, without Malaya's agreement: 'The Federation of Malaya will not agree to the Commonwealth Forces stationed in Malaya being sent to Thailand in fulfilment of the obligations of the three Commonwealth countries (United Kingdom, Australia and New Zealand) to SEATO.'[1] And, in fact, an Australian 'Sabre' squadron destined for Thailand was first withdrawn from Butterworth to Singapore.[2] While this action does not prove that British and Malayan interpretations of the agreement were identical, it raises the question whether legal rights can be enforced in the event of local political opposition.

5. *Agreement relating to Malaysia*[3]

Further uncertainty as to correct interpretation is introduced by the terms of, and comments upon, Article VI of the Agreement of 9 July 1963, signed by representatives of Great Britain, the Federation of Malaya, North Borneo, Sarawak and Singapore, The article is as follows:

The Agreement on External Defence and Mutual Assistance between the Government of the United Kingdom and the Government of the Federation of Malaya of 12 October 1957, and its annexes shall apply to all territories of Malaysia, and any reference in that Agreement to the Federation of Malaya shall be deemed to apply to Malaysia, subject to the proviso that the Government of Malaysia

---

[1] *The Times* (London), 21 May 1962, p. 10.   [2] *Ibid.* 29 May 1962, p. 12.
[3] For text, see *Select Documents on Malaysia* (no. 1 of 1963), pp. 143–5.

will afford to the Government of the United Kingdom the right to continue to maintain the bases and other facilities at present occupied by their Service authorities within the State of Singapore and will permit the Government of the United Kingdom to make use of these bases and facilities as that Government may consider necessary for the purpose of assisting in the defence of Malaysia, and for Commonwealth defence and for the preservation of peace in South-East Asia.

In view of the wide scope of the introductory clauses of this Article, applying to Malaysia as a whole what had previously applied to Malaya, it is not clear why the word 'proviso' had been used. Further, the interpretation of the latter part of the Article would not appear, *prima facie*, to be open to question. It is a matter for the United Kingdom Government, and for that Government alone, to decide whether it is necessary to use bases and facilities on the island of Singapore for Commonwealth defence and the preservation of peace in South-East Asia. Yet the Malayan Prime Minister is reported as having made the following comments on these arrangements:

...the Tunku made it clear that sovereignty over the Singapore base remained with the future Malaysian Government and... although Singapore could not be regarded as a SEATO base, it could be used for SEATO purposes if Britain considered this necessary for the maintenance of security in South-East Asia. In every case, however, the future Malaysian Government would be consulted about the use of the base.[1]

The last line of this statement leaves it quite uncertain whether or not the consent of the Malaysian Government has to be obtained before the Singapore bases can be used by the United Kingdom Government for 'SEATO purposes'.

Whatever the correct legal interpretation of the two defence Agreements it is apparent that both relate to an area where political considerations must in practice be taken into significant account. Clearly the political reactions of the Government of Malaysia, and of the Governments of the constituent parts of the Federation, will be of great importance in deciding the practical application of the two Agreements. This underlines the need for the closest liaison between the Governments of Great Britain, Australia, New Zealand and Malaysia, and

[1] *Select Documents on Malaysia* (no. 1 of 1963), p. 6.

between their respective diplomatic and service representatives, to try to ensure that action contemplated under the Agreements is supported by all concerned.

On 9 August 1965 Singapore was separated from Malaysia, and became an independent sovereign State. The terms of separation were set out in an agreement dated 7 August between the Government of Malaysia and the Government of Singapore. Article V of the agreement provides that

(1) the parties will establish a joint defence council;

(2) the Government of Malaysia will afford 'such assistance as may be considered reasonable and adequate' for the external defence of Singapore, for which purpose the Government of Singapore is to provide units of its own armed forces;

(3) 'the Government of Singapore will afford to the Government of Malaysia the right to continue to maintain the bases and other facilities used by its military forces within Singapore and will permit the Government of Malaysia to make such use of these bases and facilities as the Government of Malaysia may consider necessary for the purpose of external defence';

(4) neither party will enter into any agreement with a foreign country detrimental to the independence and defence of the territory of the other.[1]

This agreement would appear to leave the legal rights of the United Kingdom Government and of the Australian Government to use Singapore bases and facilities singularly unclear. On 10 August Sir Robert Menzies informed Parliament that the Australian Government had recognised the State of Singapore and that it would establish diplomatic relations with Singapore at High Commissioner level. The Prime Minister added that the Australian Government was consulting with other governments, including those of Malaysia and Singapore, regarding 'various aspects of the separation', and regarded the 'continued and combined defence of the region' as a 'central and most important matter'.[2] As of the time of writing all relevant Commonwealth Governments seem to have acted on the assumption that pre-separation rights to bases and facilities at Singapore remain intact, but serious post-separation disputes between the Governments of Singapore and Malaysia suggest that such rights

---

[1] Department of Information, Kuala Lumpur, Siaran Akhbar (Information Bulletin), 8/65/109 (PM), 9 August 1965.

[2] *C.N.* vol. xxxvi (1965), pp. 504–5.

may have an insufficiently secure foundation until some new agreement is entered into between the United Kingdom and Singapore direct.

6. *Australia and the Malayan and Malaysian Defence Agreements*

The Government of Australia 'associated' itself with the United Kingdom–Malaya Defence Agreement of 12 October 1957 by a letter of 24 March 1959, the contents of which were acknowledged in a reply of 21 April 1959 by the Government of Malaya.[1] The central paragraph of the former letter is as follows:

As you know, the Commonwealth Strategic Reserve referred to in the [United Kingdom–Malayan] Agreement...includes Australian forces which are or may from time to time be serving in the Federation. Accordingly, the various provisions applicable to the Commonwealth Strategic Reserve, in particular the provisions dealing with the status of forces, apply in respect of these Australian forces.

The second letter, from the Malayan Government, confirms this understanding of the Australian Government.

Similarly, in a letter of 17 September 1963, one day after the creation of the Federation of Malaysia, the Australian Government referred to Article VI of the Agreement of 9 July 1963 and sought confirmation of its view that its association with the Agreement of 1957 henceforth applied to Malaysia. This confirmation was given in a reply from the Government of Malaysia on 18 September 1963.[1] In tabling these and related documents in Parliament on 25 September 1963 the Prime Minister made a statement on the defence of Malaysia, the last paragraph of which is in the following terms:

I therefore, after close deliberation by the cabinet, and on its behalf, inform the House that we are resolved, and have so informed the Government of Malaysia, and Governments of the United Kingdom and New Zealand and others concerned, that if, in the circumstances that now exist, which may continue for a long time, there occurs, in relation to Malaysia or any of its constituent States, armed invasion or subversive activity—supported or directed or inspired from outside Malaysia—we shall to the best of our powers and by such means as shall be agreed upon with the Government of Malaysia, add our military assistance to the efforts of Malaysia and the United King-

---

[1] For text of letters see *Select Documents on Malaysia* (no. 1 of 1963), p. 206.

dom in the defence of Malaysia's territorial integrity and political independence.[1]

The subsequent separation of Singapore from Malaysia on 9 August 1965 did not change the Australian Government's policy of full support for the territorial integrity and political independence of both States. While Sir Robert Menzies' statement of 10 August indicated that the particular Australian association with 'common defence' would require study in the light of the new circumstances, he pledged Australia's willingness to play its part, with other countries concerned, 'in continuing a common resistance to attacks upon the Malaysian area, an area which will still include Singapore'.[2]

7. *Indonesia's 'confrontation' of Malaysia*

A detailed account of Australia's post-war relationships with Indonesia will be given in chapter 6, as it is against this general background that the nature and consequences of President Sukarno's policy of 'confrontation' of Malaysia can best be considered. Here it is necessary only to point out that Sir Robert Menzies' statement of 25 September 1963, promising Australian support in the maintenance of Malaysia's territorial integrity and political independence, was made with full awareness of the risks to Australian–Indonesian relationships, if in the pursuit of the 'confrontation' policy Indonesian forces should meet Australian forces in combat.

The Australian Government's decision, announced by the Prime Minister, was not taken hastily. It followed a long period of diplomatic activity during which every effort was made by the Minister for External Affairs, Sir Garfield Barwick, to maintain friendly relations with Indonesia and to induce the Government of that country to seek an agreed and peaceful solution of its differences with the Government of Malaya regarding the creation of Malaysia. Only after the rejection by Sukarno of the report of the representative of the Secretary-General of the United Nations, after investigation in the area, that 'there is no doubt about the wishes of a sizeable majority of the peoples of these territories [Sabah and Sarawak] to join in the Federation of Malaysia'[3] and after the President had

---

[1] *Ibid.* p. 203.   [2] *C.N.* vol. xxxvi (1965), p. 505.
[3] *Select Documents on Malaysia* (no. 1 of 1963), p. 201.

reiterated his intention to 'crush' Malaysia, did the Australian Government reluctantly conclude that these risks must be taken. To have acted otherwise would have been to deny the validity of the Government's policy, consistently adhered to since it came to power in 1949, that the stability of the strategic area of Malaya was a matter of primary Australian concern.

Even after the statement of 25 September Australian political leaders engaged in no public recrimination of Indonesia; nor did the Australian Government show any signs of haste to take action which would have resulted in actual combat between Australian armed forces and Indonesian infiltrators within Malaysia. In due course military encounters on a small scale did in fact take place, both in Malaya, Borneo and the waters around Malaysia. These encounters were not played up, the broad governmental policy being to assume that 'confrontation' should be regarded as a kind of aberration, that the long-term interests of both Indonesia and Australia required mutual policies of friendly co-operation, and that Indonesia would find Australia ready to extend a sympathetic hand as soon as the aberration ceased. Meanwhile Australia continued to offer technical training in Australia, under the Colombo Plan, to Indonesian students, rejecting the argument in some Australian quarters that it should be discontinued.

8. *North West Cape Communication Station*

On 9 May 1963 an agreement was signed by the Australian Minister for External Affairs and the American Ambassador to Australia providing for the establishment by the United States Navy of a communication station at North West Cape, Western Australia. The Australian Government decided to submit the agreement to Parliament for its consideration, and a Bill to approve the agreement was passed by the House of Representatives on 22 May and by the Senate on 23 May 1963.[1]

In presenting the Bill to Parliament, Barwick said that the agreement covered the establishment of 'a naval communication station, a wireless station, nothing more and nothing less'. It would be under the sole control of the United States Govern-

---

[1] See *C.N.* vol. xxxiv (1963), no. 5, pp. 10–32, for text of the agreement and also for text of an agreement concerning the Status of United States Forces in Australia, together with Barwick's second reading speech.

ment. The title to the land would remain with the Australian Government, which would charge the United States as lessee a token rental only. Australia would have the right of access to the station at all times, and Australian forces would have the right to use its communication services. The station could not be used for any purpose other than defence communication without Australian consent. The agreement, which had a currency of twenty-five years, did not give Australia control of or access to the content of messages transmitted. Under Article 3 Australia had the right to consultation on any matters connected with the station and its use, which included consultation as to the effect of the station's use on any Australian interests, national or international. This right of consultation, however, did not imply any right of control over the station.

In his speech the Minister referred frequently to the ANZUS Treaty, the importance of which to Australia 'cannot be exaggerated'. He claimed that grant by Australia of the site for the station and assent to its establishment constituted 'a most important contribution by Australia to the mutual purpose of the ANZUS pact and beyond that to the security of the free world generally'.[1] The station would 'significantly increase the capacity of the United States to perform its part of the ANZUS pact',[2] and as well to play its part in maintaining world peace.

During the debate the Labour Party Opposition criticised the grant of sole control of the station to the United States and asserted that, if it came to power, it would re-negotiate the agreement with a view to securing greater Australian participation in its control. In effect, the Opposition refused to accept the Minister's assertion that 'unless it was desired to create unilateral right of veto on the use of the station (and it is not) joint operation is impracticable';[3] nor did it accept the claim that the United States would not have agreed to establish the station on any other basis than sole American control.

In his comments on the significance of the North West Cape Communication Station, Dr T. B. Millar stresses the importance of 'complete exactness' in determining the location of a shifting base such as a submarine armed with missiles, and of the 'correct receipt of messages which detail the targets and give the signal to fire'. First-class radio communications are needed for these purposes; in particular, a station must be capable of very

---

[1] Ibid. pp. 11–12.   [2] Ibid. p. 11.   [3] Ibid. p. 14.

low frequency transmissions if its messages are to be 'received at significant ranges by submerged vessels'. The North West Cape Station would have such capacity.[1]

Millar also points out that public discussion of the issue within Australia disclosed a degree of confusion between the relaying of a message to fire nuclear weapons and the initiation of an instruction to fire them. Further confusion arose from the tendency to equate control over despatching a message with control over despatching a missile. If the Americans wished to instruct a Polaris submarine to fire a missile they would despatch a message by some means whether or not the North West Cape Station existed; its establishment would merely help ensure that an accurate message was received. In his opinion it was 'hard to see what kind of control could be envisaged which would not constitute a veto power. If there is value in having the station there at all, this value applies most in an emergency, when any delay could be fatal.'[2]

Underlying Opposition and other criticism within Australia of sole American control of the communication station was, no doubt, fear that its establishment would attract enemy attention in a nuclear war. In Europe non-nuclear Allies of the United States have evidenced a desire to maintain a 'finger on the trigger', while American nuclear weapons in Great Britain could not be fired without prior British assent. If the United States was prepared to make such an agreement with the British regarding the firing of nuclear weapons from British soil, why should she not be prepared to agree that Australian assent must be obtained prior to despatch of a message instructing a submarine not in Australian waters to fire a missile? Obviously the two sets of circumstances were not identical, but the retaliatory consequences in each case might be the same. Remembering the Manus Island controversy,[3] the Opposition suspected that the Government was too ready to accept agreements with the United States involving some derogation of Australian sovereignty, and that it did not fight hard enough to maintain Australian rights.

In general, Australian public opinion accepted the North West Cape Agreement, but with a degree of uneasiness. There was a growing realisation—similar to that developed in Europe

---

[1] Millar, *Australia's Defence*, pp. 87–91.
[2] *Ibid.* p. 90.   [3] See p. 100 above.

at a much earlier stage—that military alliances involve disadvantages as well as advantages, and that the price to be paid for protection by a nuclear ally can, in the worst case, be extremely high.

9. *Despatch of Australian troops to Vietnam*

On 29 April 1965 Sir Robert Menzies announced in Parliament the Government's decision to commit a battalion of troops to South Vietnam as 'the most useful additional contribution which we can make to the defence of the region at this time'.[1] He reminded members of the House of Representatives that the Government, as early as 1962, had sent thirty military instructors to South Vietnam at the request of the Government of that country, later increased to 100; that six Caribou aircraft had also been sent; and that economic aid to South Vietnam amounted to about £1 million a year. The decision to commit a battalion had been taken after the closest attention to defence priorities.

This decision was opposed by the Leader of the Opposition, Arthur Calwell, 'firmly and completely'. In an effective speech he strongly criticised the Government's policy on Vietnam and claimed that it rested on three false assumptions, namely an erroneous view of the nature of the war in Vietnam; failure to understand the nature of the Communist challenge; and a false notion as to the interests of America and her allies. The Labour Party did not believe the decision served the immediate strategic interests of Australia. 'On the contrary', added Calwell, 'we believe that by sending one quarter of our pitifully small effective military strength to distant Vietnam, this Government dangerously denudes Australia and its immediate strategic environs of effective defence power.'[2]

The doubts expressed by Calwell were reflected in unprecedented discussion within Australia during ensuing months as to the wisdom of governmental policy on Vietnam. Much of the discussion took place in university 'teach-ins', the form of which echoed similar 'teach-ins' within the United States and Great Britain. Two exchanges of letters took place between a group of bishops and the Prime Minister, and the Government was subjected to heavy pressure to justify its policy. Somewhat

---

[1] *C.N.* vol. xxxvi (1965), no. 4, p. 179.   [2] *C.P.D.* 4 May 1966, p. 1102.

belatedly it bestirred itself to action, presumably having come to the conclusion that much of the opposition or uncertainty was to be found amongst voters who could not simply be written off as Communist or extreme Left Wing. The Department of External Affairs published in its May 1965 issue of *Current Notes* a substantial background article on Vietnam and subsequently issued two sets of documents on Vietnam, the first of which (*Information Handbook* no. 1 of 1965) included an impressive summary of various unsuccessful efforts which had been made by non-Communist countries or organisations to secure a peaceful settlement of the Vietnam problem. Sir Robert Menzies' press conference in London on 27 June after the Prime Ministers' Conference and in Canberra on 13 July were well publicised, while Paul Hasluck, who had succeeded Barwick as Minister for External Affairs on Barwick's appointment as Chief Justice of the High Court of Australia, boldly accepted an invitation to discuss Vietnam at the 'teach-in' held at Monash University, Melbourne, on 29 July.

Gradually criticism of Government policy was weakened by the rigidity of the Communist refusal to negotiate save on unacceptable terms, particularly after American bombing of North Vietnam had been discontinued for a period of 37 days in December 1965 and January 1966 and President Johnson had instituted an elaborate diplomatic peace offensive; yet doubts remained as to the priority accorded by the Government in sending Australian troops to Vietnam, in view of the slenderness of Australian resources in trained manpower and the nearness and urgency of Indonesian confrontation of Malaysia and the despatch of Australian combat troops to Borneo. In the event of Indonesian pressure on the Trust Territory of New Guinea or the Territory of Papua, from what source could further trained units of the Australian army be found?

In fact, the Government had been slow to respond to upward pressures over an extended period for a greater defence effort. Among the newspapers, the *Sydney Morning Herald* had for long urged the need to devote a higher percentage of the budget to defence purposes, and had published special articles detailing the directions in which it believed the money should be spent. In January 1964 the Australian Institute of Political Science held a most successful Summer School in Canberra, during which five papers were read and discussed. These were subsequently published as a book which sold widely. Several of the papers provided serious evidence that a critical reappraisal of Australia's defence needs was overdue, that she had the economic capacity to do more to meet such needs, and that the Government was lagging behind informed public opinion in its estimation of the nation's preparedness to accept additional burdens in the interest of Australian security.[1]

When therefore a number of changes were introduced by the Government during 1964 to improve the size and effectiveness of the Australian army[2] public opinion supported them, even though the most important, namely the introduction of a selective national service scheme under which young men were called up for service over a two-year period, with the obligation to serve overseas if necessary, ran counter to the long Australian tradition of opposition to conscription for military service outside Australia. Public acceptance of the principle of conscription for overseas service in time of technical peace should thus be regarded as a significant development, even though the numbers of men called up have not so far been great.

Criticism of the Government's decision to send a battalion of troops to Vietnam has been directed not merely to the merits of direct Australian involvement in the undeclared war in Vietnam, but also to the failure of the Menzies Government to build up the Australian army to the point where it could be regarded as reasonably adequate to meet the various international commitments into which Australia had entered. At the political level the controversy was revived when Mr Harold Holt, who in January 1966 succeeded Sir Robert Menzies as Prime Minister and Leader of the Liberal Party, announced in Parliament on 8 March the Government's decision to increase to approximately 4,500 men the number of Australian forces in Vietnam. The existing battalion, he said, would be replaced by a self-contained Australian 'task force' under Australian command embracing all personnel serving there. It would include headquarters, two infantry battalions, a Special Air Squadron (SAS), a flight of eight R.A.A.F. Iroquois helicopters, the flight of Caribou aircraft and the team of 100 army advisers already in Vietnam, together with substantial overall combat and logistic support

[1] See *Australia's Defence and Foreign Policy*, ed. John Wilkes (Angus and Robertson, Sydney, 1964).
[2] See Millar, *Australia's Defence*, pp. 125–6, for a summary of the new measures.

units. The two battalions would contain 'a proportion of fully trained and integrated national servicemen', as would 'all future substantial Australian army units deployed overseas in any theatre'.[1] This decision did not involve any increase in the current annual intake of 8,400 national servicemen.

Holt's announcement of the expanded Australian military contribution in Vietnam was strongly criticised by the Labour Party Opposition, whose Leader demanded a referendum before conscripts were sent to Vietnam. This demand was rejected by the Prime Minister.

10. *Summing up*

No aspect of foreign policy illuminates more clearly the changed assumptions of the Australian Government since Pearl Harbor than its policy in the field of defence. '...the first duty of a government is to ensure the safety of the nation...', said Menzies in his speech to Parliament of 20 April 1955.[2] The entry of Japan into the Second World War brought a direct threat to the security of Australia for the first time in her history. In Europe France had fallen, and Great Britain, fighting alone with Commonwealth and marginal Allied assistance in Europe, the Atlantic and the Middle East, was unable to send to the Pacific area naval and air reinforcements of an order sufficient to prevent or repel the Japanese attack on Malaya and Singapore. The strongest ties of sentiment between Australia and Great Britain could not obscure the fact that the United States alone had the military power to set limits to the creeping Japanese tide.

It was a Labour Party Prime Minister, John Curtin, who on 27 December 1941 published in an Australian newspaper an unhappily phrased statement which caused misgiving and perhaps resentment in Great Britain:

The Australian Government regards the Pacific struggle as primarily one in which the United States and Australia must have the fullest say in the direction of the democracies' fighting plan. Without any inhibitions of any kind, I make it quite clear that Australia looks to America, free of any pangs as to our traditional links or kinship with the United Kingdom...[3]

---

[1] *C.P.D.* 8 March 1966, pp. 27–8.
[2] *C.P.D.*, H. of R., vol. VI (1955), p. 53.
[3] *The Herald* (Melbourne), 27 December 1941; see p. 55 above for more detailed extract and comments.

But it was a Liberal–Country Party Prime Minister, Robert Gordon Menzies, who pursued an Australian initiative which resulted in the creation of the ANZUS alliance, of which Great Britain was not a member, and whose Government pressed for the establishment of a South-East Asia Treaty Organisation, which the British Government indicated its readiness to join only after some delay and hesitation.

Again, although it was a Labour Party Government which, during the Second World War, insisted on the return of Australian troops from the Middle East (after Japan entered the war) and refused British and American requests to allow some of them to be diverted for the defence of Burma, it was a Liberal–Country Party Government which, after the war, decided that in the foreseeable future it must be assumed that the primary sphere of Australian military operations must be, not the Middle East or Europe, but South-East Asia—a view eventually accepted by Great Britain. Agreement on this basic principle has led to valuable collaboration between Great Britain, Australia and New Zealand in ANZAM, in the Commonwealth Strategic Reserve in Malaya, in joint military operations in Malaya during the 'emergency', and in military support for Malaysia against Indonesian 'confrontation'. On the other hand, the Australian Government has not shrunk from the decision to send military forces to Vietnam although Great Britain—heavily involved in Malaysia—took no similar action.

In short, the facts of international life, as they have developed during and since the Second World War, have compelled *all* Australian Governments to concentrate their military attention on the Pacific area as a whole and South-East Asia in particular. These facts have also compelled all Australian Governments to recognise the diminution of decisive British military power and the accretion of American military power in the Pacific area which Europeans, but not Australians, can think of as the 'Far East'. The readiness of the British Labour Government, under Mr Harold Wilson, to maintain substantial military forces east of Suez despite the financial and other burdens involved, and, in particular, its readiness to defend Malaysia and Singapore against Indonesian 'confrontation', has been greatly appreciated in Australia. Nevertheless, Australians are compelled to read strictly the important 'limitations' on future British military capability outside Europe announced by the British Minister

for Defence on 25 February 1966 in his statement on the British
Defence Estimates, 1966. These limitations were outlined by
Mr Denis Healey as follows:

First, Britain must not undertake major operations of war except in
co-operation with allies. Secondly, we will not accept an obligation
to provide another country with military assistance unless it is prepared to provide us with the facilities we need to make such assistance
effective in time. Finally, there must be no attempt to maintain
defence facilities in an independent country against its wishes...
Further east [of the Mediterranean] we shall continue to honour
our commitments to our allies and to play our proper part in defending the interests of the free world. But the load must be more equit-
ably shared than in the past and we shall aim to make significant
economies by deploying our forces more realistically in accordance
with the political circumstances in which they are likely to operate.[1]

There is little disposition within Australia to question the need
for these limitations, or to criticise the British Government, which
has stated them publicly. At the same time most Australians
would expect their kinsmen in the United Kingdom to understand the degree of importance which they themselves attach to
the ANZUS alliance and, in a lesser degree, to SEATO, and
the reasons which have prompted the Australian Government
to accept an increasing military burden in Vietnam.

The Menzies Government came to power in December 1949.
Its activities since that date provide strong evidence of an energetic and consistent foreign policy in the defence field. The
desirability of such a policy is, of course, open to challenge by
those who believe that Australia, as a country permanently
anchored in the south-west Pacific below the southern rim of
Asia, should abjure all military alliances, concentrate on trying
to attract the goodwill of her Asian neighbours and, perhaps,
return all armed forces to Australian shores. Critics of the policy
outlined above are also entitled to point to the limitations of
SEATO, the obscurities of ANZAM, and the uncertainty as to
the precise purposes for which the Commonwealth Strategic
Reserve in Malaysia can be used.

Even those who accept in their entirety the foreign-policy
objectives in the defence field of the Menzies Government since
1949, including Australian involvement in Vietnam, are still
entitled to question and to criticise the domestic decisions and

[1] *British Defence Review* (G 42/a/SUB), 25 February 1966, pp. 8–9.

attitudes of the Government on defence matters designed to give effect to international obligations which have been assumed. Has the proportion of the total annual budget devoted to defence been adequate? Has the proportion of annual defence votes allocated to each of the three services been justified? Has the particular expenditure within each of the services on manpower, weapons and equipment been wise? Has Australia's overall contribution to her own security and the security of her allies and friends been responsible, prompt and far-sighted? Has Australia given sufficient attention to non-military aspects of security through such avenues as economic aid to underdeveloped countries and opportunities for technical training which together contribute to the political and economic stability of neighbouring countries? Has the Government taken the Australian Parliament and the Australian community sufficiently into its confidence in explaining, ahead of the event, the reasons for the important decisions it has felt compelled to take?[1]

In his speech of 20 April 1955 the Prime Minister, Mr Menzies, laid down a general principle which few thinking Australians would dispute:

We have sometimes been tempted to think that high pay and abundant leisure and good living conditions and good fun are in some way our absolute right. The least we are to do is to recognise that if, as is true, peace is indivisible, so responsibility for maintaining the peace is indivisible. We must do our share. We must not do less than others. We must be prepared to face up to our responsibility even though a price has to be paid for the carrying of burdens and the acceptance of novel responsibility.[2]

Ten years have passed since that statement was made, with the same Government in power. It is unlikely that future historians will take the view that the practical implementation of its defence policy since 1949 in terms of trained manpower, weapons, equipment and public explanation matched the diplomatic initiatives of the Menzies Government in that vital section of the field of foreign policy which is related to defence.

---

[1] For critical comments on these questions see especially Wilkes, *Australia's Defence and Foreign Policy*.   [2] *C.P.D.*, H. of R., vol. VI (1955), p. 53.

6

AUSTRALIAN RELATIONS WITH
ASIA (1945–1965)

An examination of Australian relations with Asia during the period which has elapsed since the end of the Second World War requires, ideally, substantial consideration of such relations before 1945, in order to underline significant changes which have taken place in Australian attitudes since the foundation of Australia in 1788. Such a task is well beyond the scope of this book. In any event, much original research has still to be done in this field, although an American, Professor Werner Levi, has already made a useful contribution.[1] In this chapter it is proposed to deal only in broad, general terms with Australian attitudes before 1945, stressing immigration policy, as necessary background to post-war attitudes towards Asia. In addition, a detailed account will be given of Australian relations since 1945 to four important Asian countries, namely Japan, India, China and Indonesia.

I. GENERAL RELATIONSHIPS

1. *Introductory*

The word 'Asia' is of course a geographical expression which suggests a degree of cultural similarity, political unity, and equality of economic development which simply does not exist. Any student of the traditional cultures of India, China and Japan is more likely to be impressed by diversities than by similarities, even though Japanese culture is substantially derivative from Chinese.[2]

The absurdity of regarding Asia as a political monolith becomes at once apparent when one remembers the undeclared

[1] Werner Levi, *Australia's Outlook on Asia* (Angus and Robertson, Sydney, 1958).
[2] See *Asia and Australia*, ed. John Wilkes (Angus and Robertson, Sydney, 1961), chapter 1, 'The cultural background', by J. D. Frodsham; *The Legacy of China*, ed. Raymond Dawson (Oxford University Press, 1964), especially chapters 1 and 7; also *Encyclopaedia Britannica, Book of the Year 1965*, Australia and New Zealand Supplement, 'Australia and New Zealand's northern neighbours', special report by Alan Watt.

war between India and Pakistan over Kashmir in 1965, the incursion of Chinese troops into India in 1962, Indonesian confrontation of Malaysia, the division of Korea and of Vietnam into two parts, and the depth of Cambodian suspicion of its adjoining neighbours, namely Thailand and Vietnam. It has been suggested that the only thing common to Asian countries is poverty,[1] but even here, as the same writer admits, Japan is a notable exception to the general pattern. Indeed, it is the very diversity of Asian countries which tends to make any examination of Australia's relations with Asia mainly a study of relations with individual States.

Nevertheless there are certain features common to all Asian States, though in varying degrees, which justify brief consideration of Australian relations with Asia as a whole. All such States resent the long period of domination of Asia by European countries which began with the discovery by Vasco da Gama of the sea-route to India in 1498 and reached its peak in the nineteenth century. The greatest resentment was felt by China, where pride in the ancient achievements of the 'Middle Kingdom' whose emperors possessed the 'mandate of heaven' was outraged by 'barbarians' from Europe. The least resentment was felt in Thailand, which over the centuries had managed to avoid becoming a European colony or being subjected to the degree of humiliating control suffered by China.

In their successful revolt against European domination during the twentieth century all Asian countries have supported policies directed against 'colonialism' and 'imperialism', as evidenced by continuing pressure upon 'imperialist' Powers—especially in the United Nations—to grant self-government and independence to their respective colonies with the minimum delay. The defeat of Russia by Japan in the war of 1904–5 showed what could be done by an Asian power. The Second World War, during which European prestige in Asia was reduced to a minimum, provided the opportunity. Asian nationalism, encouraged for their own ends by Communist countries—including mainland China after 1949—provided the motive force. Henceforth, for the foreseeable future, European presence in Asia, whether political, economic, military or cultural, must be based upon the consent of the country concerned.

[1] Richard Harris, 'Communism and Asia', *International Affairs*, vol. xxxviii, no. 1 (January 1963).

European nationals living in Asia could if necessary return to their metropolitan territories. Australians, living in a continent anchored off the southern rim of Asia, must try to come to terms with Asia. In descent, culture and outlook they had been Europeans, but it was no longer possible for them to think and act merely as Europeans. The first task was to understand their northern neighbours. The second task would be to exercise imagination and take initiatives in devising and executing policies designed to lead to friendly collaboration of mutual benefit to both, provided this could be achieved without destroying their own inherited and chosen values and way of life.

2. *Before 1945*

Werner Levi's account of Australian attitudes to Asia stresses the fact that until the Second World War, most Australians 'observed their country and its environment with the eyes of the European Briton most of the time'.[1] One important reason for this was the fact that information about Asia came largely through British channels; even outstanding Australians who lived in Asia, like Dr George Morrison or W. H. Donald, wrote mainly for British newspapers. For the most part, Australians were content to concentrate on the development of their isolated island continent, relying upon the protection of the British navy. They shared the tendency of nineteenth-century Europeans to regard Asians as people who belonged to inferior races.

British and Australian attitudes about the desirability of using Asian labour in Australia, however, varied considerably. Levi reminds us that

Captain Phillip's original instructions had advised him to look to Asia for labour. Governor King in 1804 had suggested bringing 'industrious' Chinese into the colony to grow cotton for the Chinese market and generally by their presence to produce 'the most desirable consequences'. On several occasions in the following years individual colonists had received permission to import Asian labour. Wakefield in 1829 clinched his argument for the colonization of Australia with the tentative advocacy of building 'a free bridge between the settlements and those numerous over-populated countries, by which, they are, as it were, surrounded'. Indians might be induced to work and play in Australia instead of drowning their

---

[1] Levi, *op. cit.* p. 3.

children in the sacred stream; and the Chinese, 'by far the most industrious and skilled Asiatics', might in the course of a century 'perhaps' convert 'this enormous wilderness into a fruitful garden'.[1]

Despite the eventual termination of convict transportation to Australia, however, and the readiness of Australian pastoralists to look to India for cheap labour, things did not work out that way. The introduction of Indians was opposed by workers who feared reduction in wage levels. The social argument against the introduction of Asians, 'destined to become basic and typical',[2] was also raised. The homogeneity of the population must not be threatened; 'at present', it was claimed, it was 'so unmixed in its composition as to promise to supply materials for the fabrication of a social and political state corresponding with that of the country from which it derives its origin'.[3]

It is unnecessary to trace here the course of immigration restrictions upon the entry of Asians imposed by the various Australian States following the arrival of substantial numbers of Chinese, especially after the discovery of gold in Australia. What is more important, in a study of foreign relations which includes the reactions of Asians to such restrictions, is to note the more objectionable arguments used by some Australians to justify them. As Levi says, 'The racist argument...was not lacking...'[4] It is this type of argument which has done most harm to the Australian image in Asia. Non-European peoples remember it when more acceptable grounds for Australia's restrictive immigration have been forgotten or simply not heard, and it engenders strong resentment. It is therefore essential that Australians themselves should be aware of extreme statements made by their fellow-countrymen in the past, however untypical of current statements, if they are to understand the strength of Asian reaction to the so-called 'White Australia' policy.

In the second half of the nineteenth century Australian gold-miners who objected to the competition of Chinese on the gold-fields referred to Chinese in petitions for restriction of immigration as 'swarms of human locusts, Mongolians with filthy habits and repulsive to the feelings of Christians'.[5] In 1858 an attorney-general of the State of New South Wales could argue that '"so

---

[1] *Ibid.* p. 10. [2] *Ibid.* p. 12.
[3] *Ibid.* quoted at p. 12 from *Report from the Committee on Immigration, 1841*, p. 4.
[4] *Ibid.* p. 12. [5] *Ibid.* p. 13.

serious an evil as having half the population of an inferior race" could not be tolerated'.[1]

In 1894 Great Britain signed a Commercial Treaty with Japan which included a clause permitting nationals of each party freedom of entrance to and travel within the country of the other party. Under the Treaty, British colonies could accede. Despite the desire for trade between Australia and Japan, Australian reactions against possible accession were so strong that Great Britain became concerned lest her own trade with Japan be prejudiced. In Australia it was argued that any advantages from accession would be 'far outweighed by the evils accompanying an invasion of the "ungovernable multitudes of Japanese subjects"'.[2] Objection was taken to the introduction of an 'extraneous and inferior element'[3] into the population. The result would be 'lamentable degradation of race'.[3]

Even as late as 1921 individual members of the Federal Parliament still expressed themselves at times in terms which any Asian would interpret as racial. Thus, on 21 April of that year Mr Anstey (A.L.P.) declared that 'There is no government, no law, or no power which could compel the people of Australia by reason of their peculiar psychology to fight side by side with an Asiatic race against a white man's country'.[4] Some six months later Mr McGrath (A.L.P.) affirmed that 'if ...war should break out between the United States of America and Japan, with Great Britain as the ally of the latter, not one Australian youth will leave these shores to fight with any yellow race against a white people'.[5]

It is perhaps a matter for irony that Australian appreciation of the virtues of the Japanese increased considerably after Japan had demonstrated, by defeating Russia in war, her military and industrial capacity. There was in Australia and elsewhere 'much and widespread admiration of Japan's military prowess and the irreproachable behaviour of the Japanese warriors'.[6] In 1905 the Commonwealth Immigration Act was amended to make it less objectionable to the Japanese by substituting an immigration test 'in any prescribed language' for a test in a 'European language'. An extraordinary motion was actually

---

[1] Levi, *op. cit.* pp. 13–14.   [2] *Ibid.* pp. 18–19.
[3] *Ibid.* p. 19.   [4] *C.P.D.* vol. xcv (1921), p. 7,644.
[5] *C.P.D.* vol. xcvii (1921), p. 11,791.   [6] Levi, *op. cit.* p. 31.

proposed in Parliament, though without success, in the following terms:

That...in view of the facts that the Japanese people have placed themselves in the front rank of civilised nations; that they have proved themselves to be one of the most progressive peoples of the world; that, as a nation, they have become the honoured and trusted friend and ally of the British people, and therefore of the British Empire; because of their high moral character; and because they have become one of the greatest naval and military powers of the world; the time has arrived for differentiating the Japanese people from other Asiatic races with whom they have been impliedly grouped under the Immigration Restriction Act of 1901, and for placing them in their relationship to the people of Australia, upon the same footing of international amity as that which is now extended to European peoples.[1]

Official statements by Australian political leaders, especially after the foundation of the Commonwealth in 1901, did not echo the cruder grounds advanced in support of a policy designed to restrict the entry of non-Europeans for permanent residence in Australia. Speaking on the Immigration Restriction Bill 1901, the Attorney-General, Mr Alfred Deakin, denied that the Bill was 'based upon any claim of superiority' or reflected a judgement by the Australian people of 'the mental and moral status of the Japanese'.[2] He praised the 'inexhaustible energy' of the Japanese and other 'alien races', and 'their endurance'—which made them, in view of their low standard of living, formidable competitors—but claimed that they were 'incapable of being assimilated' in Australia.[3] Japan was amongst the most civilised nations in the world, but this was not the point. 'All that is necessary for us to urge...is that these people do differ from us in such essentials of race and character as to exclude the possibility of any advantageous admixture...'[4]

The various Australian States became one federal Commonwealth in 1901. During the first federal elections in that year, all three political parties agreed in supporting a policy of restriction of non-European immigration for permanent residence.[5] The experience of Queensland, which alone of the Australian

[1] *Ibid.* quoted at p. 32.
[2] J. A. La Nauze, *Alfred Deakin* (Melbourne University Press, 1965), p. 280.
[3] *Ibid.* p. 279.   [4] *Ibid.* quoted at p. 280.
[5] See A. T. Yarwood, *Asian Migration to Australia* (Melbourne University Press, 1964), p. 19.

States had adhered to the Anglo-Japanese Commercial Treaty of 1894, in the hope of securing trade benefits with Japan without risking embarrassment over the entry or presence of Japanese citizens, did not encourage the remaining States to take similar risks. An authoritative commentator has expressed the view that,

Instead of achieving an harmonious relationship with Japan, Queensland by abandoning her freedom of action in the vital field of immigration control had laid herself open to the embarrassment of continuous diplomatic intervention [by Japan]. New South Wales after accepting the 'education test' compromise, remained free from such pressures...[1]

The actual method of control adopted in the Commonwealth Restriction Act 1901 was 'a version of the so-called Natal Test, which had effected exclusion in practice by defining a prohibited immigrant as one who failed to write out, in any language of Europe, an application in a certain form'.[2] This method had been pressed upon Australian representatives at the Colonial Conference held in London in 1897 by Mr Joseph Chamberlain, Secretary of State for the Colonies, who had warned that the British Government would disallow Acts of Australian colonies restricting immigration on the ground of race or colour. It was not until 1958 that the 'dictation test' method of controlling non-European immigration to Australia was abolished.

In short, there is evidence during much of Australia's history of an Australian attitude towards Asians based upon ignorance and a sense of superiority, although it is still somewhat difficult to determine just how widespread was this attitude. As the nineteenth century ended and the twentieth century began there is evidence of greater caution and more doubt in public statements. Political leaders defended the restrictive immigration policy in more measured terms, particularly after the foundation of the Commonwealth, stressing the need to ensure that migrants were readily assimilable and the need to maintain the Australian standard of living. The shock of the Second World War was the catalyst which produced deep-seated changes in the Australian outlook upon Asia.

[1] A. T. Yarwood, *op. cit.* p. 18.   [2] La Nauze, *op. cit.* p. 281.

3. *Since 1945*

The primary cause of greatly increased Australian interest in Asia since the end of the Second World War was the Japanese threat to the security of Australian metropolitan territory. The fall of Singapore, hitherto regarded as an 'impregnable' bastion, and the occupation by Japanese forces of the Netherlands East Indies brought Australians face to face with danger to their homeland for the first time in their history. Bitter fighting took place in Papua and New Guinea, Darwin was bombed, Japanese midget submarines penetrated the defences of Sydney harbour and vessels were sunk off the coast. The naval battles of the Coral Sea and Midway relieved fears of actual Japanese invasion, but the old complacency about British ability to defend the Malayan area in a major war if Great Britain were heavily engaged elsewhere disappeared.

It was natural and inevitable that, after the war, the Australian Government should decide to concentrate upon plans for the strategic defence of the South-East Asian area, as distinct from the Middle East or Europe. The development and execution of this policy has been described in detail in chapter 5. There passing reference was made also to the view of the Menzies Government—foreshadowed to some extent by its Labour Party predecessors—that a purely military approach to the solution of Asian problems was inadequate; in addition, the basic problem of poverty must be dealt with if political stability was to be achieved. While Minister for External Affairs, Spender was personally responsible for taking a strong Australian initiative in the creation of the Colombo Plan, which under his successor, Casey, became a significant feature of Australian foreign policy. During his first visit as Minister for External Affairs to South-East Asia in 1951, Casey saw the urgent need for greatly increased Australian diplomatic representation in that area, and it is to him that the credit is due of putting such a policy into effect.

The Colombo Plan[1] stemmed from the meeting of Commonwealth Foreign Ministers in Colombo in January 1950, and was

[1] For a description of the origins, nature, organisation and practical working of the Colombo Plan, see address by Casey published in *Current Notes*, vol. xxv (1954), pp. 11–24; also L. P. Singh, *The Colombo Plan, Some Political Aspects* (Working Paper no. 3, Australian National University, 1963).

launched formally on 1 July 1951. First sponsored by Commonwealth countries alone to help improve the economies of under-developed countries in South and South-East Asia, membership gradually expanded to include not only Great Britain, India, Pakistan, Ceylon, Australia and New Zealand, but also the United States of America, Afghanistan, Burma, Bhutan, Cambodia, Indonesia, Japan, the Republic of Korea, Laos, Malaya, The Maldives, Nepal, North Borneo, the Philippines, Sarawak, Singapore, Thailand and the Republic of Vietnam. In addition, Brunei, though not an actual member, has received some assistance.

Donor members entered into bilateral arrangement with recipient members for economic development and technical assistance purposes. Under the Technical Co-operation Scheme provision was made for the establishment of a Council with headquarters in Colombo, where a Bureau for Technical Co-operation was also set up under a Director with limited co-ordinating and administrative powers. At the ministerial level annual meetings take place in a 'Consultative Committee' to review the progress of the Plan. These meetings rotate from one member country to another, with the result that interest in the Colombo Plan as a whole is stimulated in the host country, while visiting delegates gain a better understanding of the problems of the country where the meeting is held.

Australian expenditure under the Colombo Plan to 30 June 1965 amounted to £A58,641,744. Of this total, expenditure on economic development accounted for £A41,295,157, while £A17,346,587 was spent on technical assistance.[1] Under its technical assistance programme Australia had made by the same date 5,920 awards for a wide range of training in Australia, and also 4,103 correspondence training awards; 682 Australian experts had been sent to Asian countries for varying periods to act as technical advisers.[2] When there is added to the number of Colombo Plan trainees in Australia the much larger group of Asian students, whose parents have private means, studying in Australian schools, universities and other educational establishments, the significance of this post-war development in Australian–Asian relations becomes immediately apparent.

By 1965 the number of Asian (and some African) students and

[1] *Commonwealth of Australia Year Book* (1965), p. 1,226.   [2] *Ibid.* p. 1,227.

trainees actually in Australia had risen to more than 12,000. An influx of this size adds appreciably to the demand for more adequate Australian teaching resources and educational facilities. The visitors acquire technical and other skills, live with their Australian colleagues as equals—sometimes in 'International Houses'—participate in sport and other club activities, and generally get to know how Australians think and act. In return, Australian associates are gaining personal impressions of Asian ways and outlook unprecedented in Australian history. Direct contact of this kind and on this scale can scarcely fail to lower barriers to understanding.

Moreover, during the nineteenth century most Asians who came to Australia were the least educated of their fellow-countrymen. Those who now come to study under the Colombo Plan are selected by their governments for their ability and promise; while those who pay for their own training come from social groups who have been successful in their own countries.

Many thousands of Australians have visited Asian countries since 1945, especially businessmen in search of trade, tourists, parliamentarians and students. Australia now has diplomatic representation in Japan, the Republic of Korea, the Philippines, Thailand, the Republic of Vietnam, Cambodia, Laos, Malaysia, Singapore, Indonesia, Burma, India, Pakistan and Ceylon. A network of very active Trade Commissioners has been developed through this area, including Hong Kong. Through military alliances and arrangements described in chapter 5, Australian armed forces (land, sea or air) have served in or around Malaya, Singapore, Sabah, Sarawak, Thailand and Vietnam at the request of the relevant governments.

In Australian universities, substantial numbers of students study aspects of Asian history as part of their general History studies, and a growing number of specialists take courses in the Chinese, Japanese or Indonesian languages. Within the Faculty of Oriental Studies at the Australian National University, Canberra, for instance, there are Departments of Chinese, Japanese, Indonesian Languages and Literature, Asian Civilisation and South Asian and Buddhist Studies.

The dictation test was formally abolished in 1958 as the means of controlling non-European immigration to Australia. In its place the Government substituted, to use the words of the Minister for Immigration, Mr Downer, the 'simple expedient of an entry permit'.[1] Since it came to power in 1949, the Menzies Government has maintained the broad policy of restricting entry of non-Europeans into Australia for permanent residence, but on the whole it has administered the law with greater flexibility than its predecessor in office, endeavouring to avoid giving unnecessary offence to sensitive Asian governments and peoples. A greater degree of liberality and humanity in administration was particularly evident while Mr Harold Holt was Minister for Immigration from 1949 to 1956. Asians have been admitted to Australia for permanent residence under ministerial discretion, though the numbers are small and there has been official reluctance to supply detailed information about the decisions taken which might enable public opinion to understand and test the principles applied. Thus many Asians married to Australians have been admitted, including some 500 Japanese wives of Australian troops who served in Korea or Japan.

Unfortunately, any publicised exclusion of an Asian, whatever the facts may be, can in one day outweigh the goodwill built up by years of sensible decisions. Relations with the Philippines, for instance, have been seriously and adversely affected by the refusal of Australian governments to allow two particular Philippines citizens to migrate to Australia. While the Labour Party was still in power, Mr Arthur Calwell refused an application by Sergeant Gamboa, a Filipino in the United States Army. Although this decision was reversed by Mr Holt in due course, great publicity was given in the Philippines to the earlier refusal, which was greatly resented. Yet in 1964 a member of a well-known Philippine family, Mr Aurelio Locsin, was also refused permission to migrate—on this occasion with a Liberal–Country Party Government in power. Public opinion was outraged in the Philippines, where it was seriously suggested in some quarters that the entry of Australian visitors should be denied and Australian goods boycotted. The damage done to the Australian image in Asia as a whole by this one decision has been substantial.

Strangely enough, all Australian political parties have been insensitive to the deep-seated modification which has been taking place in the attitude of thinking Australians towards their Asian neighbours in the post-war years. While still determined

[1] *C.P.D.*, H. of R., vol. xix (May 1958), p. 1,396.

to maintain the basic homogeneity of their population, Australians have mixed easily with the many thousands of Asians who have entered the country for educational and other purposes. Australian involvement in the difficult problems—political, economic and military—of South-East Asia in particular and Asia in general is now so direct and substantial that one would have expected political parties to be ready to risk conceivable electoral reactions to any governmental decision to introduce a more flexible immigration policy.

Fortunately there are recent signs that the parties have sensed the wind of change affecting a widening section of Australian opinion regarding immigration policy. Recently the Labour Party removed from its official platform the offensive phrase 'White Australia', though the extent to which this decision will influence some future Labour Minister for Immigration in the direction of greater liberality towards the admission of Asians has yet to be demonstrated. On the Government side concrete evidence of readiness to move with the times is now available.

The successor to Sir Robert Menzies as Prime Minister, Mr Harold Holt, made his first general statement on Government policy in the House of Representatives on 8 March 1966. In an important section of the statement dealing with immigration, Holt said that the Government had felt that a review of the restrictive aspects of Australian immigration policy was desirable, in view of Australia's increasing involvement in Asian developments. He referred in passing to rapid growth of trade, the increasing number of aid projects in the area, the numbers of Asian students in Australia, the expansion of military effort, the scale of diplomatic contact and the growth of tourism. He then reiterated in the following words the reasons for adherence to the broad principles of policy adhered to in the past:

It is...important that there should be a clearer understanding in Asia of our policy...It is certainly not based on any false notion of superiority. We are fully aware that many of the peoples of Asia can point to cultures dating back centuries before those of Western Europe. But, in these modern times, every country reserves to itself the right to decide what the composition of its population shall be; it has regard to the preservation of standards and of national characteristics and to the maintenance of the essential homogeneity of its people. Australia derives strength from its unity and a community life free from serious minority and racial problems. All countries in

South-East Asia maintain restrictions against immigration to serve their own national policies. Our basic policy has been firmly established since the beginning of our Federation. It is widely supported. But it has been the wish of the Government, as it would be of the community at large, that the policy should be administered with a spirit of humanity and with good sense.[1]

The Prime Minister added that the Government had 'decided on some modification and a degree of liberalisation'[1] of current policy. Details would be announced by the Minister for Immigration, but he proposed to state immediately one important change. Whereas non-Europeans admitted to Australia under long-term entry permits had had to complete fifteen years in Australia before applying for resident status and Australian citizenship, in future application in such cases could be made after five years—the same length of time applicable for naturalisation application by settlers from Europe.

On 9 March Mr Hubert Opperman, Minister for Immigration, described in detail the changes now approved.[2] He reminded Parliament that 'several significant reforms' had been introduced in 1956, 1957 and 1964. In 1956 people already settled in Australia became eligible to be naturalised; admission for permanent residence of immediate relatives of Australian citizens was authorised; and it was made possible for highly qualified people to come to Australia for indefinite stay, though under temporary permits. During the following year it was decided that non-Europeans admitted on temporary permits could be naturalised after fifteen years' stay. In 1964 the rules governing entry of persons of mixed descent were eased.

In elaborating upon the Prime Minister's statement that non-European people already in Australia under temporary permit, but likely to remain indefinitely, could henceforth apply for naturalisation after five years, the Minister made it clear that not everyone admitted to Australia for limited temporary residence would be entitled to stay indefinitely. In particular, 'it would be quite wrong and most unfair to the development of countries whence they came to offer to the 12,000 Asian students in Australia the right to settle here after five years study. The objective of admitting these young people, to use educational facilities which are both expensive to the Australian Government and in great demand, is to help the students'

---

[1] *C.P.D.* 8 March 1966, p. 34.   [2] *C.P.D.* 9 March 1966, pp. 68–70.

homelands by increasing their numbers of qualified people.'[1] The two main examples of people affected by the elimination of the fifteen-year rule were

the highly qualified Asians admitted in recent years for 'indefinite stay' but on temporary entry permits; and Chinese admitted before 1956 who, if they left Australia, could only go back to Communist China.[1]

These had been allowed to stay on in Australia, but, lacking the status of settlers and citizens, had been unable to bring their wives and children.

Opperman then announced a second governmental decision under which application for entry by 'well qualified' people wishing to settle in Australia would be considered

...on the basis of their suitability as settlers, their ability to integrate readily, and their possession of qualifications which are in fact positively useful to Australia. They will be able after five years' stay on temporary permits to apply for resident status and citizenship. They will be able to bring their immediate families with them on first arrival.[2]

No annual quota was contemplated, but the numbers entering were likely to be 'somewhat greater than previously'.[3] The changes were not intended to meet general labour shortages or to permit the large-scale admission of workers from Asia.

The Minister listed seven examples of persons who, under the new decision, would be admitted in numbers greater than previously:

persons with specialised technical skills for appointments for which local residents were not available; persons of high attainment in the arts and sciences, or of prominent achievement in other ways; persons nominated by responsible authorities or institutions for specific important professional appointments, which otherwise would remain unfilled; executives, technicians, and other specialists who have spent substantial periods in Australia, and who have qualifications or experience in positive demand here; businessmen who in their own countries have been engaged in substantial international trading and would be able to carry on such trade from Australia; persons who have been of particular and lasting help to Australia's interest abroad in trade, or in other ways; and persons who by former

---

[1] *Ibid.* p. 68.   [2] *Ibid.* pp. 68–9.   [3] *Ibid.* p. 69.

residence in Australia or by association with us have demonstrated an interest in or identification with Australia that should make their future residence here feasible.

Where the governments of other countries might be concerned over loss of qualified people, there would be appropriate consultation.

The Ministerial statement concluded as follows:

Our primary aim in immigration is a generally integrated and predominantly homogeneous population. A positive element in the latest changes is that which will admit selected non-Europeans capable of becoming Australians and joining in our national development. Both the policy and the rules and procedures by which it is effected cannot remain static and must be constantly reviewed. Though redefined from time to time, they must be administered in accordance with the law, on principles decided by the Government, with justice to individuals and for the future welfare of the Australian people as a whole.[2]

These decisions of the Holt Government on immigration to Australia are of fundamental importance in the development of Australian foreign policy and the search for friendly relations with non-European countries. They will not satisfy many people, both inside and outside Australia, who believe that still more liberal conditions of entry for permanent residence should have been adopted.[3] Yet they are not only reasonable and defensible in themselves, but also suitably adapted to current Australian public opinion as a whole. They have been well received by the Australian Press, while there have already been some echoes of favourable overseas reaction. If the new rules are administered humanely and sympathetically, and are adapted from time to time to meet changing circumstances, both domestic and external, they can contribute substantially to the building-up of new, more co-operative and more stable relations with non-European countries, especially those in Asia.

In short, during the past twenty-five years the attitude of Australians towards Asians has suffered a 'sea-change'. This is not to suggest, of course, that they have suddenly cast aside their European cultural heritage and wish to become Chinese,

---

[1] *C.P.D.* 9 March 1966, p. 69.　　　　　　[2] *Ibid.* pp. 69–70.
[3] For wider proposals made by the Australian Immigration Reform Group, see *Immigration: Control or Colour Bar?*, ed. Kenneth Rivett (Melbourne University Press, 1962).

Japanese and Indians. But the old physical and intellectual isolation from Asia is dying fast if it is not already dead. The great majority of Australians are now keenly aware that the future of their own country is inevitably wrapped up with the future of Asia. If one reflects for a moment upon the influence upon the Australian outlook of the Colombo Plan; other aid projects carried out under United Nations auspices; military involvement in South-East Asia; trade developments, especially with Japan; contact with thousands of Asians studying in Australia; the activities of Radio Australia, which broadcasts programmes in several Asian languages and gives much-appreciated lessons in English to overseas listeners; improved Press and radio coverage of Asian news; recent changes in immigration policy; Australian membership of the Economic Commission for Asia and the Far East (ECAFE) and readiness to contribute substantial capital to the new Asian Development Bank; emergency food grants to India and financial contributions to the Indus Waters Scheme—it is impossible to believe seriously that Australians are still living in the nineteenth century in their outlook on Asia. Moreover, if it can justly be said that Australians have still a great deal to learn about Asia, Asians also have something to learn about Australia. It would not be strange if countries like China, India and Japan, proud of their ancient traditions, tend to regard Australia as culturally underdeveloped. It is sufficient, perhaps, to point out in reply that in many respects Australia is a very developed country with things to teach, for instance in the fields of Parliamentary Democracy and Law; nor is it wise to underestimate her achievements in certain scientific fields, such as medicine and radio-astronomy, in the arts and in industrial know-how. Respect and interest is required in both directions if mutually beneficial co-operation is to be achieved.

II. RELATIONS WITH PARTICULAR ASIAN COUNTRIES SINCE 1945

1. *Japan*

Australian relations with Japan since 1945 have an exceptional quality, both negative and positive. To all Australians Japan was *the* enemy during the Second World War. Before Pearl

Harbor, Australian forces were heavily involved in the Middle East, where they made a significant contribution to eventual Allied victory. Most foreigners and many Britishers are unaware or have forgotten the substantial Australian contribution under the Empire Air Training Scheme to the composition of the Royal Air Force. During the war members of the Royal Australian Air Force who died or were presumed dead totalled 10,562; of these, no fewer than 5,397 died in the European theatre, and 1,135 in the Middle East.[1]

But whereas the figure of Hitler tended to evoke in Australia anger, and the figure of Mussolini derision, the image of Japanese militarism stimulated a reaction approximating to hatred. There were a number of reasons for this difference of attitude towards Japan. Europe and the Middle East were far away; the Pacific and South-East Asia were on Australia's door-step. For the first time Australian metropolitan territory seemed threatened by a ruthless enemy. The fall of Singapore was a severe blow to Australian confidence, and adaptation to the notion that American rather than British power must in the foreseeable future underpin Australian security was a painful process. Finally, Japanese treatment of prisoners of war,[2] especially those who were forced to work on the Burma–Siam railway, was regarded as brutal and unforgivable.

The negative reaction of Australians to Japanese during and for some time after the war is understandable. Far more surprising is the gradual development, since signature of the Japanese Peace Treaty in 1951, of an attitude of acceptance if not of actual friendship, which has permitted a surprising degree of mutually beneficial co-operation to develop between the two countries, particularly in the field of trade. This extraordinary change in outlook within a period of less than fifteen years requires some examination.

Few countries exist which, at first sight, seem more different from one another than Japan and Australia. These differences are not limited to such features as geographical area, population and climate; they include, more significantly, language and cultural tradition. Japan has an ancient civilisation which

---

[1] John Herington, *Air Power over Europe 1944–45* (Australian War Memorial, Canberra, 1963), pp. 508–9.

[2] For detailed accounts of Japanese treatment of prisoners of war see Wigmore, *The Japanese Thrust*, Part III, written by A. J. Sweeting; also Lord Russell of Liverpool, *The Knights of Bushido* (Cassell, London, 1958).

measures its history in centuries if not millennia. Australia was founded in 1788, and thinks in terms of decades rather than centuries.

Japan's tradition was military and autocratic, practical power being exercised by hereditary commanders-in-chief (Shoguns) under the nominal sway of emperors, until the abolition of the Shogunate system in 1868. The sumurai caste followed in theory the principles of bushido, the way of the warrior, which demanded absolute and unquestioning obedience to the head of the clan of which one was a member. Warriors were supposed to die in battle or commit suicide—prisoners of war, including Japanese prisoners, had no rights.

Australia began as a penal settlement. Until the Second World War no wars had been fought on its soil. Conquest of difficult terrain developed a degree of individualism which showed itself, amongst other ways, in at least verbal lack of respect for authority. The Australian tradition is civilian, not military, members of large voluntary armies in two world wars priding themselves on disrespect for officers off the battle-field. Self-government and independence were won without revolution or domestic war, along lines determined by the British parliamentary system and British respect for the rule of law.

Even in modern Japan, form seems often as important as substance—in a good Japanese restaurant, what the food is served on or in and how it is served is almost as significant as the food itself. Etiquette is of great importance—except to members of the modern *avant garde*—and there is a highly sophisticated aesthetic tradition.

The Australian, on the other hand, has been brought up in a tradition of earthy practicality, directness of speech and distrust of etiquette and polite forms, which he often regards as hypocritical if not effeminate. Australian painting tends to reflect the clear, harsh sunlight of a dry continent; Japanese art is more subdued and suggestive; in Japanese literature meaning is often ambiguous.

Immediately after the Second World War leaders of all Australian political parties faithfully reflected public opinion at large in demanding a tough peace with Japan. This attitude was personified in the person of Dr Evatt while Minister for External Affairs, although some modification in practice rather than theory became visible after 1947. The most succinct statement of the Labour Government's views on the peace settlement in the Pacific was made by him on 17 August 1947 in a report on his recent visit to Japan:

The first principle of our policy has always been the safety and security of the Pacific, including our own country. That calls for the disarmament and demilitarisation of Japan, destruction of its capacity to wage war, and a sufficient degree of supervision under the peace treaty to prevent the regrowth of war-making capacity. The second principle has been the encouragement of democracy in Japan, which involves the gradual growth of the social, political and economic system.[1]

Evatt's energies were largely directed towards trying to ensure that the Far Eastern Commission, consisting of representatives of eleven countries which participated in the war against Japan, should adopt a Basic Post-Surrender Policy incorporating Australian views, and that General MacArthur, as Supreme Commander of Allied Forces in Japan, should put it into effect. In due course, after much debate and delay, the Far Eastern Commission did in fact adopt on 19 June 1947 a Basic Post-Surrender Policy which, while not incorporating Australian views in their entirety, can only be described as 'tough'.[2] Its broad objectives were stated in the following terms:

To complete the task of physical and spiritual demilitarization of Japan by measures including total disarmament, economic reform designed to deprive Japan of power to make war, elimination of militaristic influences, and stern justice to war criminals, and requiring a period of strict control; and

To help the people of Japan in their own interest as well as that of the world at large to find means whereby they may develop within the framework of a democratic society an intercourse among themselves and with other countries along economic and cultural lines that will enable them to satisfy their reasonable individual and national needs and bring them into permanently peaceful relationships with all nations...[3]

The means prescribed for achieving these objectives included complete disarmament and demilitarisation and elimination of the influence of militarism; encouragement of a desire for individual liberties, especially freedom of religion, assembly and association, speech and the Press; together with the formation of

---

[1] *C.N.* vol. xviii (1947), p. 470.
[2] For full text, see *ibid.* pp. 420-5.   [3] *Ibid.* p. 420.

democratic and representative organisations. Japan was to be permitted to 'maintain such industries as will sustain her economy and permit the exaction of just reparations in kind, but not those which would enable her to rearm for war'.[1] Japan was 'not to have any army, navy, air force, secret police organisation, or any civil aviation, or gendarmerie', but only adequate civilian police forces.[2] The formation of trade unions was to be encouraged, both in industry and agriculture.[3] Large family combines (Zaibatsu) were to be dissolved and individuals prohibited from holding important positions in the economic field where there were grounds for believing they could not be trusted to direct Japanese economic effort solely towards peaceful and democratic ends.[4] If much of this massive programme fell by the wayside, this was due not to any lack of effort by Evatt but to the change in the post-war situation and to the personality and power of General MacArthur. The United States came gradually to regard Japan not as a defeated enemy but as a possible ally in resisting Communist encroachment.

Evatt also pressed Australia's claims for a share of institutional responsibility for the post-war settlement. After a 'preliminary skirmish'[5] his protest against Australia being excluded was successful in securing Australian representation when the Japanese surrender was accepted on the U.S.S. *Missouri* in Tokyo Bay. He pressed strongly for the establishment in Washington of a Far Eastern Commission composed of Small as well as Great Powers, contrary to original American proposals.[6] When finally established, it was the function of this Commission to determine broad lines of policy towards occupied Japan, while an Allied Council for Japan in Tokyo, consisting of representatives of the United States, the Soviet Union, China and the British Commonwealth was to advise the Supreme Commander, General MacArthur, on matters of substance, 'the exigencies of the situation permitting'. The original Commonwealth member of the Allied Council for Japan, representing the United Kingdom, India, Australia and New Zealand, was an Australian, Professor MacMahon Ball, who held office from April 1946 until his resignation in August 1947. He was succeeded by other

---

[1] *Ibid.* p. 421.   [2] *Ibid.* p. 422.   [3] *Ibid.* p. 423.   [4] *Ibid.* p. 424.
[5] *Australia in World Affairs, 1956–60*, ed. Norman Harper and Gordon Greenwood (Cheshire, Melbourne, 1963), quoted at p. 245.
[6] For the earliest American proposals, see G. H. Blakeslee, *The Far Eastern Commission* (U.S. Department of State, 1953), pp. 2–5.

Australians, namely Mr Patrick Shaw (1947–49) and by Lt.-
Col. W. R. Hodgson (December 1949–52). When the Japanese
Treaty came into force in 1952, both the Far Eastern Commis-
sion and the Allied Council for Japan ceased to exist.

Evatt was also successful in strengthening the impact of the
Australian 'presence' in Japan during the pre-Treaty period,
when an Australian was appointed as Commander-in-Chief of
the British Commonwealth Occupation Force, and when an
Australian judge became President of the International Military
Tribunal for the Far East, which dealt with major war crimes.

Professor MacMahon Ball has given detailed accounts of the
problems he encountered on the Allied Council—one written in
1948 coloured to some extent by recent doubts and frustration,[1]
and the other written in 1963, when his views had mellowed with
time and with experience of Japanese developments during the
post-Treaty period.[2] On the latter occasion he pointed out that
'status did not necessarily give influence, still less substantial
power'.[3] As the four Great Powers represented on the Far
Eastern Commission possessed the right of veto, the United
States could always prevent a majority recommendation being
put into effect. But in such case the United States, under the
Commission's terms of reference, could issue an 'interim directive' to the Supreme Commander along whatever lines it
wished. In Japan itself, General MacArthur had no intention of
accepting the advice of the Allied Council unless he happened to
agree with it. According to Professor Ball, General MacArthur
had 'resented' the establishment of the Commission, and 'from
first to last, his senior officers treated it contemptuously...on
balance, the Allied Council was a fiasco'.[4] This judgement,
however, modestly under-estimates the substantial influence of
Professor Ball, as Commonwealth Representative, and his supporting advisers, in helping to ensure substantial rural land reform in Japan which resulted in the Japanese Diet passing legislation providing 'compulsory means to enable about two million
tenants, or three-quarters of all farmers, to acquire the land
they work'.[5]

Recently, an 'inside' account of the activities of the Council
has been given by William Sebald, who succeeded George

---

[1] Professor MacMahon Ball, *Japan, Enemy or Ally?* (Cassell, Melbourne, 1948).
[2] *Australia in World Affairs 1956–60*, chapter v.   [3] *Ibid.* p. 247.
[4] *Ibid.* p. 248.   [5] MacMahon Ball, *Japan, Enemy or Ally?*, p. 141.

Atcheson as deputy for the Supreme Commander, Chairman of the Council, and its United States Member.[1] Sebald confirms that 'MacArthur made no secret of his dislike for the Allied Council, which he regarded as an unwanted intrusion into the Occupation and an undesirable vehicle for Soviet propaganda'.[2] He himself, on the other hand, thought that 'it served as a safety valve for the release of pressures created by the aftermath of war'.[3] Proceedings were public; a Japanese representative attended sessions and reported them to the Prime Minister and the Foreign Office; the meetings were followed 'avidly' by the Japanese Press. It provided a ray of hope for the Japanese people, as it was at that time 'the only forum in which their problems and their future were discussed openly and freely'.[3]

In the immediate post-war period, therefore, while the Australian Labour Party was still in power, no country was as rigid as Australia in its efforts to ensure that Japan should never again have the capacity to commit another act of aggression. This policy was broadly supported by the Opposition and by public opinion. Until Evatt visited Japan in July 1947, as the guest of General MacArthur, he seemed to regard Japanese aggression during the war period as an unforgivable personal affront. He had no hesitation in opposing strongly American policy towards Japan, whether in the Far Eastern Commission or through his representative on the Allied Council sitting in Tokyo. This opposition for the most part proved ineffective, and in the meantime American–Australian relations deteriorated somewhat.

For reasons which are not clear, Evatt's visit to Tokyo in 1947 seems to have marked a turning-point, if not in actual policy at least in tone and degree of pressure. According to Professor Ball, reports of the meetings between General MacArthur and the Australian Minister 'exuded an atmosphere of cordiality and mutual confidence. From that point Australian official policy became remarkable resilient.'[4] Professor Rosecrance notes that there is 'evidence that Evatt and Prime Minister Chifley had decided to smooth over differences with the United States even before Evatt left for Japan... by emphasising the areas of accord and passing over those of divergence Evatt may have succeeded

[1] William Sebald, *With MacArthur in Japan* (W. W. Norton and Co. Inc., New York, 1965). [2] *Ibid.* p. 62.
[3] *Ibid.* p. 63. [4] *Australia in World Affairs 1956–60*, p. 253.

in conveying the impression that Australia was more favourably disposed towards a lenient peace than she actually was'.[1] Reporting on 17 August 1947 on his mission to Japan, Evatt stressed the 'cordiality and friendship' of his reception by General MacArthur, claimed that he had found the 'greatest goodwill towards Australia on the part of the Americans in Japan', and roundly asserted that no country had 'exercised as much influence on American policy towards Japan as Australia'.[2] It is a curious coincidence that Professor Ball's resignation as Commonwealth Representative on the Allied Council and Head of the Australian Mission in Japan took effect on the very same day.[3] A career officer of the Department of External Affairs was appointed to succeed him.

The Liberal–Country Party Government which came to power in December 1949 soon found that a 'tough' peace treaty with Japan was not procurable.[4] The development of the Cold War and the outbreak of the Korean War in June 1950 led to an American reassessment of Japan's significance. In due course the new Australian Government adjusted its policy realistically to the new circumstances, secured through diplomatic initiative an American guarantee of Australian security in the ANZUS Treaty, and consciously began to build up, as and when circumstances permitted, friendly relations with post-war Japan.

In pursuing this policy the Menzies Government had to take into account two main considerations, namely the state of public opinion within Australia and the extent to which post-war Japan provided real grounds for believing that its governments had broken with past militaristic traditions. It was under no illusion that the Japanese people and their political leaders were likely overnight to become peace-loving and democratic. Mutually beneficial co-operation was offered by Australia, but only step by step, as circumstances seemed to justify. The basic approach was well defined by Casey when, as Minister for External Affairs, he visited Japan in 1951 after a tour of South-East Asian countries. Reporting to Parliament on 27 September 1951 on the tour as a whole, Casey said:

In speaking to the Press in Japan I made it clear that it would be misleading for the Japanese to expect Australia quickly to forget the

[1] Rosecrance, *Australian Diplomacy and Japan*, p. 84.
[2] *C.N.* vol. xviii (1947), pp. 469–70.
[3] *Ibid.* p. 430.   [4] See pp. 122–3 above.

past. At the same time I expressed the view that if Japan by her actions demonstrated in the future that she had, in fact, cast off for all time the ambitions and objectives of Japanese Imperialism, then Australians would be prepared to meet the Japanese people half way.[1]

The Australian Government certainly kept this promise. By its signature and ratification of a generous Peace Treaty it helped to remove from Japanese minds the feeling that Australia, of all the enemies of the Second World War, was the least forgiving. Following the entry into force of the Peace Treaty, ambassadors selected for the Tokyo post were men of substantial experience. The Prime Minister, and subsequently the Minister for External Affairs, made goodwill visits to Japan. Australia sponsored Japan's entry to the United Nations and her addition to the list of Colombo Plan countries. The problem of war criminals was handled, to use Menzies' words, 'in a liberal and civilized way'.[2]

Three problems were less amenable to simple treatment, namely employment of Japanese technicians in New Guinea, pearl-fishing and trade. When in 1954 the United States, in accordance with the terms of an agreement with some Commonwealth countries, including Australia, to carry out certain mapping and surveying work, proposed to use Japanese technicians in operations around New Britain, the Australian Government refused its assent. Within Australia there were strong protests against permitting Japanese citizens to operate in an area where bitter fighting had taken place in the Second World War and where the indigenous people had suffered heavily from Japanese military operations. Assent to re-entry by Japanese could also have been seriously misunderstood by the inhabitants of the area. In the event, the United States substituted Filipino for Japanese crews to carry out the surveying operations.

Japanese attempts after the war to resume pearl-fishing in waters over the Australian continental shelf raised probably the most serious difficulty in post-war relations between Australia and Japan. Such fishing had taken place for some years before Pearl Harbor, during which it was feared in Australia not only that the amount of pearl shell taken had substantially depleted

[1] *C.N.* vol. xxii (1951), p. 515.
[2] Statement made at a press conference in Tokyo, 12 April 1957: *C.N.* vol. xxviii (1957), p. 305.

resources important to Australian pearl-shell operators, but that Japanese fishing operations had also covered intelligence activities of a military nature. When therefore Japan proposed to despatch a fleet to the same area in 1953, Australia exercised its power under Article 9 of the Peace Treaty to call for negotiation of an agreement on fishing rights.

Negotiations began, but moved slowly. They were broken off by Australia when Japan announced that her fleet would operate in two areas within 100 miles of Darwin and would take a tonnage of shell regarded as excessive and prejudicial to Australian fishing interests. The Australian Government thereupon passed legislation which, with subsequent proclamations, claimed Australian sovereign rights over natural resources of the sea-bed and subsoil of the Australian continental shelf and the continental shelf around New Guinea to a depth of 100 fathoms. The legislation provided that pearl-fishing within 'Australian waters' could be carried out only under licence and subject to conditions laid down, heavy penalties being imposed for unauthorised fishing.

The Japanese Government protested that this constituted a breach of international law and sought Australian assent to the issue being taken to the International Court of Justice. Australia agreed, subject to Japan entering into provisional arrangements covering each season's fishing. Such agreements were in fact entered into, but the problem of settling precise terms of reference to the Court proved difficult and the matter is now unlikely to be litigated. Two reasons contributing heavily to this were, first, the fall in the world price of pearl-shell owing to increased use of substitutes—which made pearl-fishing less profitable—and secondly, further development of the International Law of the Sea under which in 1958 a United Nations Conference adopted various conventions, including a convention on the continental shelf which contained provisions favouring the Australian case.[1]

This dispute over pearl-shell fishing rights caused a good deal of irritation on both sides. To the Japanese, the Australian attitude betrayed a lack of understanding of their pressing need in the immediate post-war period to find employment for fishermen and to reconstruct their war-shattered economy by any and

---

[1] See Sir Kenneth Bailey, 'Australia and the Geneva Conventions on the Law of the Sea', chapter x of *International Law in Australia*, ed. O'Connell.

every means; moreover, the Australian legislation seemed to them high-handed and, in practice, discriminatory—all this on behalf of a small Australian industry which could not even operate without introducing divers from overseas or using aboriginals from some of the Australian islands. To the Australians, the Japanese attitude reflected a lack of appreciation of justifiable Australian sensitiveness regarding the operation, close to Australian shores, of nationals of an ex-enemy State whose fishermen, even before the war, were believed to have abused whatever international rights they might have had.

Fortunately for both countries the pearl-fisheries dispute became of minor importance against the background of their overall trade relations. Australian exports to Japan grew rapidly as from the year 1949/50, until they reached in 1956/57 no less than £A139 million, as compared with imports from Japan of only £A12·88 million. Australia thus had a favourable balance of trade of £A126·12 million and a trade ratio in Australia's favour of 10·8:1.[1] 'By 1956/57', according to Mr P. Drysdale, 'it was clear that if Australia was to increase imports from Japan she had, in order to help correct Japan's sterling-area deficit from time to time, to consider the import of less "essential" goods which would be in competition with other overseas as well as local supplies (to some extent)...This dilemma was faced squarely in 1957.'[2]

In July 1957 the Australian Minister for Trade, Mr John McEwen, visited Japan to complete negotiations for a Trade Agreement, which was signed on 6 July. This constituted 'the major watershed in Japanese–Australian trading relations after the War':[3] indeed, it is scarcely an exaggeration to regard the Agreement as the most significant development in Japanese–Australian relations generally since the end of the war. Before the agreement Japanese exports to Australia were subject to the General Tariff, or the highest rates of duties imposed on imports. They were also severely limited by Australian licensing authorities. Under the Trade Agreement Japan obtained two major concessions. Henceforth her exports were accorded Most-Favoured-Nation Tariff treatment, and in future there was to be no discrimination against her in import licensing.

For her part Japan guaranteed that no duty would be imposed

---

[1] See *Papers on Modern Japan 1965* (Australian National University), article by P. Drysdale, p. 86. [2] *Ibid.* p. 89. [3] *Ibid.* p. 90.

on imports of Australian wool while the Agreement was in force, while freer access to the Japanese market was granted for Australian exports of wheat, sugar, barley, hides and skins, dried vine fruits and skim milk.

Under Article IV (2) of the Agreement, both governments retained the right to invoke Article XXXV of GATT, which permits, in certain circumstances, the non-application of GATT between particular contracting parties. Article V, inserted no doubt at Australia's request, specifically permitted each country to impose restrictions on imports from the other if serious injury were caused or threatened to producers in the country of importation of like or directly competitive products.[1] Prior to any such action there was to be consultation between the two parties to try to agree upon an alternative solution. In practice, Australia found little need to take special action of this character.

The Trade Agreement ran for its full three-year period, and was subsequently extended until it was revised in August 1963. Under the revised agreement Australia waived its right to invoke the provisions of Article XXXV of GATT. This involved surrender of her right, if the 1957 Agreement had lapsed, to discriminate against Japanese goods alone. While Australia in 1962 had created a Special Advisory Authority for the purpose of recommending temporary protection for Australian industry through the imposition of emergency tariff, any such action after the 1963 Agreement came into force would have to be taken against other countries as well as Japan.[2]

The effectiveness of the two Agreements is shown by the subsequent terms of trade between the two countries. For the year 1963–64, Australia exported to Japan goods to the value of £A243,905,000 and imported from Japan goods to the value of £A81,234,000. While the balance of trade was still heavily in Australia's favour, the favourable ratio of trade was reduced to 3:1.[3]

Despite strong fears of Australian manufacturers when the 1957 Agreement came into force, this significant increase in mutual trade has taken place without substantial injury to Australian industry; however, a considerable increase in the volume

---

[1] See *Australian Treaty Series* (1957), no. 15.
[2] *Papers on Modern Japan 1965*, pp. 92–3.
[3] *Commonwealth of Australia Year Book*, 1965, p. 502.

of Japanese motor-cars exported to Australia led to the announcement on 18 February 1966 of governmental decisions, based upon Tariff Board recommendations, designed to compel Japanese and other foreign companies to make provision for greater production of their cars in Australia itself. In view of the decline in the share and value of Australian exports now taken by the United Kingdom, and the further probable decline if Great Britain should be permitted to join the European Economic Community, the growth of Australian exports to Japan is of the first importance to Australia. Such exports now include coal, and will include iron ore on a massive scale when newly discovered fields are developed.

This account of steadily improving relations between Japan and Australia since the Japanese Peace Treaty came into force has for the most part stressed the attitude of the Australian Government. Mr Menzies described this attitude, during his visit to Japan in 1957, as follows: 'We have not, in spite of what may have been the problems of ten years ago, approached the problems with Japan in a spirit of hatred or unpleasantness. On the contrary, we have made our watchword, full and friendly association.'[1] But this description of developments would be misleading and unfair if nothing were said about the Japanese contribution to the development of friendly relations.

The first Japanese Ambassador appointed to Australia after the Peace Treaty came into force was Mr Haruhiko Nishi, who impressed those with whom he had official dealings by his ability and integrity. His was not an easy task, but he performed it with dignity, skill and judgement. His contribution to the gradual diminution of Australian doubts and suspicions as to Japan's post-war outlook and policy deserves specific mention. After a comparatively short period of service in Australia he was promoted to the far more responsible post of Japanese Ambassador to the Court of St James. He was succeeded in Australia by a series of able and experienced men who were able to build upon the foundations he had laid.

Reciprocal visits were made to Australia by Japanese political leaders and officials. In particular, the Prime Minister of Japan, Mr Nobusuke Kishi, visited Australia towards the end of 1957. This was a delicate operation, as Kishi had been a member of the Tojo cabinet from 1941 to 1943, and after the war had been

[1] Tokyo Press Statement of 12 April 1957: C.N. vol. xxviii (1957), p. 305.

held in confinement by the occupation forces as a suspected 'A' class war criminal. The President of the New South Wales Branch of the returned servicemen's organisation protested against the visit, and an incident occurred after Kishi had laid a wreath on the war memorial in Canberra. On the whole, however, the visit was successful and prepared the way for a subsequent visit in September 1963 by his successor in office, Mr Hayato Ikeda.

Before this latter visit took place, however, Australia had had six years experience of how the trade agreement with Japan worked in practice. This was a rewarding experience, which did much to remove Australian fears and to establish confidence in Japanese governments of the post-war period. Sir Robert Menzies paid public tribute to the Japanese attitude when, in his speech of welcome to Ikeda on 30 September 1963, he said that 'Our trade treaties with you have marked our close relations with you. Their efficacy—and I point this out with some satisfaction—has depended, not only upon the letter of the deal, but upon genuine good faith.'[1] Drysdale has made the same point in more specific terms: 'The Japanese Government honoured its undertaking scrupulously in exercising "voluntary restraint" upon exports which were imposing undue hardship upon Australian manufactures.'[2]

The speeches made by the Australian and Japanese Prime Ministers during Ikeda's visit, and the joint communiqué issued, are evidence of a closeness of association and a degree of mutual confidence which was scarcely conceivable when the Peace Treaty was signed in 1951. Menzies expressed himself in these terms:

Some years after the echoes of the war had died away, we decided, in this country, as a considered matter of policy, that security and co-operation in the Pacific should be preferred to the prolongation of enmity; that we should learn to live with each other; that we should concentrate upon our common interests and be aware of our common dangers. In the achievement of all these great objectives, Japan has shown herself a willing co-operator. In the world atmosphere of recent times, Japan has resumed her place as a great power, with remarkable economic development and skill, and with a growing willingness...to play an effective part in the solution of the world's economic problems...I think we can all agree here today

[1] *C.N.* vol. xxxiv, no. 9 (1963), p. 49.   [2] *Papers on Modern Japan 1965*, p. 92.

that we can now look back upon a decade of most civilised association. We want this association to continue, and to grow stronger, and I am sure, Sir, that you share this desire.[1]

In reply, Ikeda referred to the 'striking advance' in trade between the two countries since the first trade agreement was signed, and to the 'mutual inter-dependence' which had developed and added that 'There is not one international issue to disturb this bond between us'. Japan and Australia were both freedom-loving democracies; they were industrially advanced; they had stable governments and sound economies; and they had a common interest in maintaining peace and achieving prosperity in the region in which they share major responsibilities.[2] In a joint communiqué issued during the visit, Australia and Japan recognised 'the common destiny and responsibility of their two countries in Asia and the Western Pacific area...'[3]

It would of course be a mistake to assume that two countries with cultural traditions as diverse as those of Japan and Australia now think alike on every international question and are inevitably cast to play similar roles on the international scene as political, economic and even military allies. Four-day and four-teen-day tours of Japan by thousands of Australian tourists can bring but shallow understanding of such an ancient and sophisticated country. Of greater importance are the mutually beneficial trade ties which bring Japanese and Australian businessmen increasingly together, and which have led to the establishment of a Japan–Australia Business Co-operation Committee. These alone, however, will not be sufficient to lead to co-operative political activity in the international field.

A great deal remains to be done to put overall relations on a sound footing[4]—exchange of visits by politicians, trade unionists, academics, sportsmen; university courses in linguistics and oriental civilisation; cultural exchanges, such as art exhibitions and musical performances; closer knowledge by Australians of Japanese reaction to the use of atomic weapons, of the implications of their cultural links to China, and of a post-war inclination towards pacifism and neutrality.

Nevertheless, a substantial start has been made, and the

---

[1] *C.N.* vol. xxxiv, no. 9 (1963), p. 49. [2] *Ibid.* pp. 50–1. [3] *Ibid.* p. 51.
[4] For a recent personal interpretation by an Australian of the Japanese background and outlook, see Mildred Watt, *Japan, Land of Sun and Storm* (Cheshire, Melbourne, 1966).

results to date have been striking. The change in the Australian outlook on Japan is well illustrated by the changed views of Professor MacMahon Ball. In his book *Japan—Enemy or Ally?*, written in 1948, an examination of current American policy in Japan led him to express the belief that 'it is rash and dangerous to assume that Japan cannot in the foreseeable future again become a danger to her neighbours'.[1] Writing in 1962, however, his views had changed significantly:

It is extremely important to recognise that although Japan may still, at bottom, be an authoritarian nation in domestic politics, she is certainly no longer a militarist or expansionist nation in foreign policy. In a nuclear war, Japan would perhaps be the most vulnerable nation in the world. Recognizing this, her leaders know that peace is Japan's first national interest. They can be expected always to strive for negotiated settlements when the Cold War threatens to become a hot war in the region. Japan has the technical and industrial skills to enable her to play a big part in helping the nations of South-East Asia achieve economic growth. Her leaders, however conservative, have a good understanding of the desire of India and other non-Communist Asian nations to follow a foreign policy of non-alignment. On all counts it would seem good sense for Australia to work as closely as possible with Japan.[2]

2. *India*

Relations between India and Australia since 1947, when it became clear that India would shortly achieve independence, deserve close study, both for their own sake and also for the light thrown upon the difficulty of making predictions in the international field ten to twenty years ahead.

Under the Australian Labour Government, which was still in power from 1947 to 1949, relations were close and sympathetic; they deteriorated somewhat—though not disastrously—under the Menzies Government between 1950 and 1962; they improved substantially under the Menzies Government between 1962 and 1965, after Indian–Chinese border disputes led to an incursion of Chinese troops into Indian territory, and after China gave active support to Pakistan when the Kashmir dispute erupted into undeclared war between India and Pakistan in 1965.

It is not surprising that the Indian attitude towards Australia

[1] Ball, *op. cit.* p. 201.   [2] *Australia in World Affairs 1956–60*, pp. 267–9.

immediately before and after independence was comparatively sympathetic while the Labour Party Government was still in office, despite a degree of aristocratic disdain by leaders of an ancient and sophisticated civilisation for a young country thought to be *nouveau riche* and materialistic. At San Francisco the Australian Delegation had fought for inclusion in the United Nations Charter of wide provisions reflecting the application of the principle of international accountability for trustee and non-self-governing territories. Later, in 1947, Australia strongly supported the broad principle, though not the details, of the Soviet Resolution against 'war propaganda' at the Second Session of the United Nations General Assembly, and pursued a successful diplomatic initiative on the same subject at the Conference on Freedom of Information and the Press, held at Geneva in 1948.[1]

The Australian Government welcomed the decision of the British Government, announced by Mr Attlee on 20 February 1947, to transfer power to responsible Indian authorities by June 1948, and accepted, if with some reluctance, the Indian decision to become a sovereign republic within the Commonwealth, recognising the Crown only as the Head of the Commonwealth.

In 1947 an Asian Relations Conference[2] was held in New Delhi from 23 March to 2 April. Invitations were issued by the Indian Council of World Affairs, and Australia was represented by two observers, one from the Australian Institute of International Affairs and one from the Australian Institute of Political Science. These observers subsequently wrote a report in which they noted that Nehru, in his opening speech, welcomed observers from Australia and New Zealand. '...we have many problems in common,' he said, 'especially in the Pacific and in the South-East region of Asia, and we have to co-operate together to find solutions.'[3] Although 'migration' was a specific item on the agenda, the same report states that 'The established

---

[1] See *C.N.* vol. XIX (1948), pp. 497–8.

[2] For details of the Conference and comments see *C.N.* vol. XVIII (1947), pp. 162–7, and *Australian Outlook*, vol. I (June 1947), pp. 3–7.

[3] See *Australian Observers' Report on Asian Relations Conference, New Delhi, March 1947*, p. 6 (copy held by Victorian Branch, Australian Institute of International Affairs). (For text of Nehru's Inaugural Speech at the Conference, see *Jawaharlal Nehru's Speeches*, vol. I (1946–49), Indian Ministry of Information, pp. 297–304.)

immigration policy of the Australian Government was not challenged and Australia was mentioned once only and then only as one of a number of countries which claim the right to exclude immigrants who are not likely to be assimilated'.[1]

On the other hand, there was strong evidence during the Conference of Ceylonese and Burmese fears of Indian migration, and of Malayan fears of Chinese migration. The Australian observers reported that there was general acceptance of the view that every State must be its own judge of the composition of its nationhood, and must consequently be granted the right to restrict or control immigration. Certain qualifications to this principle, however, were suggested. Some delegates advocated a quota system to prevent ill-feeling and objected to total exclusion of any Asian national as such.[2]

In July 1947 both India and Australia brought the Indonesian situation to the attention of the United Nations Security Council, while in 1949 Australia accepted an Indian invitation to be represented officially at an Asian Conference on Indonesia held at New Delhi to which neither the United Kingdom nor the Netherlands was invited. Acceptance of the invitation was challenged in Parliament by leading members of the Opposition, while doubts as to the propriety of Australian participation in the Conference were expressed in several Australian newspapers.[3]

India recognised Communist China in December 1949 and the Australian Government might well have done likewise had not impending elections in New Zealand and Australia led to a postponement of such a decision for tactical domestic reasons. In these elections, the Australian Labour Party suffered a heavy defeat and lost office.

Two differences of opinion between the Australian Labour Government and the Government of India deserve to be recorded. First, India did not support the Australian view that the right of veto accorded by the United Nations Charter to the Permanent Members of the Security Council should be abolished or severely restricted. The Indian Government regarded any 'regulation' of the use of the veto as 'a matter for the Big Five themselves to consider'.[4] Secondly, the Australian Labour Party

---

[1] *Australian Observers' Report on Asian Relations Conference, New Delhi, March 1947*, p. 14.   [2] *Ibid.* p. 13.

[3] See *Australian Opinion on World Affairs*, January 1949 (published by the Victorian Branch of the Australian Institute of International Affairs).

[4] *India and the United Nations* (Manhattan Publishing Co., 1957), p. 42.

wanted the Peace Treaty with Japan to be 'tough'. When in Opposition it voted against ratification by Australia of the Peace Treaty signed at San Francisco on 8 September 1951 by forty-nine nations. Further, it was a Labour Government which appointed Sir William Webb, a Justice of the High Court of Australia, to the International Military Tribunal for the Far East, of which he was President. Sir William Webb found none of the sentences passed upon Japanese War Criminals 'manifestly excessive or manifestly inadequate', and, indeed, stressed in a separate statement his view that the Emperor of Japan, who had not been prosecuted, could not be absolved from responsibility for the outbreak of war on the alleged ground that he was bound to act on advice.[1] While the President of the Tribunal no doubt expressed his own opinions and was not acting upon political instruction, his views were broadly consistent with those which had been expressed at various times by the Australian Minister for External Affairs, Dr Evatt.

The Indian Government, on the other hand, refused to attend the San Francisco Conference of 1951, and did not sign the Treaty accepted by that Conference. India thought that the Ryuku Islands should be returned to Japan, and did not approve the policy of stationing American troops in Japan after the Treaty.[2] Further, the Indian representative on the International Military Tribunal, Mr Justice Pal, held in a dissenting judgement that all of the accused should have been acquitted. In his opinion a union of victor nations had no authority to legislate and promulgate a new law of war crimes as this would constitute a 'revolutionary creation of *ex post facto* international law'.[3]

As mentioned earlier,[4] the Menzies Government came to power in December 1949 on a strongly anti-Communist platform after strikes on the coal-fields, Communist-inspired, had caused some 600,000 Australian industrial workers to become idle. The Korean War broke out in June 1950. When later in the same year Communist Chinese 'volunteers' crossed into North Korea and became heavily engaged against United Nations forces, any inclination of the new Australian Govern-

---

[1] *C.N.* vol. xx (1949), p. 337.

[2] See Rosecrance, *Australian Diplomacy and Japan*, p. 223.

[3] See *C.N.* vol. xx (1949), pp. 338–41, for a summary of the dissenting opinion.

[4] See chapter 5, p. 106 above.

ment to recognise Communist China was restrained or suppressed indefinitely.[1]

While in Opposition, the Liberal and Country Parties had been critical of the Labour Party's support for Indonesia against the Dutch. Although they accepted the fact of Indonesian independence when they came to power, the old close and sympathetic relationships between Indonesian and Australian political leaders were not maintained. Independent Indonesia continued to press for control over West New Guinea; no Australian political party supported this claim, but inevitably the parties in power had to bear the brunt of growing Indonesian resentment at Australian pro-Dutch policy on this issue. India, on the other hand, fully supported Indonesia's claim to West New Guinea.

The international priorities of the new Australian Government were different from those of its predecessor. In particular, it was less optimistic as to the probable results of action within the United Nations and more disposed to seek the practical support of Great Britain and the United States, Australia's 'great and powerful friends'—as the Prime Minister frequently described them. The Minister for External Affairs, Sir Percy Spender, made his primary objective signature of a military alliance of Pacific Powers including the United States. Although he was well aware of the importance of ameliorating poverty in Asia, and was substantially responsible for the creation of the Colombo Plan, which was directed to this end, Australia's commitment to a policy of military alliance made a deeper impression on non-aligned India than her marginal contributions to economic development and technical training in underdeveloped countries. In the circumstances it was almost inevitable that Indian and Australian policy should diverge and that relations between the two countries should be less close than they had been when the Australian Labour Party was in power.

By 1955 Australia had become 'committed' to three military alliances or arrangements, namely the ANZUS Treaty, the South-East Asia Collective Defence Treaty (SEATO), and Commonwealth arrangements under ANZAM, including the decision to station Australian troops in Malaya as part of the Commonwealth Strategic Reserve. India, on the other hand,

---

[1] For a fuller discussion of the attitude of the Menzies Government towards recognition of Communist China, see pp. 240–4 below.

was strongly opposed to proposals for a Pacific Pact. Prime Minister Nehru informed Parliament on 2 March 1950 that India would not join a South-East Asian or Pacific Pact.[1] India, deeply conscious of her historic past and of her cultural relations with other Asian countries before the period of European domination, was primarily concerned to oppose the continuance in Asia and Africa of European 'imperialism' or 'colonialism'. Her resentment at past domination, and suspicion that European Powers might try by indirect means to maintain their influence in Asia and Africa even after countries in these geographical areas had achieved political independence, were stronger than her fears of Communist domination.

It is scarcely surprising that Nehru shared such resentment, fears and suspicion. Despite his English education at Harrow and Cambridge University, he had fully identified himself with the Indian nationalist movement and spent years in prison. Unlike Gandhi, with whom he was for long associated, Nehru was a politician rather than a saint. The policy he laid down for India incorporated his conception of what was in the best interests of his country. Despite a tendency to moralise and to imply that the best policy for India was the best policy for other countries too, if not for the world at large, there were times when he expressed himself in frankly realistic terms. Thus, in a speech on non-alignment made in the Constituent (Legislative) Assembly as early as 4 December 1947, he admitted that 'whether a country is imperialistic or socialist or communist, its foreign minister thinks primarily of the interests of that country'.[2] 'We are not going to join a war if we can help it', he declared, '...and we are going to join the side which is to our interest when the time comes to make the choice.'[3] But he distinguished between a 'short-distance view' of a country's interests, and 'long-term policy', and asserted that 'we propose to look after India's interests in the context of world co-operation and world peace'.[4]

Nehru's inaugural address at the Asian Relations Conference, New Delhi, on 23 March 1947 reflects both pride in the long cultural tradition of Asia—especially India—and determination to pursue independent policies in the future. Asia, he told the

[1] Peter Calvocoressi, *Survey of International Affairs 1949–50* (Oxford University Press, 1953), p. 35.   [2] *Jawaharlal Nehru's Speeches*, vol. i, p. 206.
[3] *Ibid.* p. 202.   [4] *Ibid.* p. 207.

assembled delegates, after a long period of quiescence, had suddenly become important again in world affairs.

Far too long have we of Asia been petitioners in Western courts and chancelleries. That story must now belong to the past. We propose to stand on our own legs and to co-operate with all others who are prepared to co-operate with us. We do not intend to be the playthings of others...The countries of Asia can no longer be used as pawns by others; they are bound to have their own policies in world affairs.[1]

These brave words were spoken before Nehru had taken over the reins of government. Later experience made him more aware of the difficulty of pursuing an 'independent' policy in this interdependent world, particularly as Prime Minister of a country with a low average standard of living and exploding population which needed at least substantial economic assistance from more affluent or more authoritarian societies which were able or willing to provide it. But he continued to pursue the objective of independence with courage and determination, developing his policy of 'non-alignment' with either Communist or anti-Communist Powers, accepting aid from either camp provided 'political strings' were not attached. He did not fear to criticise roundly policies of Western Powers with which he disagreed, and, if his criticism of Communist countries was rather more muted, he did not hesitate to deal severely, on occasion, with the activities of Communists within India itself.

Signature of the ANZUS Treaty by the United States, Australia and New Zealand does not appear to have excited much antipathy in India.[2] On the other hand, signature of the South-East Asian Collective Defence Treaty (SEATO) was strongly criticised. The most violent criticism came from Mr Krishna Menon, the Prime Minister's *alter ego* in the field of foreign policy, especially in meetings of the United Nations General Assembly. During a debate on foreign affairs in the Indian Council of States, Menon said on 28 August 1954:

...by no stretch of imagination or interpretation can SEATO come under the U.N. Charter...The Charter provides for regional organization, but this is not a regional organization but...a modern version of protectorate. It is an organization of certain imperial Powers, and some others, who may have an interest in joining together to

---

[1] *Jawaharlal Nehru's Speeches*, vol. I, pp. 298–301.   [2] See pp. 136–8 above.

protect a territory which they say is in danger. We are part of that territory and we say that we do not want to be protected.[1]

Menon's attack may be discounted in some degree because he is scarcely given to under-statement when dealing with 'colonial' themes. More surprising are two important omissions from Nehru's speech in the Lok Sabha on 29 September, three weeks after signature of the treaty at Manila. The Prime Minister first mentioned two strong reasons why India could not participate in the Manila Conference. In the first place, participation would have involved giving up India's basic policy of non-alignment. Secondly, participation at Manila would have affected India's position as Chairman of the International Commissions established at the Geneva Conference on Indo-China, 1954, to help assure that the terms of the Geneva Agreements were in fact carried out. For the rest, he claimed not to understand the reasons for the 'special urge' towards the Manila Conference, or the basis of fears of aggression in the area. The Treaty itself, in his opinion, had not added to the strength of the signatory parties: on the other hand, it had added 'definitely to the tensions and fears of the situation'.[2]

Nehru thought that the Manila Treaty was 'inclined dangerously in the direction of spheres of influence to be exercised by powerful countries'.[3] He was disturbed by the fact that the Treaty area, as defined in the Treaty, did not comprise merely the territory of the countries party to the Treaty, but could also include additional areas unanimously designated by the parties. This was a dangerous extension of the idea of defence. He reminded his listeners that the North Atlantic Treaty Organisation had extended its interests from the North Atlantic area to the Mediterranean, to the coasts of Africa, to Eastern Africa and to distant countries which had nothing to do with the Atlantic community. Portugal had claimed that NATO included Goa in its scope. The Prime Minister wondered whether the South-East Asia Treaty too would extend likewise.[4]

It will be noted that Nehru nowhere referred to paragraph 3 of Article IV of SEATO, which states that 'It is understood that no action on the territory of any State designated by unanimous agreement under paragraph 1 of this Article or on any territory

[1] *Keesing's Contemporary Archives*, p. 13,763.
[2] *Jawaharlal Nehru's Speeches*, vol. III, pp. 265–6.
[3] *Ibid.* p. 267.   [4] *Ibid.* pp. 268–9.

so designated shall be taken except at the invitation or with the consent of the government concerned'. Nor is there any reference to the fact that Pakistan was a signatory of the Manila Treaty, and that one of the strong reasons impelling her to become a party was her hope to secure support in her dispute with India over Kashmir. During the debate in the Australian Parliament on the ratification of SEATO, the Australian Minister for External Affairs made it completely clear that SEATO would not oblige Australia to take military action against any other member of the Commonwealth, and added that the Foreign Minister of Pakistan had been so informed before the Treaty was signed.[1] Nevertheless, membership by Pakistan of a military alliance in an Asian area was undoubtedly displeasing to India, which would assume that Pakistan would become more intransigent in pursuing an anti-Indian line on such issues as Kashmir and disposal of the waters of the Indus.

In fact the creation of SEATO cut across Indian foreign policy in several respects. Basically, it was a defensive military alliance against Communist aggression, especially possible aggression by Communist China. But India had chosen, before Chinese incursions into Indian territory in 1962, to adopt towards Communist China a policy of peaceful co-existence, enshrined in the Five Principles (Panchsheel) first proclaimed in the preamble to the agreement between India and China in regard to Tibet and signed on 29 April 1954. Until Chinese pressure upon the frontiers between the two countries became so obvious that it could no longer be ignored, Indian faith in the efficacy of the Five Principles enabled her to concentrate upon the problems of economic development and to limit her military expenditure.

Secondly, India aspired to leadership of the non-Communist Asian world. Membership of a military alliance by three Asian countries, namely Pakistan, Thailand and the Philippines, was inconsistent with acceptance by these countries of Indian leadership, with its policy of non-alignment. Further, it did not suit Indian policy that the United States should enter into military commitments in regard to areas on or near the mainland of Asia. She preferred Asian problems to be settled by Asian Powers in accordance with Asian interests.[2]

Yet Indian criticism of SEATO was not directly aimed at

[1] See p. 156 above.
[2] See Greenwood and Harper, *Australia in World Affairs 1950–55*, p. 279.

Australia. Indeed, with one notable exception, Nehru's statements about Australian policy and Australian political leaders were, on the whole, remarkably restrained. Reference has already been made[1] to the specific welcome extended by Nehru to Australia and New Zealand at the Asian Relations Conference 1947. In his speech at the concluding session of the Bandung Conference, 1955, to which Australia and New Zealand had not been invited, he said:

We send our greetings to Australia and New Zealand. And indeed Australia and New Zealand are almost in our region. They certainly do not belong to Europe, much less to America. They are next to us and I should like Australia and New Zealand to come nearer to Asia. I would welcome them because I do not want what we say or do to be based on racial prejudices.[2]

One would not have been surprised if Indian political leaders had indulged in public criticism in regard to a number of important matters on which Indian and Australian policy differed. First, one might have expected Australian immigration policy to come under official attack; but although severe Indian criticism of this policy is to be found,[3] Professor R. G. Neale is able to comment that 'The Indian Government has taken the attitude that Australia's migration policy is a matter for [sic] domestic jurisdiction'.[4]

This policy is, of course, consistent with the basic policy approved by the 1921 Imperial Conference—South Africa dissenting—in the following terms:

This Conference, while reaffirming the resolution of the Imperial War Conference of 1918 that each community should enjoy complete control of the composition of its population by means of restrictions on immigration from any of the other communities, recognises that there is an incongruity between the position of India as an equal member of the British Empire and the existence of disabilities upon British Indians lawfully domiciled in some other parts of the Empire.[5]

At that time the Australian Prime Minister, Mr W. M. Hughes, like other Commonwealth leaders, had been impressed by the Indian contribution to the war effort during the First

---

[1] See p. 221 above.
[2] *Jawaharlal Nehru's Speeches*, vol. III, p. 291.
[3] See extracts from the *Eastern Economist*, vol. xv (25 August 1950), quoted in *Australia in World Affairs 1950–56*, pp. 265–7.
[4] *Ibid.* p. 265.   [5] Quoted in Yarwood, *Asian Migration to Australia*, p. 137.

World War. He not only voted for this resolution, but invited Mr Srinivasa Sastri, President of the Servants of India Society, to visit Australia in 1922. The visit of Sastri, a gifted speaker, was successful, and he was informed by Hughes that his speeches had 'brought those reforms covered or suggested by the resolutions of the 1918 and 1921 Conferences within the range of practical politics'.[1] While it took some years before necessary legislative changes were in fact made, in due course Indians in Australia acquired 'a civil status superior to that of any other Asian minority. They were permitted to bring out their immediate families. Facilities were available for visits by merchants, students and tourists that were as generous, comparatively, as they were little used. In this respect they had replaced the Japanese as the most favoured Asian nation.'[2] No doubt this favourable treatment of Indians already in Australia was a factor contributing to the restraint shown in official Indian comments upon Australian immigration policy.

Secondly, the Indian and Australian attitudes towards the Commonwealth of Nations were poles apart. Whereas Sir Robert Menzies had a deep sense of personal attachment to the Crown, had argued in 1938 that the Crown was indivisible—so that when the United Kingdom was at war Australia too was automatically at war—and believed that the British Empire should speak with one concerted voice,[3] for Mr Nehru, Indian policies were 'in no way conditioned or deflected from their normal course' by the Commonwealth association.[4] Nehru's publicly expressed attitude towards the Commonwealth seemed at times casual in the extreme: 'If...it does not come in our way in the slightest degree and in fact gives us certain opportunities, helpful opportunities to serve the larger courses that we have at heart then it is worth while being there.'[5]

Thirdly, the Australian attitude towards the Kashmir problem in the early 1950s must have been strongly resented by India. The Australian Government was seriously disturbed by the dispute by India and Pakistan over Kashmir. The fact that Sir Owen Dixon, a judge of the High Court of Australia, had been induced to accept the thankless task of United Nations Mediator

[1] Yarwood, *Asian Migration to Australia*, p. 139.
[2] *Ibid.* p. 140. See pp. 124–40 for a detailed account of Indian immigration to Australia from 1896 to 1923.   [3] See p. 20 above.
[4] *Australia in World Affairs 1956–60*, quoted at p. 350.
[5] *Ibid.* quoted at p. 351.

in the Kashmir dispute suggests the personal interest of Sir Robert Menzies in this issue. The Dixon report, presented to the Security Council on 19 September 1950, recommended that, as all efforts by the Mediator to secure a settlement had failed, the parties themselves should be left to negotiate a settlement.

While the Australian Prime Minister was on his way to attend a Prime Ministers' Conference in London in 1951, he broke his journey *en route* at New Delhi and Karachi and had informal discussions on Kashmir with both the Indian and the Pakistan Prime Ministers. Menzies was largely responsible for the fact that the Prime Minister of Pakistan, Liaquat Ali Khan, attended the London Conference; he also encouraged the holding of private talks on Kashmir outside the Conference itself which were unsuccessful.[1] In 1951 Australia provided a number of military observers in Kashmir under the aegis of the United Nations, an Australian General being appointed to command the United Nations team of observers as a whole.[2] Although India formally accepted the appointment of Sir Owen Dixon as United Nations Mediator, none of these Australian initiatives could have been welcome to Nehru—particularly the discussions on Kashmir outside the Prime Ministers' Conference in London; yet Nehru's public reactions showed considerable restraint.

Fourthly, India and Australia had very different attitudes towards the Korean War. While both countries supported the United Nations condemnation of North Korean aggression, India limited its contribution to medical aid, pressed the need for admission of Communist China to the United Nations, opposed the crossing of the 38th parallel by United Nations forces in the process of recovery from attacks by Chinese 'volunteers', opposed the United Nations resolution declaring Communist China an aggressor and, in general, saw the Korean problem 'primarily as an Asian question to be settled by Asian nations by Asian methods in Asia's interests'.[3] Australia, on the other hand, was the first country to announce that it would send ground forces to Korea to assist American troops, and made available R.A.A.F. units in the earliest stages of the war. Australia supported the decision to cross the 38th parallel and voted for the United Nations resolution condemning Communist China as an aggressor. The Indian view that the Korean war

[1] See *C.N.* vol. xxII (1951), pp. 56–7, 161–2. [2] *Ibid.* pp. 700–1.
[3] *Australia in World Affairs, 1950–55*, p. 252.

was linked to the question of the admission of Communist China to the United Nations was disputed by Australia,[1] which joined other Commonwealth countries, however, in supporting—in face of South Korean and United States opposition—Indian participation in a political conference on Korea after signature of an armistice. In the result, India requested withdrawal of her nomination when it became clear that the necessary two-thirds vote in her favour would not be obtained.[2] Indian objections to United Nations policy in the Korean War were objections primarily to American policy; by comparison, Australian support for American policy would in Indian eyes have only marginal significance.

On one occasion, however, the Indian Prime Minister appears simply to have lost his temper over Australian policy, and clashed personally with the Australian Prime Minister in the United Nations General Assembly. The circumstances were as follows. The Summit Meeting of President Eisenhower, Mr Harold Macmillan, Mr Khruschshev and President de Gaulle, scheduled to open in Paris on 16 May 1960, broke down before its opening session on the issue of American U 2 flights over the Soviet Union. This breakdown was regarded as a serious threat to world peace. When the United Nations General Assembly met in September 1960, a Resolution sponsored by Ghana, India, the United Arab Republic, Yugoslavia and Indonesia was presented to the Assembly. The preamble to this Resolution expressed concern at the deterioration in international relations and referred to the need to reduce world tension. In its operative part the Resolution requested that, 'as a first urgent step', President Eisenhower and Mr Khruschhev should 'renew their contacts' to facilitate the solution of outstanding problems by negotiation.

Menzies, who was then both Prime Minister and Minister for External Affairs, arrived at the United Nations on 30 September to find that Eisenhower and Macmillan were 'troubled about the Resolution'. While the terms of the preamble were unexceptionable, the operative part appeared to accept the view that 'the real world issue is between the Soviet Union and the United States', a view with which Menzies disagreed. In his judgement a meeting between all 'four atomic powers' should

[1] *C.N.* vol. xxi (1950), p. 580.
[2] *Australia in World Affairs 1950-55*, pp. 253-4.

be recommended. Called to Washington for consultation with the American President and the British Prime Minister, Menzies suggested that an amendment should be moved which, while accepting the preamble to the Five-Power Resolution, would substitute for its operative part of a series of clauses, the main purpose of which was to urge that a meeting of the Heads of Government of the United States, the Soviet Union, Great Britain and France should be held at the earliest practicable date. This suggestion was accepted by the other parties to the discussion, and Menzies, returning to New York, put forward his amendment.[1]

In a speech delivered on 5 October Nehru strongly opposed the Australian amendment and in the process used words implying that the amendment either had no meaning or covered unjustifiable suspicions that the five sponsors of the original Resolution had 'fallen into some Communist trap'.[2] The Australian amendment received only five affirmative votes (France, the United States, Great Britain, Canada and Australia), but no less than forty-three countries registered abstentions—two less in number than those which voted in the negative. Amongst those which abstained was the Soviet Union. Although the Australian amendment was roundly defeated, the five sponsoring powers withdrew their substantive resolution because it had become clear that it would not receive the necessary majority.

On his return to Australia, Menzies defended himself in Parliament with dignity and humour against criticism which had been levelled within Australia against his activities at the United Nations Assembly. In a speech delivered on 20 October 1960 he recounted the circumstances in detail, and claimed that he had pursued the right course at New York. By that date he was able to disclose that he had seen Khrushchev some days after the voting, and that Khrushchev had 'made it abundantly clear that he wanted a Summit Conference'—presumably a Four-Power Conference. Menzies expressed the hope that such a Conference would in fact take place after the American elections.[3]

Nehru's public criticism of Menzies' intervention in the United Nations in October 1960 on the above-mentioned issue

[1] See C.N. vol. xxxi (1960), pp. 529–33.
[2] Jawaharlal Nehru's Speeches, vol. IV, pp. 327–34.
[3] For text of speech, see C.N. vol. xxxi (1960), pp. 529–43.

is, however, the exception which proves the rule. In fact, both Indian and Australian Prime Ministers and Foreign Ministers normally exercised considerable restraint when referring publicly to each other's foreign policy. Australian leaders, while insisting upon Australia's right and need to enter into military alliances, made it clear that if India decided in her own interests to pursue a policy of non-alignment that was a matter for India herself to decide.

Indian representatives in the United Nations did indeed criticise Australian policy in New Guinea, Papua and Nauru, and this sometimes brought a tart reply.[1] Nor was Australia always silent when it disagreed strongly with an Indian point of view. Thus Spender, as Minister for External Affairs, referred to the 'casuistical argument' that Communist China's representation in the U.N. Security Council was related to the Korean dispute, although he refrained from indicating that the argument had been put forward by India.[2] In general, however, India and Australia pursued their separate policies without recrimination at a level or intensity likely to disturb basically friendly relations.

International developments after 1960 proved the wisdom of this mutual restraint. When in 1962 the border disputes between India and Communist China became acute and serious fighting erupted between the two countries, Chinese troops penetrating deeply into the North-East Frontier Agency, Australian sympathy for India was expressed immediately and practical aid speedily offered. On 28 October Menzies sent a message of 'sympathy and support' to Nehru.[3] This message presumably crossed with a letter of 27 October sent to Menzies by the Indian Prime Minister which revealed the depth of Indian disillusion with the Peking regime. The latter stated, *inter alia*, that it was a matter of deep regret that the Chinese, in their relations with India, had 'paid back evil for good'. Nehru continued:

Friendly and peaceful relations with China have been our basic policy ever since India became independent. We have consistently followed this policy and gone out of our way to support China's case in the councils of the world. We regret that in their relations with India, China has not merely shown a hostile attitude, but has also

---

[1] See *Australia in World Affairs 1950–55*, pp. 260–2.
[2] *Ibid.* quoted at p. 252. For text of speech see *C.N.* vol. XXI (1950), pp. 578–82.
[3] *C.N.* vol. XXXIII (1962), no. 10, p. 41.

resorted to dissimulation...The issue involved is not one of small territorial gains one way or the other, but of standards of international behaviour between neighbouring countries, and whether the world will allow the principle of 'might is right' to prevail in international relations...This crisis is not only of India, but of the world, and will have far-reaching consequences on the standards of international behaviour, and on the peace of the world. We cannot submit to this law of the jungle...[1]

The Indian Prime Minister sought Australian sympathy and support 'directed to the elimination of deceit, dissimulation and force in international relations'.[1]

Whatever reservations the Australian Government may have had about Indian policy on Kashmir and the use of force by India when Goa was incorporated as part of Indian territory, the reply sent by Menzies on 8 November asked whether there were ways in which 'the Australian Government could be of help'.[2] This was followed by a public statement on 22 November by Sir Garfield Barwick, Minister for External Affairs, disclosing that Australia had offered to make a gift of blankets, military clothing and wool tops to the value of £300,000 and, on a credit basis, small arms and ammunition valued at £800,000. The latter offer was subject to the condition that arms and ammunition supplied should be used only for the purpose of resisting Chinese Communist aggression.[3] On 10 March 1963 the Minister announced that the Australian Government had decided to raise the level of assistance to approximately £A2,000,000 and that the earlier credit for rifles and ammunition had been changed to a gift. He added that India had given assurances that such aid would be used only for the purpose of resisting Communist Chinese aggression.[4]

Subsequently, Australia participated in the joint United States–Commonwealth Mission that went to India to look into the problems of its air defences,[5] while a number of exchanges of visits between the two countries took place at both the political and official levels, notably visits by experts in the fields of defence and defence production.

The quality of Australian diplomatic representation in India also deserves mention. While this was inevitably varied over the

[1] *C.N.* vol. xxxiv (1963), nos. 1 and 2, pp. 48–9.   [2] *Ibid.* p. 50.
[3] *C.N.* vol. xxxiii (1962), no. 11, pp. 64–5.
[4] *C.N.* vol. xxxiv (1963), no. 3, p. 22.   [5] *Ibid.* no. 7, p. 61.

period since India acquired her independence, on the whole the standard has been high as compared with many other Australian posts overseas. Since 1952, for instance, Australians appointed to the post have all had wide diplomatic experience. Mr W. R. Crocker served two terms in New Delhi. Educated at Adelaide, Oxford and Stanford Universities, he served for a time in Nigeria as a member of the British Colonial Service before transferring to the staff of the International Labour Office in Geneva. After war service he was for a time attached to the United Nations Secretariat, and then became first Professor of International Relations at the Australian National University. His inaugural lecture on 'The Race Question as a Factor in International Relations' had a marked influence not limited to Australia. Mr Peter Heydon was a career officer of the Department of External Affairs who had served in London, Washington, Moscow, Rio de Janeiro and Wellington, New Zealand. Subsequently he became Permanent Head of the Department of Immigration.

The two appointments since 1962 are, however, of particular interest, clearly indicating the importance attached by the Australian Government to the New Delhi post. In March 1963 Sir James Plimsoll was transferred to New Delhi from the post of Australian Ambassador to the United Nations, New York. After some two years as High Commissioner to India, he was recalled to Canberra to take over responsibility as Permanent Head of the Department of External Affairs. He was succeeded in New Delhi in May 1965 by Sir Arthur Tange, who for some eleven years had been Secretary of that Department.

To sum up: relations between Australia and India in the post-war years have been generally satisfactory. While the Labour Government was still in power relations were close and sympathetic, despite differences of outlook in regard to Japan. There was less sympathy and substantial divergence of policy under the Liberal–Country Party Government from December 1949 to the second half of 1962, but mutual restraint in criticism—for the most part—made easier the establishment of much closer relations during the period 1962–65, after Communist pressure on India had brought about a new situation. There is no present reason to assume that the greater degree of understanding and co-operation now developing is likely to be diminished in the foreseeable future.

3. *China*

For most Australians China is *terra incognita* as compared with India. Although traditional India is to them no less strange than traditional China, they find modern India easier to focus than modern China. The long period of British rule in India, bringing with it for the *élite* use of the English language, subjection to British educational processes in England or India itself, the spread of British legal and administrative practices, the gradual growth of a British-type parliamentary system—not to mention common membership of the Commonwealth of Nations, helped Australians to think of India as a country reasonably familiar. Very few Australians, of course, appreciated the rigidities of the caste system, or knew the facts of Indian village life. Nevertheless, India was not regarded as a 'foreign' country, but as an 'Eastern' part of the Empire or Commonwealth.

China, on the other hand, was completely strange. Australians who knew it well could be counted upon the fingers of two hands. One of these was Dr George Ernest Morrison (1862–1920)—'Chinese' Morrison—the story of whose life as explorer, correspondent in Peking of the London *Times* and political adviser to Yuan Shih-ka'i reads like an improbable work of fiction.[1] Another was W. H. Donald (1875–1946)—'Donald of China'—a journalist who eventually became Managing Director of the *China Mail*, Hong Kong, correspondent for British and American newspapers, adviser to various Chinese authorities and a friend of Chiang Kai-shek. He was interned by Japanese forces in the Philippines during the Second World War and was released when the Philippines were liberated. The Japanese regarded him as a bitter enemy, but never learned his identity while he was in captivity—either from Donald himself or from fellow prisoners.[2]

Most Australians, however, knew little or nothing of traditional China, of her imperial power and cultural achievements during millennia before European domination in the nineteenth and early twentieth centuries and before an Asian power, Japan, joined the search for special privileges. To the average Australian, Chinese were immigrants, mainly of the coolie

[1] See *Australian Encyclopaedia*, ed. Chisholm (1958 ed.), vol. VI, pp. 156–8.
[2] *Ibid.* vol. III, pp. 268–9.

class, who had come to Australia during the gold rushes of the nineteenth century. Later, they were known as market-gardeners, furniture makers or businessmen—the largest Asian population in Australia, and a constant headache to the Department of Immigration because of their skilful and obstinate evasiveness.[1]

An Australian Trade Commissioner was appointed to Shanghai as early as 1921, but the appointment was soon terminated. A further appointment to this post was made in 1935. Diplomatic relations between China and Australia were not opened until after the outbreak of the Second World War. Reference has already been made to the establishment by the Menzies Government of the first Australian diplomatic mission to a foreign country when, early in 1940, Casey was sent as Minister to Washington. This was followed in August 1940 by the appointment of Sir John Latham[2] as Minister to Tokyo, and in July 1941 of Sir Frederic Eggleston[2] as Minister to Chungking.

The Australian Government, which in 1938 had supported the Chamberlain policy of appeasement of Hitler at Munich, agreed with the British decision, made under Japanese pressure just after the fall of France, that the Burma Road should be closed for a period of three months. This policy did not reflect any lack of sympathy for China or any lack of realism in judging Japanese ambitions; it was rather a desperate attempt to gain time during which some Far Eastern Settlement might be negotiated with Japan or at least some promise obtained of United States support against Japan if and when she moved south. Australia also concurred in the British decision to reopen the Burma Road, shortly after Japan joined the 'Axis Pact' on 28 September 1940.[3]

When in late November 1941 the negotiations in Washington between Japan and the United States broke down, China strongly opposing acceptance by the United States of a *modus vivendi* proffered by Japan, Casey made a last-minute call upon the chief Japanese negotiator, Kurusu, offering to act as an intermediary between Japan on the one hand and the United States and Great Britain on the other if Kurusu had any further proposal to make.[4] This personal intervention came to nothing and

[1] See Yarwood, *op. cit.* chapter 6, for the history of Chinese immigration 1896–1923.　　[2] For brief details of their careers, see p. 25 above.
[3] See Hasluck, *Government and People*, p. 525.　　[4] See p. 40 above.

was probably unknown at the time to the Chinese Embassy in Washington. On 7 December Pearl Harbor was bombed by the Japanese. On this occasion the Labour Party Government, taking a different constitutional view from that followed by Menzies when Great Britain declared war against Germany in 1939, issued a separate declaration of war against Japan.[1] Australia and China found themselves allies.

China and Australia had a common interest thereafter in endeavouring to ensure that American involvement in the European War and adoption by the United Kingdom and the United States of the policy of 'Beat Hitler First' did not result in such a diminution of Allied—especially American—military aid in the Pacific as to defer indefinitely the defeat of Japan or greatly to increase the cost of such defeat. The difference in status between the two countries, however, led to the exclusion of Australia (and New Zealand) from the Cairo Conference of November 1943, attended by President Roosevelt, Mr Churchill and Generalissimo Chiang Kai-shek. Reference has been made already[2] to the effect of this exclusion upon Australia and New Zealand, and to the part which it played in stimulating the two dominions to enter into the 'Anzac Pact' of January 1944, in which they expressed in somewhat vehement terms their own vital interest in any Far Eastern Settlement.[3]

Diplomatic representation between Australia and China was maintained at a high level during the post-war years. When Sir Frederic Eggleston, the first Australian Minister to China, was appointed to Washington in 1944, the Australian Legation in China was under the control of Mr F. K. Officer, as Chargé d'Affaires. Officer was at that stage the most senior member of the Department of External Affairs serving overseas.[4] In 1946 Professor D. B. Copland[5] was appointed Australian Minister, and he was succeeded in 1948 by Officer as Ambassador, the two countries having in the meanwhile raised their missions to the level of embassies. Officer remained in China until the Australian Mission was withdrawn, following the defeat of the Kuomintang forces by the Chinese Communists and the

---

[1] For details as to the constitutional procedures adopted, see *C.N.* vol. XII (1942), no. 1, pp. 3–7. [2] See p. 73 above. [3] See pp. 74–6 above.
[4] At that date he had already served in London, Washington, Tokyo and Moscow.
[5] Professor of Commerce (1924–44) at the University of Melbourne; Commonwealth Prices Commissioner (1939–45); Vice-Chancellor (1948–53), Australian National University; Principal, Australian Administrative Staff College (1956–59).

departure of Chiang Kai-shek and his supporters to the island of Formosa.

The subsequent history of Australian diplomatic relations with China is peculiar, and requires close investigation,[1] as interpretations have been placed upon Australian policy which the facts do not justify. The Australian Diplomatic Mission was withdrawn from Nanking in October 1949, the Ambassador and his staff returning to Canberra except for a small group which was left in Hong Kong. This group showed continuing interest in the availability of embassy premises in Peking. After the outbreak of the Korean War, the group was returned to Australia.[2] From 1949 to 1966 Australia had no diplomatic mission either in Peking or Taipei; yet Nationalist China was continuously represented in Canberra at the level of Ambassador or Chargé d'Affaires![3]

In these circumstances it has been claimed that the new Liberal–Country Party Government which came to power in Canberra in December 1949 originally intended to recognize Communist China, probably in two stages. During the first stage diplomatic relations with Nationalist China would be severed; during the second stage recognition would be accorded to the Communist Chinese regime in Peking. The legend has been developed that this Australian policy was frustrated by the United States Government, which made its acceptance of the ANZUS military alliance conditional upon a promise by the Australian Government not to recognise Communist China.

The main support for this latter claim, is a statement by Dr John Burton, Permanent Head of the Australian Department of External Affairs from 1947 to early June 1950. In his book

[1] An exhaustive study of relations between Australia and China in the post-war period has been made by Henry S. Albinski in his book *Australia's Policies and Attitudes towards China* (Princeton University Press, 1965). This is based, *inter alia*, upon investigations carried out in Australia itself while Dr Albinski was a Visiting Fellow in the Department of International Relations, Australian National University. For preliminary studies by the same author, see also *Australia and the China Problem during the Korean War* (Working Paper no. 5, Department of International Relations, A.N.U.); 'Australia and the China Problem under the Labor Government', article in *Australian Journal of Politics and History*, vol. x (August 1964), pp. 149–72; 'Australia and the Chinese Strategic Embargo', article in *Australian Outlook*, vol. xix, no. 2, pp. 117–28.

[2] Albinski, *Australian Policies towards China*, p. 64.

[3] In June 1966 the Holt Government, without convincing explanation, decided to open a mission in Taipei; see *C.N.* vol. xxxvii (1966), p. 379.

The Alternative, published in 1954 after his resignation from the Commonwealth Public Service, Burton wrote as follows:

...six months after being in office, the Liberal Minister (Mr Spender) asked his advisers for suggestions as to how recognition could be accorded in politically tactful stages, and was prepared to accord *de facto* recognition of the Communist Government as a first step, though not to support immediate recognition by the United Nations. The Prime Minister (Mr Menzies), then in London, was asked to assent to recognition, and left the impression that he would. However, in February 1951, before Mr Menzies had returned, Mr Dulles visited Sydney, and the last vestige of Australian independence vanished. Australia promised not to recognise China...in exchange for the A.N.Z.U.S. Pact.[1]

The publisher's note on the back cover of the book states that Dr Burton 'was Secretary of the Department of External Affairs from 1947 to 1951, when he was appointed High Commissioner to Ceylon'. The general reader would assume from this description that Burton was Secretary of the Department when Dulles visited Canberra in February 1951; as such he would, of course, have been in the best possible position to know what Dulles said.

In fact, Burton ceased to be Secretary of the Department when in June 1950 he sought and was accorded six months' leave of absence; a successor was appointed Secretary in his place. In January 1951 he was nominated Australian High Commissioner to Ceylon,[2] and left Australia for Colombo on 2 February. In March of the same year he returned to Australia[3] to contest unsuccessfully a Federal seat on behalf of the Australian Labour Party, and was not subsequently a member of the Department of External Affairs. Burton was not present at any meeting between the United States, New Zealand and Australian delegations which, after Dulles's arrival in Canberra on 14 February 1951, discussed the proposed Japanese Peace Treaty and a possible ANZUS Pact.

The second main proponent of the assertion that the United States accepted the proposal for an ANZUS Pact only on condition that Australia agreed not to recognise Communist

---

[1] Burton, *The Alternative*, p. 91.
[2] See *C.N.* vol. xxii (1951), p. 65.
[3] *Ibid.* p. 182.

China is Professor C. P. Fitzgerald, of the Australian National University.[1] He has written as follows:

...Mr John Foster Dulles visited Canberra in February 1951 in order to discuss with Australian political leaders the prospective Japanese Peace Treaty...In international relations small powers may propose, but great powers dispose. It soon became clear that America was determined to go forward with a Japanese Peace Treaty framed on lenient lines...America was...ready to meet Australian fears to some degree, but only if Australia for her part would conform to American policy in the Pacific. The United States was not prepared to recognise Communist China, which since October 1950 had been actively intervening in the Korean war. It was made plain that Australia also must refrain from such recognition if she wished to gain from America any guarantee of security to offset the re-emergence of Japan.[2]

Professor Fitzgerald gives no source for this important statement, but subsequently repeats it, claiming in the following words that Casey, as Minister for External Affairs, admitted the charge in 1953:

Just as the close connexion between the Japanese Peace Treaty and the ANZUS Pact had been recognised by both political parties, so the Minister for External Affairs admitted that the price for ANZUS also included the non-recognition of China.

Quoting the resolution of the ANZUS Council in November 1953 Mr Casey said, 'Under present circumstances no recognition of Communist China or admission of its representatives to the United Nations would be entertained'.[3]

Read in its full context[4] Casey's statement of 27 November 1953, two years after discussions in Canberra, cannot justifiably be interpreted as an admission that, in 1951, Dulles demanded, as part of the price for ANZUS, a promise by Australia not to recognise the Peking regime. Professor N. C. H. Dunbar has repeated this charge as recently as 1965 in the following words: 'But the reward of Australia for her agreement to a lenient Japanese Peace Treaty and for her refusal to have relations with the Communist Government of China was a Treaty [ANZUS] framed in somewhat less compromising terms.'[5] Of the two authorities cited for this comment, however, Dr Evatt

[1] Professor of Far Eastern History, Research School of Pacific Studies.
[2] *Australia in World Affairs 1950–55*, p. 207.
[3] *Ibid.* p. 213.   [4] *C.P.D.*, H. of R., vol. II (1953), p. 664.
[5] *International Law in Australia*, p. 402.

was dealing solely with the relationship between ANZUS and the Japanese Peace Treaty, while Professor Fitzgerald's claim remains unsubstantiated.

That Australia continually took into account, both before and after ANZUS, the attitude of the United States towards recognition of Communist China was both natural and inevitable. But any suggestion that Australian policy towards China, even after ANZUS was ratified, was completely rigid and merely echoed American policy is a gross over-simplification. Fortunately, Dr Albinski has considered this question at some length and with remarkable objectivity. He draws attention to a number of issues on which Australian and American policy diverged. Thus, although the policy of the two countries coincided as regards support for United Nations action in Korea, the crossing of the 38th parallel by Allied Forces and the declaration by the United Nations that Communist China had committed aggression, Australia consistently refrained from setting up a diplomatic mission on Formosa,[1] and opposed suggestions by General MacArthur that targets across the Yalu River should be bombed and Nationalist Chinese troops used in Korea. The Australian Prime Minister stated publicly that Australia would not think that the destiny of the 'off-shore' islands between Formosa and the mainland of China 'were worth a great war'.[2] When in April 1953 Burma complained to the United Nations about the continuing presence of Chinese Nationalist irregular troops, Spender, by then Australian Ambassador to Washington, was extremely active and vocal in his criticism of delays in their withdrawal from Burma. 'Time and again Australia openly scolded the Nationalists, urged meaningful measures against the arms shipments, and hardly hesitated to differentiate herself from the more conciliatory tone of the American delegation.'[3] Dr Albinski has rightly called attention to the importance, for an understanding of certain reservations in the attitude of Australians towards the Government of Nationalist China, of critical reactions, first, to misuse of very substantial UNRAA aid sent from Australia to China after the Second World War, and, secondly, to Nationalist China activities on Manus Island after the war which were prejudicial to Australian interests.[4]

[1] See now page 240, note 3.
[2] *C.N.* vol. xxvi (1955), p. 117.
[3] Albinski, *Australia's Policies towards China*, p. 89.   [4] *Ibid.* pp. 5–9.

Further, Australian policy towards trade with Communist China has not been identical with American policy, although American feeling on this subject has obviously been taken into account.[1] Despite strong American objections to such trade, Australia has sold to Communist China not only wool but large quantities of wheat. In 1957 a second-hand rolling mill was sold,[2] and in 1958–59 some iron and steel plate.[3] According to Albinski Australia maintains three lists of goods in relation to exports to China. The first contains items which may be exported freely, including beeswax, earthenware, kitchenware, sulpha drugs, toys, wheat, agricultural machinery and implements (not including tractors). The second sets out goods which can *not* be exported to China. The third is an 'intermediate list' of goods, which can be exported to China only if an export licence is granted. Licences for these may or may not be granted, depending on circumstances, policy being decided by the Department of External Affairs, often in consultation with the Department of Trade and Industry.[4] In short, Australia in her trade with Communist China stands somewhere between the United States on the one hand and Great Britain, Japan and some other countries on the other. She takes into serious account American objections to trade, especially in what are clearly strategic items; yet within these limits trades substantially in what she regards as non-strategic items. Albinski sums up:

The nature of Australia's strategic embargo against China is...a very successful exercise in *realpolitik*. The Government's position can variously be regarded as inconsistent, secretive, or hypocritical. But at bottom it is pretty much a case of having one's cake and eating it too. Maintaining a stiff strategic materials policy helps to placate America, to make her more sympathetic towards expressed Australian views on international questions in general, and perhaps even softens her objections to Australia's non-strategic trade with China. Maintaining the 'China differential' also serves to deter potentially embarrassing political criticism at home.[5]

Sufficient evidence has been presented to dispel the charge that, in its policy towards China, the Australian Government has merely echoed or followed the views of the United States,

---

[1] Albinski, *Australia's Policies towards China*, chapters VI, VII.
[2] Albinski, 'Australia and the Chinese strategic embargo', p. 121.
[3] Albinski, *Australia's Policies towards China*, p. 258.   [4] *Ibid.* pp. 305–8.
[5] Albinski, 'Australia and the Chinese strategic embargo', pp. 127–8.

and that such a policy of automatic acceptance of American policy flowed from a condition allegedly laid down by Dulles before signature of the ANZUS Treaty. The credibility of the charge has in the past been increased not insubstantially by the policy of the Menzies Government in deliberately choosing to reduce to a minimum the occasions upon which differences with 'great and powerful' friends have been disclosed publicly to the Australian electorate—with the notable and remarkable exception of differences over many aspects of trade policy! Thus the Minister for External Affairs, Sir Garfield Barwick, said in 1964:

> ...I do not believe in diplomacy by statements in newspapers...I prefer direct communication, preferably face to face, which lacks the embarrassment of publicity and engenders confidence in the continuous quiet exchange of significant views, not merely, though particularly, in times of crisis or approaching crisis...overall it is the course best calculated to advance national interests and avoid unnecessary conflict and exacerbation of difficult situations.[1]

While there is much force in this attitude as a statement of general principle, two comments should be made. When the Australian Government refrains from informing its own public opinion of occasions when its policy differs from that of its friends and Allies, it not only deprives Australians of important information, but affects the Australian image in other countries and deprives itself of the opportunity of affecting public opinion favouring the Australian point of view in countries whose governments hold opposing or divergent views. Thus 'non-aligned' countries may the more readily believe that Australia is an 'American stooge'; while opinion in the United States opposing official American policy on a particular issue is deprived of the stimulus and support of confirmatory Australian views. Such knowledge would be helpful in strengthening efforts by majority or minority opinion in the United States to seek relevant changes in American policy.

Secondly, the phrase 'diplomacy by statements in newspapers' is ambiguous. Few if any would argue that the best means of communication between Foreign Ministers is through statements in national newspapers. But newspapers also report ministerial statements in Parliament. Explanation to Parlia-

---

[1] Wilkes, *Australia's Defence and Foreign Policy*, pp. 8-9.

ment, subsequently reflected in mass media of communication, and followed up in occasional press conferences, is not only an essential aspect of democratic government, but can on selected occasions be a valuable means of conveying to foreign governments the limits of flexibility within which Australian foreign policy operates.

It must be remembered, however, that the interpretation by the Australian Government of Communist Chinese policy frequently coincided with the interpretation of the United States Government. When Australian fears of a resurgent militarist Japan within the foreseeable future gradually subsided and Australian political leaders surveyed the Asian scene, it was on Peking that their attention focused. While they had no ambition to become involved in a full-scale war with Communist China, whether through bombing or 'hot pursuit' on the northern side of the Yalu or through American support for Nationalist Chinese operations against the mainland, they did in fact regard the Peking regime not only as an aggressor in Korea but also as the main threat to long-term stability in South-East Asia. The Liberal–Country Party Government under Sir Robert Menzies was strongly anti-Communist in outlook, and interpreted Chinese Communist policy as the most belligerent form of Communism. When Chinese troops invaded Indian territory in 1962, Australian sympathies were wholly on the side of India, whatever reservations might be held about some aspects of past Indian policy.

Naturally, there were more immediate preoccupations from time to time, such as Vietnam, Indonesia, Malaysia, and undeclared war between India and Pakistan over Kashmir in 1965. But the Australian Prime Minister and successive Ministers for External Affairs since December 1949 have all at one stage or another seen the Peking regime as Australia's greatest long-term threat.

The present Minister for External Affairs, Mr Paul Hasluck, has expressed himself forcibly on this theme on several occasions. In a press statement issued in Washington on 25 November 1964 he spoke as follows:

The rising power of China, its aggression and subversion against its neighbours, and its political activities in other continents, make it the major danger to peace today.

South-East Asia is threatened by the Communist Chinese and

unable to gain either stable government or to bring social and economic progress to its peoples because of the fear of Communist China.

The aggressive intent of the Communist Chinese government, shown blatantly by actions in India and Tibet and in the plain declarations of its leaders, is a threat to the world. This is not just a regional or an Asian question. It is part of a world conflict. It is the most significant factor in the long-term problem of world peace.[1]

It is not without interest that Nehru in his letter to Menzies of 27 October 1962 disclosed a similar interpretation of Communist Chinese policy when he wrote: 'This crisis is not only of India, but of the world, and will have far-reaching consequences on the standards of international behaviour, and on the peace of the world.'[2] Australian critics of the attitude of the Menzies Government towards Communist China who tend to regard it as bigoted, parochial, conservative and unimaginative might do well to ponder upon the fact that the creator of the policy of 'non-alignment' and the apostle of faith in Communist Chinese readiness to adhere to the Five Principles, including peaceful co-existence, felt impelled by harsh experience to adopt a far more critical attitude towards the policy of Peking.

Addressing the House of Representatives on 23 March 1965 after China had exploded its first nuclear device, Hasluck reiterated the views he had expressed some four months earlier:

Some time may elapse before Communist China becomes a front-rank nuclear power, but the cause for concern is that China has repeatedly spoken and acted in a way that reveals an aggressive intention to try to dominate the life of other nations, a readiness to achieve her purposes by any means at her command, and an unwillingness to contemplate peaceful relationships with other great powers except on her own terms. In the hands of such a nation, nuclear weapons become more dangerous and the prospect of nuclear control of disarmament less hopeful.[3]

The same view was underlined and elaborated by Hasluck in a speech in Parliament on 10 March 1966, after the retirement of Sir Robert Menzies and the formation of the new Holt Government.

We want to see an Asia free from fear and insecurity in which the independent nations will be able to develop for themselves the kind of society and the forms of government that they believe are best suited

[1] *C.N.* vol. xxxv, no. xi (1964), p. 33.
[2] See p. 235 above.   [3] *C.N.* vol. xxxvi (1965), p. 119.

to themselves, where human welfare can be advanced more rapidly, and where economic progress will strengthen the means by which each country will be able to support its own independence. We want to see the conditions in which such free and prosperous nations will be able by their own decision to co-operate more fully in measures for common welfare and security. This means that it must be an Asia free from the domination of any single great power and safe from the persistent subversion of a communism which is being used deliberately as an instrument of imperialist power...What threatens this freedom and independence...is the dread of domination by the new imperialism of China and the throttling grip of Communist aggressors. It is the Communists who have themselves announced their plans. Are these so-called liberation fronts—the National Liberation Front of Vietnam, the Malaysian Liberation Front or the Thailand Liberation Front, all of whom have lodging and blessing in Peking—created to ensure that peoples of Asia will be free to choose for themselves?...They have been formed and dedicated to the purpose of bringing these countries, without free choice, under Communist rule.[1]

The assumptions which lie behind this interpretation of Communist Chinese policy may be questioned, but it is unwise either to doubt the sincerity of the governmental attitude so expressed or to under-estimate the evidence upon which it is based.

A review of policy towards China since 1949 makes it clear that the attitude of the Australian Government towards the Peking regime is based upon factors wider and deeper than any mere desire to avoid American displeasure. These include moral disinclination to take any action which could have the result of incorporating in a Communist State, against their will, the population of Formosa.

4. Indonesia

Few international problems in the post-war period have proved as difficult for Australia as the development of a friendly and effective policy towards Indonesia. Australians could not but associate Indonesia in their minds with the Japanese thrust southwards, and they found it hard to forget that many Indonesian nationalists, like Sukarno, had collaborated with the Japanese. The nearness of Indonesia, the size of its population and the economic potential of its soil all underlined for Australians the long-term need for friendly relations between the two

[1] *C.P.D.* 10 March 1966, p. 173.

countries. On the other hand, Indonesia's political instability in the years after she acquired independence in 1949; the chaos of her economy; the authoritarian substitution of 'guided democracy' for Western parliamentary democracy; and the strident nationalism fostered by President Sukarno's 'confrontation' policies made a deep and uncomfortable impression on Indonesia's southern neighbour. Australians had to consider two serious alternatives, neither of which they liked. Would Indonesia become a unified and effective authoritarian State, aggressive and expansive in outlook; or would economic chaos give the powerful Communist Party its opportunity to seize power, with the support and assistance of China or the Soviet Union or both?

During the period 1945–49, while the Australian Labour Party was still in power, relations between the two countries were exceptionally close and friendly. Such relations were facilitated by the fact that the long-drawn-out and bitter dispute between the Netherlands and Indonesia over the West New Guinea issue had not come to a head. They were not adversely affected by the invitation extended by the Australian and New Zealand Governments to the Netherlands to attend the South Seas Commission Conference which opened in Canberra on 28 January 1947. This Conference, consisting as well of representatives of the United States, the United Kingdom and France, established a South Pacific Commission as 'a consultative and advisory body to the participating Governments in matters affecting the economic and social development of the non-self-governing territories within the scope of the Commission and the welfare and advancement of their peoples'.[1] The Dutch representative made it clear at the Second Plenary Session of the Conference that 'only that part of the Netherlands Indies known as Dutch New Guinea' came within the scope of the Conference.[2]

The Round Table Conference at The Hague between the Netherlands and Indonesia, held in 1949, agreed that Indonesia should acquire sovereignty over the Netherlands Indies; but the issue of West New Guinea was not resolved: it was sidetracked by agreement to maintain the *status quo* pending determination of its political status through negotiations within the succeeding year. If the Australian Labour Party had remained

[1] For text of agreement, see *C.N.* vol. XVIII (1947), pp. 97–105.   [2] *Ibid.* p. 16.

in office during the period when the unresolved dispute over West New Guinea became a serious current problem, Australia's relations with Indonesia would have suffered, just as they did under the Liberal–Country Party Government; for the Labour Party at no time endorsed the Indonesian claim to West New Guinea—indeed, when in Opposition it was often critical of the Menzies Government for not being sufficiently tough and decisive on this issue.

Reference has already been made[1] to collaboration between Australia and India in regard to the problem of Indonesian independence. Both countries brought the issue before the United Nations Security Council on 30 July 1947. Australia asked the Council to determine the existence of a breach of the peace, to call on the parties to cease hostilities and withdraw troops, and to recommend that the parties should seek a solution by arbitration. In the event, a somewhat milder Resolution proposed by the United States was adopted, but the Australian action must have given great satisfaction to Indonesian leaders.

On 25 August 1947 a joint Australian–Chinese proposal on the observance of a cease-fire was adopted by the Security Council.[2] On the same date the Council tendered its good offices to assist in the pacific settlement of the dispute, and expressed its readiness, if the parties so requested, 'to assist in the settlement through a committee of the Council consisting of three members of the Council, each party selecting one and the third to be designated by the two so selected'.[3] Indonesia nominated Australia to this committee, the Netherlands nominated Belgium, while Australia and Belgium together nominated the United States as the third member. On 28 January 1949 this committee was converted by the Security Council into a Good Offices Commission, with power to assist the parties in implementing a further Council Resolution of that date.

The first Australian representative on the committee was Mr Justice Kirby.[4] In 1948 he was succeeded by Mr T. K. Critchley,[5] a career officer of the Department of External Affairs, 'who remained until after the transfer of sovereignty and came to be regarded by many Indonesians as a symbol of Aus-

---

[1] See p. 222 above.   [2] *C.N.* vol. XVIII (1947), p. 465.   [3] *Ibid.* p. 466.
[4] Now Sir Richard Kirby, President, Commonwealth Conciliation and Arbitration Commission.
[5] Later, Australian High Commissioner to Malaya (1955–57) and to Malaysia (1957–65).

tralia's sympathy towards the Republic'.[1] Nor was other evidence of Australian sympathy for the Indonesian cause lacking. An invitation from the Indian Government to attend the New Delhi Conference on Indonesia, held in January 1949, was accepted, Dr J. W. Burton, Secretary of the Department of External Affairs, attending with another official representative. Acceptance of this invitation to a conference to which neither the United Kingdom nor the Netherlands had been invited was strongly criticised by members of the parliamentary Opposition.[2] Further, after the second Dutch 'police action' in December 1948 had strengthened the determination of the Australian Government to take more vigorous action, the Australian representative in the Security Council, Lt.-Col. W. R. Hodgson,[3] delivered a bitter attack upon Dutch policy and demanded the expulsion of the Netherlands from the United Nations.[4]

It is unnecessary to trace in detail the significant steps taken by the Good Offices Committee and Commission in helping to bring about eventual agreement between the Netherlands and Indonesia on the issue of independence for the territory of the old Netherlands East Indies, with the exception of West New Guinea. The important point is that the nomination of Australia to the Committee by Indonesia represents the high-water mark of close and sympathetic relations between the two countries in the post-war years. In December 1949 the Menzies Government came to power. As relations between Indonesia and the Netherlands became more and more exacerbated because of the West New Guinea issue, relations between Indonesia and Australia gradually deteriorated.

While in Opposition, leaders of the Liberal and Country Parties had from time to time criticised the Government's policy as anti-Dutch and pro-Indonesian. By the time the Menzies Government came to power in December 1949, however, the Round Table Conference at The Hague had ended and the Netherlands Government had promised to transfer sovereignty over the Netherlands East Indies to Indonesia, with the exception of West New Guinea. One of the first acts of the new Gov-

[1] Comment by J. A. C. Mackie, in *Australia in World Affairs 1956–60*, p. 278.
[2] For text of New Delhi Resolutions, see *C.N.* vol. xx (1949), pp. 283–5.
[3] Secretary, Department of External Affairs, 1935–45; Australian Minister, later Ambassador, to France 1945–49; British Commonwealth Representative, Allied Council for Japan 1949–52; High Commissioner to South Africa 1952–57; died 24 January 1958.   [4] *Australia in World Affairs 1956–60*, p. 280.

ernment in Canberra was to accord recognition to Indonesia, thus accepting independence as a *fait accompli*.[1]

The Minister for External Affairs, Mr Spender, spent several days in Djakarta on his way to the Conference of Commonwealth Ministers held in Colombo from 9 to 14 January 1950. He met President Sukarno and most of his cabinet, and 'formed the conclusion that they were able men with moderate views and a sober realisation of the immensity of the tasks in front of them'.[2] This early and somewhat naïve opinion was expressed in the course of the Minister's first review for Parliament of the international situation on 9 March 1950. During the speech he made a brief though indirect reference to the West New Guinea issue when he said that 'New Guinea...is an absolutely essential link in the chain of Australian defence. The Australian people are deeply interested in what happens anywhere in New Guinea.'[3] In the context it is clear that Spender was referring not merely to Australian New Guinea, but to the Island of New Guinea as a whole.

A considered statement of the Government's policy on Dutch New Guinea was made by Spender in the House of Representatives on 8 June 1950.[4] The Minister referred back to his earlier statement of 9 March in which he had 'said that, for security and strategic reasons, Australia had a vital interest in the question of the future status of Dutch New Guinea'.[5] It was the Government's view that, should discussions between the Netherlands and Indonesia 'trend' towards any arrangement which would alter the status of West New Guinea. the matter was no longer one merely for the Netherlands and Indonesia themselves. West New Guinea was an integral part of New Guinea as a whole, both ethnically and strategically. 'In the future of Western New Guinea, Australia has direct and vital interests, and feels strongly that those interests are entitled to be considered.'[6]

Spender became Australian Ambassador in Washington in 1951, and he was succeeded in the portfolio of External Affairs by Casey. It was Casey's ambition to keep the problem of Dutch New Guinea in 'cold storage'. He contested Indonesian legal claims to the territory, stressed the differences between the

[1] *C.N.* vol. xx (1949), pp. 248–9.   [2] *C.N.* vol. xxi (1950), p. 159.
[3] *Ibid.* p. 164.   [4] *Ibid.* pp. 416–17.
[5] *Ibid.* p. 416.   [6] *Ibid.* p. 417.

Papuans of West New Guinea and the Indo-Malayans of the 'Indonesian islands' as regards ethnic origin, language and culture, and reaffirmed the strategic importance for Australia of the whole island of New Guinea. Australia had a 'vital and legitimate interest in the future of Dutch New Guinea...a right to a voice in any discussions which would change its present status'.[1] In his view Indonesia had 'complicated and intractable economic and political problems to solve, which must provide distinct limits to its ability to ensure the proper administration, development and defence of New Guinea'.[2] Australia wanted to be friends with Indonesia, and to see her 'peaceful and prosperous'.[2] She was ready to help Indonesia under the Colombo Plan by gifts of equipment and provision of technical assistance. But this would not prevent Australia co-operating with the Dutch in West New Guinea at the administrative level, discussing problems common to Dutch and Australian New Guinea in the fields of health, agriculture, education and social development, and improving transport and communications between the two territories.[2]

Unfortunately, the West New Guinea problem could not be kept in 'cold storage', because President Sukarno was determined to oust the Dutch from their last European colonial territory on the eastern flank of Indonesia. Both the Netherlands and Australia under-estimated his determination to achieve his objective, and the amount of support given by his colleagues, the army and the Indonesian Communist Party (PKI).

Indonesia took the problem on numerous occasions to the General Assembly of the United Nations, and there, as also in Afro-Asian Conferences, obtained increasing support for her case. She failed, however, to secure the necessary two-thirds majority in the General Assembly for Resolutions proposed by her, although she came close to doing so. Australia on each occasion supported the Dutch, stressing the right of the Papuans of West New Guinea to self-determination.

After a rebel Government was set up in Sumatra on 15 February 1958, Australia adopted an official policy of non-interference. The rebellion failed, and the United States quickly adjusted itself to the new situation in Indonesia, sending to Djakarta as Ambassador Mr Howard P. Jones, who remained

[1] Casey, *Friends and Neighbours* (1954 ed.), p. 102.
[2] *Ibid.* pp. 102–4.

there until 1965 and symbolised American efforts to retain friendly links with Indonesia despite Sukarno's 'confrontation' of the Dutch and of Malaysia, his purchase on credit from the Soviet Union of substantial military equipment, and his NASAKOM policy under which the Communist Party was regarded as an essential element in the Indonesian community.

During 1959 Australia, too, made efforts to improve relations with Indonesia. The Indonesian Foreign Minister, Dr Subandrio, was invited to visit Australia, and he and Mr Casey issued a joint statement which caused much controversy. After referring to the different views of their two countries regarding West New Guinea, the two Ministers declared:

This difference remains, but the position was clarified by an explanation from Australian Ministers that it followed from their position of respect for agreements on the rights of sovereignty that if any agreement were reached between the Netherlands and Indonesia as parties principal, arrived at by peaceful processes and in accordance with internationally accepted principles, Australia would not oppose such an agreement.

A further paragraph stated that 'force should not be used by the parties concerned in the settlement of territorial differences'.[1]

This joint declaration was attacked in Parliament and in the Press as indicating a change in Australian policy on West Irian, as a concession to Indonesia and as an invitation to Indonesia to mount pressure on the Dutch. The Government stoutly denied that there had been any change, but the strength of the attack must have discouraged any tendency towards change if the Government had wished to move in a direction more conciliatory to Indonesia on this issue. In December of the same year the Australian Prime Minister visited Indonesia, but little resulted from the visit other than a restatement of diverse attitudes towards West New Guinea and the endorsement by President Sukarno of Dr Subandrio's undertaking that force would not be used to settle the problem.

Meanwhile a conservative Dutch Government came to power in March 1959. This Government, having decided after soundings that the Australian Government was not prepared to commit itself to a common solution for both Dutch and Australian New Guinea in the form of a Melanesian Federation, and feeling

---

[1] *Australia in World Affairs 1956–60*, quoted at p. 305.

the need to take an initiative in view of growing anti-colonial pressures in the United Nations, decided to increase the pace of the movement towards self-government in Dutch New Guinea.

In 1961 the Dutch Foreign Minister took the bold step of informing the United Nations General Assembly that the Netherlands Government was prepared to hand over control of West New Guinea to the United Nations. He proposed, first, the creation by the Assembly of a United Nations Commission to organise a plebiscite in West New Guinea to enable the inhabitants to decide their own future, and, secondly, replacement of the Netherlands by the United Nations as administering authority in the territory. He offered on behalf of his Government to continue to contribute $30 million a year as financial aid, and to urge Dutch officials to continue as international civil servants. Indonesian opposition led to the rejection of these proposals, while other resolutions on West New Guinea also failed to attract the necessary two-thirds majority.

In November 1961 the Dutch Government announced the provision of finance for a considerable build-up of its defence forces in West New Guinea. Shortly afterwards the Indonesian cabinet decided to purchase large quantities of Russian arms. On 18 December India seized by force the Portuguese territory of Goa. Portugal referred the issue to the United Nations Security Council immediately, without success. On 19 December President Sukarno alerted Indonesian forces to await his call for the 'liberation' of West New Guinea and Dr Subandrio made the following official statement:

While previously the West Irian problem as well as other problems involving Indonesian–Dutch interests have been handled in the spirit of achieving agreement by negotiations on the give and take basis, now the Government adopts a policy of confrontation in all fields, which means we will confront the Dutch hostility with a similar attitude, in the political, economic, and if necessary in the military field.[1]

The Acting Secretary-General of the United Nations, U Thant, intervened as early as 19 December when he sent cables to The Hague and Djakarta expressing concern at the serious situation which had developed, and the hope that the parties

---

[1] *Indonesia on the March*, vol. II, pp. 260–1 (Indonesian Department of Foreign Affairs).

could negotiate a peaceful solution. As fighting in and around Dutch New Guinea developed in January 1962, U Thant requested that the Governments of the two countries should instruct their representatives at the United Nations to discuss with him possibilities of a peaceful settlement. Such discussion did in fact take place, and specific proposals were put forward by Mr Ellsworth Bunker, an American business-man and ex-diplomat, acting as a 'third-party observer'[1] designated by the Acting Secretary-General.

By 15 August 1962 the Dutch—faced by Indonesian armed forces greatly strengthened by Soviet weapons; unsupported by any military alliance with Australia; and keenly aware that their two NATO allies, the United States and Great Britain, were determined not to burn their fingers in the fire of such an internationally unpopular and, to them, relatively unimportant issue—yielded. An agreement based upon the principles of the Bunker proposals was signed with Indonesia under which the latter would take over control of West Irian as from 1 May 1963 following an interim period of United Nations control. Under this agreement Indonesia undertook to make arrangements by 1969 for the population of West New Guinea to exercise a right of free-choice or self-determination—an undertaking which subsequent Indonesian statements and actions have called in question. The Australian Government felt that there was no alternative to acquiescence in the terms of the agreement.

President Sukarno was exultant. In his Independence Day Address of 17 August 1963 he described the preceding twelve months as the 'Year of Triumph'. History, he declared, was on the side of Indonesia, which typified the new emerging forces opposed to the old established order. The policy of 'confrontation', 'continuous' confrontation, was the key to success.[2] The method had been tested against the Dutch. Political and economic difficulties within Indonesia made it useful to focus national attention upon another external 'enemy'. By the time the President made his speech 'confrontation' was being applied against the inhabitants of the area designated to constitute the new Federation of Malaysia. In these circumstances, Menzies

[1] *C.N.* vol. xxxiii (1962), no. 7, p. 28.
[2] For an analysis of Sukarno's ideology and of Australian reactions to 'confrontation' of the Netherlands on the one hand and Malaysia on the other, see *World Review*, vol. iii, no. 2 (July 1964), published by the Jacaranda Press, Queensland, article on 'The Australian commitment to Malaysia', by Alan Watt.

announced on 25 September 1963 the Australian Government's decision to help maintain Malaysia's political independence and territorial integrity against Indonesian pressure.

Australian policy on West New Guinea has been strongly criticised by Professor B. D. Beddie.[1] He has commented as follows:

...even when allowance is made for all the complexities and unforeseen changes that entered into it, the West New Guinea dispute still seems to me to stand as a striking instance of a failure to co-ordinate foreign and defence policies. If the original statements of 1950, declaring West New Guinea to be of vital importance to the defence of Australia, were seriously meant the Government had but one path to follow—to build up defences and to win allied support by all means possible. If the original statements were not meant seriously there would probably have been considerable advantage in explicitly rejecting them and seeking a negotiated settlement while it was still possible. As it was, we attempted to combine vague military threats, based more on the power of Dutch than Australian arms, with the half-conciliatory diplomacy of cold storage. It is possible, of course, that Government policy in the dispute was in essence an attempt to find the line of least resistance between Australian public opinion, Indonesian claims and Allied pressures. But assuming that this was not so, it is plausible to argue that an effective cabinet committee, continuously weighing up the diplomatic and military factors involved in the situation, could have provided an alternative to the sorry outcome of 1962.[2]

Professor Beddie's views on international problems command respect; yet it is at least open to argument that scope for other Australian initiatives was very limited and that the developing situation was not under Australian control. The fundamental reason why Dutch and Australian policy on West New Guinea failed was lack of support by a Great Power able and willing to back it up, in the last resort, by armed force. Neither the United States nor Great Britain had any intention of becoming embroiled in a 'colonial' war, even though the 'imperialist' power was a NATO ally. It is inconceivable that the Australian Government did not exhaust the possibilities of support from both Washington and London. In these circumstances Australia could not risk entering into a military alliance with the Dutch to defend West New Guinea, one of the few remaining outposts

[1] Professor of Political Science, School of General Studies, Australian National University.   [2] Wilkes, *Australia's Defence and Foreign Policy*, p. 136.

of European colonialism, against pressure from a permanent neighbour of growing military power; indeed, it is clear that the Menzies Government throughout its period of office resisted Dutch pressure in this direction. Even if the Australian Government continuously believed that Australian 'vital interests' were involved, it could not have succeeded in protecting them.

However, it is quite conceivable that Spender used this phrase somewhat loosely on 9 March 1950, and that defence assessments of the significance to Australia of Dutch retention of West New Guinea either in 1950 or later might have substituted the word 'important' for 'vital'. But it is easier to create a phrase and state it publicly than to modify it afterwards, without untoward effects. If while the Dutch still remained in West New Guinea an Australian political leader had said that Australian interests in the territory were no longer vital but only important, this would have been an open invitation to Indonesia to bring further pressure to bear upon the Dutch. Such action would have been justified only if Australia had been ready to advise the Dutch to settle with the Indonesians, in the hope of acquiring some credit with the latter in the process. Professor Beddie's comments may imply that this is precisely what Australia should have done.

Viewed without benefit of hindsight, Australian policy on this issue was not clearly irrational. Indonesia in the post-war years has seemed a land of instability and uncertainty. Any Indonesian Government would have had to cope with tremendous difficulties. Devastation and dislocation due to the war with Japan was increased by two Dutch 'police actions'. Indonesia inherited no substantial and highly trained indigenous civil service, as did India. Centrifugal tendencies in different regions complicated the task of building up a unified nation. Parliamentary Democracy in the Western sense did not work well, and in due course Sukarno substituted for it Guided Democracy. But his own gifts were political and psychological, not administrative or economic. He invented the national symbols, and stirred up national emotions.[1] In the resulting political and economic chaos rebellion broke out in 1958, and until it was crushed foreign countries had grounds for wondering whether Indonesia

---

[1] See Herbert Feith, *The Decline of Constitutional Democracy in Indonesia* (Cornell University Press, 1962), especially chapters I and XI.

might not split into several parts. Had this happened, Dutch retention of West New Guinea for a substantial period of years was a distinct possibility.

Casey's invitation to Subandrio to visit Australia in February 1959 strongly suggests some Australian re-assessment of the Indonesian situation, and an initiative designed to draw closer to Indonesia. The text of the joint statement of the two Foreign Ministers[1] points even more strongly in this direction. The resulting spate of criticism, not only by members of the Labour Party and by the Press, but also by a senior member of the Liberal Party, was unlikely to strengthen any governmental inclination to try to reach a 'negotiated settlement' with the Indonesians at the expense of the Dutch. Australian public opinion at this stage was too strongly opposed to such a change in policy and the only charge which can reasonably be directed against the Government is that any government in the last resort has to take the responsibility for the state of its own public opinion. Here criticism rests on firmer ground.

J. A. C. Mackie has justly pointed out that Australians' 'image of Indonesia had been formed very largely from newspaper accounts of her failures and inefficiencies rather than of her achievements'.[2] 'A tendency to underrate the Indonesians ...was also a factor in creating a sense of comfortable moral superiority in regard to our talk of self-determination' for West New Guinea.[2] In his opinion it was by no means self-evident that the Papuan population would be better off under a Dutch ten-year 'crash-programme' ending in self-determination, particularly 'if the outcome was likely to be an unviable economy for the half-island, over-stimulated expectations and a built-in antagonism with Indonesia'.[2] This latter argument, however, ignores the overwhelming climate of opinion in the United Nations General Assembly in regard to 'colonial issues', as endorsed by paragraph 3 of the 'Declaration on the Granting of Independence to Colonial Countries and Peoples', adopted by the Assembly on 14 December 1960.

On 22 January 1960 it was announced in London and Canberra that the Queen had conferred a life peerage on Mr R. G. Casey, who thereupon resigned his portfolio of Minister for External Affairs. Menzies then became Minister for External Affairs as well as Prime Minister, and held both offices until,

[1] See p. 254 above.   [2] *Australia in World Affairs 1956–60*, p. 317.

after Federal elections in December 1961, Sir Garfield Barwick was appointed Minister for External Affairs as well as Attorney-General. Casey had held the portfolio for a period of almost nine years. His wide experience as British Minister of State at Cairo and as British Governor of Bengal, together with his frequent visits to Asian countries as Australian Minister for External Affairs, had given him a closer understanding of Asian problems and reactions than any other member of the Australian cabinet. By contrast, Menzies had little personal experience of Asia. A convinced 'Commonwealth' man, relying for Australian security primarily upon two 'great and powerful friends', namely Great Britain and the United States, his manifold preoccupations as Prime Minister left only restricted time to devote to the problems of international affairs—particularly the taking of new initiatives towards Asian countries.

Yet by chance the years 1960 and 1961 were crucial for Australian–Indonesian relations, based as they primarily were on Australian policy towards Dutch New Guinea. As already indicated,[1] the new Dutch Government which came to power in March 1959 decided to force the pace towards self-government for West New Guinea. This decision threw an uncomfortable light upon the relatively slow or uncertain pace towards self-government in Australian New Guinea. The Australian Government, however, could not complain at the Dutch decision, because the Netherlands gave Australia every opportunity to co-ordinate the rate of political development in the two territories, and indeed to pursue a common objective for those territories, namely a Melanesian Union.

Mr Mackie has pointed out that the Dutch Under-Secretary for West New Guinea Affairs, Dr Bot, visited Canberra and on 15 February 1960 'spoke approvingly of union as an ultimate solution'. A statement along similar lines was made by Mr Toxopeus, Dutch Minister of Home Affairs, after an Australian–Netherlands administrative conference held at Hollandia from 3–9 March of the same year.[2] 'But no sign was forthcoming from Canberra that the Australian Government was prepared to accept the implications of a Melanesian Federation.'[3]

Uncoordinated if not conflicting statements made by the

---

[1] See p. 255 above.
[2] *Australia in World Affairs 1956–60*, p. 310 and note 96, pp. 324–5.
[3] *Ibid.* p. 310.

Prime Minister and by the Minister for Territories, Mr Hasluck, indicated that the Government had still formulated no clear picture of the future time-table for self-government in Australian New Guinea. In a press conference given in Sydney on 20 June after an overseas visit, Menzies said for the first time that he would sooner grant independence to New Guinea too early than allow hostilities to develop. 'At one time it was thought better to move slowly towards independence. The school of thought now is that it is better to go sooner than later. I belong to that school, although I did not always.'[1] Yet Hasluck was reported on 19 June as having told the Washington correspondent of the *New York Times* that Papua and New Guinea would not be ready for self-government for 30 years.[2] This statement drew from the *Sydney Morning Herald* of 21 June the following tart comment:

To declare...that Papua–New Guinea will not be ready for self-government for 30 years is doubtless accurate enough. It would, however, be extremely foolish to suppose that Papuan or world opinion will be prepared to wait for that period. Mr Hasluck is no better qualified than King Canute to turn back the tide, and the tide is setting strongly against the perpetuation of colonial rule.[3]

On 17 June a Bill for the establishment of a New Guinea Council, partly elective and partly nominated, was introduced into the Netherlands Parliament. By September the Dutch Foreign Minister had confirmed reports that the Netherlands Government was considering the handing over of the supervision of West New Guinea to the United Nations at some future date, subject to guarantees of its territorial integrity and of the free development of the Papuan population.[4] One year later, on 26 September 1961, the Foreign Minister, Dr Luns, informed the United Nations General Assembly of his Government's readiness to hand over control of West New Guinea to the United Nations, but, as already indicated,[5] the necessary majority for approval of a formal resolution along these lines was not forthcoming.

The Dutch initiative in the United Nations General Assembly in 1961 marked a turning-point in Indonesian policy towards West New Guinea. Frustrated in attempts to solve the issue in

[1] *The Times* (London), 21 June 1960.   [2] *Sydney Morning Herald*, 20 June 1960.
[3] *Sydney Morning Herald*, 21 June 1960.
[4] *Keesing's Contemporary Archives*, p. 17,796.   [5] See p. 255 above.

their favour in the United Nations, faced with a 'crash pro-gramme' under which the Dutch proposed to hasten progress towards self-government in West New Guinea, and noting Dutch reinforcement of military strength in the territory, Indo-nesian leaders decided to acquire arms from the Soviet Union and to 'confront' the Dutch by force to the extent necessary. Undertakings given to Australia at the highest level not to use force to solve the issue were conveniently forgotten or ignored: if India could use force to conquer Goa without suffering effec-tive international condemnation and restraint, why should Indonesia pay any greater attention to its obligation under the United Nations Charter (Article 2, 4) to refrain from the use of force? Indonesia cast the die on 19 December 1961. It was the misfortune of Sir Garfield Barwick to take over the portfolio of External Affairs on 22 December, too late to turn back the clock. One of his first ministerial acts was to issue a statement on 30 December 1961, expressing shock and dismay that Indonesia should openly declare its intention to resort to force, and plead-ing for negotiations between the Netherlands and Indonesia to settle the issue, preferably under the aegis of the United Nations.[1]

If there has been any period since 1949 to which Professor Beddie's criticism of Australian policy on West New Guinea justly applied, the period 1960–61 calls for closest scrutiny. It is difficult to believe that by this time Australian defence assess-ments would have regarded the retention of West New Guinea in non-Indonesian hands as of 'vital interest' to Australia. In his statement of 30 December 1961 Sir Garfield Barwick speaks only of Australia having '*a great interest* [emphasis added] in the ability of the indigenous people of West New Guinea to have the ultimate choice of their own future, whether it were for integra-tion with Indonesia or for independence, with or without any relationship with the people of East New Guinea'.[2] If, on the other hand, the Government really believed Australia's vital interests did require action to keep the territory out of Indo-nesian hands, the case for active espousal of a Melanesian Union, and for an offer of military support for the Dutch, would have been strong. The fact that the Government re-jected Dutch approaches seeking common action for a Melan-esian Union suggests that West New Guinea was regarded as important to Australia, but not vital.

[1] *C.N.* vol. XXXII (1961), no. 12, pp. 16–17.   [2] *Ibid.* p. 16.

But when the Dutch took the logical step, in view of Australia's attitude, of offering to place West New Guinea under a United Nations trusteeship, could not Australia at this stage have taken an equally logical step by notifying Indonesia that she no longer supported Dutch control or Dutch proposals? At this stage, such action would not have justified a charge of knifing the Dutch in the back. It could have been taken as early as September 1960, when Dr Luns publicly confirmed reports that the Netherlands Government was considering United Nations trusteeship. An approach by Australia to Indonesia then might well have helped to foster Indonesian goodwill. Instead, Australia fell between all stools. By failing to back the Dutch she forfeited any remaining Dutch respect; by failing to support Indonesia she failed to improve her relations with that country. When on 17 August 1963 Sukarno boasted of his 'Year of Triumph', and claimed that history was on the side of the new emerging forces, no doubt he believed that he had triumphed over the Australians as well as the Dutch, and that Australian hesitation and inaction helped to justify inclusion of Australia as part of the 'old established order', doomed in due course to wither away.

Sir Garfield Barwick did his best to improve relations with Indonesia, and to influence Australian public opinion in the direction of greater and more sympathetic understanding of the emotional background of countries newly come to independence. Thus, in a speech on 'Ourselves and our Neighbours', delivered in March 1963 as one of a series organised by the New South Wales Branch of the Australian Institute of International Affairs, the Minister urged that 'in judging what our neighbours say, we try to place their words in their historical and local setting'.[1] He stressed that among peoples who have had to fight for their independence, anti-colonialism is an emotion deeply and sincerely felt—something which touches their hearts more than their minds. Australians had not had this emotional experience, because their own colonial regime ended quietly and amicably; but this should not lead them to underrate the sincerity of others when they showed real emotion at the possibility of liberating someone else from a colonial yoke. Colonialism in Australia was a much easier yoke than many other nations knew; we were of the same stock as those who colonised

[1] *Living with Asia* (Anglican Press, Sydney, 1963), p. 44.

us. We had to be ready to understand and give credence to a different point of view.[1]

The Minister made frequent calls at Djakarta, explaining with patience the Australian attitude towards West New Guinea and stressing the need to avoid the use of force in seeking a solution of Dutch–Indonesian differences over this issue. When Sukarno moved from confrontation of the Netherlands to confrontation of Malaysia, Barwick's public comments on Indonesian policy still showed considerable restraint. He praised the 'spirit of conciliation and responsible statesmanship'[2] shown by President Macapagal of the Philippines, President Sukarno and the Prime Minister of Malaya, Tunku Abdul Rahman, during their discussions of the Malayan issue in Tokyo on 31 May and 1 June 1963, and commended the subsequent successful meeting of the Foreign Ministers of the three countries in Manila from 7–11 June. The communiqué issued by the Foreign Ministers stated, *inter alia*, that they had examined the Philippines' proposal to establish a 'confederation', and agreed to recommend to a meeting of Heads of Governments 'the establishment of machinery for regular consultations among their Governments at all levels on problems of common concern, such as security, stability, and economic, social, and cultural development'.[3] The Australian Minister for External Affairs 'noted with satisfaction the indications that the three countries look forward to setting up machinery to achieve these objectives'.[4]

The proposed meeting at Head of Government level took place in Manila from 31 July to 5 August and resulted in agreements conceding a great deal to the Indonesian point of view. Tunku Abdul Rahman made two major concessions. In the first place, he yielded to pressure to postpone beyond 31 August the publicly announced date for the creation of Malaysia. Secondly, he agreed that the Secretary-General of the United Nations 'should ascertain prior to the establishment of the Federation of Malaysia the wishes of the people of Sabah (North Borneo) and Sarawak'. Each of the three governments were to be permitted to 'send observers to witness the carrying out of the task'. Much of the terminology of the agreements reflected Sukarno's views on 'new emerging forces', use of bases by 'big powers', and primary responsibility of the signatory

[1] *Living with Asia*, p. 49.   [2] *C.N.* vol. xxxiv (1963), no. 6, p. 43.
[3] *Keesing's Contemporary Archives*, p. 19,715.   [4] *C.N.* vol. xxxiv (1963), no. 6, p. 44.

powers for the security of the so-called 'Maphilindo' area, i.e. an area comprising Malaya, the Philippines and Indonesia.

The Prime Minister of Malaya made these concessions, presumably, in the expectation that the United Nations investigation would confirm the wishes of the people of Sabah and Sarawak to join Malaysia, and in the hope that President Sukarno, supported for different reasons by President Macapagal of the Philippines, would thereupon cease his opposition to the establishment of the new Federation. It would seem that the Australian Government shared this hope. When the President of Indonesia made unreasonable demands for privileges for the Indonesian observer team, which strongly suggested that he intended its members to do more than 'witness' the investigation, and some of these demands were equally strongly opposed by Great Britain, in whose territory the investigation was being carried out, Australia did its best to compose the differences, acting almost in a mediatory capacity.[1]

It was not until Sukarno refused to accept the verdict of the United Nations investigatory team and announced his intention of crushing Malaysia despite its creation on 16 September 1963 that the Australian Government took its first firm stand against Indonesia previously described.[2]

It remains a matter for speculation why Sukarno did not accept Malaysia as a *fait accompli*, proceed with the establishment of 'Maphilindo' (a proposed loose confederation between Malaya, the Philippines and Indonesia) and pursue his objective of securing Indonesian domination of the area from within the confederation itself. He rejected this alternative, however, and against the background of direct Indonesian threat to the stability of a strategic area which the Menzies Government, since 1951 at least, had consistently regarded as of primary Australian concern, Australia too cast the die.

Subsequent developments need not be described in detail. While showing firm determination to help Malaysia, the Australian Government continued to show restraint in public criticism of Indonesian policy, and, while building up its military strength, showed no haste to take any action which might in-

[1] These comments are based upon personal impressions formed at the time during a visit to Djakarta, Singapore and Kuala Lumpur.
[2] For an extract from the Prime Minister's statement of 16 September 1963, see pp. 178-9 above.

volve Australian troops in direct combat with Indonesian troops. The first Australian army units sent to the Borneo territories of Malaysia were engineers, and it was a considerable time before combat units joined British and Malaysian forces in Borneo.

Further Australian involvement in Indonesia's undeclared war with Malaysia has been limited by two unforeseen developments. Decisions by the Australian Government to send a battalion to Vietnam, and later a 'self-contained Australian task force under Australian command...of some 4,500 men',[1] restricted substantially the numbers of Australian forces available to fight in defence of Malaysia. Secondly, the continuing effects of the attempted *coup d'état* in Djakarta on the night of 30 September/1 October 1965 and of the successful counter-*coup* by the Indonesian army necessitated so much concentration by Indonesian leaders upon domestic affairs that Malaysia gained some time in which to breathe. This, indeed, was badly needed, as disputes between Singapore came to such a head that the Government of Malaysia ejected Singapore from the Malaysian Federation as from 9 August 1965, Singapore becoming an independent sovereign State.

Since 30 September the Australian Government has shown great caution in public comment upon Indonesian developments. The new Minister for External Affairs, Mr Paul Hasluck, who on 24 April 1964 was appointed to the portfolio when Sir Garfield Barwick was translated to the post of Chief Justice of the High Court of Australia, has made it clear that the *coup* and counter-*coup* were internal matters for Indonesia herself to handle. The situation was so 'fluid' that 'it would be neither prudent nor helpful...to engage in comment or speculation about it'.[2] He has also reiterated Australia's desire to maintain friendly relations with Indonesia, and stated that the only existing dispute between the two countries arises from the Indonesian policy of confrontation against Malaysia.

It is too early to predict the eventual significance of the *coup* and counter-*coup* upon Australian–Indonesian relations. At the time of writing there is no doubt that the power of the Indonesian Army has been greatly increased, the power of the Indonesian Communist Party substantially diminished, and the dominant position of President Sukarno placed in jeopardy.

---

[1] Statement by the Prime Minister, *C.P.D.* 8 March 1966, p. 27.
[2] *C.P.D.* 10 March 1966, p. 179.

While Indonesia still maintains publicly her intention to crush Malaysia[1], and while it would be foolish to assume that the Indonesian army is 'pro-Western' in outlook as well as anti-Communist, recent attempts to set the Indonesian economy on its feet suggest greater concentration in the foreseeable future upon domestic matters and less adventurism abroad. This is of great significance to Australia, which is fortunate to have some time and opportunity to re-think its policy towards Indonesia, in the light of developments which have taken place within Malaysia and in Vietnam, and which are likely to take place within Australian New Guinea and Papua.

[1] An agreement between Malaysia and Indonesia to end the state of confrontation between the two countries was signed in Djakarta on 11 August 1966: see *Commonwealth Survey*, vol. 12, no. 18 (2 September 1966), pp. 919–20.

7

THE COMMONWEALTH OF NATIONS

As its most recent name implies, the Commonwealth of Nations has suffered a 'sea-change' during the period 1938–65. The Balfour Report of 1926 described Great Britain and the Dominions as 'autonomous communities within the British Empire, equal in status, in no way subordinated one to another in any respect of their domestic or external affairs, though united by a common allegiance to the Crown, and freely associated as members of the British Commonwealth of Nations'. In 1926 it did not seem incongruous to use in one and the same paragraph the two phrases 'British Empire' and 'British Commonwealth of Nations'. In Australia at least—a Dominion which did not exercise its right to establish diplomatic missions in foreign countries until 1940—Menzies in 1938 still chose to use and emphasise the phrase 'British Empire', and few Australians who listened to him felt any urge to explode with national indignation at the affront to their international status. On the other hand they, and Menzies, were also content with the phrase 'British Commonwealth', which reflected the predominantly but not exclusively British character of the Old Commonwealth, consisting of the United Kingdom and its empire in the more limited sense, Canada, Australia, New Zealand and South Africa, before South Africa ceased to be a member in 1961. If those of Dutch descent in South Africa and of French descent in Canada felt other or additional loyalties, these were loyalties to European countries of broadly similar cultural traditions.

The Statute of Westminster 1931 gave due legal authority for the transfer to the Dominions of full sovereignty over their own affairs recognised in principle by the Balfour Declaration, though Australia felt no urgent need to adopt the Statute until 1943. The Statute, like the Balfour Declaration, still referred to 'common allegiance to the Crown' as a distinguishing feature of Commonwealth communities. But the post-war decision to permit independent India to become a republic within the Commonwealth permitted those members who so wished to forgo in future allegiance to the British Crown, merely recognising

instead the Crown 'as the symbol of the free association of...
independent member nations and as such the Head of the
Commonwealth'. Field-Marshal Smuts was 'dismayed' at this
development, and warned that: 'Great care should be taken
not to empty the concept of the Commonwealth of all substance
and meaning and not to whittle it away until nothing but the
word remained with no real meaning or significance. Far better
would it be to drop it altogether.'[1]

Acceptance of India, Pakistan and Ceylon as members also
made it necessary to substitute 'The Commonwealth of Nations'
for 'The British Commonwealth'—although the latter phrase is
still used from time to time in some Old Commonwealth countries, especially Australia.

By 1965 the 'British' element in the Commonwealth had
become more and more attenuated; the Commonwealth had
grown increasingly 'multi-racial', and resembled more and
more a miniature United Nations. No fewer than twenty-one
members were represented at the Prime Ministers' Conference in
London, held in June 1965, the alphabetical list of countries
being as follows: Australia, Canada, Ceylon, Cyprus, Gambia,
Ghana, India, Jamaica, Kenya, Malawi, Malaysia, Malta,
New Zealand, Nigeria, Pakistan, Sierra Leone, Tanzania,
Trinidad and Tobago, Uganda, United Kingdom, Zambia.
By this time South Africa had withdrawn from the Common-
wealth because of opposition to her policy of apartheid. On
9 August 1965 Singapore was separated from the Malaysian
Federation and became an independent State within the
Commonwealth of Nations, making the total membership 22.

The change in outlook amongst Commonwealth members as
of 1965 can best be judged against a background of developments in the United Nations. On 14 December 1960 the United
Nations General Assembly adopted, by a vote of 89 to 0, with 9
abstentions, a 'Declaration on the Granting of Independence to
Colonial Countries and Peoples'. The countries abstaining were
as follows: Australia, Belgium, Britain, Dominican Republic,
France, Portugal, South Africa, Spain and the United States.
This resolution includes the following two paragraphs:

(5) Immediate steps shall be taken, in trust and non-self-governing territories or all other territories which have not yet attained

---

[1] Quoted by Menzies in *The First Smuts Memorial Lecture*, delivered at Cambridge
16 May 1960. See *C.N.* vol. xxxi (1960), p. 258.

independence, to transfer all powers to the peoples of those territories, without any conditions or reservations, in accordance with their freely expressed will or desire, and without any distinction as to race, creed, or colour, in order to enable them to enjoy complete independence and freedom.

(3) Inadequacy of political, economic, social, or educational preparedness should never serve as a pretext for delaying independence.

It will be noted that all Afro-Asian members of the Commonwealth at that date supported the resolution, while three Old Commonwealth members in effect opposed it.

The disruptive effect of 'colonial' issues upon the Commonwealth of Nations is best illustrated by events which followed the Unilateral Declaration of Independence made on 11 November 1965 by the Government which represents the white minority of Rhodesia. Although the British Prime Minister, Mr Harold Wilson, himself flew to Rhodesia in a last-minute attempt to prevent such a declaration, and although the British Government took the issue to the Security Council of the United Nations and advocated the imposition of economic sanctions against Rhodesia, African opinion was dissatisfied with what it regarded as the inadequacy of British efforts to protect the rights of the Rhodesian non-white majority. A meeting of the Organisation of African Unity, held at Addis Ababa in the first week of December, decided to request member States to break off diplomatic relations with Great Britain if the latter failed to bring the Smith Government of Rhodesia to heel by 15 December 1965. When the deadline passed, with the Rhodesian Government still successfully defying the British Government, a number of African governments did in fact break off relations with the United Kingdom. These included two members of the Commonwealth, namely Tanzania and Ghana. At the request of the British Government, Australia undertook the responsibility of representing British interests in Ghana until such time as diplomatic relations between the two countries were restored following the *coup* in February 1966 which ousted President Nkrumah from office.

Extreme tension, however, was not limited to issues which divided 'colonial' from anti-colonial members of the Commonwealth. While an informed observer could write as late as 1961 that 'At least it is unthinkable that members of the Commonwealth should go to war against each other',[1] during 1965 India and Pakistan found themselves in a war over Kashmir none the less real because it was undeclared. From the point of view of the significance attached to membership of the Commonwealth of Nations one need refer only to the ironical circumstance that India and Pakistan proved ready to accept, at a conference in Tashkent, the good offices of the Soviet Union—not of the United Kingdom—in effecting a cease-fire and mutual withdrawal of forces!

In addition, the decision of the British Government in 1961 to apply for membership of the European Economic Community caused serious strains in relations not merely between the United Kingdom and members of the Commonwealth newly come to independence; older members of the Commonwealth, New Zealand and Australia in particular, experienced a sense of shock not substantially alleviated by a promise that 'entry by Britain into the Common Market would be conditional upon her securing special arrangements to protect the important trading interests of Australia and other Commonwealth countries'.[2] The application was rejected, chiefly because of the influence of President Charles de Gaulle, but it was impossible for inter-Commonwealth relations to return to their erstwhile state.

In all the circumstances it became more and more difficult to define the Commonwealth. Stress was laid on its multi-racial character, and on its infinite variety and diversity; but it was difficult to find any single special feature of Commonwealth relationships between Australia and Britain, for instance, which did not also pertain to relationships between Britain and the United States.[3] Surely Professor K. C. Wheare's quip about the Commonwealth seemed to be justified—'If it did not exist, you could not invent it.'[4]

Changes in the Australian attitude towards the Commonwealth during the period under review are best traced, in the first instance, through statements made by Australian political

---

[1] C. M. Woodhouse, *British Foreign Policy since the Second World War* (Hutchinson, London, 1961), p. 232.

[2] Statement to Parliament on 3 May 1962 by Mr McEwen, Minister for Trade: *C.N.* vol. XXXIII (1962), no. 5, p. 140.

[3] For an analysis of the 'special relationship' between Britain and the United States, see H. C. Allen, 'The Anglo-American relationship in the sixties', *International Affairs*, vol. XXXVIII, no. 1 (January 1963), pp. 46–7.

[4] *Commonwealth Perspectives*, ed. N. Mansergh (Duke University Press, 1958), in Preface.

leaders, particularly Menzies. A consecutive summary of significant views on the Commonwealth by such leaders already dealt with incidentally in earlier chapters will be followed by a detailed examination of Menzies' statements on this theme during his long rule as Prime Minister from December 1949 to January 1966.

During the debate on the Munich agreement in October 1938 Menzies, then Attorney-General, held stoutly to the opinion that the Crown was indivisible: when the United Kingdom was at war Australia was automatically at war. It was not possible for Australia to be neutral in a British war. Australia could merely decide the extent to which she would fight, and where she would fight—provided the enemy allowed her to choose. Further, the 'British Empire' should speak with one concerted voice. Australia should be consulted by Great Britain on important questions, in time for her to express an opinion. How she was to be able to make intelligent judgements and comments in the absence of a variety of information which a developed diplomatic service could alone provide was not explained.[1]

Hitler seized Prague on 15 March 1939. The Australian Prime Minister, Joseph Lyons, died on 7 April and he was succeeded by Menzies, who issued his first statement to the Australian people as Prime Minister in a broadcast made on 26 April. The events of the six months between Munich and Prague led Menzies to lay a new emphasis in his broadcast upon Australia's 'primary responsibilities and primary risks' in the Pacific, and upon the need for Australia to provide herself with her own information and to maintain her own diplomatic contacts with foreign powers. She should still, however, 'act as an integral part of the British Empire'.[2] No one could have adhered more loyally to this principle than Casey while he held the post of Australian Minister to the United States, but the advent of the Labour Party to power in Australia and the strains and stresses imposed by Japan's entry into the war led to greater assertion of separate Australian interest and the development of a more independent foreign policy.

On 27 December 1941 the new Prime Minister, Mr John Curtin, published his direct appeal to the United States 'free of any pangs as to...traditional links of kinship with the United

[1] See pp. 19–20 above.   [2] See p. 24 above.

Kingdom'.[1] The words were unfortunate, and reflected the calm judgement neither of Curtin nor of the Australian people. There followed unhappy disputes between Curtin and Churchill over the proposed diversion to Burma of the Australian 7th Division, then *en route* to Australia from the Middle East, and over the appointment of Casey as British Minister of State in Cairo.[2] Dr Evatt began his numerous war-time visits overseas as Minister for External Affairs, pressing for greater Australian participation in war-time strategy and for a greater allocation of military supplies to the Pacific area.[3]

After the battle of Midway, Evatt turned his energies more and more to the problems of the post-war settlement, determined to leave no stone unturned in an effort to ensure that Australian influence on the settlement should correspond to the contribution she had made to the Allied war effort. Decisions taken by the United States, the United Kingdom and China at the Cairo Conference of November 1943, without any prior consultation with the Pacific Dominions, stimulated Australia and New Zealand to publish their own joint views in the Australia–New Zealand Agreement of February 1944.[4] These were developed and pressed by Evatt at the United Nations Charter Conference held at San Francisco in 1945, with a somewhat ruthless disregard for British (or American) susceptibilities.[5] In relation to the Japanese settlement, Evatt pursued energetically the notion that Australia had a special role to play representing Commonwealth interests as a whole. He succeeded in securing the appointment of an Australian as 'Commonwealth' representative on the Allied Council for Japan. Senior Australian Army Officers were successively appointed to command the Commonwealth Occupation Forces in Japan, while an Australian judge acted as President of the International Military Tribunal for the Far East, which tried major Japanese war criminals.[6]

On the other hand, the Labour Party Government showed a sympathetic understanding of Great Britain's acute economic difficulties in the immediate post-war period.[7] Mr J. B. Chifley succeeded to the Prime Ministership on the death of Curtin in April 1945. His unassuming simplicity, personal integrity and

---

[1] See p. 55 above.
[2] See pp. 56–9 above.
[3] See pp. 61–8 above.
[4] See pp. 73–7 above.
[5] See pp. 83–93 above.
[6] See pp. 209–10 above.
[7] See p. 50 above.

firmness of character won the confidence of the Australian electorate and the respect of the political leaders of other members of the Commonwealth.

On 4 March 1947 Chifley announced his Government's decision to make a gift to the United Kingdom Government of £A25,000,000 (£S20,000,000) to help meet British balance of payments problems. His attitude towards Great Britain and the part she played in the Second World War was clearly stated in Parliament in the following words:

The mother of all the British Commonwealth of Nations, which carried the greatest burden throughout the war and bore the greatest loss of life and suffering, came out of it the world's greatest debtor nation, although she had gone into it one of the world's greatest creditors. Do the Dominions say: 'We have done well out of the war, and you must not do anything which will worsen our position in the future, no matter what may be the price economically to you. You ought to be prepared to sacrifice your country so that we may continue on our money-making way'?[1]

The Prime Minister saw to it that Australia played its due part in conserving dollar funds on behalf of the Commonwealth of Nations as a whole, and in maintaining the strength of sterling as an international currency.

Chifley's standing within the Commonwealth is evidenced by an approach made to him in 1950, when he had become Leader of the Opposition, to ascertain whether he would act as mediator in the Kashmir dispute. He rejected the overture, for sound reasons, commenting humorously to a friend, 'I would look too silly riding an elephant around New Delhi'.[2]

It is conceivable that Evatt's insistence, when approached by the United States after the Second World War about future American use of the Manus Island base, that any such agreement must provide for joint use of Commonwealth and American bases in the Pacific—a proposal which the United States rejected[3]—was due substantially to the influence of Chifley. According to Professor Crisp, Chifley was not only 'firm that co-operation with the United States must be on a two-way access to bases', but also held the view that 'no Australian–United States reciprocity on bases like that at Manus Island was acceptable...unless Britain was brought fully into the

---

[1] Quoted in Crisp, *Ben Chifley*, pp. 281–2.
[2] *Ibid.* p. 287.   [3] See p. 100 above.

arrangement'.[1] In any event, on this particular issue the Labour Government followed a Commonwealth rather than a more limited Australian line. It should be remembered, also, that informal ANZAM arrangements between Great Britain, Australia and New Zealand for the defence of the Malayan area started when Chifley was Prime Minister.[2]

Chifley's overseas visits, especially to Britain and America, 'did much to offset the unfortunate impression which Evatt's manner and methods had sometimes made on Ministers and officials in those countries'. This effect was achieved by the Prime Minister without ever failing in 'loyalty to his brash, mercurial and sometimes difficult colleague'.[3] While he lacked the intellectual training of his Minister for External Affairs, Chifley also lacked Evatt's burning ambition, avid desire for publicity, and capacity to antagonise those with whom he disagreed. The Prime Minister did not possess either the knowledge or the expertise of Evatt in the field of international affairs, but his simple integrity and rugged common sense served Australia well. Chifley's contribution to cohesion within the Commonwealth of Nations was substantial.

Since December 1949, when the Liberal–Country Party came to power in Canberra, Australian attitudes to the Commonwealth of Nations are inevitably linked with the name of Robert Gordon Menzies, Prime Minister from that date until January 1966. While the views expressed by the Prime Minister from time to time do not necessarily coincide with the views of the average Australian, his comments upon Commonwealth developments well reflect the changes which have been taking place.

In 1950 Menzies gave the first Roy Milne Memorial Lecture for the Australian Institute of International Affairs, on the subject 'The British Commonwealth of Nations in International Affairs'.[4] He reiterated his reservations as to the effectiveness in maintaining world peace of international organisations such as the League of Nations and the United Nations, and stressed the need for Australia to be 'In the big matters...intimately associated with Great Britain, with our sister Dominions, with the United States and with the democratic powers of Western

---

[1] Crisp, *Ben Chifley*, p. 283.   [2] See p. 164 above.
[3] Crisp, *Ben Chifley*, p. 287.
[4] Printed by the Australian Institute of International Affairs.

Europe'.[1] Of these, 'the British Empire must remain our chief international preoccupation'.[2]

The Prime Minister expressed some dissatisfaction with the adequacy of inter-Commonwealth consultation, and it is clear that he had in mind primarily consultation between London and Canberra. '...I remain convinced', he said, 'that no system of consultation can be regarded as adequate which has left many people in Australia, including myself, satisfied that decisions of great moment in this country have occasionally been presented to the Australian Government and to the Australian people as *faits accomplis*.'[3] No particular illustrations were given; nor was there any discussion of the problem inherent in any system of effective consultation, namely the speed at which world events move and the impossibility of any British Government avoiding all major decisions until the views of members of the Commonwealth had been ascertained, including the least well-equipped and the most dilatory. As a partial cure Menzies suggested that a Committee on Imperial Foreign Policy should be established, to sit in London and to be composed of the British Foreign Secretary and Dominion High Commissioners or visiting Dominion Ministers. In addition, a small British Empire secretariat might be established in each Dominion capital.[4]

Menzies clearly did not like the structural changes which had taken place in the Commonwealth following upon the decision that India could become a republic and remain a member of the Commonwealth. The citizens of India no longer owed allegiance to the Crown. He deplored the possibility that the Commonwealth might become 'a purely functional association based upon friendship and common interest but...lacking the old high instincts and instantaneous cohesion which sprang from the fact that we were, all over the British world, as indeed we remain in the old Dominions, the King's subjects and the King's men'.[5] But time should not be wasted in 'vain regrets'; instead, everything possible should be done 'to preserve the many good things that are left'.[6]

The Prime Minister concluded by affirming that the Commonwealth was more than a group of friendly powers, and more than a series of concerted economic interests.

[1] *Roy Milne Memorial Lecture*, 1950, p. 14.   [2] *Ibid.* p. 9.
[3] *Ibid.* p. 18.   [4] *Ibid.* p. 19.   [5] *Ibid.* p. 3.   [6] *Ibid,* p. 4.

It is and must be a living thing—not a corpse under the knives of the constitutional dissectors. It would be the tragedy of our history if what began as a splendid adventure and grew into a proud brotherhood should end up as a lawyer's exercise. When the Empire ceases to be an inner feeling as well as an external association, virtue will have gone out of it.'[1]

On 7 March 1951 Menzies reported to the House of Representatives upon the Prime Ministers' Conference held in London in January of that year. After referring to the structural alterations which had taken place in the Commonwealth, he still felt able to affirm that 'there is no meeting of any group in the world quite so intimate, so significant, so informed, so representative, as a meeting of Prime Ministers who can speak for so many different races'.[2] He had been 'moved to feel that if any group of men could provide a bridge between East and West, between the New and the Old',[2] the assembled Prime Ministers should be able to do so. Everyone at the Conference had felt that the British Commonwealth, so far from being outmoded, was still a special and precious association of nations, and as such had a unique common task and common responsibility. The influence of the nine nations represented, speaking with a common voice on some great issue, was 'much greater than the mere mathematical sum of the various influence of the individual members'.[2] The British Empire was no longer a single organism. The old points of unity had become looser and the old common allegiance was qualified. The Prime Minister proceeded as follows:

I for one have no vain tears to waste upon this process, because in common with all Honourable Members of this House I believe that the problems of mankind are in the future and not in the past. But I do venture to say this. We must not, at our peril, allow this precious family association...to cease to be a family association; to become no more than a loose association of nations who are in temporary alliance but who spiritually have no common roots in the ground.

As members of the Commonwealth we have obligations as well as rights. The continuance of the world influence and effectiveness of the British Commonwealth will continue to depend upon the readiness of every member to contribute to that Commonwealth's welfare as a whole and to share with it in the great task of forwarding the welfare of mankind.[3]

---

[1] *Ibid.* p. 24.   [2] *C.N.* vol. xxii (1951), p. 158.   [3] *Ibid.* pp. 158–9.

Five years later Menzies published in *The Times* of London on
11 and 12 July 1956 two articles on the Commonwealth.[1] The
Prime Minister again referred to the 'momentous change'
which took place when India became a republic within the
Commonwealth:

Clearly the 'new' Commonwealth had emerged. Superficially, it
may look like the old one, but in reality we no longer have a Commonwealth fully integrated on the basis of the Crown. Indeed, it
might be more accurate to say that we have now a Crown Commonwealth within a total Commonwealth...That the Queen remains the head of the Commonwealth is no doubt important. But a
new name for a new office doesn't assure the continuance of the
significance of the Crown. On the contrary, it draws sharp attention
to the fact that there is a world of difference between Australia's
relationship to the Throne and that of India...[2]

The new Commonwealth had become internally anomalous.
Nehru, for instance, had 'made it quite clear that for India
neutrality has become almost an article of faith'.[3] Menzies, on
the other hand, found it 'an astonishing thought that Australia
or New Zealand should put forward and practise a policy of
neutrality',[3] It was necessary, however, 'not to dwell on the
anomalies, but to make the whole association work for the good
of all'.[3]

What were the working problems of the new Commonwealth,
asked the Australian Prime Minister. As regards defence, it was
an open secret that defence talks at Prime Ministers' Conferences did not take place in full session, but were confined to
those member countries which regarded their defence problems
as joint and not merely several. Indeed, defence arrangements
had already ceased to have an overall Commonwealth character and were becoming selective and regional. For instance,
Pakistan, but not India, was a member of SEATO. Similarly
with trade. New members of the Commonwealth did not support the concept of 'imperial preference'. We could not reasonably expect to have any new multilateral arrangements
operating only inside the Commonwealth. Trade agreements
would inevitably be made bilaterally, general limitations upon
any treaties arrived at being found in such broad international
agreements as G.A.T.T. 'In short, it is hard to think of any great

---

[1] Quotations given are taken from the version published in Menzies, *Speech is of
Time.*   [2] *Ibid.* p. 27.   [3] *Ibid.* p. 28.

matter of international policy which will lend itself instantly, as in the old days, to joint discussion among all the British countries designed to produce a single joint conclusion.'[1] The time had come 'when, in the British Commonwealth, we must give ourselves furiously to think about where we are going and what road or roads we should take'.[2]

Contacts between Commonwealth countries, Menzies continued, might well come to depend upon periodical meetings of Prime Ministers without agenda, bilateral trade talks, and periodical meetings of Finance Ministers. Whether such instruments could serve to continue something identifiable as the British Commonwealth, with a powerful voice in world affairs, would depend largely on the importance attached to such contacts and the goodwill and resolution brought to them. Everything would turn upon means and spirit of contact and consultation: 'one text might be boldly printed in every Department in London, New Delhi, Canberra, and the other Seats of Government—'Will any decision I am today contemplating affect some other nation of the Commonwealth? If so, have I informed or consulted it?'[3]

On 16 May 1960 the Australian Prime Minister delivered the first Smuts Memorial Lecture at the University of Cambridge.[4] At this date South Africa had still not withdrawn from the Commonwealth.

Menzies, who had a tremendous admiration for Smuts, found comfort in the latter's doctrine of 'holism', and claimed that the Commonwealth was the best proof of Smuts's central thesis that 'the whole is greater than the sum of its parts'.[5] Having again reviewed the changes which had taken place since allegiance to the Crown ceased to be a mark of all citizens within the Commonwealth, he boldly essayed to 'ascertain the present nature of the structural and dynamic elements in Commonwealth development', not, as he declared, for the purpose of sitting in vain judgement upon the past, or in order to be censorious or gloomily retrospective, but as someone optimistically forward-looking.[6]

The Prime Minister spoke at some length about the continuing significance of the Crown. He described King George V as

---

[1] *Ibid.* p. 29.   [2] *Ibid.* p. 32.   [3] *Ibid.* pp. 30–1.
[4] For text, see *C.N.* vol. xxxi (1960), pp. 255–63.
[5] *Ibid.* p. 256.   [6] *Ibid.* p. 258.

the first great constitutional monarch. 'By the force of his own personality George V did much to preserve the true significance of the Crown and to make his many millions of subjects think of the Crown, not as an obstacle to democracy but as a living element in it. This example was superbly followed by King George VI and his great Queen and, of course, by our Sovereign Lady of today.'[1] The influence of the Crown, though intangible, was, he declared, 'the most profound of all the unifying influences for the Crown Dominions'.[1]

Menzies then asked rhetorically what were the operative factors which continued to make the Commonwealth a special association of nations with a mutual relationship distinguishing it from other world groups. In giving his reply he forestalled and admitted the charge that his approach was 'sentimental'. He spoke of the 'sense of community between the Crown members and the Republican members', the 'special atmosphere' in which Commonwealth Ministers and officials meet 'which induces both frankness and friendliness', a 'quality of intimacy about...meetings', the tempering of 'intolerance engendered by long-range and imperfect knowledge'.[2]

No doubt with the South African problem particularly in mind, Menzies stressed as well certain negative aspects of Commonwealth meetings. Members of the Commonwealth did not meet 'to sit in judgement upon each other or to ventilate and pass upon intra-Commonwealth issues'.[2] They were not a super-state; nor did they constitute a court.

The Prime Ministers' Conference would break up in disorder and the new Commonwealth would disintegrate if we affected to discuss and decide what we thought to be the proper measure of democracy in our various countries; whether particular groups should or should not have the vote; whether oppositions should be respected; whether a Parliament should control the Executive. On all such matters, 'autonomous' or 'independent' nations must have the right to manage their own affairs in their own way.[3]

He contrasted this description of the Commonwealth of Nations with proceedings in the United Nations, to the detriment of the latter. In the United Nations large numbers of delegates met, of necessity, almost as strangers. There, of necessity, resolutions were tabled, amendments drafted, votes canvassed and majority

---

[1] *C.N.* vol. xxxi (1960), p. 260.   [2] *Ibid.* pp. 260–1.   [3] *Ibid.* p. 261.

decisions taken. There one found inevitable bargaining which tended to weaken mutual trust.[1] The Prime Minister summed up his 'faith' as follows:

We of the Commonwealth are no longer a single integrated structure with a common foundation and a powerful organic association. Our strength is that we meet as equals, without vote or lobby; we speak to each other with freedom and friendliness; we seek to understand each other but we do not sit in judgement on each other; we take an interest in each other but respect the fact that each member has achieved self-government; hence we seek to co-operate with each other but not to invade the sovereignty of each other. We seek agreement on purpose and principle but leave to each the decision on how to achieve or apply them. For, though so much has changed, the nations of the Commonwealth remain 'autonomous' and 'freely associated'. We derive strength from the knowledge that we are not like other associations, that our rules may be unwritten but our true relations written into our hearts and our consciousness.[2]

Two major developments in Commonwealth affairs during 1961 and 1962 deeply disturbed the Australian Prime Minister. The first was the situation which led South Africa to withdraw from the Commonwealth; the second was the decision of the British Government to seek admission to the European Common Market.

The inferences to be drawn from the circumstances surrounding South Africa's decision, at the Prime Ministers' Conference held in March 1961, to withdraw its application to remain a member of the Commonwealth, though as a republic, are open to dispute. Menzies has affirmed[3] that at the 1960 Prime Ministers' Conference all the Commonwealth representatives were agreed that South Africa's racial policy was a matter of domestic jurisdiction. On the other hand, South Africa in 1961 waived the general rule which would have precluded discussion of this subject at formal meetings. In these circumstances it can be claimed that no precedent was set in 1961 for discussing any other matters falling within the domestic jurisdiction of any member of the Commonwealth. Further, it can be argued that South Africa was not expelled from the Commonwealth; she herself withdrew her application to remain a member.

These were not the views of the Australian Prime Minister.

---

[1] *Ibid.* p. 261.   [2] *Ibid.* p. 262.   [3] *The Times* (London), 20 March 1961, p. 12.

In his report to Parliament on 11 April 1961[1] Menzies described the impending withdrawal of South Africa as 'an event of great historic importance'.[2] 'Technically', he said, 'Dr Verwoerd withdrew. But in substance he had to withdraw unless he was prepared to depart from policies which however criticised are the settled doctrine of his own Government.'[3]

The Prime Minister quoted the British Prime Minister, Mr Harold Macmillan, as saying 'There are some who think that the Commonwealth will be gravely and even fatally injured by this blow. I do not altogether share this view. I do not share it at all.' Menzies added that he deeply respected Macmillan's opinion, and hoped it turned out to be right. Nevertheless he still retained his own opinion that the Commonwealth had been 'injured and not strengthened by the departure of South Africa'.[3] The issue concerned more than South Africa; it concerned the whole character and future of the greatest international partnership the world had yet seen. He knew of nothing which had happened since the issue of the Conference Communiqué in 1960 to convert the internal affair of South Africa into a matter warranting intervention by the Commonwealth.[4]

In a press conference given in London on 19 March 1961 under the immediate emotional stress of the events of the Prime Ministers' Conference, the Australian Prime Minister had been even more forthright and less guarded in his criticism. He complained that a lot of people seemed to think that the British Commonwealth was a court of judgement.

Even though there has been a great deal of international agitation, this [apartheid] is still a matter of domestic policy in South Africa which South Africa does not seek to apply to any other country. It is as much a matter of domestic policy to South Africa as Australia's migration policy is a matter for us.

To have a member of the Commonwealth virtually excluded from the Commonwealth on a matter of domestic policy presents, in my opinion, a rather disagreeable vista of possibilities for the future.

We may object very strongly to racial discrimination practised in one country, we may equally object very strongly to the absence of any form of democracy in another, we might take exception to the absence of parliamentary machinery or the presence of imprisonment

---

[1] *C.N.* vol. xxxii, no. 4, pp. 19–35.
[2] *Ibid.* p. 20.   [3] *Ibid.* p. 23.   [4] *Ibid.* p. 29.

without trial—any of these things lend themselves to examination if we adopt the attitude that one of our tasks is to examine each other's policies. That is why I think this is a very unhappy development.[1]

But it was the British Government's decision to apply for entry into the European Economic Community which caused the Australian Prime Minister greatest disquiet regarding the future of the Commonwealth of Nations. While he was far from insensible of the important damage to the Australian economy which could occur if the United Kingdom proved unable, during her negotiations, to maintain what Australia would regard as her vital economic interests, Menzies alone of Australian political leaders showed deep concern for the possible *political* effects upon the Commonwealth of Nations should the British application be accepted.

No speech delivered by the Prime Minister during his preceding record period in that office reflects more clearly his stature as a British Commonwealth statesman than his report to Parliament on 16 October 1962 regarding the Prime Ministers' Conference which had opened in London on 10 September to discuss Common Market problems. While tenaciously holding to his own estimate of the serious political risks to the Commonwealth of Nations of a successful British application, and while unconsciously expressing a depth of sadness that the Commonwealth he would have preferred no longer existed in many respects, he exhibited a degree of tolerance and restraint and a readiness to accept and make the best of whatever the future might hold which perceptive listeners found extremely moving.

Menzies did not question the British Government's right to decide that 'entry into the European Economic Community was of essential importance to Great Britain for both political and economic reasons'.[2] But he had informed the London Conference that Australia 'had reservations in respect of the possible implications for the Commonwealth itself'. These reservations would not lead Australia into 'a position of blind opposition'. 'The whole decision was one of historic and almost revolutionary importance. It would fall for decision by the Mother Nation...'[3]

The Prime Minister readily admitted that, since the days of the Balfour Declaration and the Statute of Westminster, the

---

[1] *The Times* (London), 20 March 1961, p. 12.
[2] *C.N.* vol. xxxiii (1962), no. 10, p. 32.   [3] *Ibid.* p. 33.

Commonwealth had become 'a loose association of nations who value their friendship with each other, who recognise, for the purpose of their association, even though they may be republics, that the Queen is head of the Commonwealth, and who, with some notable exceptions, enjoy somewhat similar institutions and traditions of government'.[1] But it was still true, however tenuous the nature of the association, that each member was, itself, sovereign and independent.

What would be the effect upon the Commonwealth of Nations, he asked, if the European Economic Community, including Britain, should become a federation? True, at present it was far from being a federation. True, the British Government said that it was not contemplating a federation in Europe, that it looked at its political association with a European Economic Community in *ad hoc* terms, with periodical discussions at the ministerial level but without the creation of federal institutions. He himself, however, was not aware of any history of confederations or political associations in which there had not been either a tendency to break up or a tendency to become more concerted. Mr Macmillan had expressed the view that the European Community would be more likely to develop and to grow in political strength than to fall apart. In the Australian Prime Minister's judgement, unless the association disintegrated 'there must be, at the centre, more and more a body of elected persons exercising the powers and performing the administration involved in the further working of the Treaty of Rome'.[2] Should the day come when the European Community became a federation, with Great Britain as a constituent State, then Great Britain would cease to be a sovereign community. It was no more feasible to say that Great Britain's position in the Commonwealth would be unaffected by participation as a constituent State in a European federation than it would be to say that Australia could join another great federation and still remain an independent sovereign member of the British Commonwealth.

The Prime Minister continued as follows:

I think that twenty years ago I might have become more impassioned about this matter, but the Commonwealth has changed a lot since then. Its association has become much looser. For most of its members, the association is, in a sense, functional and occasional. The old hopes of concerting common policies have gone. Under these

[1] *C.N.* vol. xxxiii (1962), pp. 33–4.   [2] *Ibid.* p. 34.

circumstances, it may well prove to be the fact that even if federation should be achieved in Western Europe, the anomalous position of Great Britain in the Commonwealth which would then emerge, would be regarded as no more anomalous than many other things which have been accepted, and with which we have learned to live. In any event, so far as Australia is concerned, nothing can shake us in our allegiance to the Throne, an allegiance which will always give us a very special relationship to many other millions of people in Great Britain and elsewhere.[1]

It is doubtful whether Menzies' attitude towards the British application to join the Common Market faithfully reflected the approach to the problem of the ordinary Australian, whose ears were attuned rather to the insistent warnings by the Minister for Trade and Leader of the Country Party, Mr McEwen, of the extent of the economic damage which might result to the Australian economy. When Mr L. H. Bury, a member of the Liberal Party who at that time was Minister for Air and also Minister Assisting the Treasurer, made bold to question publicly whether such damage was likely to be as serious as Government spokesmen had suggested, he was speedily compelled to resign from the Ministry. Australian fears were primarily economic, but for the Prime Minister the political risks to the Commonwealth of Nations were at least equally important.

It is ironic that one of the most important decisions of the Government which it fell to Menzies to announce in the final days of his Prime Ministership was criticised in several parts of the Commonwealth[2] as 'anti-Commonwealth'. This was the decision that Australia would be represented only by an observer at the Commonwealth Conference to be held in Lagos in January 1966, to discuss the problem of Rhodesia. On 7 January the Prime Minister announced that the cabinet had made a complete review of the proposals of the Prime Minister of Nigeria to hold the Conference. The Australian decision to seek representation only at observer level had been based upon grounds of important principle. Menzies continued as follows:

We put them in this order because—
   1. Our prime duty is to Australia.
   2. If the modern Commonwealth, on the initiative of some or many of its members, begins to claim the right to intervene in and give orders in relation to matters which are the proper concern of

---

[1] *Ibid.* p. 35.   [2] See p. 112 above.

some individual member of the Commonwealth, good relations cannot long continue, nor can the present Commonwealth structure long endure.[1]

He pointed out that the 1965 Prime Ministers' Conference had unanimously declared that 'the authority and responsibility for leading her remaining colonies, including Southern Rhodesia, to independence must continue to rest with Britain'. Was it for other members of the Commonwealth to give Britain instructions as to how she was to use her authority and discharge her responsibility? The Australian Government strongly believed that it was not: 'For if Britain can be instructed or coerced by the Commonwealth—or most of its members—in a matter which is, by concession, hers and hers alone to deal with, then Australia can some day be instructed or coerced on some matter in which the sole jurisdiction resides with Australia.'[1]

This statement by Menzies is unique, and can only be interpreted as reflecting deep disillusion and caution in the person who throughout his political career was proud to proclaim himself a Commonwealth man and who had not hesitated on significant occasions, of which the Suez crisis is the supreme example, to support British policy through thick and thin, sometimes, in the opinion of many Australians, to the detriment of vital Australian interests.

It is not proposed here to consider, with benefit of hindsight, whether the Government's policy was justified by subsequent developments at the Conference itself—to say nothing of subsequent developments in Nigeria and Ghana, where constituted authority was overthrown by force. Developments in the Commonwealth of Nations as a whole, as distinct from the Australian attitude towards the Commonwealth, will be considered further in the next chapter. Here it is perhaps sufficient to add that editorial opinion within Australia showed uneasiness about the decision, quoting arguments both for and against, tending on the whole to agree with the decision, but at times contesting the validity of the reasons advanced by the Prime Minister to support it.

Until the problems of the Common Market forced upon their attention the changes which had taken place in the Commonwealth during the preceding twenty years—not least in the

[1] *Melbourne Age*, 7 January 1966, p. 1.

attitude of the United Kingdom towards the Commonwealth—comparatively few Australians gave thought to their significance. Yet there were some who saw the new trends clearly and tried to warn Australians of their nature, and one or two who exposed an angry desire to turn back the clock. Of the latter probably the best known is Sir Alexander Downer, now Australian High Commissioner in London.[1] While still a private member of Parliament, Mr Downer made known in Parliament in March 1957 his reservations about the new Commonwealth in the following forthright terms:

In the last eleven years we have all been too painfully aware of startling instances of divergent policy [within the Commonwealth]. One member has attacked every major move of Britain, Canada, Australia and New Zealand to circumvent Communism. We have listened like meek oxen to strictures on NATO, on the Bagdad Pact, on SEATO and only recently the joint United Kingdom, Australian and New Zealand view on Suez . . . In striving to accommodate many diverse policies, conflicting ambitions, irreconcilable philosophies, in maintaining that opponents are our friends, there is a danger that the whole thing will dissolve into thin air . . . more than anything else I believe in the Commonwealth, but it must be a co-operative Commonwealth in fact not just a historical fiction. However much we hope that the emergent colonial states will take their place by our side and that the large and populous Asian nations now within shall remain, yet this also must be said: If their ways are not our ways, if their aims are not our aims, if they feel we are so wrong as one of them continually claims, then I say that for the sake of an effective Commonwealth of the future it would be better if a dissident member gracefully retired and continued on its own course, in the full exercise of its own judgement but without corroding our own joint councils.[2]

Oddly enough it was the same Mr Downer who, as Minister for Immigration, displayed in his Roy Milne Memorial Lecture for 1950, entitled 'The Influence of Migration on Australian Foreign Policy', a realistic understanding of the long-term effects upon Australian attitudes towards the British Commonwealth of the heavy proportion of non-British migrants who have come to Australia in the post-war years. Since the end of the Second World War all Australian political parties have agreed upon the necessity for the maximum immigration from

[1] Australian Minister for Immigration, 1958–63; K.B.E. (1965).
[2] Quoted in *Australia in World Affairs, 1956–60*, pp. 347–8.

Europe which the country could absorb. As a result, no fewer than 2,408,403 immigrants had entered Australia for permanent residence by December 1965, and of these 1,139,941, or approximately 47·3% were non-British. In his lecture the Minister commented that, to practically all non-British migrants, 'Britain has no emotional meaning whatsoever'.[1] He continued as follows:

...I believe our immigration programme will, in course of time, attenuate our British ties, and place our Commonwealth membership more on a basis of practical self-interest. To those of us who are fond of England, and proud of our British institutions, and the Commonwealth association, this conclusion may come as a surprise. But it is better to recognise these tendencies now than to remain unaware of them.[1]

Sir Frederic Eggleston, a distinguished Australian of wide governmental and diplomatic experience who died in November 1954, had pointed to the risk of over-estimating the current significance of the Commonwealth in a chapter on 'The Commonwealth and its value' printed as part of a book entitled *Reflections on Australian Foreign Policy*, published in 1957:

The disadvantages of the Commonwealth are that the association tends to be taken as somewhat more real than it actually is; sacrifices may be made to preserve it, which may be vital, but which may secure no corresponding support from others; members of the Commonwealth, though not bound to do so, may abandon positive policy, which they think necessary, for fear of alienating other members.[2]

To Sir Frederic Eggleston the British Commonwealth tie had now 'no political significance whatever'.[3] It did not fetter the independent initiative of any member, or involve any agreement to confer on policy, or any obligations of mutual support. It did not imply any likelihood that the members would adopt a common policy.[3] On the other hand, speaking of the advantages of the Commonwealth, he still felt able to say that all members of the Commonwealth tried, in their own way, to preserve democratic principles; all were genuinely interested in a peaceful and free world order, though they might differ as to the means by which that objective was to be pursued; all

---

[1] Published by the Australian Institute of International Affairs. See pp. 19–20.
[2] F. W. Cheshire, Melbourne, 1957, p. 205.   [3] *Ibid.* p. 204.

would settle their own problems by peaceful means, except, perhaps, India and Pakistan. Eggleston felt that 'we ought...to work out principles of behaviour between members of the Commonwealth, norms and conventions...which...give life and effectiveness to the association, without impairing the freedom of the members', and he himself made a number of suggestions to this end.[1]

Professor J. D. B. Miller described the Commonwealth of Nations in 1958 as a 'concert of convenience'.[2] The prime consideration of each member was its own interest; national self-assertion was the aim of everyone. Yet a certain common element connected them, namely the influence of their connexion with Britain, as revealed in many fields besides the political. 'It does not go so far as a common set of values', he wrote, 'but it is sufficiently embodied in institutions and modes of expression to make the business of consultation and discussion more congenial for the members than it might be with foreign countries.'[3]

Professor Gordon Greenwood has expressed in thoughtful and restrained terms growing doubts of thinking Australians about the trend of Commonwealth affairs in recent years. Writing in 1962, he said:

The growing concern about the contemporary character of the Commonwealth centres around three issues—the loss of cohesion, the lack of international influence, and the divisions of outlook among the members. Diversity as opposed to uniformity is not necessarily a fault and may indeed have much to commend it, but when diversity regularly produces fundamental differences of outlook and policy then it must inevitably stultify both action and influence. It is perhaps for this reason that the international impact of the Commonwealth is in no sense commensurate with the expectations which were aroused when the initial post-war transformation first took place.[4]

The most influential Australian voice on the present state of the Commonwealth of Nations has been that of Lord Casey,[5] who retired from the portfolio of External Affairs in January 1960 when a life peerage was conferred upon him, and who in 1963 published a book on *The Future of the Commonwealth*.[6]

---

[1] *Ibid.* p. 205.
[2] *The Commonwealth in the World* (Duckworth, London, 1958), p. 275.
[3] *Ibid.* p. 302.   [4] *Australia in World Affairs 1956–60*, p. 49.
[5] Now Governor-General of Australia.   [6] Frederick Muller, London.

Whereas most other observant Australians had been content to note the changes within the Commonwealth, and to give warnings that its influence was declining, Casey wanted to stir up the citizens of every member of the Commonwealth, especially those in the United Kingdom, to do something about the present situation and to take those steps which were practicable to rebuild its power and prestige.

In the preface to his book he says that it has been 'deeply distressing' to watch the decline of the Commonwealth, which was 'on the way to becoming not much more than a paper conception, with little reality or practical usefulness...'[1] He presents his book as an argument for 'the interdependence of the Commonwealth countries' and he seeks a change in attitude of mind in all Commonwealth countries designed to revive the cohesion of the Commonwealth if not its unity.[1] In his opinion the Commonwealth was not going to break up, but it might well 'fade out through inaction'.[2] He concluded with the following paragraph: 'Do not let us continue to speak of the Commonwealth in soothing terms. It is not tranquillisers that are wanted but stimulants. Either we should all stop talking about the Commonwealth or do our utmost to make it worth talking about.'[3]

In chapter 6 of his book Casey summarises the numerous suggestions he has made for the purpose of generating a far greater interest in the Commonwealth than now exists. These range from the grant of more economic and technical aid by old to new Commonwealth countries, through scientific research in Britain into appropriate means of coping with excessive population growth in new Commonwealth countries, to the creation of regional Commonwealth universities and technical colleges in Asia, Africa and the West Indies. But it is clear that the author regards such proposals as useless unless based upon a common will to sustain and strengthen the Commonwealth in all practicable ways.

This chapter has been concerned primarily to describe the changes which have taken place in the *Australian* attitude to the Commonwealth during the past twenty-eight years. It would be incomplete without again referring briefly to Australia's own responsibility for changes which have taken place in the Commonwealth of Nations. Too frequently have Australian spokes-

[1] *The Future of the Commonwealth*, p. 10.   [2] *Ibid.* p. 12.   [3] *Ibid.* p. 165.

men implied that the growing lack of cohesion within the Commonwealth has been due to, or followed directly from the growth of the multi-racial Commonwealth and the attitudes of mind of the 'new' members of the Commonwealth. But as it has been pointed out earlier,[1] both Labour and Liberal–Country Party governments of Australia have contributed to centrifugal forces within the Commonwealth when vital Australian interests seemed to be at stake. It is desirable to remember this in order to maintain proper perspective when considering current actions by new members of the Commonwealth which seem likely to reduce still further Commonwealth cohesion and influence. If, to use Shakespeare's phrase, 'the caterpillars of the commonwealth' are to be weeded and plucked away,[2] it is desirable to call in aid the microscope as well as the telescope in order to find them.

[1] See pp. 186–7 above.   [2] *King Richard II*, act ii, scene iii, ll. 166–7.

8

A RE-APPRAISAL OF AUSTRALIAN FOREIGN POLICY (1938–1965)

I. GENERAL

The primary purpose of the preceding chapters has been to try to *describe* the evolution of Australian foreign policy during the period under review, although here and there questions were raised as to the correctness or adequacy of such policy when this seemed specially appropriate at the time. In this concluding chapter an attempt at a more critical appraisal of some important aspects of policy and methods will be made, remembering, of course, that it is much easier to be wise after the event. On the other hand, it would not be profitable to list problems current as of the date of writing and to make dogmatic pronouncements on desirable governmental action in regard to such problems. International events do not stand still between dates of writing and publication, and a policy which may have seemed eminently desirable at one time may be open to objection later. Constructive criticism, therefore—apart from an analysis of some past actions—should deal with principles and the correct approach to problems, rather than with particular facts or sets of facts which change from week to week.

During the twenty-eight years which elapsed between 1938 and 1965, inclusive, Australian foreign policy—wise or foolish, right or wrong—became distinctive and adult. In 1938 Australia relied primarily on British initiatives and upon such information and comments, collected and tendered by the British Foreign Service at home and overseas, as the British Government chose to pass on to Canberra in communicating that Government's own views and decisions.

True, an embryo Foreign Office was in existence in Canberra from 1935, when External Affairs was re-established as a separate department to which a few career officers were appointed with reasonable educational qualifications and, occasionally, overseas experience. In London, there was a large staff at Australia House under a High Commissioner, including a senior adviser from the Department of External Affairs whose main additional function was to act as liaison with relevant British Ministries, especially the Foreign Office and the Dominions Office. The experiment was being tried of attaching an Australian Counsellor to the staff of the British Ambassador, Washington. Further, Trade Commissioner Posts were established in Toronto (1929), Wellington (1934), Batavia, Shanghai and Tokyo (1935), and Cairo, New York and Calcutta (between 1937 and 1939). Earlier appointments to Shanghai (1921) and to Singapore (1922) had been terminated shortly afterwards.[1] Officers appointed to these Trade Posts were not selected by or under the control of the Department of External Affairs or attached to Australian Diplomatic Missions.

As pointed out in chapter 1, at the time of the Munich Agreement in 1938 Australia had no Embassies or Legations in Germany, France, the Soviet Union, Japan or the United States regularly reporting on and interpreting from a basically Australian point of view developments within these countries. No doubt reports came from the Australian Counsellor at the British Embassy, Washington, but at this stage the United States was itself heavily isolationist in outlook and not well placed to advise on what should be done with Hitler. In the circumstances it was inevitable that the Liberal–Country Party coalition government in Canberra would echo the policy of the Neville Chamberlain Government in London. It was not isolationist in outlook, as was the Australian Labour Party at that date. Moreover, it had confidence in British Conservative Party policy, and it was content to let Britain take the initiative in foreign affairs, expecting due consultation by London and reserving the right to express opinions from time to time for Britain to take into consideration in formulating policy for the Commonwealth as a whole.

By the end of 1965 this Australian outlook on world affairs had changed almost unrecognisably, due mainly to the entry of Japan into the Second World War and her military victories in the Pacific and South-East Asian areas. The war forced a reluctant Australia into diplomacy, until she has now[2]

---

[1] *Commonwealth of Australia Year Book* (1965), p. 496.
[2] August 1966: the Australian High Commissioner to Kenya is also High Commissioner to Uganda and accredited as Ambassador to Ethiopia. The Australian High Commissioner to India is also accredited as Ambassador to Nepal.

twenty-eight Embassies in foreign countries, twelve High Commissions within the Commonwealth of Nations, Missions to the United Nations (New York and Geneva) and to the European Economic Community (Brussels), Consulates-General in Madrid, Geneva, New York and San Francisco, Consulates in Denmark, New Caledonia and Portuguese Timor, and a Commission in Fiji. It is necessary to read the list of countries where Embassies and High Commissions have been established to realise the scope, burden and responsibility which Australia has undertaken in the diplomatic field in the short period of twenty-five years. There are High Commissions in Britain, Canada, Ceylon, Ghana, India, Kenya, Malaysia, New Zealand, Nigeria, Pakistan, Singapore and Tanzania. Embassies have been opened in Argentina, Austria, Belgium, Brazil, Burma, Cambodia, France, Federal Republic of Germany, Greece, Indonesia, Ireland, Israel, Italy, Japan, Korea, Laos, Mexico, Nepal, The Netherlands, the Philippines, South Africa, Sweden, Taiwan, Thailand, Union of Soviet Socialist Republics, United Arab Republic, United States of America, the Republic of Vietnam and Yugoslavia. The Australian Ambassador in Bonn is also Head of an Australian Military Mission in Berlin.[1] On the other hand, there are 34 non-Commonwealth countries and 9 Commonwealth countries represented by diplomatic Missions in Australia, including 29 Embassies, 5 Legations, and 9 High Commissions.[2] In addition, the Australian Trade Commission Service has expanded greatly and has representatives abroad not only in most capital cities where Australian diplomatic missions are placed, but often in additional cities within such countries and, in a few cases, in cities such as Hong Kong where there is no formal Australian diplomatic post.[3]

This great expansion of formal contacts with Commonwealth and foreign countries has involved, of course, a large increase in the recruitment and training of diplomatic personnel. Taking the Department of External Affairs alone, as of 4 March 1966 there were 103 professional officers and 291 others in the home establishment and 134 professional officers and 157 others

---

[1] *Commonwealth of Australia Year Book* (1965), pp. 1,229–30. Later information supplied by the Department of External Affairs has been added to the list given therein.

[2] *Ibid.* pp. 1,231–2, as amended by the Commonwealth of Australia Diplomatic List for June 1966.   [3] *Ibid.* pp. 1,232–3.

posted overseas. Unofficial observers from amongst all Australian political parties who have travelled abroad, together with occasional Commonwealth and foreign observers, have paid tribute to the general keenness and competence of the members of the Australian Foreign Service, many of whom are reasonably fluent in the more obvious European languages such as French and German, and some of whom have specialist qualifications in Russian, Japanese, Chinese, Indonesian and Arabic. In the gathering of facts and their interpretation in the light of wide personal experience in different regions overseas, most Australian diplomats can now at least compete on the world stage with foreign professionals. Although a few individual weaknesses can still be found in particular areas, Ministers for External Affairs cannot in general justly complain either of lack of access to a variety of information gathered by native Australians or of lack of skilled advice. Evidence of this can be gleaned from the speech made in Parliament on 10 March 1966 by the present Minister, Mr Paul Hasluck:

Australian diplomatic work...is growing both in range and in intensity. After nearly two years' experience with the portfolio, I am personally greatly heartened at the repeated signs I have found in all parts of the world that in most of the 40 capitals in which Australia is represented we have established ourselves in truth and regard, and that we do have access to places of influence because we, or those who represent us, have earned the confidence of others. I believe from my observations that we Australians are thought of as a reliable people and I hope that nations who are undergoing trial are also thinking of us as a nation that is trying to understand and to help and to respect the rights of others.[1]

Additional evidence from non-Australian sources is provided by the fact that Australia now represents American interests in Cambodia, and Cambodian interests in the Republic of Vietnam; for a time she also represented British interests in Ghana during the temporary breach in diplomatic relations between that country and the United Kingdom. Further, Australia now conducts each year a three-months' Foreign Service Training Course. In 1966 trainees have come from eight Afro-Asian countries.

In Australia as a whole substantial changes have also taken place since 1938. The percentage of any community which

[1] *C.N.* vol. xxxvii, no. 3 (March 1966), p. 134.

takes a close interest in international, as distinct from domestic, problems is comparatively small in most countries. Twenty-eight years ago the percentage in Australia was particularly small, due largely to remoteness from the actual scene of international crises and from the centres of world communications media. This is no longer true. Japan's march southwards during the Second World War made Australians acutely conscious of direct threats to their own security, while developments in Asia since the end of the war have made them realise that they live in a country which is close to the southern rim of one of the most turbulent and unstable regions in the world.

Since 1945 public opinion has been particularly conscious of developments in Indonesia. Two Dutch 'police actions' were followed by an unsuccessful Communist revolt, a civil war, substitution of 'guided democracy' for parliamentary democracy, confrontation of the Dutch over West New Guinea, confrontation of Malaysia and, most recently, *coup* and counter-*coup* in 1965. In Malaya Communist uprisings led eventually to co-operation between British, Malayan and Australian troops against the 'terrorists' in the jungle. There has been intermittent turmoil in Laos since 1954, while in Vietnam the Geneva Agreements of that year failed to settle bitter disagreements between North and South. In due course American forces became increasingly involved in the fighting, and they were joined during 1965 by Australian combat units. During the Korean War Australia accepted land, sea and air commitments in and around that country. Public opinion was also uneasily aware of the possibilities of escalation of fighting between Communist China and Nationalist China—the latter protected by American air forces and fleets—after agreement had been reached on a Korean armistice. All these developments have been, on the whole, reasonably well reported in the Australian Press and over radio and television. While the number of special Australian correspondents in the region is not large, their influence has become increasingly significant even though important gaps in reporting still remain.

In these circumstances it would be strange if Australian interest in and understanding of developments in Asia had not grown greatly during the past twenty years. Experience during the war itself made the Australian electorate accept almost without question the Government's post-war decision that military plans in any foreseeable future must be based upon the assumption that Australian strategic involvement would be in South-East Asia, and not, as in the past, in the Middle East or Europe. The widening of Australian diplomatic contacts in Asia after Casey became Minister for External Affairs in 1951 led not only to more sophisticated reporting of the Asian scene by officials, but also brought increasing publicity about Asian problems as Ministers for External Affairs visited the area and attended frequent conferences. Business-men seeking new outlets for Australian exports and tourists seeking pleasure increased general comprehension.

Australians as a whole accepted governmental policy under the Colombo Plan, though strong minorities pressed for a greater allocation of funds for the purpose of aid to under-developed countries. Technical assistance under the Plan contributed substantially to the vast increase in the numbers of Asians studying in Australian schools, universities and technological institutions, and resulted in significant numbers of Australian scientists, technologists and teachers visiting various Asian countries to advise on local problems. Brief reference has already been made to changes within the universities tending to reduce the old dominance of European subjects in the Humanities.[1]

In addition, for more than thirty years two non-profit institutes have made continuing and substantial contributions to Australian understanding of national and international problems. The Australian Institute of Political Science was founded in 1932 to provide education and research facilities for people interested in the study of the political, economic and social problems of Australia. Every year, with the exception of some of the war years, it has held a Summer School where papers have been read on some chosen subject, widely discussed, and subsequently published in book form. While the focus of problems has for the most part been domestic, they have included immigration, foreign policy, the marketing of primary products, Asia and Australia, New Guinea and Australia's defence and foreign policy. Discussion of the last topic in 1964 had a significant influence upon opinion within the country as a whole. The Institute publishes a well-established journal, *The Australian Quarterly*.

[1] See p. 199 above.

The Australian Institute of International Affairs was formed in 1933 to promote the objective study and discussion of international problems. It is an unofficial, non-party body affiliated with Chatham House, London, as are also sister institutes in a number of Commonwealth countries. There are branches in the capital cities of each of the six Australian States, and also at Canberra, Armidale and Townsville. Over the years it has published books[1] and periodicals[2] and brought to Australia distinguished overseas speakers as Dyason Lecturers,[3] while the branches hold regular meetings where lectures on international problems are followed by discussion. In recent years the Institute has substantially expanded its activities, due partly to the grant by the Ford Foundation of $75,000 for a three-year research programme, and partly to the appointment of a full-time director with a central office in Canberra. It has held some seminars and conferences, and plans to expand activities of this kind. Annual Roy Milne Memorial Lectures under Institute auspices have been given by leaders of the Liberal, Country and Labour Parties—all of whom have given support to the organisation, by other cabinet ministers, deputy leaders of political parties and other distinguished Australians. The precise extent and degree of its influence is difficult to measure, but there is no doubt that, through the dissemination of different points of view, it has contributed significantly to the formation of a more informed and questioning public opinion.

Nor have newspapers and radio stood still in the period under review. Old established newspapers like the *Sydney Morning Herald* and the *Melbourne Age* have played essential parts in expounding and testing governmental policies and in commenting on the factual overseas information which they provide for their readers. In Canberra itself, with a population which is increasing rapidly but has still not quite reached the 100,000 mark, *The Canberra Times* and the *Australian* have each essayed to

[1] For instance, *Australia in World Affairs, 1950–55*, and *1956–60*; F. W. Eggleston, *Reflections on Australian Foreign Policy*; *International Law in Australia*, ed. O'Connell; C. P. Fitzgerald, *The Third China*.

[2] *The Australian Outlook*, ed. Professor J. D. B. Miller; *World Review*, ed. Charles Grimshaw; *Australia's Neighbours*.

[3] These have included Bertrand Russell, Arnold Toynbee, Julian Huxley, Gunnar Myrdal, Salvador de Madariaga, Dr V. K. R. V. Rao, Mrs Margaret Ballinger, Kenneth Younger, Alastair Buchan, and, most recently, Professor Merle Fainsod (Harvard), Professor Shigeto Tsuru (Hitotsubashi), Sir Robert Scott (United Kingdom) and Senator Raul S. Manglapus (Philippines).

become, in different senses, national newspapers—the latter attempting the extremely difficult task of wide daily delivery in all States of the Commonwealth. Feature articles in the more important Australian newspapers have increased in range and depth, reflecting, *inter alia*, closer links between the Press and members of the staffs of universities. The news services of the Australian Broadcasting Commission, whose finances derive from licence fees and not from advertising, have added to the range and quality of other information media. The Commission draws heavily upon the universities for commentaries on the news. Its extensive short-wave programmes beamed overseas, not only in English but also in French, Indonesian, Japanese, Mandarin Chinese and Cantonese, Vietnamese and Thai, have awakened a lively interest in Australian programmes, especially lessons in English. This has improved somewhat the sharpness of the Australian image projected into neighbouring countries of the Pacific. Television is of more recent vintage in Australia, while talent, experience and finance are limited. Both the A.B.C. and Commercial Television Stations are, however, endeavouring to cope more effectively with the outstanding need for better documentaries on domestic and international problems.

In all these circumstances no one could reasonably deny that the stage has been set within Australia for public response to effective Government leadership and initiative in the field of foreign affairs. Yet there have been significant gaps in such leadership, and a degree of rigidity in some aspects of policy, the causes of which require analysis. Within recent years, indeed, pressure for increased defence preparedness, for greater flexibility in immigration policy and for larger contributions towards foreign aid has come upwards from minority groups and the grass roots rather than downwards from the cabinet or parliamentary level. Moreover, important government decisions which have been taken in the defence field, especially those relating to the question whether Australian combat forces should be sent to Borneo and to the Republic of Vietnam, have been made without adequate preparation of public opinion in advance. As a result, many Australians, though disposed to support both decisions, have been confused and uncertain in their reactions. This hiatus between Government and electorate and, indeed, between cabinet and Parliament, seems to have been more evident during the past ten years than during the preceding ten years, and some review of the two periods is thus desirable.

The Labour Party lost office at the end of 1949, by which year Australia, like other countries, had scarcely emerged from the post-war doldrums. At the United Nations Charter Conference at San Francisco in 1945 Dr Evatt had pursued a somewhat personal policy on highly technical, constitutional problems not easily capable of simple explanation to public opinion, even if serious effort had been made. Most Australians knew that Evatt had achieved prominence at San Francisco; many probably approved his attacks upon Great Power 'veto' rights and the demand for increased Middle and Small Power responsibility, his pressure for guarantees of 'full-employment', his insistence on the doctrine of 'accountability' for non-self-governing territories and his urge towards United Nations involvement in all important international issues. It would have required exceptional insight to foresee that a vast increase in membership of the United Nations could lead to majority decisions of the General Assembly modifying in practice the meaning of the Charter without formal amendment, and to realise in advance that some of these decisions, especially on colonial issues, would in due course be directed against Australia.

Evatt's 'hard' line towards a Japanese Peace Treaty was without doubt strongly supported at the time by the electorate, and needed little detailed public explanation. Stalin's 'cold-war' policy, however, together with the outbreak of the Korean war and the victory of the Communists in China, revolutionised American policy towards Japan and made it impracticable for Australian policy towards a Japanese Peace Settlement to be realised.

Since December 1949 Australia has known only one Government, a Liberal–Country Party Coalition under the leadership of Menzies. Prior to his retirement in January 1966 Sir Robert Menzies had been Prime Minister of Australia for an unprecedented length of time in Australian political history. His unrivalled capacity for effective speech, which showed out like a beacon light amongst both his colleagues and political opponents, his flair for parliamentary debate and his capacity for withering repartee made him the dominant political personality of post-war Australia. He was never popular, and he has made serious mistakes, yet his native ability, vast experience and courage in adversity have combined with the inadequacies of political leadership within the Labour Party to make it possible for him to recover from the verge of political disaster. Over the years, and particularly from 1956 onwards, the foreign and Commonwealth policy of the Government has been predominantly that of the Australian Prime Minister.

There is no doubt that, during the first five years of office, the Menzies Government took vigorous initiatives, and went to some pains to expound its policy to public opinion at large. Sir Percy Spender was Minister for External Affairs for a short period of approximately eighteen months; yet during that time his pertinacity and skill were largely responsible for the Colombo Plan coming into existence, and especially for the degree of emphasis in the Plan upon technical assistance. In addition, Spender is entitled to claim credit, before becoming Australian Ambassador to Washington, for completion of the basic work which resulted in the ANZUS Alliance. These two significant initiatives were overwhelmingly approved by the Australian electorate.

Spender was succeeded by Casey, who maintained the previous initiative in regard to the ANZUS Treaty, the SEATO Treaty, and the Colombo Plan, which Casey expanded in various directions and always regarded as a highly important aspect of Australian foreign policy. Perhaps his own most distinctive achievement, however, resulted from his frequent trips to Asia, especially South-East Asia, whose personalities and background conditions he probably knew better than any other Foreign Minister in the world. Casey was a man who learned more by personal contact and conversation than by reading documents and reflecting deeply upon their contents. His judgement of messages received was strongly influenced by his visual and audile memory of the persons who sent them or whose activities they described.

His first goodwill visit to South-East Asia in 1951 made a deep impression upon him, and convinced him that Australia must build up its diplomatic representation in the area. On his return to Canberra he took the necessary initiatives to convince cabinet, Parliament and public opinion of the justification for this policy, and he subsequently put it into effect. Nor was any opportunity lost to explain policy to the general public. Casey made almost a fetish of 'public relations'; he was always available to the Press, both in Australia and abroad, and any failure to make clear the bases of Australian foreign policy cannot be ascribed to lack of effort or will. While Minister for External Affairs he published in both Australian and American editions of *Friends and Neighbours* short accounts of Australian policy in regard to a variety of international problems.[1] These are the first connected accounts, written for the general reader, of modern Australian foreign policy.

Why then did Australian initiatives in the international field during a period of approximately ten years, from 1955 to 1965, flag or correspond less well to the rapidly changing international situation? And why did a growing gap develop between the Government on the one hand and public opinion on the other? Only speculative answers can be given to these questions, but it is important that answers should at least be sought. An acute observer, Professor Gordon Greenwood, President of the Australian Institute of International Affairs from 1962 to 1965 and co-editor of two volumes of *Australia in World Affairs*, has drawn attention to the difference between the two periods 1950–55 and 1956–60. He has written as follows:

Looking at the period 1956–60, it is difficult to avoid the conclusion that policy had become stereotyped, that it proceeded along familiar routes and was simply continuing or repeating earlier initiatives without devising new techniques or discovering fresh possibilities. A good deal of the imagination, the probing, the experimentation, the search for new ways of applying policy, which characterized the Government's approach five years before, had been lost. This more imaginative and adventuresome policy needs to be recaptured. There are possibilities for much greater manœuvrability, for accommodation between the west on the one hand and Asia and Africa on the other, and for fertile suggestion in international policy-making—always provided the level of thinking is high enough.[2]

The hypothesis which appears to fit most closely to the available evidence places primary responsibility for rigidity in foreign policy upon the personality and outlook of the Australian Prime Minister, Sir Robert Menzies, although Government political parties, Parliament and the Department of External Affairs must take some share of the blame.

[1] Cheshire, Melbourne, 1954, and Michigan State University Press, 1958.
[2] *Australia in World Affairs 1956–60*, p. 102.

If one looks at the Australian domestic scene during the ten-year period 1955–65, Menzies bestrides it like a colossus. Within his own political party, few approached him in ability and none could compete against his determined opposition. He personally has been predominantly responsible for Government success in every federal election since 1949. Only one man in his cabinet, namely, McEwen, Minister for Trade and Industry and Leader of the Country Party, was tough and skilful enough on occasion to advocate publicly policies which were not always quite in line with cabinet views as announced by relevant ministers—for instance, regarding the amount and kind of overseas investment in Australia and the sale to overseas interests of unprocessed raw material like iron ore. Whenever Menzies was abroad and McEwen was Acting Prime Minister, one quickly became conscious that McEwen was no mere stop-gap. Yet one felt that he respected Menzies and was prepared to work with him, while taking all necessary steps to ensure that Country Party interests did not suffer in the process.

But McEwen's portfolio is Trade and Industry—by now, it would seem, by Australian habit and tradition, almost a Country Party preserve. Menzies, however, has always been less interested in trade problems than in the Commonwealth of Nations and foreign policy, including defence. In these related fields the Prime Minister has strong convictions, and if there were a conflict of opinion, his views prevailed. The outstanding illustration of this was his complete support for the disastrous policy of Anthony Eden during the Suez crisis of 1956, which isolated Australia not only from Afro-Asian nations, but also from the United States! If strong rumour is to be believed, the Menzies policy on Suez was unsuccessfully opposed in cabinet by Casey as Minister for External Affairs. A distinguished British diplomat, Sir William Hayter, sometime Ambassador to Moscow and now Warden of New College, Oxford, has written of Britain's need 'to preserve above all a capital of respect for her wisdom, maturity, moderation and skill, a capital well built up in the decade that followed the end of the Second World War but then wildly dissipated in the crazy gamble of Suez.'[1] Australian historians of the future may well see in Menzies' unswerving support for British policy on this occasion the most serious misjudgement of Australian post-war foreign policy—a mistake

[1] *The Diplomacy of the Great Powers* (Hamish Hamilton, London, 1960), p. 48.

which made far more difficult the necessary adjustment of Australian policy to the changed position of Asian countries, in the shadow of which Australia, but not the United Kingdom, must inevitably continue to live.

Menzies' speeches and comments on the Suez Canal issue make painful reading today.[1] As late as 8 July 1957 the Prime Minister roundly declared that he was 'utterly unrepentant about anything that was done or said over this great issue on our side'.[2] No Australian should minimise his courage in pursuing a policy which was extremely unpopular internationally and strongly questioned within Australia, or fail to respect his intense loyalty to Britain in a situation of great strain and difficulty, even to the extent of refusing to criticise Eden's failure to consult with Australia before the ultimatum to Egypt was issued. In the result, however, British policy failed, despite Eden's half-hearted and *ex post facto* attempt—later echoed by Menzies—to justify it on the ground that Franco-British action against Egypt was necessary in order to galvanise the United Nations into sending a United Nations force into the Canal Zone.[3] Australian support for British policy was, therefore, not only ineffective, but damaging to vital Australian international relations with other countries.

It is of interest to note that whereas Canada acquired great international prestige through the proposal of its Secretary of State for External Affairs, Mr Lester Pearson, that the United Nations should send an emergency force to the Suez area to secure and supervise the cessation of hostilities—a proposal later incorporated in a resolution jointly submitted by Canada, Colombia and Norway—Australia was one of nineteen countries which abstained from voting. Her eighteen colleagues in abstention were as follows: Albania, Bulgaria, Byelorussia, Czechoslovakia, Egypt, France, Hungary, Israel, Laos, New Zealand, Poland, Portugal, Rumania, Turkey, Ukraine, South Africa, the U.S.S.R. and the United Kingdom. Of these nine were Communist countries—who had no desire to establish a precedent for United Nations intervention in Hungary; four were interested parties; while Portugal and South Africa had special grounds for avoiding approval of United Nations intervention. Of the remaining three, New Zealand alone could be

---

[1] See Menzies, *Speech is of Time*, pp. 81–180.   [2] *Ibid.* p. 171.
[3] *Ibid.*: Eden's statement is quoted on p. 159.

regarded as a country with problems and outlook substantially similar to those of Australia.

There is no point in considering here the rights and wrongs of the Suez affair—whether President Nasser acted illegally or immorally; whether or not Dulles at various stages led Eden up the garden path while eventually spear-heading the attack upon Britain and France in the United Nations; whether or not Eden deliberately kept the United States Government uninformed of British intentions, in the hope that the American administration would be so preoccupied with its presidential elections that it would be unable to take dissuasive or preventive action. The simple test is that, international as well as domestic politics being the art of the possible, British, French and Australian judgement was seriously at fault in overestimating British and French power and capacity, in the postwar world, to use force to prevent an Afro-Asian country from nationalising the Suez Canal—at least in the absence of full backing by the United States.

Moreover, there are several specific passages in the Australian Prime Minister's statements on the Suez issue which need recalling. In his speech to Parliament of 25 September 1956 Menzies quoted with approval two extracts from Eden's speech during the debate in the House of Commons on 2 August:

> ...the industrial life of Western Europe literally depends upon the continuing free navigation of the Canal as one of the great international waterways of the world...No arrangements for the future of this great international waterway could be acceptable to Her Majesty's Government which would leave it in the unfettered control of a single Power which could, as recent events have shown, exploit it purely for purposes of national policy.[1]

The event has shown that, despite Egyptian control of the canal, the industrial life of Western Europe continues to develop, while Her Majesty's Government has accepted, with whatever reluctance, the unfettered control of a single Power.

Far more important, however, in a South-East Asian context, is Menzies' defence of the use of force outside the provisions of the United Nations Charter as a means of settling international problems. He describes as a 'suicidal doctrine' the argument that 'force can never be employed (except presumably in self-

---

[1] *Ibid.* pp. 121–2.

defence) except by and pursuant to a decision of the United Nations Security Council.'[1] For him it had been 'an astonishing experience to find that there are people who reject force out of hand, reject economic action on the ground that it is provocative, and so, being opposed to action of either kind, are prepared to accept the new tyranny, with regret perhaps, but without resistance'.[2] In the same speech he underlined this point of view in the following words:

We must avoid the use of force if we can. But we should not, by theoretical reasoning in advance of the facts and circumstances, contract ourselves out of its use whatever those facts and circumstances may be. We are to seek peace at all times, but we are not bound to carry that search so far that we stand helpless before unlawful actions which, if allowed to go unchecked, can finally dissipate our own strength and deprive the world of that power and authority, both moral and physical, which reside in the free nations, and are still vital to the free world and the human interests which the free world protects.[3]

There may be much common sense in this reasoning—from the point of view of the 'free nations'. Unfortunately it is difficult for any country supporting this philosophy to deny a similar right to unfree or less free nations. In the first place, there may be some slight disagreement as to which countries are 'free' and which are 'unfree'. Secondly, a nation which claims the right, in its own vital interests, to use force without United Nations authority and without the justification of self-defence can scarcely criticise any other nation which claims a similar right. Was the use of force at Suez by Britain and France justified, but the use of force by India in Goa unjustified? Was Australia entitled to charge Indonesia with bad faith in breaking her undertakings not to use force to settle the West New Guinea dispute or with breach of the United Nations Charter in confronting Malaysia by force? One would have thought it extremely unwise for a country in Australia's situation to advance publicly a philosophy justifying the use of force to protect national interests, other than in accordance with United Nations decisions, or in self-defence, or at the request of a friend or ally itself exercising the right of self-defence.

The Australian attitude towards the Suez crisis has been

[1] Menzies, *Speech is of Time*, p. 137.   [2] *Ibid.* p. 141.   [3] *Ibid.* p. 139.

dealt with at some length, first, because it was identifiably the policy of the Prime Minister himself, and, secondly, because the result was not to benefit Britain but to isolate Australia both from her American ally and from Afro-Asian opinion. It was Canada, not Australia, which found the compromise, short-term solution which, in the long term, made it possible to rebuild those harmonious British–American relationships which Australian Ministers for External Affairs had in the past unanimously regarded as a vital Australian interest. Most disturbing of all was the rigidity and obstinacy shown by Menzies in claiming, as late as 8 July 1957, that he was 'utterly unrepentant' regarding the line pursued on this issue. One is forced to the conclusion that his emotional attachment to Great Britain (where, incidentally, public opinion was seriously split over the Suez issue), his intellectual distrust of paper constitutions and international organisations such as the United Nations, and his instinctive leaning towards 'great and powerful friends' clouded his judgement.

A further illustration has already been given of a bold but unwise interposition by Menzies, though not on the Suez scale. This was the initiative he took in the United Nations General Assembly in October 1960, when the Prime Minister was his own Minister for External Affairs.[1] On this occasion he was at least acting with the approval of both the United States and the United Kingdom in trying to prevent the Assembly from passing a resolution, sponsored by Ghana, India, the United Arab Republic, Yugoslavia and Indonesia, the effect of which would have been to urge Khruschhev and Eisenhower to 'renew their contacts' after the disastrous breakdown of the attempted Summit Meeting in Paris in the preceding May. The amendment he proposed was overwhelmingly defeated, but it was successful in the sense that the five-power resolution was withdrawn for lack of adequate support.

Yet an Australian is compelled to ask why an Australian initiative, rather than that of any other country, was thought necessary and justified, at the cost of attracting the literal anger of Nehru and the disapprobation of a large number of Afro-Asian States? Why not Canada, which voted for the resolution? Why not Belgium, New Zealand or any of the other dozen or more allies of Great Britain and the United States? Why did

[1] See pp. 232–3 above.

Australia have to lead with *its* particular and rather vulnerable chin?

It is impossible to believe that a person of the stature and international experience of Sir Robert Menzies feels impelled always to act internationally in accordance with the dictates of his personal conscience or the considered policy of his country *irrespective of the consequences*. This, at any rate, was not the view of the Australian Prime Minister when his Government advised the British Government on 25 July 1940 that the best line would be to give way to Japan, under *force majeure*, on questions which were not absolutely vital, while trying to secure a settlement with Japan, working in as close co-operation as possible with the United States.[1] Thus Australia concurred in the temporary closing of the Burma Road by Great Britain for a period of three months, as she also concurred in its reopening. It is well known to anyone who has attended international conferences that Great Powers themselves do not always leap to the rostrum and declare publicly the policy they believe the conference should follow; they not infrequently prefer Middle and Smaller Powers to commit themselves first, before suggesting some broad compromise solution.

Was it a vital Australian interest, or even a vital American or British interest, to prevent the five-power resolution being passed? It is difficult to support such an argument. If it had been passed, it would have been merely a recommendation which the United States and the Soviet Union might or might not have accepted. If they had accepted it, and if, as Menzies reported to Parliament, his subsequent interview in New York with Khrushchev led him to believe that Khrushchev himself wanted a four-power conference, Khruschhev and Eisenhower only had to meet for three minutes to decide that a four-power rather than a two-power conference should be held. This would not have been inconsistent with the five-power resolution, which recommended a two-power conference 'as a first urgent step'.

It would seem reasonable to conclude, therefore, that Menzies' intervention was based once again upon his emotional attachment to the United Kingdom, whose prestige he felt to be at stake, and to the priority given by him to the views of 'our great and powerful friends', namely Great Britain and the

[1] Hasluck, *Government and People*, p. 525.

United States, over the views of other members of the United Nations. If so, he can scarcely complain if India and other Afro-Asian countries have found it difficult, at times, to distinguish the voice of Australia from that of Britain or the United States, and have placed some Australian interests rather low in their list of international priorities. In short, the price paid by Australia on this occasion seems disproportionate to the benefit gained for her two great allies.

In January 1960 Mr R. G. Casey was appointed a Life Peer, and the Prime Minister took over the portfolio of External Affairs. Casey was then approaching the age of 70, and had held the portfolio since 1951. It is not a matter for surprise that anyone of his age, experience, and range of service to his own country and to the Commonwealth of Nations should have decided to retire, although his subsequent acceptance at the age of 75 of the onerous post of Governor-General of Australia somewhat belies this interpretation. In these circumstances, one is tempted to speculate whether a contributing cause of retirement was the belief that Australian foreign policy by this time had become too rigid to meet the challenge of a rapidly changing Commonwealth of Nations and world at large.

The British Prime Minister, Harold Macmillan, had felt the 'wind of change' blowing and was trying to adapt British policy to meet it, especially in relation to the Commonwealth of Nations and to the European Common Market. Menzies was not unaware of serious changes within the Commonwealth, but he was more nostalgic and less flexible than his British counterpart. While he was wise enough not to try to resurrect the past, and was prepared to try to make the best of the present, he could not cast an active, fertile and imaginative mind towards the future. Menzies' beliefs were deep-rooted. British wisdom supported by American power should be supreme. The parliamentary system; the common-law approach; British justice ensuring equality before the law—these were the great achievements of world civilisation, standing above all others. These were the traditions which Australia must follow, irrespective of her geographical situation or her limited power. Robert Gordon Menzies lived in the world of Anglo-Saxon governance, largely untouched by non-European cultural traditions.

A third illustration of the rigidity of Australian foreign policy during the last ten years of the Menzies administration can be found in the field of immigration. It is not surprising that the Prime Minister, as an experienced and wary politician, should not have sought to introduce dramatic changes in an area of domestic policy as sensitive as this by widening significantly the scope for admission to Australia for permanent residence of people of non-European origin. Some liberalisation did of course take place during this period. The dictation test was abolished in 1958 as a method of restricting immigration, while two years earlier the Government did relax in some degree the conditions for entry and stay of non-Europeans and persons of mixed descent. Yet it seems significant that, within less than two months after Sir Robert Menzies announced his retirement, the Holt Government introduced important changes in Australian immigration policy which gained all-party support in the House of Representatives and were accepted by public opinion almost without challenge. The new policy was distinctly more liberal in its approach to non-European immigration than any which had taken place during the Menzies regime. It seems reasonably clear that the Menzies outlook on non-European immigration was more rigid than that of the Prime Minister's colleagues, and that it was thought practicable to put their policy into effect only after his retirement.

As pointed out earlier,[1] the Prime Minister's dominance in cabinet and in the Liberal Party ensured that his views on foreign policy prevailed on matters in which he was interested or felt deeply. The Country Party was chiefly interested in trade, and was content for its leader, Mr McEwen, to determine basic policy in this field. The Labour Party Opposition was divided and comparatively ineffective under both Dr Evatt and Mr Calwell. The Government's mistakes were not sufficiently made clear to the electorate. The Australian Parliament itself suffered, as in some other countries, from an increasingly dominant executive which, secure in office, grew somewhat complacent and disinclined to consult Parliament in the creation of policy as distinct from its endorsement.

The need for parliamentary reform in Australia has been well and effectively argued by a back-bench member of the Liberal Party in the federal House of Representatives, Mr H. B. Turner.[2] As Chairman of the Parliamentary Committee on

[1] See pp. 303 above.
[2] *The Australian Quarterly*, vol. xxxvii, no. 4 (December 1965), pp. 56–64.

Foreign Affairs, he is well aware of the tremendous changes which have taken place in the post-war world, and disturbed by the 'failure of Parliament to focus great issues':

...increasingly in recent years, Parliament has failed in its primary tasks; and one cannot but detect a growing awareness of this among thinking people. True, the Australian government has, broadly, done the right things, if in general too little and too late. But, above all, it has failed to carry the people with it. There is too little understanding in the community at large of the perils of our position, especially in the fields of foreign relations, defence and trade. More and more the government seems to act on the assumption that policy is a matter for it alone and that action by it is alone necessary; that Parliament is merely a rubber stamp...Debates on major matters of foreign policy have too often been relegated to the initiative of private bodies, not always disinterested. When conscription for overseas service was introduced, this great issue was obfuscated— whether deliberately or not one does not know—by the emotive minor issue whether wet canteens should be established in National Service camps. Debate on our future relations with New Guinea has been smothered, one cannot help suspecting, of set purpose...[1]

Turner makes 'a plea for light, a drawing aside of the curtains, the opening of a door of communication between government and the people's representatives'. In his opinion Parliament should insist upon having essential information at its disposal, mainly by bringing legislators face to face with administrators and experts at the committee table, and, where possible, by making available from the departments background documents that form the basis of policy decisions.[2] He strongly urges the appointment of a joint Select Committee to review the machinery of Parliament in such a way as to make possible an appreciable return of power to Parliament itself.

Some attempt to introduce a degree of greater flexibility into Australian foreign policy was undoubtedly made by Sir Garfield Barwick when in December 1961 he took over from the Prime Minister the portfolio of External Affairs. An outstanding barrister of proven reputation, not specially tied to party politics, he entered Parliament in 1958 and brought renewed distinction to the post of Attorney-General. Evidence of this is his initiative in such unrelated fields as divorce and restrictive trade practices. He held the External Affairs portfolio for a

[1] *Ibid.* pp. 59–60.　　　　　　[2] *Ibid.* p. 63.

short period of just over two years before accepting appointment as Chief Justice of the High Court of Australia, and
cannot be said to have left as clear a mark upon it by way
of personal initiative as did Sir Percy Spender during an even
shorter term of office. Nevertheless, his policy towards Indonesia,
which has been described earlier, showed subtlety, imagination
and a degree of determination to avoid adopting a distinctively
'Western' approach to the problems of Asia.

Unfortunately, the critical West New Guinea issue made it
impossible for the Minister to gain sufficient time to test fully the
scope of establishing better working relationships with Indonesia, whose confrontation of Malaysia forced an Australian
cabinet decision to help that Commonwealth country defend its
political independence and territorial integrity. While Australian verbal attacks on Indonesian policy remained muted and
attempts were made not to preclude the resumption of more
friendly relations between Canberra and Djakarta, specific initiatives in this direction had eventually to be postponed.

In one respect at least, however, Barwick showed himself in
advance of the Government of which he formed part. Though
cautious, if not critical of the Press, he was seriously concerned
about the state of public opinion and did his best to enlighten
it both through his own speeches and by encouraging institutes
and other organs of study and communication to play an active
part. In a paper read to the Summer School of the Australian
Institute of Political Science in January 1964 he boldly declared
that 'foreign policy will be more effective and stable if it enjoys
public support based on an informed and educated, and indeed
a questioning, public opinion'.[1] He pointed out that foreign
policy must always in its general direction be related to, and be
tempered by, the domestic situation of the nation. If Australian
foreign policy was to be stable, it must always be broadly in
accord with the general will. Governments had their own responsibilities in educating public opinion, but 'a government-
induced state of public information' was most undesirable. He
continued as follows:

The public education in this field needs the assistance of such bodies
as this Institute of Political Science, the Institute of International
Affairs, the United Nations Associations, the Universities, and re-

[1] *Australia's Defence and Foreign Policy*, p. 5.

sponsible news and information media—including broadcasting and television. The process of public education is particularly necessary...in this country because our people have no 'inherited' information or inherited international attitudes relevant to our immediate international region. We have not lived with our neighbours in the same sense that European countries have lived with theirs for 2,000 years. This calls for much factual material descriptive of the ways of life, the problems and the historical background of neighbouring countries and peoples as a means of exciting interest, promoting understanding and providing a proper basis for evaluation. By focusing public awareness on the great issues of the day in the setting of this background information, the domestic reaction to foreign policy will be of an increasingly mature nature, increasing in maturity as the public becomes better informed. Naturally this is not likely to be achieved by sensationalism. We cannot, of course, deny to a free press the right to sensational and headline-promoting stories, particularly as advertising, and therefore circulation for its own sake, bulks so large in newspaper economics. But this makes it all the more necessary that the Universities and the various informed Institutes play their unremitting part in keeping current events in their perspective and in encouraging what is, as I have said, a most responsible public to weigh the news of the day calmly and carefully.[1]

It was unfortunate that Barwick did not hold the post of Minister for External Affairs long enough to feel as much at home in dealing with international problems as he did in dealing with legal problems. While overseas experience gradually brought increasing understanding of foreign affairs to a man of subtle intellectual capacity, he had scarcely time, while Minister, to learn to identify tigers in the international jungle which a simpler man might have recognised more quickly. Thus, even as late as January 1964, in the address to the Australian Institute of Political Science already mentioned,[2] Barwick quoted with approval a statement by Lord Strang, sometime British Permanent Under-Secretary for Foreign Affairs, that a foreign policy depended for its implementation on three things: effective and available military power, remembered military prowess, and sheer diplomatic skill. The Minister commented that, despite Australia's growing population, industrial progress and political stability, she was not a great military power. Her record in two world wars had indeed built up 'remembered military

---

[1] *Australia's Defence and Foreign Policy*, p. 5.   [2] *Ibid.* pp. 8–9.

prowess'. Nevertheless, Australia must depend heavily upon sensitive and skilful diplomacy to explain and maintain her place in the world. He admitted that diplomacy needs some military capacity to lend it credibility, but felt that Australian diplomatic skill would be the main factor in securing a stable and tranquil region around her.

In underlining the importance for Australia of skilful diplomacy, especially at a time when public opinion was highly critical of the Government for failing to build up its military establishment to a sufficient level, Barwick underestimated the extent to which the success of the most expert diplomacy depends upon military and economic strength. This was well understood by Lord Attlee, who wrote of Ernest Bevin as Foreign Secretary as follows:

Bevin...was a first-class negotiator...He was very conscious always of the economic issues that underlay so many international questions and worked in close co-operation with successive Chancellors of the Exchequer. Our economic weakness was a great handicap to him in his work. I have often heard him say that a few million tons of coal at his disposal would have made all the difference to the outcome of some of his negotiations.[1]

An illustration from Australian experience pointing in the same direction is the negotiation of the ANZUS Treaty, during which Sir Percy Spender exhibited a high level of skilful diplomacy; yet he himself would probably be the first to admit that success at the diplomatic level was made possible only by common American–Australian effort and suffering in the Second World War, and by speedy and valued Australian military assistance during the Korean War which helped to create a political climate within the United States favourable to a military alliance with Australia. In short, while skilful diplomacy is highly desirable, it can never be regarded as a substitute for military and economic power. Over-emphasis upon diplomacy risks creating the illusion that a people can through its skilful exercise avoid substantial sacrifice and effort—blood, toil, tears and sweat—outside the immediate compass of diplomacy. Few illusions are more dangerous.

An encouraging feature of the current official scene has been growing evidence, particularly since the appointment of Sir

---

[1] C. R. Attlee, *As it Happened* (Odhams, London), n.d., p. 197.

James Plimsoll as Secretary, Department of External Affairs, at the beginning of 1965, of an increasing realisation by that Department of its 'public relations' responsibilities. Whereas in the United States it has long been taken for granted that senior members of the State Department, in addition to the Secretary of State himself, should play an important and direct part in the education of public opinion in the field of foreign policy, and while in the United Kingdom close and flexible contacts between the Foreign Office and mass media such as the Press, Radio and Television contribute significantly in spreading information and comment about Government policy, no such traditions have been built up in Australia until recently.

The Department of External Affairs has indeed produced for over thirty years monthly editions of *Current Notes on International Affairs*, which are an invaluable source of accurate information for the research student and specialist. This publication is distributed without charge and its circulation in December 1965 was 7,200, with a waiting list of 400, including 72 from overseas.[1] The Australian community takes this unspectacular but essential work too much for granted. In recent years the Department has had its Public Information Officer, who is available to give guidance to journalists and commentators. It has also begun to issue an important series of select documents on international affairs which, especially those covering Malaysia and Vietnam, contain a wide range of material too detailed for publication in *Current Notes*. Moreover, there now appears to be a stronger trend for senior officers to address private meetings of organisations interested in foreign affairs,[2] and to participate to some extent in non-official conferences and seminar discussion groups. This is a valuable development, because, while officials do not and would not be expected to reveal State secrets, the information available to them makes it possible for them to influence views of others which are not soundly based.

II. RE-EXAMINATION OF ASSUMPTIONS

This general review of Australian foreign policy during the twenty years which have elapsed since the end of the Second

[1] See *C.N.* vol. xxxvi (1965), p. 841.
[2] See, for instance, speeches by Sir James Plimsoll: 'The United Nations Charter 1945 and 1962', *C.N.* vol. xxxiii (1962), no. 6, pp. 42–9; 'A. N. Smith Memorial Lecture, November 23, 1965', *C.N.* vol. xxxvi (1965), pp. 745–57.

World War now enables us to re-examine some of the more important assumptions underlying that policy in the light of current and foreseeable international facts. These will be considered under four broad headings: (1) the Commonwealth of Nations, (2) the United Nations, (3) relations with the United States, and (4) relations with Afro-Asia, especially Asia.

1. *Commonwealth of Nations*

In chapter 7 a broad account was given of changes which have taken place within the Commonwealth of Nations during the post-war period, while changes in Australian attitudes to the Commonwealth were described in some detail. Although, as has been seen, Australians from the Prime Minister down have not been unaware of basic alterations in the Commonwealth of Nations, few can still be said to have reached the stage of clear understanding of the significance of developments during the past ten years. Emotional attachment to the Crown, especially among the older generations, combines with ties of kinship with people in Great Britain to cloud a realistic appreciation of how people in the United Kingdom themselves now regard the Commonwealth. For Australians the primary Commonwealth tie has been to Great Britain. It is essential therefore to underline some of the doubts as to the current nature or value of the Commonwealth which have been expressed in the United Kingdom itself.

One of the most perceptive accounts of the present Commonwealth of Nations given by an Englishman is that of Sir Ivor Jennings, an outstanding constitutional lawyer who was Master of Trinity Hall, Cambridge, at the time of his death in 1965.[1] According to Jennings, the reality of the Commonwealth is better shown, not by relations between governments, but by relations between persons and institutions. 'The foundation on which the Commonwealth rests', he declares, 'is seldom mentioned. It is community of culture.'[2] He acknowledges that this statement may seem surprising, in view of the diverse cultural background and vast populations of some of the newer members of the Commonwealth, but he defends his claim by underlining the extent to which the English language is used within the Commonwealth for purposes of education and administration,

---

[1] See *The British Commonwealth of Nations* (Hutchinson, London, 1961 ed.).
[2] *Ibid.* p. 206.

and by stressing the influence of British university systems, both in Britain and in British-type universities outside the United Kingdom, in training students from Asian and African members of the Commonwealth. He reminds us that of the 'sixteen Prime Ministers in the Asian countries of the Commonwealth between 1947 and 1960, eight had been educated at Cambridge and two at Oxford. Most of the others had been educated at Indian universities founded on English models.'[1] Nor had British influence been limited to presidents and prime ministers. The ideas of Mahatma Gandhi, 'of Lincoln's Inn, barrister-at-law', were 'profoundly influenced by his reading in English and his experience of people in England and South Africa'.[2] According to Jennings, 'self-government was possible in the Asian countries because there was an English-educated minority ready and anxious to assume responsibility'.[2]

On the negative side, Jennings declares flatly that 'So far as policies are concerned the nations of the Commonwealth require no leadership and the British Government has given up the attempt...The United Kingdom provides for the Commonwealth not policies but a reservoir of knowledge and experience which can be drawn upon freely as occasion requires.'[3] As an academic accustomed to the long-term point of view, he evinces no particular concern about the current state of the Commonwealth of Nations. His legitimate pride in British contributions to world society appears in his comment that 'if our civilization were wiped out and centuries hence archaeologists began digging about in the ruins of any city from Vancouver to Singapore or from Hong Kong to Accra, their first remark would be, "The English were here".'[4]

Such a detached attitude, however, is scarcely typical of the man in the street or of his political masters. As Jennings himself recognises, 'Politicians are...always in a hurry because they have to create the New Jerusalem before the next election...'[5] A harsher judgement based upon the short-term situation was expressed in an article published in the The Times of London on 2 April 1964 by an unidentified writer who assumed the pen-name of 'Conservative'. Appealing for patriotism based upon reality, not dreams; deploring humbug; and stressing the change in Britain's relative power and position in the world since 1939, he describes the current Commonwealth as 'a gigantic farce'.

[1] *Ibid.* p. 207.　[2] *Ibid.* p. 209.　[3] *Ibid.* p. 216.　[4] *Ibid.* p. 217.　[5] *Ibid.* p. 210.

Britain, he declares, is a power, but a European power, an industrial and technical power. She needs the forces and the defence policy appropriate to such a power. Existing commitments of Britain's armed forces 'bespeak a fixed determination to remain blind to the true facts of Britain's altered power and role in the world. All around the globe...Britain has commitments which combine the maximum chance of involvement, embarrassment, expense, and humiliation with the minimum effect on the course of events.' Britain ceased to be a power in the Far East years ago; she was incapable of guaranteeing the defence of Malaysia. Nor was she any longer a Middle Eastern power. She should renounce 'the relics of world empire', and recast her forces and defence policy on European lines. Britain had to make a clean break with her imperial past, divest herself of the pretences of a world-wide Commonwealth of Nations 'with the overtones of hostility and suspicion that they carry in great tracts of the world', and dedicate herself to the cultivation of her own industrial and technical strength as a European power. As such, she would be not less but more influential in the United Nations and in the world outside.

This article created a considerable stir inside the Commonwealth of Nations, and accentuated uncertainties outside the United Kingdom arising from Britain's application to join the Common Market. The views expressed in it can scarcely be said to represent official Conservative Party policy, although they are indicative of important trends of opinion. It is to be noted, for instance, that Mr Enoch Powell, at present 'Minister for Defence' in the 'shadow cabinet' of the Conservative Party (now in Opposition) under the leadership of Mr Edward Heath, has raised substantial doubts as to the justification for maintaining Britain's military commitments east of Suez, at any rate on their present scale. He is also reported to have said:

What I believe has been profoundly and generally resented [in Great Britain] is to be told at every stage that this or that action must be taken, not necessarily because we regard it as right or just or in the interests either of this country or of Rhodesia, but because, if we do not, 'it will mean the break-up of the Commonwealth'.

Many people on being told this say to their neighbours or under their breath: 'Let it break up then, so much the better.'[1]

[1] *The Times* (London), 15 January 1966, p. 6.

On the other hand, Mr Harold Wilson's Labour Government has given notable support to the defence of Malaysia against Indonesian confrontation, despite the strains and stresses upon Britain's balance of payments. As already indicated,[1] the British Government's Defence Review outlined by Mr Denis Healey in his statement of 25 February 1966 confirms British determination to continue to play an important military role in the Far East and South-East Asia, where 'the greatest danger to peace may lie in the next decade'.[2] This policy, however, is to be subject to more equitable sharing of the load than in the past, and readiness of independent countries to permit Britain to maintain necessary defence facilities in their territories.

Nevertheless, the extent and depth of British reappraisal of the significance and value of the Commonwealth of Nations today is seriously underestimated amongst Australians, who tend to cling to the illusion that dissatisfaction with many Commonwealth developments since the war is a prerogative of their own. This illusion, of course, is not peculiar to Australians: it is shared by Indians, Malaysians, Ghanaians, some Canadians and others. The Director-General of the Canadian Institute of International Affairs, Mr John Holmes, found it necessary to remind his fellow countrymen in 1965 that 'Those Canadians who can never get rid of the idea that the Commonwealth is a plot of the English gentry to enslave poor gullible Canadians ought to read what they are saying in London about the way the Commonwealth is exploiting poor gullible Britain'.[3]

Most Australians, preoccupied with their own affairs and problems, simply do not appreciate the difficulties of Britain's situation during the post-war years. The United Kingdom entered two world wars as a Great Power, and spared neither blood nor treasure in an effort not merely to survive but also to preserve a democratic way of life in which the rights of individual citizens are recognised and guaranteed under a rule of law. Unlike the United States, she was involved in both wars from the very beginning. She ended the Second World War with her overseas assets exhausted, her cities and factories damaged and her largest colonies clamouring for independence.

---

[1] See p. 160 above.
[2] *British Defence Review*, 25 February 1966, paragraph 32.
[3] Lecture to the Empire Club, Toronto (1 March 1965), entitled 'The Commonwealth: White Man's Burden or Blind Man's Bluff [*sic*]'.

Soon there were two Super-Powers, the United States and the Soviet Union, whose military and economic resources she could no longer match. Two defeated enemies, Germany and Japan, who were both prostrate at the end of the war, speedily rebuilt their economies (with considerable assistance) and became welcome allies of the United States. France, which had surrendered to Germany, regained her economic strength and her pride under General de Gaulle and barred British entry to the European Economic Community. In the United Nations, Communist countries and others which had newly achieved independence (including Commonwealth countries) were constant critics of the alleged slowness with which Britain carried out her decolonising process. Indonesia accused her of 'neo-colonialism' in Malaysia. Dean Acheson, sometime American Secretary of State, used in a public speech the wounding phrase 'Great Britain has lost an empire and has not yet found a role'.[1] He described the Commonwealth as a body 'which has no political structure, or unity, or strength'.[1]

Australians have to make a positive effort of imagination to view the post-war Commonwealth from the vantage point of London as it must have appeared to many Englishmen. Colonies were disappearing with great speed, blown along by the 'wind of change'. For the most part they brought headaches, due to pressures on Britain by domestic opinion within colonies and by international opinion outside. On 'The Morning After' independence (the ingenious title of a book by Brian Crozier)[2] they have often discovered that political independence does not necessarily bring economic independence. As 'non-aligned' countries, they are ready to accept economic aid from both Communist and non-Communist countries, provided no political 'strings' are attached. They insist upon their right to vote in favour of proposals like General Assembly Resolution 1514, xv (Declaration on the Granting of Independence to Colonial Countries and Peoples),[3] and to press for the creation of still more completely independent countries, irrespective of their size, power and resources, except perhaps 'under very exceptional circumstances by their own free will'.[4]

---

[1] *The Times* (London), 6 December 1962, p. 12.
[2] Methuen, London, 1963.   [3] See pp. 269–70 above.
[4] See *International Law in Australia*, ed. O'Connell, p. 378, where a statement by Mr Quaison-Sackey of Ghana is quoted in footnote 48.

As to the Old Commonwealth, Australia and New Zealand entered into a military alliance with the United States in ANZUS, from which the United Kingdom was excluded, and joined with Canada in pressing Britain to maintain their special trading rights in the British market, thus complicating Britain's application for membership of the European Economic Community, which the Conservative Government at least had come to regard as essential in her long-term political and economic interests.

Is it surprising if British sentiment towards the Commonwealth moved towards an all-time low? *Great Britain or Little England?* is the title of a book written by an Englishman, John Mander, published in 1963. In it he writes: 'Why should John Bull fret if his empire has "exhausted the mandate of heaven?"' He urges his fellow countrymen to abandon the 'siege mentality' caused by 'the physical expulsion of Britain from Europe' at Dunkirk. 'What we should aim for', he writes, 'is an equal place for Britain in a directorium of Europe's major powers. It is a more modest prospect for John Bull than some he has been offered; but I believe it is the only realistic one. *Faisons-nous l'Europe!*'[1] Is it surprising, to quote John Holmes again, that 'One of the new realities of the Commonwealth is that the will to preserve it has to be encouraged not only at the periphery but also at the heart'?[2]

This problem has not been made any the less acute by the events of 1965, during which India and Pakistan have indulged in substantial if somewhat restricted fighting against one another over the Kashmir issue, and both countries have decided to accept Russian good offices in Tashkent rather than British good offices in London in an attempt to settle their differences; while two other countries, Tanzania and Ghana, broke off diplomatic relations with Great Britain to mark their dissatisfaction with Britain's handling of the Rhodesian situation, although Ghana renewed contacts after the overthrow of President Nkrumah. Failure to solve the Rhodesian problem on terms acceptable to African countries could easily disrupt the multi-racial Commonwealth as we know it today.

A number of Prime Ministers have found themselves unable to attend the meeting of Commonwealth Prime Ministers

---

[1] Penguin Books, London, 1963, pp. 203–7.
[2] Lecture to Empire Club, Toronto, *op. cit.*

WAF

scheduled for September 1966, and already representatives of some African States have referred to the possibility of withdrawal from the Commonwealth unless Mr Harold Wilson agrees at that Conference to some more effective and forceful method of compelling the Smith regime to yield to Commonwealth opinion on the Rhodesian issue. These warnings of withdrawal led to an unprecedented comment in the Australian Parliament by a member of the Liberal Party, Senator M. C. Cormack. On 2 September he told his colleagues that he was rapidly reaching the stage where he found it intolerable to be faced with a situation where groups of nations issue constant threats that they are going to leave the Commonwealth. In his opinion the time had come when we (Australia) should consider whether we should leave it. The mere fact that any such view could be ventilated in any responsible Australian quarter is significant of changes which are taking place in outlook, however unlikely it may be that such a suggestion could become official policy.

During the past two years the attitude of Malaysia towards the Commonwealth has in some respects been distinctly offhanded. Singapore was ejected from the Malaysian Federation without any prior notification to the United Kingdom, Australia or New Zealand, whose military aid—especially that of the United Kingdom—was vital to the survival of Malaysia in face of Indonesian confrontation. The long-term consequences of this decision can well prove to be extremely serious for the continued stability of the area, affecting vital Australian interests. Further, following refusal by Great Britain of an application by Malaysia for a substantial loan, the Malaysian Government announced, in August 1966, decisions to peg the Malaysian dollar to gold rather than to sterling, and to abandon Commonwealth preference on a number of imports. These decisions, announced somewhat blandly after the ending of physical confrontation by Indonesia made Malaysia less dependent upon Commonwealth military forces, scarcely reflect the gratitude which Tunku Abdul Rahman expressed on 31 August to those Commonwealth countries which had stood by Malaysia during the difficult period when Indonesian pressure against Malaysia was at its peak.

Clearly what is required today throughout the Commonwealth is a realistic assessment of what it is and what it is not, and what it can reasonably be expected to become. 'We must keep the quota of hypocrisy to an acceptable level.'[1] Let us recognise that no member of the Commonwealth is totally committed to anything other than its own vital interests, though these, of course, often include some of the interests of some other members.

In the circumstances described above I suggest that Australian policy towards the Commonwealth of Nations should be based upon the following assumptions:

(1) The Commonwealth is a multi-racial society, the objectives of whose members differ greatly. Agreement by every single member of the Commonwealth on any common purpose, decision or action is extremely unlikely and not to be expected. The ties are so loose that it is possible for two members to be at war with one another, or to remain neutral when, for instance, Britain is at war. Yet the overall objective should be to display tolerance and understanding of the problems of every member and to maintain trust amongst the different members, even when they differ. Pursuit of this objective to the maximum practicable extent would be of great significance in reducing the greatest danger to world peace outside an atomic war, namely a world divided upon a basis of race or colour.

(2) Within the total Commonwealth close co-operation is possible between some members. For instance, Australia and New Zealand have acted together with Great Britain in the military defence of Malaysia. Again, African and Asian members have their own specially close relationships for certain purposes, such as voting within the United Nations, and the espousal of certain policies arising out of non-alignment. Further, richer members have a responsibility towards 'developing' members, in regard to both aid and trade.

(3) Great Britain can be expected to bear economic and military burdens on behalf of the Commonwealth only within strict limits, and to a decreasing extent. Members like Australia must undertake a greater share of the burden. It is essential to counteract the attitude towards the Commonwealth reflected in the ironic phrase describing it as 'a cow to be milked, but never to be fed'.

(4) Australia must not only have an independent foreign policy, but must also appear to have one. It must not appear to

---

[1] Lecture to Empire Club, Toronto, *op. cit.*

be merely the echo or the tool of Great Britain (or the United States); this means that opportunities must be found, from time to time, to make known publicly occasions on which Australian policy differs from that of Britain (or America). In particular, Australia must demonstrate a constant and co-operative interest in the problems of the newer members of the Commonwealth, mixing politeness with frankness.

(5) Relations between Australia and some foreign countries, the United States in particular, are likely to be closer than relations with some members of the Commonwealth. This is no more unnatural than that a country like Ghana has closer relations with some African countries than with Australia. Common cultural traditions and common interests point in such directions. Each member will have a series of specially close relations, some within the Commonwealth, some outside it, some bound up with regional responsibilities.

(6) Finally, all human institutions are subject to change and adaptation. Nostalgia for the past is no basis for a foreign policy. The present should be scanned realistically and the future approached with imagination with a view to making maximum use of opportunities within the Commonwealth for fruitful co-operation in any practicable field. Both wishful thinking and blind pessimism are to be condemned. Few members of the Commonwealth seem to appreciate sufficiently that they all have, in different degrees, a magnificent instrument at their disposal in the English language, which carries with it a heritage of important common tradition. It would be wise to cherish and foster this world language, not in substitution for one's own, but as an avenue leading towards greater understanding within the Commonwealth and within the international community as a whole.

2. The United Nations

The part played by the Australian Minister for External Affairs, Dr Evatt, in the creation of the United Nations Charter at San Francisco in 1945 has been described in some detail.[1] Subsequently, Evatt supported maximum use of organs of the United Nations to help solve international problems, both when he was still Minister for External Affairs, and later as

[1] See pp. 78–93 above.

Leader of the Labour Party Opposition. While the Menzies Government asserted that it fully supported the principles and purposes of the United Nations, it had a lower estimate of the capacity of the world organisation to maintain international peace and security, and in practice accorded a lower priority to the United Nations than to close relations with its 'great and powerful friends', Great Britain and the United States.

In this chapter it is not proposed to discuss in detail the part played by Australia over the full course of United Nations activities in the post-war years. Much of this information is already available elsewhere.[1] Here attention will be focused predominantly upon the most important and most contentious field of United Nations activities, namely the maintenance of international peace. Many Australians are still insufficiently aware of what the Charter was designed to establish in the security field, what in fact the two main organs of the United Nations have done during the first twenty years of its existence, and the difficult situation in which the United Nations still finds itself.

The Charter accepted at San Francisco by all signatories, and by all countries subsequently admitted to membership of the organisation, accorded to the Permanent Members of the Security Council, namely the United States, the Soviet Union, Great Britain, France and China, a privileged position evidenced by their right of veto over Council activities in matters of substance, subject to the proviso set out in Article 27 (3) that in decisions under chapter VI and under paragraph 3 of Article 52, a party to a dispute shall abstain from voting. The only concession made to Middle and Small Power sensitivities or pretensions on this issue was Great Power agreement that veto rights should not prevent placing an item on the agenda or discussion of any such item.

Evatt fought tenaciously to secure abolition of the veto on procedures relevant to the pacific settlement of disputes (chapter VI), but he was unsuccessful in this battle. The Great Powers argued that the organisation must be based upon the principle of their unanimity: which implied, of course, that the Security Council could not act to carry out its primary responsibility for international peace and security if any one of the

---

[1] See Harper and Sissons, *op. cit.*, and chapters by Professor Geoffrey Sawer in *Australia in World Affairs 1950–55*, and *1956–60*.

five Powers disagreed with the course of action proposed. In short, subject to the proviso of Article 27 (3), when the substantial interests of any of these Powers were involved, action in the Security Council could at once be stultified by a negative vote by one of them. Further, the same Powers insisted on the application of the principle of their unanimity even in regard to amendments to the Charter, so that, whereas at San Francisco the various Articles were accepted by a two-thirds vote, no single word or comma could subsequently be altered unless a two-thirds vote included the votes of all the Permanent Members of the Security Council. In justifying their stand the privileged Powers publicly deplored any imputation that they would exercise their special rights irresponsibly.

In the event, the Soviet Union used its veto on more than 100 occasions. This abuse of rights, together with the development of Stalin's cold-war policy after 1945, was substantially responsible for the failure to create the overall security system envisaged by the Charter. Articles 43–47 had provided for special agreements to be entered into between all Members (or groups of Members) of the United Nations on the one hand and the Security Council on the other hand, under which Members would have made available to the Council 'armed forces, assistance and facilities' to be used by the latter for the purpose of maintaining international peace and security, in accordance with the advice of a Military Staff Committee composed of representatives of the Permanent Members. Failure to establish this security system undoubtedly stimulated the creation of military alliances such as NATO, ANZUS and SEATO, whose members were impelled to try to provide for their security by collective measures of their own. Further, stultification of Security Council action on important issues, together with the complete rigidity of the Charter provisions for amendment, led in practice to the assumption by the General Assembly of a degree of responsibility for the maintenance of international peace and security which had never been envisaged at San Francisco.

On 3 November 1950 the General Assembly, by a majority of 57 votes to 5 (the U.S.S.R., Poland, Czechoslovakia, Ukraine and Byelorussia), with 2 abstentions (India and Argentina), adopted what has become known as the 'Uniting for Peace' Resolution (377, v). Under its provisions a Peace Observation

Commission and a Collective Measures Committee were established to observe, study and report on situations and methods
of dealing with them, and United Nations Members were
urged to maintain armed forces trained and equipped for such
service in United Nations units as might be decided by the
Security Council or the General Assembly. Thus, when the
Suez crisis occurred in 1956, no fewer than 6,000 men from the
armed forces of ten nations were sent,[1] in accordance with a
decision of the Assembly, to 'secure and supervise the cessation
of hostilities' in the Suez area between Great Britain, France
and Israel on the one hand and Egypt on the other.

It should be noted in passing that the Soviet Union was one
of nineteen countries whose representatives registered abstentions when the vote on the establishment of a United Nations
Emergency Force (UNEF) was taken in the Assembly. Explaining his abstention, the Soviet Representative argued, *inter
alia*, that the composition of the proposed international force
was not in accordance with the Charter.[2] An unsuccessful
attempt was also made by the Soviet Union to present to the
Security Council a Resolution calling upon Britain, France and
Israel to cease military action against Egypt within twelve
hours and to withdraw their troops from Egyptian territory
within three days—failing which the United States, the Soviet
Union and other Member States should aid Egypt by sending
to her assistance armed forces in conformity with Article 42 of
the Charter. This article empowers the *Security Council*, not the
General Assembly, to impose military sanctions.[3]

Russian objections to the proposed composition of the international force may well have stemmed partly from the fact that
contributions to the force by Permanent Members of the
Security Council were specifically excluded by the terms of the
Assembly Resolution. Nevertheless, it is at least open to question whether the General Assembly was ever intended to exercise authority under the terms of the Charter to establish and
despatch such a force. Basically the Charter envisaged unanimous agreement between the Permanent Members of the
Security Council on action to be taken by the United Nations

[1] Arthur Burns and Nina Heathcote, *Peace-Keeping by U.N. Forces* (Pall Mall
Press, London, 1963), p. 9.
[2] *Keesing's Contemporary Archives*, p. 15,202. Australia voted for the Resolution, in
spite of earlier 'misgivings' as to whether some parts were *intra vires* (see *C.N.*
vol. XXI (1950), pp. 697, 736).   [3] *Ibid.* p. 15,219.

for the maintenance of international peace and security—especially the despatch of military forces. Even though an Assembly Resolution constituted a recommendation only, acceptance by a majority of the Assembly of a Resolution to send a peace-keeping force had the practical effect of evading a possible veto in the Security Council, if that organ had been dealing with the issue.

Agreement by Great Britain, France and Israel to an earlier call by the General Assembly for a ceasefire in the Suez area and to the peace-keeping operations of the international force was due far less to acceptance of the view that the General Assembly had wide executive powers and authority to maintain international peace than to political, economic and military factors outside the United Nations affecting the vital interests of these three countries. In particular, public opinion in Britain was seriously divided on the issue of military action against Egypt; Britain's special relationship with the United States was endangered; world opinion was extremely critical; and many Commonwealth countries directly opposed British policy which, if pursued, could have led to reassessment in some cases of willingness to remain Members of the Commonwealth of Nations.

The success of United Nations intervention in the Suez crisis must therefore be judged cautiously. It established a precedent for U.N. peace-keeping operations which set the stage for greater, different, and more serious United Nations intervention in the Congo in 1960 and 1961, as a result of which the organisation was brought to a state of near-bankruptcy and—at one stage at least—its continued existence threatened.

The problems of the Congo since it gained independence and the various interventions of the United Nations as part of peace-keeping operations in that country are too vast to attempt adequate description and assessment here. Books have been written on the subject[1] and authors differ as to whether or not the Congo operation set a precedent for United Nations intervention in the internal affairs of a member country, despite the 'domestic jurisdiction' clause of the Charter (Article 2 (7)). In any event, the precedent could be of serious importance to Australia should intervention by the United Nations ever be

---

[1] See Catherine Hoskyns, *The Congo since Independence* (Oxford University Press, 1965); Burns and Heathcote, *Peace-keeping by U.N. Forces.*

proposed in relation to an Australian territory (such as Papua) which had acquired independence but was experiencing difficulty in maintaining it. Here, consideration will be limited to a comparison of peace-keeping operations in regard to Suez on the one hand and the Congo on the other in order to make clear the greater degree of intervention on the latter occasion and its effects upon the stability of the world organisation.

In the Suez case, U.N. Forces were used to secure and supervise the cessation of clearly *international* hostilities between the armed forces of different States. Moreover, the forces of the contestants were relatively disciplined and under the effective control of their national political leaders. Further, the United Nations Forces were not intended to be used for 'offensive' purposes; indeed, they were equipped only for self-defence. In a report to the Assembly the Secretary-General, Mr Hammarskjold, interpreted 'self-defence' as implying that

men engaged in the operation may never take the initiative in the use of armed force, but are entitled to respond with force to an attack with arms, including attempts to use force to make them withdraw from positions which they occupy under orders from the Commander, acting under the authority of the Assembly and within the scope of its resolutions.[1]

In other words, in this case the U.N. Forces were in reality a kind of 'police force' interposed between contending international parties while supervising an agreed cessation of hostilities.

In the case of the Congo, peace-keeping operations were first authorised by the Security Council without, however, invoking the provisions of chapter VII of the Charter under which sanctions may be imposed in case of a threat to peace, breach of the peace or act of aggression. Subsequently, the General Assembly passed various Resolutions on the Congo, endorsing and at times supplementing Security Council decisions.[2] On 20 September 1960 the General Assembly specifically endorsed the Security Council Resolution of 9 August 1960, which in paragraph 4 reaffirmed 'that the United Nations Force in the Congo will not be a party to or in any way intervene in or be used to influence the outcome of any internal conflict, constitutional or otherwise'.

---

[1] Quoted in Burns and Heathcote, *op. cit.* p. 21.
[2] See Catherine Hoskyns, *op. cit.*, appendix II, for full texts of U.N. Resolutions.

Yet in due course the United Nations became involved, without invoking the sanctions provisions of the Charter under chapter VII, not merely in trying to secure the cessation of hostilities between Congolese forces and foreign (Belgian) troops (and the repatriation of Belgian troops and foreign mercenaries) but also in trying to end hostilities, by methods eventually including the use of substantial force, between armed groups operating on behalf of different *Congolese* claimants to legitimacy or power or the right to secede.

After the unexplained death of Hammarskjold in an air crash while on a personal visit to the Congo in an attempt to ensure better control of a deteriorating situation, U Thant was appointed Acting Secretary-General. In his first statement to the Security Council U Thant declared:

Everything possible must be done to avert civil war, *even by the employment of force* [emphasis added], should this prove necessary as a last resort. This I believe necessarily implies a sympathetic attitude on the part of UNOC [U.N. Operations Congo] toward the efforts of the Government to suppress all armed activities against the Central government, and all secessionist activities...[1]

Burns and Heathcote interpret this statement as implying that Hammarskjold's ''"non-intervening" policy' had been 'buried' and also, perhaps, his 'scruples about compliance with the Charter'.[1] Catherine Hoskyns, while rejecting the conclusion that the Congo operation set a precedent for U.N. intervention in internal affairs, nevertheless admits that 'a precedent was set for authorising a force established in these circumstances to use force beyond self-defence', and for the very concept of self-defence to be much expanded.[2]

The result of the Congo operation was to throw upon the United Nations a tremendous burden of debt and to set up strong centrifugal forces within the organisation when two of its most powerful members, namely, the Soviet Union and France, refused to pay their share of the costs. It is scarcely surprising that the United States, whose contributions over the years to United Nations activities and to international aid for developing countries have been generous in the extreme, tried to invoke

---

[1] Quoted in Burns and Heathcote, *op. cit.* p. 128.

[2] Hoskyns, *op. cit.* p. 477. For a discussion of the applicability of the principle of non-intervention to the operations of ONUC, see also D. W. Bowett, *United Nations Forces* (Stevens and Sons, London, 1964), pp. 196–200.

the provisions of Article 19 of the Charter in an effort to compel all members of the United Nations to pay their allotted share of the debt. This dispute made it impossible for the 19th Session of the General Assembly to function normally.

In 1965 it became clear that a majority of members of the Assembly (which had endorsed the Advisory Opinion of the International Court of Justice, approved by a majority of 9 to 5, that all members were liable to contribute to the costs of the Congo operations) was unwilling to force the issue to the point of invoking Article 19 of the Charter for the purpose of depriving defaulters of two-years' standing of their voting rights in the Assembly. Eventually the United States reluctantly accepted this unsatisfactory situation in the wider interests of the organisation and of international co-operation as a whole. In announcing this decision, however, the American representative warned the Assembly that the United States would now reserve the right to refuse to pay for any United Nations activity if, in its view, 'strong and compelling reasons' exist for doing so.[1] It would appear from a statement made by Sir James Plimsoll, Leader of the Australian Delegation, to the General Assembly on 29 September 1965 that Australia too has now made a similar reservation.[1]

How the United Nations' debt in respect of the Congo operation is to be met is still uncertain, though some countries not in default have made voluntary contributions to help meet it; but at least the General Assembly is functioning once again.

The Advisory Opinion of the International Court of Justice on 'Certain expenses of the United Nations (Art. 17, para. 2)', handed down on 20 July 1962, decided the issues raised on somewhat narrow grounds. The Separate Opinion of the Australian Judge Sir Percy Spender—now President of the Court—who agreed with the majority view, contains important *obiter dicta* which deserve close consideration.[2] One section of his judgement deals with the subject 'Practice within the United Nations—its effect on or value as a criterion of interpretation'. Spender rejects arguments put to the Court stressing the importance of past practice of the General Assembly or the Security Council in interpreting their own powers under the

---

[1] For United States views, see *U.N. Monthly Chronicle*, vol. II, no. 8 (August–September 1965), p. 18; for Australian views, see *C.N.* vol. xxxvi (1965), no. 9, pp. 551–2.   [2] See generally *I.C.J. Reports*, 1962, pp. 182–97.

Charter, and the relevance of the general principle that a treaty provision should be interpreted in the light of the subsequent conduct of the contracting parties. In his opinion, arguments of this kind, firstly, would only be relevant if the meaning of the text were not clear. Secondly, multilateral treaties such as the United Nations Charter differ from other treaties in important respects. In Spender's words:

I find difficulty in accepting the proposition that a practice pursued by an *organ* of the United Nations may be equated with the subsequent conduct of *parties* to a bilateral agreement and thus afford evidence of intention of the parties to the Charter (who have constantly been added to since it came into force) and in that way or otherwise provide a criterion of interpretation. Nor can I agree with a view sometimes advanced that a common practice pursued by an organ of the United Nations, though *ultra vires* and in point of fact having the result of amending the Charter, may nonetheless be effective as a criterion of interpretation.[1]

Spender points out that, even if the parties to a multilateral treaty are fixed and constant, where only one or some but not all of them by subsequent conduct interpret the text in a certain manner, that conduct stands upon the same footing as the unilateral conduct of one party to a bilateral treaty. The conduct of such one or more could not by itself have any probative value or provide a criterion for judicial interpretation. In any event, it was not in his opinion 'permissible to move the principle of subsequent conduct of parties to a bilateral or multilateral treaty into another field and seek to apply it, not to the *parties* to the treaty, but to an *organ* established under the treaty'.[2] Nor did he accept the contention put to the court on behalf of several States, namely that the probative value of the practice followed by the General Assembly and the Security Council in interpreting their functions under the Charter had already found 'authority...in the jurisprudence of this Court and its predecessor'.[2] After examining the relevant cases, he came to the conclusion that 'The extent to which a practice pursued by an organ of the United Nations may be held resort to by the Court, if at all, as an aid to interpretation...' had '...yet to receive deliberate consideration by...the Court.'[2]

Judge Spender agreed that an organ of the United Nations

---

[1] *I.C.J Reports*, 1962, pp. 189–90.   [2] *Ibid.* p. 192.

had in practice to interpret its authority in order that it might effectively function. It could interpret Charter provisions so as to permit action in circumstances and situations never contemplated by those who framed the Charter. But

...the Charter...cannot be altered at the will of the majority of the Member States, no matter how often that will is expressed or asserted against a protesting minority and no matter how large be the majority of Member States which assert its will in this manner or how small the minority...

So, if the General Assembly were to 'intervene in matters which are essentially within the domestic jurisdiction of any State' within the meaning of Article 2 (7) of the Charter, whatever be the meaning to be given to these words, that intervention would be the entering into a field prohibited to it under the Charter and be beyond the authority of the General Assembly. This would continue to be so, no matter how frequently and consistently the General Assembly had construed its authority to permit it to make intervention in matters essentially within the domestic jurisdiction of any States. The majority has no power to extend, alter or disregard the Charter.[1]

The judgement of Judge Spender in the above-mentioned case has been referred to in considerable detail because the issue raised is of the first importance, not only to Australia as a country which still has responsibility for 'colonial' territories, but to all members of the United Nations and, conceivably, relevant to the question of the survival of the organisation itself. The contrary view has been argued with force by Dr Rosalyn Higgins.[2] Commenting upon the nature of general international law, she points out that it includes customary rules evidenced by the practice of States:

The emergence of a customary rule of law occurs where there has grown up a clear and continuous habit of performing certain actions in the conviction that they are obligatory under international law... Collective acts of states, repeated by and acquiesced in by sufficient numbers with sufficient frequency, eventually attain the status of law. The existence of the United Nations—and especially its accelerated trend towards universality of membership since 1955—now provides a very clear, very concentrated, focal point for state practice.[3]

[1] *Ibid.* pp. 196–7.
[2] See generally Rosalyn Higgins, *The Development of International Law through the Political Organs of the United Nations* (Oxford University Press, 1963).
[3] *Ibid.* pp. 1–2.

Dr Higgins admits that 'it is often far from easy to see...the point at which a repeated practice has hardened into a rule of law'[1] and that 'Resolutions of the Assembly are not *per se* binding: though those rules of general international law which they may embody are binding on member states, with or without the help of the resolution'.[2] She argues, however, that the body of resolutions as a whole, taken as indications of a general customary law, 'undoubtedly provide a rich source of evidence'[2] and claims that 'where unanimous resolutions are concerned—such as the Assembly Declaration on the Granting of Independence to Colonial Countries (GA res. 1514 (xv)) a question of estoppel and *mala fides* may well arise'.[3] In her opinion the International Court of Justice 'has indicated its approval' of the Charter being in part interpreted by the 'subsequent practice' of the parties, when looked at from the point of view of treaty law.[4] In view of the 'lack of opposition' to the General Assembly's Declaration on Colonialism of 14 December 1960 and to certain other resolutions on colonialism, it seems to her 'academic to argue that as Assembly resolutions are not binding nothing has changed, and that "self-determination" remains a mere "principle", and Article 2 (7) is an effective defence against its implementation'.[5]

The significance of such an interpretation of the legally binding force of General Assembly Resolutions in certain circumstances is apparent when one reflects that there has been a determined and sustained effort by anti-colonial and non-colonial powers since the Charter was framed in 1945 to expand the powers of United Nations Committees dealing with 'colonial' matters, backed in the last resort by decisions of ruling majorities in the General Assembly. In an illuminating article on 'Non-self-governing territories: the law and practice of the United Nations' published in 1964, J. A. de Yturriaga expresses the opinion that the month of December 1960 marked the end of a period of United Nations control by Western countries, and the beginning of a new era. He states bluntly that

...the anti-colonial countries are currently abusing their majority position within the General Assembly and using the Colonial Declaration as a political weapon against colonial countries, regardless of their adequacy or inadequacy to discharge their obligations as

---

[1] *Ibid.* pp. 5–6.   [2] *Ibid.* p. 5.   [3] *Ibid.* p. 7, n. 20.
[4] *Ibid.* p. 4, n. 9.   [5] *Ibid.* p. 101.

governing Powers. Consequently, on some occasions, the measures taken to implement Resolution 1514 (xv) have gone too far, persistently ignoring the provisions of Article 2 (7) of the Charter.[1]

He reminds us that, during the San Francisco Conference of 1945, the Philippines delegation proposed to grant legislative power to the General Assembly, so that it could establish rules of international law binding upon Member States after approval by the Security Council. 'This proposal was, however, rejected by an overwhelming majority.'[2] He sums up the problem in the following words: 'The constitutional issue is whether member States are bound to accept every interpretation of the Charter which a majority of the Assembly may at any time desire to apply to it, and may be charged with violating the Charter if they do not do so.'[3] One might add that, on Dr Higgins's interpretation of the significance of the practice of States in the United Nations, it would appear to be unsafe for the representative of a Member State ever to register an abstention in regard to an Assembly Resolution, instead of casting a negative vote, since it is likely to be argued that a majority decision of the Assembly implies acceptance of the validity of the Resolution not only by those who voted for it, but also by those who abstained! If no Member State specifically objects by casting a negative vote, past conduct and practice of the Assembly is all the more likely to be regarded as having converted some political decision into a binding rule of law.

Adequate examination of the issues raised above is far beyond the scope of a book on the evolution of Australian foreign policy. Their relevance to such policy is however immediately apparent when one considers Australian responsibility for colonial areas, especially New Guinea, Papua and Nauru.

Will the General Assembly be content with anything less than complete independence for Papua–New Guinea, even if the majority of the populations of these two territories prefer some other form of self-government? If the territories prefer complete independence, but wish Australia to maintain defence forces and facilities in Papua–New Guinea, will the General Assembly take the view that this would be evidence of neo-colonialism and must not be permitted?[4] If Australia and

---

[1] *The Year Book of World Affairs*, 1964, at p. 200.
[2] *Ibid.* p. 209.   [3] *Ibid.* p. 211.
[4] *International Law in Australia*, ed. O'Connell, p. 385.

Papua–New Guinea insist on such co-operation with Australia to increase their mutual security, will the Assembly agree to termination of the trusteeship agreement on these terms? If the people of the Trust Territory of Nauru, an area of 8½ square miles with a population of about 5,000, should opt for sovereign independence with a vote in the General Assembly equal to that of the United States and the Soviet Union, will the Assembly insist upon 'independence. . . in accordance with their wishes'?[1]

What conclusions should be drawn from the developments within the United Nations described above? First, that the United Nations Organisation is not a world government where national representatives dispense even-handed justice on the basis of agreed principles of morality. It is a political organisa-tion in which national representatives vote in accordance with instructions drafted against a background of what are con-ceived to be national interests. The morality of United Nations decisions will be no higher than the morality of member govern-ments, or of the peoples who elect such governments in those cases where an elective choice is permitted.

Secondly, experience has shown that Congo-type operations would appear to be impracticable (whatever their legality) unless unanimity can be achieved amongst the Permanent Members of the Security Council regarding the operations proposed and undertaken. This would seem to necessitate a return to the Security Council of *primary* responsibility for the maintenance of international peace and security, in accordance with the intention of the Charter.

Thirdly, such a diminution in the practical powers of the General Assembly, so far as executive responsibility is con-cerned, should be accepted by United Nations members who do not hold permanent seats on the Security Council as part of the price payable to ensure the effective survival of the orga-nisation. The Assembly was intended to be a general forum for discussion and recommendation, not an executive substitute for a Security Council whose action or inaction it disapproved. After all, the smaller Powers elect their own representatives to the Council, the original seven having been increased to ten in 1965. Nine affirmative votes are now necessary before the Council can take any action, and there are only five members with permanent seats. In this sense the smaller Powers sitting as

[1] See G.A. Resolution 2111 (xx) of 21 December 1965, operative paragraph 3.

members of the Council themselves possess a right of veto on positive Council action which Great Powers support.

Fourthly, it is impossible to view without concern, since the growth of U.N. membership to the present total of 117, the increasing divorce between power and responsibility in the General Assembly. Every member has an equal vote, irrespective of size, population, economic or military strength—the Maldive Islands, with its population of less than 100,000, has the same vote as India with its hundreds of millions; the vote of El Salvador is equal to the vote of the Soviet Union.

While one can readily admit that power and wisdom are not synonymous and do not inevitably march hand in hand, it is more tempting for the weak than for the strong to pass resolutions if the burden of carrying them out falls primarily upon Member States with strong economies and powerful military forces. It was pointed out in 1961 that a simple majority could be found in the General Assembly among countries which between them contributed less than 2·5% of the budget; while a two-thirds majority (which, theoretically at least, is still required to decide 'important questions') could be obtained from countries who pay only 6·22% of the budget.[1] This may not be an argument for weighted voting, but it is a strong argument in favour of Small-Power restraint and for greater consideration of the probable consequences of voting in favour of Resolutions than has been preceptible in recent years.

Fifthly, a realistic approach to the United Nations is necessary, avoiding the two extremes of wishful thinking and unjustified pessimism. Some enthusiastic supporters tend to regard any criticism of U.N. activities as a form of treason—a betrayal of the cause of humanity. Yet it would be a blind man who did not see weaknesses in the world organisation in the carrying out of its political as distinct from its 'welfare' functions, and correction of faults surely requires constructive criticism. We can take some heart from the opinion expressed by Conor Cruise O'Brien in a lecture given in 1963 when he said:

The United Nations...is by no means so fragile as...critics would suggest...No light we can shed on the organisation's actual ways of working is likely to bring it to an untimely end...On the con-

[1] 'Impact of New Members on the Structure and Efficiency of the U.N.', Lecture by Sir Patrick Dean, University of British Columbia, 15 March 1961.

trary...it is in the common interest that such light should be shed. It is by the shedding of light that practice is most often encouraged to move up a little closer to profession.[1]

Finally, we should resist the temptation to believe that every international issue should be brought before the United Nations and that adoption of such a policy would inevitably lead to a strengthening of the Organisation. No one is likely to accuse the Prime Minister of Canada, Mr Lester Pearson, of lack of sympathy for or active interest in the United Nations. His services to the world community were formally recognised when he was awarded the Nobel Peace Prize in 1957. Yet, speaking in 1961 on 'The United Nations and peace', he said: 'the best way of strengthening the United Nations is by asking it to do things of which it is capable, not those which it cannot do and where failure in the attempt would discredit and weaken it'.[2] This is the voice not of pessimism or cynicism but of wisdom and experience.

The great majority of Australians support the United Nations Organisation; but support does not require uncritical acceptance of everything it does or fails to do—rather does it imply an attempt to channel its activities in directions, and by methods, which are likely to succeed. In many fields of activity the United Nations has a record of which it can be proud—especially those fields in which the Specialised Agencies operate, such as Health, Food and Agriculture and Civil Aviation. It has also had important successes in handling international political problems; for instance, the problems of Iran, Northern Greece, Indonesia, Palestine, Suez, Lebanon and Cyprus. On the other hand, its inability to intervene effectively in the case of Vietnam, the most explosive international issue, it would seem, of 1966, appears to have been a major factor in the recently announced decision of U Thant, not to offer to serve for another term as Secretary-General. In these circumstances, while working to improve the efficiency of the United Nations in the field of international peace and security, it is necessary to recognise its present limitations and to exhaust *all* means of avoiding war and securing peace, both inside and outside the world organisation.

[1] 21st Montague Burton Lecture on International Relations, Leeds, 1 March 1963.
[2] University of British Columbia, 2 February 1961.

3. *The United States*

Australian relations with the United States since 1941 have been dominated by one fact, namely the overwhelming contribution made by America to the defeat of Japan. At a stage when Britain was fighting for survival in Europe after the fall of France and when she was heavily engaged in the Middle East, it was impossible for her to provide the air- and sea-power which would have been necessary to prevent Japan from capturing Singapore and the Netherlands Indies. Despite the agreement between Roosevelt and Churchill to 'beat Hitler first', the United States was able to fill the Allied power vacuum in the Pacific, although the disaster of Pearl Harbour and her overall strategy involved considerable delay in deploying the necessary forces. The supply line between Australia and the United States was kept open. General MacArthur was sent to Australia before the fall of Corregidor in the Philippines and his brilliantly executed strategy of 'island hopping', combined with the havoc done primarily by American forces to Japanese air- and sea-power, immobilised large numbers of Japanese troops until the surrender ceremony took place in Tokyo Bay.

As a result, Australian Governments and the Australian people felt and still feel deep gratitude to the United States for the protection afforded against the consequences of Japanese aggression. In Canberra there stands a memorial erected after the war by the Australian–American association. It consists of a very tall column surmounted by an American eagle, which appears to brood over the complex of Australian defence and services buildings erected in recent years. It does not occur to the average Australian, as it may to the visitor from a country newly come to independence, that the memorial so situated could be regarded as symbolising satellite or 'colonial' status for Australia.[1] Australian gratitude towards the United States is real and deep. Strange as it may seem to the citizens of many countries, 'America' has still not become a rude word for the overwhelming majority of Australians.

Every Australian political party accepts the American alliance in some form as a vital part of Australian foreign policy. No

---

[1] In his book *Australia's Defence*, Dr T. B. Millar refers on p. 9 to the 'over-patent symbolism' of the defence buildings being grouped around the Australian–American war memorial.

party represented in the federal parliament advocates abandon-
ment of the alliance,[1] although the attitude of the Labour
Party is ambivalent and leaves the party open to the charge that
it is happy to enjoy the benefits of the alliance but reluctant to
share the burdens. This reluctance has been most evident in
regard to Australian military involvement in Vietnam. A
statement issued by the foreign affairs committee of the Labour
Party issued on 12 May 1966 roundly declares that an Australian
Labour Government will direct the army to bring home without delay the conscripted men already there, and to return all
Australian forces from Vietnam as soon as practicable. An
attempt is made to sugar these pills to suit the taste of the Australian electorate by adding that, in bringing back the conscripts, full regard will be paid to the safety and security of the
Australian forces still in Vietnam. Moreover, volunteer forces
will not be returned to Australia without considering both the
situation in Vietnam at the time and the importance of maintaining future co-operation with the United States, while the
United States will be consulted about the proposed withdrawal.
An Australian Labour Government would also be ready to
provide forces for peace-keeping operations in South Vietnam
under the auspices of the United Nations or such other agency
as is established for the purpose.

We have already seen that the present Australian Government has disagreed with particular aspects of American policy,
but that, with the notable exception of trade matters, it normally prefers to make known its disagreement in Washington
through private representations at the political and diplomatic
levels. As pointed our earlier,[2] this attitude deprives those
Americans who differ from their own Government's policies of
the encouragement and stimulus of knowing that others abroad
share their views. It also deprives Australian public opinion
of precise knowledge of its Government's attitude to some international problems, and makes it appear to Communist and
many Afro-Asian nations that Australia is merely an American
'stooge'—an impression likely to be greatly strengthened by
Mr Harold Holt's unfortunate use of the Presidential electoral

---

[1] In his inaugural 'H. V. Evatt Memorial Lecture', 16 May 1966, Mr Arthur
Calwell, Leader of the Australian Labour Party, asserted that the support of
members of the Party for the American alliance 'has never been in doubt'.
[2] See p. 245 above.

slogan 'All the way with L.B.J.' during his visit to Washington in June 1966. Other Commonwealth Governments, especially British Governments, manage by one method or another, direct or indirect, to make public their doubts or differences about certain American policy, without destroying their fundamental ties with the United States.

Public Australian criticism of American policy is restricted, therefore, mainly to private individuals or representatives of institutions and organisations. Any visitor to Australia will find substantial criticism, from time to time, in the Press or over radio and television. There are certain features of American policy which many Australians question or find distasteful. These have included The Bay of Pigs fiasco during the first Cuba crisis in April 1961; many of the reported overseas activities of the C.I.A.; rigidity of outlook personified in the person of John Foster Dulles, who seemed at times able to combine in one and the same person a sense of moral outrage at the policies of other countries (including allies) and great toughness and considerable evasiveness in support of American interests; and brinkmanship in the Straits of Formosa. But Australians for the most part (excluding the extreme left-wing fringe and intellectual 'progressives') are equally aware of the unprecedented generosity of American Governments and people in contributing vast quantities of aid to allies and 'non-aligneds' alike, and of the value of American courage, determination and effort in support of principles in which most American citizens and most Australians believe.

Vast power and responsibilities have been thrust on the United States since the Second World War, and these responsibilities have on the whole been accepted. This attitude contrasts greatly with American reversion to isolationism after the First World War. It is scarcely surprising if important mistakes have been made by a country without centuries of experience of international power and responsibility. After all, it would not be difficult to find examples of grave mistakes of judgement by older countries. Fortunately for the world, dissident opinion within the United States is extremely vocal and effective. Changes of policy, and of governments, can be brought about by pressure from below—a state of affairs which a number of countries opposing American policy would do well to envy.

So far as British peoples are concerned, and especially Englishmen, the most fatal and dangerous attitude towards Americans is to regard them as misguided Englishmen. One has to live in the United States to realise that it is essentially a foreign country which speaks one of the varieties of the English language. An Englishman who, consciously or unconsciously, despises the American accent, reacts adversely against an American who wears yellow socks, and resents American intrusion upon English privacy as bad-mannered, should ask himself why he does not react in similar ways when, on the continent of Europe, he meets a Ruritanian wearing red socks and an embroidered shirt whose customs are often vastly different from those of England.

The United States has in truth been a 'melting-pot' of many different peoples, and the resulting national outlook is distinct from that of any other country. Moreover, non-Americans are often confused by the fact that the voice of America seems plural rather than singular, except during war or other national emergency. Who is speaking for the United States—the President, the Secretary of State, Congress, the Pentagon? Which represents fundamental American opinion—the East Coast, the South, the Mid-West, the Far West? Which is typical of the American outlook—the vast generosity of Marshall Plan aid to Europe and to developing countries; or the toughness of American trade and civil aviation policies and practices? Foreigners could perhaps accept more easily the inconsistencies and even the mistakes of American policy if it were not so often couched in terms of morality rather than national interest. Yet was not Great Britain in the heyday of her power known to much of continental Europe as 'perfidious Albion', and regarded as sanctimonious in the pursuit of her national objectives?

So far as the majority of Australians are concerned, friendly and co-operative relations with the United States seem natural and unnecessary to justify. Sharing in a broad sense a common cultural tradition, including a common language; allies in two World Wars; operating under constitutional and legal systems which are roughly similar—most Australians see in their ties to America nothing stranger than ties between Islamic countries, or Arab countries, or African countries, or Asian countries. All of these groupings agree on some things and differ on others; all have links outside their own particular group; none finds it necessary to apologise for giving support, at times, to other members of the 'group'. There are some Australians, however, who believe that Australia's geographical position off the southern rim of Asia demands, in her own long-term interest, that she should detach herself from the American alliance and concentrate upon the creation of friendly ties with Asian countries. This important point of view, which has been touched upon earlier, will be considered further in the final section of this chapter.

At the time of writing, Australian attitudes towards the United States revolve primarily around the problem of Vietnam. An important section of Australian opinion is uncertain as to the justification of Australian involvement in the undeclared war in that unhappy country, while many Australians are uneasy at the break with Australian tradition in the Government's decision to include in the forces sent there twenty-year-old 'conscripts'. Majority opinion endorses the decision of the Government, some of whose supporters, however, are critical of the somewhat bland and complacent manner in which the decision to send the original battalion was announced, without adequate preparation of public opinion, prior parliamentary debate or sufficient statement of reasons. The Labour Party, beset with internal difficulties and divisions, has exacerbated feeling on the 'conscript' question, in the hope that here at last it has found a national and popular issue which might consolidate electoral support and perhaps even return the party to power at the next Federal elections. Demonstrations against sending conscripts have been encouraged by the party leadership, despite the fact that they have occasionally got out of hand—no doubt with the aid and support of the small, hard core of Communists within the Australian community.

The Vietnam issue is, of course, several issues. Should the Americans be in Vietnam? Should Australian forces support the Americans there? Should Australian national-service trainees be included in any Australian forces sent to support the Americans? These questions can best be considered in reverse order.

On the assumption that the second question is to be answered in the affirmative, opposition to sending Australian 'conscripts' seems out of date and illogical. It is true that the Australian tradition of sending only volunteer forces overseas is a proud tradition. During the First World War, 'Of the 416,809 who entered the services...331,781 had taken the field. Of these, 59,342 were killed, 152,171 were wounded.'[1] In 1916 and again in 1917 the electorate twice rejected conscription when the question was put to it in referenda. The Second World War was a different kind of war, and casualties were proportionately lower. Nevertheless, 34,376 Australians were killed—amongst them more than 7,000 members of the Royal Australian Air Force, of whom over 5,000 died in the European theatre and over 1,000 in the Middle East. On this occasion, however, Prime Minister John Curtin succeeded in prevailing upon his party—after the entry of Japan into the war—to pass legislation imposing conscription for service overseas within the South-West Pacific area south of the Equator.[2]

So far as the current Vietnam problem is concerned, government efforts to build up the Australian army by attracting volunteers had indisputably failed to secure the necessary numbers in an era of full-employment. Opposition to conscription in these circumstances must rest therefore upon one of two propositions, provided one still accepts the assumption that Australian volunteers should be sent to Vietnam. Either Australians are not as other men; it is all right for American conscripts to be sent and not Australian—a proposition which rejects itself without further argument; or conscripts should be sent only in the event of 'national emergency', whatever that phrase may mean. Although Labour Party speakers have hinted that their attitude might be different if Australia were really at war, and if in such circumstances conscription were applied to wealth as well as to manpower, it is impossible to take such hints at their full face value. The precise meaning of 'national emergency' is not made clear—if, indeed, such a phrase is capable of definition in modern times, when wars take place without formal declaration and peace can no longer be regarded as an interval between wars. No Australian would choose to send any military forces to Vietnam if he believed the decision could responsibly be avoided—still less would he wish to send conscripts. At the same time the electorate as a whole has, to date, shown no sign of accepting the proposition that it is all right to send American conscripts but all wrong to send Australian conscripts to a

[1] Manning Clark, *Short History of Australia* pp. 197–8.
[2] Millar, *Australia's Defence*, p. 22; *Australia, A Social and Political History*, p. 376.

country the security of which, as the Minister for External
Affairs, Mr Hasluck, has argued, is more important to Australia
than to the United States.

The second question raises more difficult considerations,
although the answer is scarcely in doubt. On the assumption
that American forces should be in Vietnam, should Australian
forces, conscript or not, support them there? The answer to this
question depends, in the first place, upon what Australian
forces are available for a variety of purposes, and what priorities
are to be accorded these purposes. The Australian Government
and Australian opinion were reluctant to take decisions which
would have brought combat troops into collision with Indonesian forces. Yet, as Indonesian confrontation of Malaysia
continued, affirmative decisions were made with the support of
most Australians. Vietnam was in a different category. It was
not a member of the Commonwealth of Nations, as was Malaysia; the British Government, while supporting American action
in Vietnam, sent no combat troops itself; Vietnam was farther
away from Australia; troops sent to Vietnam would not be
available for use in Malaysia or, for that matter, in New Guinea
or Papua. On the other hand, British abstention from direct
involvement was understandable in terms of the scope of her
responsibilities in Malaysia and elsewhere, and the desirability,
if practicable, of her retaining somewhat greater influence to
negotiate a political settlement in her capacity of one of the two
chairmen of the Geneva Conference 1954. Refusal by Australia
to bear a proportion of the direct military burden in Vietnam
could have been interpreted by the United States as meaning,
first, that Australia was content for American rather than Australian lives to be lost in support of a policy closer to Australian
than to American interests, or, secondly, that Australia contemplated with complacency or indifference American withdrawal from the mainland of Asia. This could scarcely have
strengthened American readiness to give Australia maximum
support in the event of more immediate threat to Australian
security. So far as the Menzies and Holt Governments are concerned, of course, a strong additional factor in their decisions has
been a shared belief in the correctness of American support for the
Republic of Vietnam, and a common judgement as to the adverse
effects in South-East Asia as a whole of an American withdrawal.

The most difficult to answer of the three questions posed is whether American forces should be in Vietnam. Diverse views can in all honesty be held on this issue. For those who really believe that the fighting in Vietnam is just another civil war; that all governments in the Republic of Vietnam have been corrupt and authoritarian, indistinguishable—at least in the latter respect—from the Hanoi regime; that Ho Chi Minh is basically a Nationalist and not a Communist; that even if an American withdrawal brought to power in the whole of Vietnam a Communist regime, this would quickly show signs of independent 'Titoism' with which the West has learned in Europe to live; that Asia must solve its own problems in its own ways; and, finally, that the present situation in Vietnam is due to breach of the Geneva Agreements of 1954 by both the South Vietnamese and the Americans—for those who hold such views Australian military participation can well be regarded as undesirable and perhaps morally wrong.

To attempt to answer all these points adequately is beyond the scope of this book. The story of Vietnam is complicated, and extends over a period of more than 2,000 years, and few Australians have the time and energy to study it. Here it is practicable only to draw attention to some significant facts which throw doubt upon the validity of the beliefs set out in the preceding paragraph.

The history of Vietnam is one of resistance to Chinese pressure and of internal struggle for power between contending groups. What we now call North Vietnam was a Chinese colony for over 1,000 years—from 111 B.C. until about 940 A.D. After independence was achieved in the tenth century, Vietnam spread southwards and by about 1500 A.D. most of the Indianised Empire of Champa had been incorporated. As the southwards pressure continued, it became impossible for the Government of the North to exercise effective control over the South. A long civil war took place which lasted almost two centuries. Bernard Fall has drawn our attention to the situation which developed in the 1630s:

In this indecisive struggle, the south remained largely on the defensive. In the 1630s, the Nguyen rulers built two huge walls across the Vietnamese plain of Quang-Tri near its narrow waist at Dong-Hoi—barely a few miles to the north of the present dividing line at the 17th parallel—and for 150 years the country remained divided on that line, just as it now has been since 1954.[1]

[1] Bernard B. Fall, *The Two Vietnams* (Pall Mall, London, 1963), p. 17.

During the long struggle the north received help from the Dutch, while the Portuguese helped the south with artillery and military advisers. Eventually a representative of the Nguyen family in the south, Nguyen Anh—'with the help of a French force of Katanga-type adventurers',[1] defeated his rivals and had himself proclaimed Emperor in 1801. In the nineteenth century France intervened and in 1884 Vietnam accepted a French protectorate. China protested against the arrangement, but after French landings in Formosa and the Pescadores China in 1885 recognised French suzerainty over Vietnam.

Vietnamese mentality cannot be understood unless we remember the predominant influence of China and Chinese civilisation in Vietnam over many centuries. Chinese traditions greatly influenced the Vietnamese court at Hue—Confucianism; a scholar class of administrators recruited through Chinese-type examinations; the notion that the Emperor holds the 'mandate of heaven', but that revolution becomes a 'meritorious act'[2] if he loses the mandate by oppressing the people. 'In the name of this right to revolution, the Nguyen were eventually victorious over the decadent Le and Trinh; Ho Chi Minh defeated the French; Ngo Dinh Diem overthrew the discredited Nguyen ruler, Bao-Dai; and the Communist-led "Southern Front of Liberation" now seeks to gather a popular following against the stagnant Ngo Dinh Diem regime.'[2] Since that comment was made, President Diem has been overthrown and killed, not by the Viet-Cong but by those who oppose the Viet-Cong; successive governments, mostly military, have been overthrown by pressure from Buddhists, students and others; and violent demonstrations have taken place against the current government under Air-Vice Marshal Ky as Prime Minister, although, at the time of writing, these have been brought under control. Despite the instability of governments in the Republic of Vietnam, however, it is noteworthy that the South Vietnamese critics and protestors have never, so far, proposed the formation of a government incorporating members of the Viet-Cong.

If Vietnamese psychology needs study by the Westerner, inquiry is also necessary to understand the psychology of some Western critics of various governments of the Republic of Vietnam. What seems strange is the concentration of criticism on

[1] *Ibid.* p. 19.   [2] *Ibid.* p. 18.

faults in the south, and the almost complete indifference to the
nature of the regime in the north. It is not difficult to establish
the fact that southern regimes have been authoritarian in outlook; that movement towards parliamentary democracy has
been too slow; that governments have not had sufficient 'grass
roots' support; and that there have been areas of corruption.
Oddly enough, criticism centred especially upon President
Diem—an able official who chose retirement in preference to
service under French control and who accepted the eventual
call to power neither because he sought power for its own sake
nor because of riches which power could bring. Diem *was*
authoritarian—a Chinese mandarin (he has been called 'the
last Confucian'[1]) influenced in addition by his Catholic religion and his 'personalist' philosophy. He did much for his
people during the earlier years of his regime; unfortunately his
incredible obstinacy in believing that he alone knew what was
best for his country, together with increasing reliance upon the
advice and assistance of a family entourage whose integrity did
not match his own, gradually diminished his popular support
to such an extent that he too was regarded as having lost the
mandate of heaven. It is unwise, however, to underestimate the
difficulties he had to meet—the dislike of the French; the unpleasant power of sects with private armies which had to be
broken; and continuing insurgency in the country which was
eventually stepped up into a deliberate campaign of terror by
the Viet-Cong supported by Hanoi, designed to eliminate
physically headmen of village, teachers and others who would
not submit to domination. In a message to Congress in 1961,
President Kennedy estimated the number of assassinations by
the Vietcong during the preceding twelve months as 'four
thousand civil officers'.[2]

Yet it is a strange phenomenon that Western critics of southern weaknesses or inadequacies rarely do more than pay lip-
service to recognition of a catalogue of 'weaknesses' in the
north, despite the fact that the record is there for all to read.
Bernard Fall, a Frenchman by birth who is no admirer of
American policy in Vietnam, has demonstrated beyond perad-
venture that Ho Chi Minh joined the French Communist
Party in 1920 and ever since has advanced the cause of Com-

[1] See Denis Warner, *The Last Confucian* (Penguin Books, Angus and Robertson, Sydney, 1964).   [2] *The Two Vietnams*, p. 472, no. 19.

munism consistently and without mercy.[1] Amongst his many other activities he ran a training school for Vietnamese political agitators at Whampoa, China, and betrayed those whom he did not regard as reliable from the Communist point of view by transmitting their names to French Intelligence, which promptly collected the men so named on their return to Vietnam.[2] The picture sometimes painted of 'Uncle Ho' as a kindly old gentleman who would have been a Nationalist if the French and Americans had not forced him into the arms of Communism does not correspond to reality.

If the slow pace towards parliamentary democracy in the south is to be deplored, what evidence of democracy is visible in the north? Bernard Fall states that the 'land-reform' movement in the north in the middle 1950s was carried out with the 'utmost ferocity'.[3] He estimates that about 50,000 North Vietnamese were executed, and that at least twice as many were arrested and sent to forced labour camps.[4]

Local Party officials began to 'deliver' veritable quotas of landlords and rich peasants even in areas where the difference between the largest and the smallest village plots was a quarter-acre. Special 'People's Agricultural Reform Tribunals' (Toa-An Nhan-Dan Dac-Biet) began to mete out death sentences to individuals who in any case were not landlords, and who in many cases had loyally served in the war against France or had even been members of the Lao-Dong [Communist Party]. By the summer of 1956, the Lao-Dong was for the first time confronted with a severe internal crisis: A menace to life and property from whose arbitrariness no one any longer felt safe produced a wave of disobedience and outright hatred for the Party cadres throughout the country.[3]

If it should be suggested that this is the kind of defamation which anyone would expect from a Frenchman who at one time fought in Vietnam, doubters may refer to Ho Chi Minh's own admission of 'errors' which had led to wrong classification as landlords and rich peasants[4] and to the following extract from a statement on the same subject by General Vo Nguyen Giap:

We attacked the landowning families indiscriminately, according no consideration to those who had served the Revolution and to those families with sons in the army. We showed no indulgence towards landlords who participated in the Resistance, treating

[1] Ibid.; see especially pp. 81–103.   [2] Ibid. pp. 93–4.
[3] Ibid. p. 155.   [4] Ibid. p. 156.

their children in the same way as we treated the children of other landlords.

We made too many deviations and executed too many honest people. We attacked on too large a front and, seeing enemies everywhere, resorted to terror, which became far too widespread...

...Worse still, torture came to be regarded as a normal practice during party reorganisation.[1]

Further details as to the harshness of the land reform movement are given by Hoang Van Chi in the same book from which this quotation is taken. He was a member of the Vietminh Resistance movement who in 1955 decided to escape from North Vietnam when he realised the nature of the policy being enforced by Ho Chi Minh and his Communist supporters after independence from France had been won. It is not surprising that, after the Geneva Agreements of 1954, some 860,000 inhabitants of the Red River Delta, including about 600,000 Catholics, migrated to the south.

As to the Geneva Agreements 1954 which, *inter alia*, provided for general elections in July 1956 in circumstances permitting 'free expression of the national will',[2] a number of Australians do not believe or choose to ignore the fact that the Republic of Vietnam refused to be a party to the Agreements. It is necessary therefore to quote from President Diem's statement on this subject of 16 July 1955.

We have not signed the Geneva Agreements. We are not bound in any way by these agreements, signed against the will of the Vietnamese people...We do not reject the principle of free elections as peaceful and democratic means to achieve...unity. However, if elections constitute one of the bases of true democracy, they will be meaningful only on the condition that they are absolutely free.

Now, faced with a regime of oppression as practised by the Viet Minh, we remain sceptical concerning the possibility of fulfilling the conditions of free elections in the north. We shall not miss any opportunity which would permit the unification of our homeland in freedom, but it is out of the question for us to consider any proposal from the Viet Minh, if proof is not given us that they put the superior interests of the national community above those of communism...[3]

[1] Hoang Van Chi, *From Colonialism to Communism* (Praeger, New York, 1964), pp. 209–10.
[2] *Vietnam Since the 1954 Geneva Agreements* (Department of External Affairs, Select Documents on International Affairs, no. 1 of 1964), p. 16.   [3] *Ibid.* p. 22.

Nor did the United States subscribe to the Final Declaration of the Geneva Conference made on 21 July 1954. Instead, in a separate declaration, its representative took note of the agreements of 20 and 21 July, and stated that:

(i) it would refrain from the threat or the use of force to disturb them, in accordance with Art. 2 (4) of the Charter of the United Nations dealing with the obligations of members to refrain in their international relations from the threat or use of force, and

(ii) it would view any renewal of the aggression in violation of the aforesaid agreements with grave concern and as seriously threatening international peace and security.[1]

The precise extent of aid from the north given to the Vietcong at any particular time is open to dispute; what is not disputable is the direction, control and incitement of the Viet-Cong from Hanoi, especially since 1959. Professor Fifield summarises as follows:

...in May 1959 the Central Committee of the Communist party in North Viet-Nam called for the creation of a unified Viet-Nam through all 'appropriate means'. In July of the same year the party assumed responsibilities for the 'liberation' of Viet-Nam south of the seventeenth parallel, and in September 1960 the Third Congress of the party approved a resolution which called in effect for the direct overthrow of South Viet-Nam's government as an 'immediate task'. Toward the end of January 1961 broadcasts from Radio Hanoi referred to the creation in the previous month of a 'National Front for Liberation of South Vietnam', to destroy the 'U.S.–Diem clique'. As a tactic, the Communists later called for the establishment of a neutral regime in Saigon pending unification. The Communist party in South Viet-Nam is without question an extension of the northern party.[2]

The facts described above throw great doubt, to say the least, upon the validity of the view that what is happening in Vietnam is just one more civil war; that the Vietcong are merely indigenous southerners discontented with an authoritarian regime unwilling to introduce necessary democratic reforms; and that aid and advice from Hanoi and China is peripheral and unimportant. The Australian Government, in any event, completely rejects this interpretation. In its judgement 'What is happening in South Viet Nam is not a local rebellion caused by internal discontent but the application of the methods and

[1] Ibid. p. 17.   [2] Fifield, Southeast Asia in U.S. Policy, p. 206.

doctrines of Communist guerilla warfare first evolved in China and then successfully used in North Viet Nam'.[1] It believes that China regards a victory by the Vietcong in South Vietnam as of the first importance to the cause of world Communism—a test-case for wars of national liberation. If the Americans can be forced to withdraw from Vietnam by insurgency tactics while avoiding escalation into a world war, there is no reason to suppose that the same tactics cannot be successful in other parts of South-East Asia. 'The United States', Mr Hasluck has declared, 'could not withdraw without necessarily considering the world-wide impact of such a withdrawal on the broader strategies of world politics.'[2]

For the American and Australian Governments, therefore, Vietnam is also something of a test-case. Can non-Communist countries, through aid to nations which have recently achieved or regained independence, make it possible for them to gain sufficient time in which to overcome political and economic instabilities and to acquire sufficient strength to decide their own future for themselves? An authoritative statement of Australian objectives was that made by the Prime Minister, Mr Holt, on 31 March 1966, when he endorsed five points previously outlined by the Minister for External Affairs on 10 March:

(1) To help the Government of South Vietnam, at its request and in the light of Australia's own assessment, to resist armed aggression from the Communist North.

(2) To free the fifteen million people of South Vietnam from the threat of oppression and terror and help establish conditions for democratic government.

(3) To leave no doubt that Australia is resolved to honour its treaty commitments and alliances.

(4) To check the spread of Communism and encourage the work of modernisation and economic and social progress in South Vietnam.

(5) But not to overthrow the North Vietnamese regime or destroy the livelihood of its people.[3]

No foreign policy is immutable. What are the circumstances in which present Australian policy towards Vietnam could conceivably be modified? Following is a suggested list:

(a) If the United States should decide to withdraw its forces

---

[1] *Select Documents on International Affairs*, no. 1 of 1965, p. 3.
[2] *Ibid.* p. 4.   [3] *Canberra Times*, 1 April 1966.

from Vietnam, for whatever reasons, good or bad, Australian forces will inevitably be withdrawn also.

(*b*) If the Government of South Vietnam should at any stage decide to yield to pressure and to accept unification on terms dictated by the Vietcong and the Hanoi regime, it will presumably request the withdrawal of allied forces. Such withdrawal, whatever its consequences, would at least not be attributable to lack of allied will, but to circumstances beyond control.

(*c*) If South Vietnam proves unable to create or to maintain a government with sufficient prestige and power to exercise the degree of control of centrifugal forces in the population necessary for effective prosecution of the war, a point of time would presumably come when allied forces could not continue to operate and would have to be withdrawn.

(*d*) If, on the other hand, aid from the north is withdrawn and the Vietcong show willingness to abandon the policy of terror and readiness to accept decisions taken in free elections—both extremely improbable developments—a phased withdrawal of allied forces could presumably take place.

(*e*) Agreement could conceivably be reached between the contending parties for negotiations on the basis of a return to the Geneva Agreements, i.e. a cease-fire, withdrawal of forces north of the 17th parallel, and supervised arrangements for 'free elections' on a national basis. Presumably the Government of South Vietnam would be unlikely to agree to such conditions if the only guarantee of their being implemented is the 'goodwill' of their present opponents. The presence of allied or United Nations forces on some substantial scale would probably be required until the elections had been held.

It is inappropriate to close this section without paying some tribute to the courage, patience and restraint of American soldiers fighting in Vietnam the kind of war which, by temperament and tradition, they are least fitted to fight. A war of insurgency in a tropical jungle minimises the effectiveness of sophisticated weapons and techniques. True, the Americans use some unpleasant weapons, and, since the attack upon United States warships in international waters in the Bay of Tongking in 1964, they have bombed selected facilities in North Vietnam. But the United States Government has deliberately refrained so far from using all the power at its disposal in an effort to win quickly the undeclared war in which it is engaged. It has endeavoured to minimise the risks of escalation of the war into a world war which could become atomic. No doubt this restraint is due in substantial measure to judgements of broad American national interests, and European countries—especially France —may well feel that the risks of escalation are still too great to justify, in European terms, current American policy in Vietnam. Nevertheless, the history of two world wars and of the period since 1945 suggests that there is cause for relief that power of this magnitude can still be exercised with caution and with a sense of responsibility.

4. Asia

Future historians viewing international developments in the period 1900–65 may well conclude that the three most significant events, apart from the outbreak of two world wars, were (i) the advent of Communist Governments in Russia in 1917 and in China in 1949; (ii) the invention of the atomic weapon; and (iii) the revolt of Asia against European domination. Of these three the least understood in the Western world, including Australia, is the third.

In his book *Asia and Western Dominance*,[1] published in 1953 and written by K. M. Pannikar, the late Indian historian and diplomat, the story is told of the expansion of European influence and control in Asia from the time when Vasco da Gama found the sea-route to India around the Cape of Good Hope in A.D. 1497–98. Portugal built up a colonial empire which included Goa and Malacca. Spain added the Philippines to its Latin American empire. The Dutch took over the Netherlands Indies. Britain ousted the French from India, and became master of Malaya. The French gained control of Indo-China. The American Commodore Perry forced Japan to abandon its long-cherished policy of isolation. Britain, France, Germany and Russia acquired concessions and carved out spheres of influence in China. The peak of European overseas power was reached in the nineteenth century, based upon the industrial revolution in Europe and the development there of scientific and technological skills. No Asian country could compete with European military power, solidly based upon economic power. Great Britain ruled the waves, Queen Victoria became Empress of India, and Rudyard Kipling wrote of 'lesser breeds without the Law'.

---

[1] Published by George Allen and Unwin, London.

But time marched on. Japan read correctly the signs of the mid-nineteenth century, abandoned her policy of isolation, began to industrialise and imitated European military methods. By 1905 she had defeated Russia, a 'European' power, and had gained significant concessions in Manchuria, Korea, Sakhalin and the Liaotung Peninsula.

Japan's success was of primary importance in stimulating the hopes and ambitions of other Asian countries to free themselves from European dominance as and when opportunity occurred. Students from China and elsewhere flocked to Japan. In 1911 the Manchu dynasty in China collapsed and Sun Yat Sen became provisional President. Soon afterwards the National People's Party (Kuomintang) was organised, and the new Communist Government in Russia decided in 1923 to back it. Sun Yat Sen died in 1925. In 1926 Chiang Kai-shek brought off a *coup* which gave him control of the Kuomintang. He restricted Communist influence within it and eventually broke with the Communists. Chiang's successes in his northern expedition did much to unify the country and to make real independence for China a reasonable hope.

But Japan did not wish China to be unified. In 1931 Japan began the long series of incursions and interventions in Manchuria and China which led to Japan's withdrawal from the League of Nations and total military involvement in China during the Second World War. After the war Nationalist China collapsed under the combined pressures of exhausting war, domestic mistakes and Communist intransigence, until Mao Tse-tung, leader of the Chinese Communists, ejected the Nationalists by force from mainland China to Formosa in 1949.

Meanwhile victories in the Pacific after Pearl Harbor led to Japanese occupation of Indonesia, the Philippines, Malaya, Singapore, Borneo, the Netherlands Indies, Thailand and Burma. The defeat of British and Dutch 'imperialist' forces, and French acceptance of Japanese occupation of Indo-China caused an irrecoverable loss of prestige in areas where they had formerly ruled. After the war Asian countries achieved independence in quick succession: Philippines, 1946; India and Pakistan, 1947; Ceylon and Burma, 1948; Indonesia, 1949; Laos, Cambodia and Vietnam (North and South), 1954; Malaya, 1957. In 1963 Malaya joined with Singapore and the Borneo territories of Sabah and Sarawak to create the new

State of Malaysia, from which Singapore was ejected in 1965 to become itself a separate State.

By 1965, therefore, the countries of East, South and South-East Asia had escaped from the yoke of their European over-lords, due partly to their own increasing efforts but primarily to internecine strife in Europe in two world wars and the under-mining of European prestige by Japan despite her own eventual defeat. In the United Nations the newly independent countries joined with other Afro-Asian Members (for Africa too has successfully revolted against European dominance) to denounce all remaining forms of 'imperialism' and 'colonialism' and demand early independence for all remaining non-self-govern-ing territories. With Communist support, Afro-Asian countries now command a majority in the General Assembly, and they have used this majority deliberately and persistently to reinter-pret the Charter and expand the power of the Assembly and committees dealing with colonial questions to force the pace of decolonisation. On this one theme they have displayed impressive unity, which, however, fails to conceal the deep divisions among themselves to which reference was made in chapter 6.

Seen in restrospect, the revolt of Asia against European domination seems natural and almost inevitable. It would be unrealistic to assume that a proud nation like China, with an ancient civilisation which led it to regard itself as the Middle Kingdom surrounded by barbarians, and whose emperors held the mandate of heaven, should tolerate European overlords any longer than compelled to by internal weakness. The impli-cation of European superiority has been deeply resented, and European peoples would do well to show sympathetic under-standing of Asian or African sensitiveness to suspected evidence of 'neo-imperialism' and to the desire of newly independent peoples to assist others to attain independence.

Nevertheless, attacks upon 'colonialism' and 'neo-colonial-ism' have reached the point where it is time for so-called 'imperialist' countries to defend themselves in polite but clear and frank terms. When it is implied that imperialism and colonialism pertain to European countries only, and to those countries only whose populations possess white skins, it is time to remind the critics that Asia, too, has its long record of attemp-ted domination of Europe. Thus the Persians invaded Greece;

the Arabs occupied much of Spain for a long period; the Tartars raided Russia off and on for some 250 years; and the Turks captured Constantinople and came close to taking Vienna. In fact, imperialism is a manifestation of power, not of morality, and the Asian record is no better than the European.

Nor should Europeans admit, even by silence, the charge that all manifestations of colonialism have been evil in all their effects. It may indeed be true that good government, in such cases as it occurred in colonial territories, is no substitute for self-government. Yet in many cases European powers brought order out of anarchy, improved the local standard of living and greatly increased the security of the individual under law; most important of all, they sowed the seeds of democracy which had scarcely been typical of Asian regimes. The demand for self-government, for equality of voting rights for all citizens, for the right of the majority to control the future of the nation—these are predominantly European ideas. There is deep irony in the failure of some newly independent governments to maintain the forms of constitutional democracy after independence has been obtained. Indonesia, for instance, abandoned parliamentary for 'guided democracy', and has had no national elections since 1955. Yet President Sukarno demanded that Sabah and Sarawak should not form part of Malaysia unless a plebiscite was held, under conditions which he approved, proving beyond doubt the desire of their peoples to be part of Malaysia! On the other hand, until the curtailment of the President's power following upon the successful counter-*coup* of October 1965, all the indications were that Indonesia thought it quite unnecessary for the Papuans of West New Guinea to be allowed before the end of 1969 'the opportunity to exercise freedom of choice' as to whether they wish to remain with Indonesia or to sever their ties—an 'act of self-determination' guaranteed by the terms of the Treaty of 1962 between The Netherlands and Indonesia.[1]

Australia's relations with her northern neighbours are indeed of vital importance to her. Their population, their past achievements and their future economic and military potential make the objective of friendly relations a matter of plain national self-interest. During the post-war years she has given some tangible proof of her interest and goodwill. The preceding pages

[1] For the terms of the Treaty, see *C.N.* vol. xxxiii (1962), no. 8, pp. 25–31, especially p. 28.

have shown that her attitude towards Asia has been far wider and wiser than a mere attempt to find allies able and ready to assist in the military defence of Australia. The Colombo Plan was due substantially to her initiative, and she has found places in her educational establishments, despite the pressure of local demands, for some 12,000 Asian students. Her diplomatic representation in Asia is substantial, and she has sought to increase trade in this area by every possible means. Indonesia was given positive help to secure independence from the Dutch.

Australia is a full member of the Economic Commission for Asia and the Far East, and has undertaken to contribute to the establishment of an Asian Bank. Her substantial contributions to the Indus Basin Development Fund and her participation in the Lower Mekong River Development Project have not been based upon narrow self-interest.[1] So far as the Trust Territory of New Guinea and the Territory of Papua are concerned, she has announced the objective of self-government while Australian political leaders have publicly approved 'complete independence' in due course if so desired by the local inhabitants. Australia is spending on these territories far more than she can reasonably hope to obtain from them. Her efforts in any or all of these directions can be criticised as insufficient, but it cannot be denied that substantial efforts have been made.

Yet a vocal minority of Australians seems almost to suffer from a guilt-complex towards Asia, a complex which, of course, is greatly encouraged by Communist countries and by many Asian countries themselves. For the latter, it is easier and simpler to attribute all difficulties they continue to experience, after political independence has been won, to the 'imperialists' of the past or the 'neo-imperialists' of the present, ignoring such manifestations as the 'new imperialism'[2] of the Soviet Union and the neo-imperialism of Indonesia under Sukarno's leadership.

It is not difficult to understand the outlook of those Australians who are spiritually disturbed at the contrast between living standards in most Asian countries, as compared with those at home, and who wish every possible step to be taken to

---

[1] For a statement of Australia's contributions to International Economic Development and Relief to 30 June 1964, see *Select Documents on International Affairs*, no. 1 of 1965 (Department of External Affairs), pp. 56–8.

[2] See Hugh Seton-Watson, *The New Imperialism* (Bodley Head, London, 1961).

improve health, increase the expectation of life and diminish poverty in Asia. The question at issue, however, is not the desirability of this objective, but precisely how it is to be reached. Merely to provide economic aid, without 'strings', for a country which is unable to take effective steps to control its own population explosion suggests that charity is being preferred to cure. Such a diversion of economic resources from other desirable objectives is not necessarily justified. Moreover, if the primary motive is the laudable desire to minimise suffering and loss of human life, one would expect the same people to show greater interest than is normally apparent in the appalling loss of life and in the casualties on Australian roads.

Questions can also be asked of those Australians who find it 'natural' that Communist China should dominate South-East Asia at least as far south as Singapore. Where China has exercised some form of suzerainty in the past, they argue or assume, it is natural that she should exercise it again in the future. Yet they would reject as ridiculous the logical extension of this argument to support any claim by Italy to suzerainty over Britain, or by Spain and Portugal to suzerainty over the countries of Latin America. American pretensions to suzerainty over Cuba, for instance, would also be rejected.

The belief that Australian problems in relation to Asia would, in the long-term at least, be solved if the Americans went home and were speedily followed by their allies is simple and attractive; it reflects, however, extraordinary distrust of the policies and actions of a country which, predominantly, was responsible for the emergence of Australia from the dangers of the Second World War, and equally extraordinary faith in the 'natural' goodwill of Asian countries towards an Australia which stays at home and minds its own business. Relationships between China and India, India and Pakistan, Indonesia and Malaysia, Cambodia, and Thailand or Vietnam do not suggest that there is any 'natural' goodwill between Asian countries themselves, but that their actions are likely to be based upon somewhat rugged interpretations of their respective national interests.

The further 'realistic' view that domination by mainland China of neighbouring countries is 'inevitable', taking into account its enormous population and its distinguished past civilisation, is also surprising. It connotes an indifference towards the small or the weak which would be philosophically acceptable only if Australia were included in the list. If Formosa is automatically to be handed over to Communist Chinese control without any recognition of a right of self-determination which would imply prior ascertainment of the wishes of the local inhabitants, equally any claims by Australia to maintain its independence against conceivable pressure from a populous and powerful Indonesia should be ignored. Indeed, New Zealand would have no right to complain if Australia decided to exercise suzerainty over that country!

Sometimes the 'realistic' approach is recommended also as a means of settling the problem of Vietnam. The moral questions involved in accepting a negotiated settlement which may well result in the unification of Vietnam under Communism tend to be blurred by the optimistic assumption that, basically, the Hanoi regime and the Vietcong are simple nationalists who have been forced into the arms of Communism by Western blindness and stupidity. Sufficient has already been said about the 'nationalism' of Ho Chi Minh himself;[1] nor does the past record of the Hanoi regime engender confidence in its adopting a 'nationalist' as distinct from a Communist approach to a unified Vietnam.[2] It is of course conceivable, and perhaps likely, that a Communist Vietnam will endeavour to follow a Titoist, independent line, although the common border with China makes this difficult. What happens, however, to the non-Communists in the south who have committed themselves over the years against Communism? Does the world stand by, indifferent to their fate—or offer them immediate asylum?

There is, in my opinion, a fundamental misjudgement in assuming that any country, including Australia, must commit itself totally in one international direction or another. Total commitment by Australia to the United States in all conceivable circumstances and for ever would be folly; but so also would severance of the American–Australian alliance and total commitment to a 'pro-Asian' policy based upon the doubtful assumption that goodwill inevitably engenders goodwill in return. Australian goodwill towards Asia may be a pre-requisite of our long-term survival, but it will not necessarily in itself ensure our survival. In any event, foreign policy is plural, not singular. A country has many objectives, and it is usually possible to pursue several of these at one and the same time. In

[1] See pp. 348–9 above.   [2] See pp. 349–50 above.

practice all Australian Governments in the post-war years have sought, in different ways, both friendly relations with Asia as well as an alliance including the United States. In particular circumstances, in particular directions inconsistency between the two policies may from time to time arise, and a choice will have to be made. But by and large, divergent objectives may be pursued at one and the same time, greater emphasis being given to one rather than the other as and when circumstances require. It is possible to conceive a more populous and industrially developed Australia which would be far less dependent upon the American alliance than it is now. Even short of this, it is possible to conceive a situation in which our northern neighbours have demonstrated by their actions such a friendliness towards Australia, including respect for its political and territorial integrity, that the importance of the American alliance will be greatly diminished. A third possibility is that regional co-operation in the Pacific area will increase, bringing together, in the pursuit of specific aims, countries which in the past have chosen their friends more exclusively. Two recent trends in this direction are worth noting. First, representatives of Japan, the Philippines, Nationalist China, South Korea, Thailand, South Vietnam, Malaysia, Australia and New Zealand met in Korea in June 1966 and established an Asian and Pacific Council (ASPAC) to increase economic, social and cultural co-operation and improve the exchange of information. Secondly, General Suharto is reported to have expressed Indonesian interest in the possibility of closer co-operation between the countries of the proposed Maphilindo confederation (Malaysia, the Philippines and Indonesia) and the members of the Association of South-East Asia (ASA), which includes Thailand, as well as Malaysia and the Philippines.

In short, Australian governments should explore relentlessly every possible means of co-operation, not only with countries within the Atlantic community, but also with those outside it. In particular, constant interest in and sympathy with the problems of Afro-Asian countries 'should be displayed, and readiness to help within practicable limits. Thus, the Holt Government's offer in March 1966 of $A200,000 worth of rice to help victims of floods in Indonesia, despite the fact that Indonesian confrontation of Malaysia had not formally ended, was a sensible and imaginative act. Further economic assistance to

Indonesia was foreshadowed by Mr Hasluck when he visited Djakarta in August.

On the other hand, Australian relations with other countries can never be based upon silent acquiescence in their policies irrespective of the question whether such policies are or are not justified, or are contrary to Australian interests. The claim that non-European countries have a more 'spiritual' and less 'materialistic' outlook than countries of European tradition needs to be challenged, politely but firmly. Both attitudes, in varying degrees, can be found in all countries. So far as Asian and African countries are concerned, the serious disputes which exist between many of them provide little evidence of a more 'spiritual' approach to the solution of international problems than the approach of European countries.

For Australia, the age of innocence, isolation and complete dependence upon Great Britain is long since past; increasingly she will have to learn to stand on her own feet, earn a living by the sweat of her brow and accept more of the burdens of international responsibility. She must expect criticism of her policies on the world stage, and stand ready to justify them or adapt them where necessary. But so too must nations newly come to independence be brought to understand that for them the age of 'sensitivity' and 'inexperience' must increasingly be regarded as past. The old argument that their 'sensitivity' to colonial and other problems absolves them from critical examination of their policies which is normal in regard to older countries, or that some of their attitudes and decisions are due to 'inexperience' is increasingly unlikely to convince. Having claimed the privileges of independence they too must adapt themselves to international responsibilities, and learn to practise the arts of restraint as well as the arts of accusation.

To conclude: any person is entitled to express views on the broad ends of foreign policy which he believes his government should pursue, and to question the suitability of the means adopted by a government to achieve its stated objectives. But actual decisions upon current problems, as pointed out earlier, have to be made by governments in the light of detailed confidential and public information available at any one point of time. Decisions, therefore, are not taken in a vacuum, but in a particular international context, so that what makes sense in 1965 may not make sense in 1966, and vice versa. In these circumstances any private citizen who is sufficiently confident of his own opinions to tell a government precisely what it should do from day to day demonstrates not only his courage but also his rashness and perhaps his vanity. There are, however, a few general principles, not tied to time and place, which it is permissible to suggest that political leaders and their advisers would do well to keep constantly in mind. However obvious they may seem, they are important enough to need reiteration:

(1) Narrow nationalism is no longer a sufficient loyalty in the atomic age. As Arnold Toynbee has written: 'We are living in an age in which, for the first time in history, the whole human race, over the whole surface of our planet, is growing together into a single world-society... We have been, first and foremost, adherents of some local nation, civilisation or religion. In future, our paramount loyalty has to be transferred to the whole human race.'[1] The long-term objective should be to build up some system of world organisation which will command the loyalty of every man and woman.

(2) National interests should be judged by governments in the long term as well as the short term. Every nation has to learn that it may well be in the long-term interest of any one country to take into just account the interests of other countries. Thus, demands for 'unconditional surrender' are out-dated. As François de Callières, the distinguished French diplomat and theorist of diplomacy of the early eighteenth century, wrote long ago: 'The secret of negotiation is to harmonise the real interests of the parties concerned.'[2] It was the same writer who propounded the sage proposition which all diplomats should have engraved upon their memories, namely that sound diplomacy is based not upon trickery or bluff, but upon the creation of confidence, which can be inspired only by good faith.

(3) Governments, or individuals such as dictators, may be good or bad, wise or foolish. They rule over peoples who, despite differences of race, creed, colour and tradition, have a very wide range of common human qualities. Edmund Burke, speaking in 1775 on Conciliation with America, gave the neces-

---

[1] *Larousse Encyclopaedia of Ancient and Medieval History* (Paul Hamlyn, London, 1965), in foreword.
[2] Quoted in *The Evolution of Diplomatic Method*, by Harold Nicolson (Constable, London, 1954), p. 63.

sary caution and advice when he said: 'I do not know the method of drawing up an indictment against a whole people.'[1]

(4) No country can remain for ever an island of prosperity in an ocean of poverty and discontent. In the modern world of interdependence, it is impossible to separate domestic policy from foreign policy. Inconsistencies between the two must gradually be resolved, however slowly and painfully. In the long-run, international prosperity may well be found to be as indivisible as international peace.

When we tend to despair of the ability of mankind to preserve its own future against a background of atomic power, racial differences, national chauvinism and the personal vanity and ambitions of particular leaders, it is wise to reflect upon the short time since *homo sapiens* can be presumed on present evidence to have come into existence, and the tremendous advances made by him during this period—as compared with the very much longer period since an animal distinguishably human first appeared upon the earth.

As mentioned previously,[2] in 1939 Sir Robert Menzies pointed out that 'What Great Britain calls the far east is to us the near north'. This brilliant shorthand phrase, subsequently much repeated by others, is however somewhat one-sided and misleading. It suggests apprehension, which is not a sufficient basis for relationships between peoples. Nearness may bring risks, but it also provides opportunities. Australian foreign policy should concentrate as much effort and imagination upon ways of exploiting to the full opportunities for friendly international co-operation as it does upon means of avoiding dangers. The world community will judge Australia, not by what it is able to obtain for its own people by way of creature comforts and security, but by the extent and significance of the contribution it makes towards easing burdens on the long, hard road leading towards peace, justice and well-being for mankind.

[1] *Burke's Speeches and Letters on American Affairs* (Everyman, London, 1919 edition) p. 104.   [2] See p. 24 above.

SHORT BIBLIOGRAPHY

Albinski, H. S. *Australia's Policies and Attitudes towards China* (Princeton University Press, 1965).

Ball, W. M. *Japan, Enemy or Ally* (Cassell, Melbourne, 1948).

Casey, R. G. (Lord Casey). *Personal Experience 1939–46* (Constable, London, 1962).

—— *Friends and Neighbours* (Cheshire, Melbourne, 1954; Michigan State University Press, Lansing, 1958).

—— *The Future of the Commonwealth* (Frederick Muller, London, 1963).

Eggleston, F. W. *Reflections on Australian Foreign Policy* (Cheshire, Melbourne, 1957).

Evatt, H. V. *Foreign Policy of Australia* (Angus and Robertson, Sydney, 1945). Selected speeches of Dr Evatt from November 1941 to February 1945, with an introduction by Professor W. MacMahon Ball.

—— *Australia in World Affairs* (Angus and Robertson, Sydney, 1946). Selected speeches of Dr Evatt from March 1945 to May 1946, with a foreword by Sir Frederic Eggleston.

Grattan, C. H. *The United States and the Southwest Pacific* (Harvard University Press, Mass., 1961).

Greenwood & Harper (eds.). *Australia in World Affairs 1950–1955* (Cheshire, Melbourne, 1957).

—— *Australia in World Affairs 1956–60* (Cheshire, Melbourne, 1963).

Harper & Sissons. *Australia and the United Nations* (Manhattan, Publishing Co., New York, 1959).

Hasluck, P. *The Government and the People 1939–41* (Australian War Memorial, Canberra, 1952).

—— 'Australia and the formation of the United Nations' (*Royal Australian Historical Society, Journal and Proceedings*, vol. XL, Part III, pp. 133–178).

Horne, D. *The Lucky Country* (Penguin Books, Adelaide, 1964).

Levi, W. *Australia's Outlook on Asia* (Angus and Robertson, Sydney, 1958).

Menzies, R. G. (Sir Robert Menzies). *Speech is of Time* (Cassell, London, 1958). Selection of speeches, articles and extracts.

Millar, T. B. *Australia's Defence* (Melbourne University Press, 1965).

Modelski, George (ed.). *SEATO: Six Studies* (Cheshire, Melbourne, 1962).

O'Connell, D. P. (ed.). *International Law in Australia* (The Law Book Co. Ltd., Sydney, 1966).

Rosecrance, R. N. *Australian Diplomacy and Japan 1945–1951* (Melbourne University Press, 1962).

Starke, J. G. *The Anzus Treaty Alliance* (Melbourne University Press, 1965).

Warner, D. *The Last Confucian* (Penguin Books, Angus and Robertson, Sydney, 1964).

Watt, A. *Australian Defence Policy 1951–63; Major International Aspects* (Working Paper of the Department of International Relations, Australian National University).

—— *The Changing Margins of Australian Foreign Policy* (Roy Milne Memorial Lecture 1964, published by the Australian Institute of International Affairs.).

—— 'Australia and New Zealand's northern neighbours' (*Encyclopaedia Britannica Book of the Year 1965*, Australia and New Zealand Supplement).

Wilkes, J. (ed.). *Australia's Defence and Foreign Policy* (Angus and Robertson, Sydney, 1964).

—— *Asia and Australia* (Angus and Robertson, Sydney, 1961).

Yarwood, A. T. *Asian Migration to Australia* (Melbourne University Press, 1964).

OFFICIAL PUBLICATIONS

Commonwealth Parliamentary Debates.
Department of External Affairs
Current Notes on International Affairs (1938–1965).
Select Documents on International Affairs
Malaysia (no. 1 of 1963).
Viet Nam Since the 1954 Geneva Agreements (no. 1 of 1964).
Viet Nam: First Half of 1965 (no. 2 of 1965).
Information Handbook: Studies on Viet Nam (no. 1 of 1965).

JOURNALS

Australian Institute of International Affairs: *Australian Outlook; Australia's Neighbours; World Review.*
Australian Institute of Political Science: *The Australian Quarterly.*

INDEX

United Nations (*cont.*)
Australian amendments, 83–4; Australian preparations and discussions prior to conference, 73–6, 80–2; Australian delegation, 81; internal divisions within, 81–2; Great Power attitude towards veto, 86, 325, concessions to Small Powers, 86–7. Australian policy—towards veto generally, 83, 87; veto on amendment, 88; domestic jurisdiction, 88–90; trusteeship and non-self-governing territories, 84, 91; powers of Economic and Social Council, 84, 91; full-employment, 91–2; regional arrangements, 92; powers of General Assembly, 92–3; criticism of Evatt's methods by Hasluck, 94–5, Menzies, 95–6, McEwen, 96–7

Since 1945: Evatt's 'commitment' to maximum use of U.N. organs, 104–5, 324; change in Evatt's attitude to domestic jurisdiction regarding Indonesian, Spanish and religious trials issues, 90–1, Liberal–Country Party reservations towards United Nations—Menzies, 109–10, Spender, 113–14; U.N. and 'power politics', Menzies' comments, 169. Abuse of veto by Soviet Union, 326; effects of failure of security system envisaged by Charter, 326; whether SEATO conforms with Charter, 157; Uniting for Peace Resolution (1950), 326–7; U.N. Emergency Force (Suez), 327–9; use of force not authorised by U.N., Menzies' views, 305–6; U.N. operations in Congo (UNOC), 329–31; Advisory Opinion of International Court of Justice on payment of expenses of Congo operation, 331; power of U.N. organs to interpret their authority, 332–3, 356; evidence of new customary rules of international law in U.N. Resolutions, 333–4; Spender's criticism of alleged capacity of U.N. Assembly to exceed powers under Charter, 331–4; comments by de Yturriaga on unconstitutional action in U.N., 334–5; Declaration on Granting Independence to Colonial Countries (1960)—generally, 269–70, whether legally binding, 334, effect of Resolution as regards independence for New Guinea, Papua and Nauru, 335–6. Indonesian independence, Australian support in Security Council, 222, 250–1. West New Guinea problem in U.N.—generally, 253–6, Bunker mediation proposals, 256, 'freedom of choice' for Papuans, 256, 357. Indonesian confrontation of Malaysia, U.N. investigation of wishes of peoples of Sabah and Sarawak, 179, 265. Successes of U.N. in political field, inability to deal with Vietnam problem, views of Lester Pearson regarding matters to be brought before U.N., 338; realistic approach to U.N. political activities, 336–8

United States of America: *General*, a 'melting pot', many different voices, a foreign country, generous yet tough, un-English, 342, power of dissident opinion, acceptance of world responsibilities, 341

Relations with Australia: prior to Pearl Harbor (1941), Sudeten German problem, conversation between Officer and Moffat (1938), 15; projected diplomatic relations (1939), 24; Casey presents credentials (1940), 30; U.S. Cabinet reaction to possible attack on Australia, 67–8, 132; lack of American knowledge of Australia, 33; Casey's 'public relations' activities, 33; Casey's contacts with Wallace, Knox, Stimson, Dean Acheson, Hopkins, Frankfurter, 36, with British Ambassadors, Washington, 37; U.S.–Japan negotiations, knowledge of by ABCD powers, 39; Australian efforts to secure U.S. warning to Japan, American 'presence' in South-East Asia, gain time, 38; Casey as occasional intermediary between Americans and British, 34–6; interview between Casey and Kurusu, 40; burning of Japanese Embassy papers, 40; importance of public opinion in determining U.S. foreign policy, 131–2; Roosevelt's view regarding need to fight 'holding' war in Pacific if at war with Germany and Japan, 52

Pearl Harbor to San Francisco Conference (1945), Pearl Harbor, 41; change in Australian objectives regarding U.S., 41; Curtin's direct appeal to U.S. (1941), 55, 63; Eisenhower's advice to Marshall to defend Australia as base, 68; American forces for Australia, 56, 58; Evatt's first overseas visit in search of military supplies and influence on Allied strategy, 61–7; Churchill's appointment of Casey as British Minister of State, Middle East—generally, 58–9, attitude of